Arapahoe Politics, 1851-1978

Symbols in Crises of Authority

Loretta Fo

Foreword by Fred Eggan

University of Nebraska Press
Lincoln and London

Publication of this book was aided by a grant from the
National Endowment for the Humanities

Library of Congress Cataloging in Publication Data

Fowler, Loretta, 1944–
    Arapahoe politics, 1851–1978.

    Bibliography: p.
    Includes index.
    1. Arapaho Indians–Tribal government. 2. Indians of North America–
Wyoming–Tribal government. I. Title.
E99.A7F68   323.1'197'0787   81–10368
ISBN 0–8032–1956–3   AACR2

The paper in this book meets the guidelines for permanence and durability of the Committee on Production Guidelines for Book Longevity of the Council on Library Resources.

For my parents

Contents

List of Tables

List of Maps and Figures

List of Plates

xiii

Foreword

Loretta Fowler's *Arapahoe Politics, 1851–1978* is an outstanding contribution to the field of political anthropology, and to our knowledge of Plains Indians in the historic period. It is clear from her account that the Northern Arapahoes have made the most successful adjustment to white culture of any Plains tribe, and how it was done has important lessons, both for other Indian groups and for the U.S. government and its agencies.

When Dr. Fowler went to the Wind River Reservation in the late 1960s, she was primarily interested in studying the contemporary economic and political organization of the Arapahoes, and their relations with their Eastern Shoshone neighbors, but she gradually discovered that Arapahoe history served as a charter for the decisions in the present, and set out to combine fieldwork and ethnohistory in a highly productive way. This is ethnohistory at its best.

The organization is in terms of "political history, 1851–1964" and "politics today, 1965–1978," and within these two parts, is largely chronological, beginning with the role of the Arapahoes in the Plains warfare of the 1850s and ending with the current reservation situation. In contrast to other Plains tribes, the Northern Arapahoes have managed to avoid serious factional divisions and particularly those between the generations, and have been able to maintain a united front against the Bureau of Indian Affairs and other agencies of government.

The Arapahoes, along with their close kinsmen, the Gros Ventres, are among the handful of Plains tribes with an age-grade social structure, in which age-sets, or peer groups, go through a series of ceremonial age-graded societies which include all the males, and in which ceremonial knowledge is acquired. Dr. Fowler shows how this age structure is continued in modified form in Arapahoe society and how its values determine social and political behavior today. The Arapahoes have become experts in the manipulation of political symbols for the benefit of the whole tribe, and her account may well change many people's minds as to the capability of American Indian tribes to govern themselves on their own reservations.

FRED EGGAN

Preface

When I first went to Wind River, I did not intend to study Arapahoe history; my interest then was in contemporary economic and political organization. Arapahoes informed me that if I were interested in economic matters I should "go to the Business Council," but if I wished to ask about Arapahoe history or religion, I must obtain the consent of "the old people." I was eventually to discover that although important economic and social matters were discussed and voted on in council meetings, even these kinds of decisions were made only if they were compatible with the views of the old people, praying in a tipi or room far from the tribal business office. Slowly I came to realize that, for Arapahoes, history—in the keeping of (that is, interpreted by) elders— serves as a charter for the decisions and relationships of the present. This realization helped me, first, to see that in many ways Arapahoe politics was extraordinarily different from Plains politics in general, and then to understand how these differences came about.

In this book I examine the way in which the Arapahoes, since as long ago as the early nineteenth century, have legitimized new authority relations and attempted to resolve the problems that have come about as a result of new political relationships with whites. To do so I have had to analyze the meanings that the Arapahoes attribute to events and relationships through time, to explore the symbolic dimension of politics. In studying political history, I have found it essential to combine fieldwork and ethnohistory: each approach contributes to the success of the other.

The search for explanations as to how Arapahoe culture and social organization, the historical circumstances in which the Arapahoes found themselves, and United States policy influenced present-day political relations among Arapahoes and between Arapahoes and whites led me to historical documents and to the ethnohistorical method. My approach to ethnohistory—the study of primary documents from an anthropological perspective—encompasses the critical comparison and piecing together of reports and journals of government agents, travelers, missionaries, and local whites; transcripts of councils attended by Arapahoes; newspaper stories; and the writings of literate Arapahoes. I have also used anthropological sources somewhat differently from the way they have been used by many historians of Native American societies. I used anthropologists' field notes and correspondence (as well as published works) not merely as sources of "traditional culture," but as historical documents themselves: accounts and interpretations that in many ways reflect moments in time and personal experience just as do the writings of government officials and others. I also found that documents that archivists have classified under "dances," "artifacts," or "boarding schools," for example, may have critical bearing on politics. I have tried to peruse historical documents in the way that an ethnographer observes a society, seeking an understanding of politics not merely in council meetings or elections but in religion, kinship, art—in all aspects of the Arapahoe way of life.

My fieldwork on the Wind River Reservation in Wyoming began in 1967, when I was a graduate student studying social change. The reservation is occupied by the Eastern Shoshone and Northern Arapahoe tribes. I became acquainted with the elected council leaders from both tribes, although I did fieldwork only among the Arapahoes. One of the Arapahoe council members, Nell Scott, helped me to gain permission from the joint Arapahoe and Shoshone Business Council to attend its meetings during the summer and during my subsequent trips to the reservation. Father Jerome Zumach of St. Stephen's Mission introduced me to Mary Hungary, who kindly let me live with her and her grandchildren. I stayed with this Arapahoe family on all of my return visits to the reservation during the next ten years. It was in the context of family life and through participation in community activities and visits with people of varying ages and backgrounds that I learned to communicate at a rudimentary level in the Arapahoe language, became familiar with social organization and political process, and learned from elders what the "Arapahoe way" means to Arapahoes. I found fieldwork necessary to interpret the past as well as the present.

Intensive fieldwork is important in the exploration of a people's past because it reveals something of their ethos—their style, motivations, orientations, their tendency to view problems and come to terms with them in culturally characteristic ways. An understanding of ethos can give important clues to the interpretation of past as well as present events. Fieldwork gives historical inquiry other kinds of clues: personal histories, including accounts of the acquisition of ritual statuses that are not documented in written sources; genealogical information that clarifies political behavior; knowledge of the native language, which sheds light on a speaker's interpretation of events, even though in transcripts the speaker's words may be translated into English; and oral history, which (while not necessarily factual) provides the researcher with valuable new questions and directions that then can be pursued through the ethnohistorical method.

The research for this book has spanned eleven years and has been greatly facilitated by the help of several institutions and individuals. My fieldwork in 1968–69 and during subsequent summers was funded by a Doris Duke grant administered through the Department of Anthropology, University of Illinois at Urbana. In 1974–75 I received support from the City University of New York Faculty Research Award Fund. A postdoctoral fellowship with the Department of Anthropology, National Museum of Natural History, Smithsonian Institution, from 1976 to 1977 enabled me to begin the book manuscript. Smithsonian illustrators Edward Schumacher, JoAnn Moore, and Robert Lewis drew the maps. James Glenn and Paula Fleming of the National Anthropological Archives assisted in locating and identifying photographs. During 1977–78 I held a postdoctoral fellowship at the Center for the History of the American Indian at the Newberry Library, Chicago, where I completed the manuscript. My research has taken me to several archives: I wish to thank Richard Crawford and his staff at the National Archives, Katherine Halverson and her staff at the Wyoming State Archives, John Aubrey at the Newberry Library, Phyllis Rabineau of the Field Museum in Chicago, and Martin Steinwand and Clyde Hobbs and their staff at the Bureau of Indian Affairs, Fort Washakie, Wyoming.

Demitri Shimkin, Fred Eggan, and Edward Bruner gave me encouragement and direction in the early stages of my research. I also thank John C. Ewers, Mildred Mott Wedel, Peter J. Powell, and Raymond J. DeMallie for their assistance with the ethnohistorical inquiry. I am grateful to Ives Goddard, who corrected my linguistic transcriptions and helped with translations. Sara Hunter-Wiles kindly took photographs of the Arapahoe community at my request. I also thank Nancy Foner and Lawrence Rosen, who read the manuscript and made insightful comments. And I especially want to convey my appreciation to Karen I. Blu, who gave the manuscript a painstakingly critical reading that greatly improved the final product. To the Arapahoe tribe, with whom I have spent many happy and enlightening times, and the

Arapahoe Business Council, for whose encouragement and assistance I am grateful, I offer my observations about political history with the hope that they will find them interesting and useful. I thank the Arapahoe people for their patience, their good humor, and their company through the years.

Arapahoe Politics, 1851–1978

Introduction

In their political behavior the Northern Arapahoes of the Wind River Reservation appear to be atypical, even perplexing. Unlike many other tribes of the Northern Plains, they have readily accepted the electoral process, and the elected business council is fully institutionalized and accepted as the legitimate tribal government. In the Washington office of the Bureau of Indian Affairs (BIA), the staff of the Branch of Tribal Relations is amazed that year after year the file for the Wind River Arapahoes remains empty of letters protesting election results or actions of business council leaders. The files of many other tribes, in contrast, are filled with such complaints and requests for investigation or federal intervention.[1] In their success in legitimizing new criteria of authority and new leadership roles, the Arapahoes contradict many of the generalizations made about political change among native Plains peoples and challenge the observations of social scientists who studied the tribe in former times.

By and large, students of Native American and particularly Plains culture and history have observed that intergenerational relations, native religious organization, and the introduction of the political middleman role present obstacles to the formation of an effective tribal government, one that has popular support and also is able to cope with contemporary political needs and realities. Conflicts between generations, religious discord, and disputes over the legitimacy of the authority of middlemen have been regarded as inevitable products of the colonial experience, and eventually sources of bitter political conflict among native peoples. Anthropological studies of the Northern Arapahoes in the 1930s concluded that Arapahoe elders and ritual leaders were a hindrance to "modernization" (or "acculturation"),

1

and that if political innovation were to occur, the status of the elders would decline and the native religion would be abandoned.[2] The intermediary leadership role—specifically, that of the federally recognized "chief" in the nineteenth century and the business councilman in the twentieth century—has been generally characterized as incompatible with traditional concepts of authority among Plains peoples. It has also been argued that Anglo-American domination has resulted in the "powerlessness" of intermediaries, who face an apathetic electorate unable to believe that the intermediaries can work effectively on their behalf. In the view of one author, the deprivation and powerlessness of Plains peoples "broke the Indian spirit, leaving despair and a sense of futility."[3]

In fact, however, the Northern Arapahoes were not "broken." Such general characterizations of the fate of Plains peoples do not fit them. The differences between generations (or more specifically, Arapahoe age categories) have worked to facilitate rather than hinder adaptation to new political realities. Native religion remains a focal point of Arapahoe life and plays a key role in the legitimization of secular authority and the validation of political innovation. Rather than being riven with devisive conflicts or immobilized by apathy, the Arapahoes have managed to achieve tribal unity in the face of unsettling social change and to perpetuate a sense of continuity of political ideals despite a series of potentially devastating crises of authority precipitated by subordination to whites during the past 130 years.

In this book I attempt to explain how, in response to new and often painful social realities, the Arapahoes succeeded in legitimizing new authority relations and resolving the political problems of formulating realistic tribal goals and organizing people in relation to those goals. The obstacles to success were formidable: the federal government was persistent in its attempts to weaken the political and economic position of the tribe and to undermine the authority of its leaders. These efforts precipitated a series of crises of authority; that is, the actions of native leaders and their right to take such actions were challenged by other Arapahoes, federal officials, or both. To understand the Arapahoe style of coping with political problems and the way crises of authority were resolved, I argue, it is necessary to analyze the meanings, articulated in symbols, that the Arapahoes ascribed to political events through time. In the course of this study, I explore the ways ideas about politics shaped social action and the ways events themselves shaped Arapahoe concepts and interpretations of political life. Concepts concerning politics and authority were expressed and made emotionally convincing through symbolic forms; the interpretation of those symbolic forms motivated Arapahoes (and whites as well) to act in particular ways. Through the creation and use of effective political symbols Arapahoe leaders were able to legitimize their leadership roles and to mobilize political consensus. The symbolization process enabled the Arapahoes to interpret innovations as cultural continuities and cultural continuities as innovations—an accomplishment particularly adaptive when a group is forced to operate within a larger political system that it does not control.

The way Arapahoes coped with political problems and the nature of their political symbols were greatly influenced by the fact that at the time of contact Arapahoe society was age-graded, and in a special way. (Age grades are formalized life-stage categories, with which particular statuses and roles are associated.) As in many age-grade systems, Arapahoe authority roles were associated with men's age grades, with men's stages in life. For example, men of the seventh and most prestigious grade were elderly, and only those men could serve as priests. The position of band headman normally was held by men in their late forties and fifties who occupied the sixth grade. Also as in many age-grade systems, unified tribal action was facilitated by the creation of ties between males of the same grade which cut across kin groupings.[4] Not typical was the fact that the Arapahoe age-grade system represented a hierarchy of *ceremonial* authority, not political or economic power. Relations among men of senior and junior grades ideally were complementary; in fact, reciprocal respect and aid were institutionalized in several ways and were buttressed by supernatural sanctions. Men in each grade performed some roles distinct from but necessary to the roles of the others.[5] Concepts concerning age and the relationships among culturally defined age groups shaped Arapahoe authority relations even after the age-grade system itself ceased to exist. In this book I argue that Arapahoe ideas about the relationship of one age category to another facilitated adaptive political reorganization. The Arapahoes' success is not fully comprehensible without an understanding of the ways in which those symbols associated with age categories motivated and reassured the Arapahoes in various political contexts.

The Arapahoes not only succeeded in legitimizing new criteria of authority and mobilizing consensus, but also at times were remarkably effective in influencing federal representatives. The Arapahoe case points to a need to revise generalizations made about the response of Native Americans to the imposition of controls by a dominant society. Some researchers have argued that unlike colonized peoples in Africa, where men in power would respond to appeals to "tradition," Native Americans, subjected to unyielding assimilationist federal policies, were not able to use the rhetoric of tradition in order to accomplish political change and to enhance self-determination. According to this argument, Native Americans instead had to depend on legal efforts (that is, constitutional guarantees, treaty rights, and so on).[6] My study of Arapahoe politics illustrates how the Arapahoes used symbols of "progress" to accomplish many of the same ends—enhanced self-determination, for example—that other peoples achieved by using symbols of tradition. As we shall see in the chapters that follow, customs offensive to white authorities were disguised in ways that made those practices appear "progressive" and therefore acceptable to whites. No doubt the Arapahoes were not the only Native American group to exploit whites' commitment to assimilation in this manner.

POLITICAL SYMBOLS

In this work, culture is viewed as "socially established structures of meaning" in terms of which social action occurs. Culture is articulated through symbolic forms and activities. I follow Clifford Geertz's definition of symbol: "any object, act, event, quality, or relation which serves as a vehicle for a conception—the conception is the symbol's 'meaning'." The construction, apprehension, and use of symbolic forms are not simply occurrences in the mind, but are manifested in social events, hence are public and observable. Symbols express conceptual frameworks and at the same time impel belief and motivate action; that is, symbols "both express the world's climate and shape it."[7] In this book I examine how Arapahoe political culture partly stimulates and is partly stimulated by the events and new social relationships that have accompanied political domination by the federal government. In the chapters that follow, I trace through time the ways in which new political realities are perceived, accepted, and resisted through the articulation of meanings attached to symbols. And I examine the ways political symbols also are manipulated by individuals in generating support, validating status, and undercutting the positions of others. For the Arapahoes, ritual objects, personal names, clothing and body decoration, language, and such ceremonies as the "giveaway" are a few among many symbolic vehicles that articulate concepts about authority and its legitimization and instill an emotional commitment to the shared interpretations that order political life.

    The ambiguity of symbols, their potential for multiple meanings and for gaining and shedding meanings, helps make possible the resolution of the crises of authority with which the Arapahoes had to cope.

Arapahoes and whites "understood" certain words, acts, gestures, and objects differently; Arapahoe leaders, aware of the variant meanings of political symbols, attempted to manipulate symbolic associations to the tribe's advantage in their dealings with whites. Similarly, the flexibility inherent in religious symbols facilitated the priests' creative reorganization of native religion to meet the challenges of changing times. The Arapahoes resolved problems of legitimization of authority and advocacy of tribal interests by interpreting new social realities in ways that were culturally acceptable as well as adaptive. Symbols emerged that worked to revitalize or reassert traditional values and relationships, yet at the same time reassured whites that the Arapahoes were neither dangerous nor uncooperative. At the same time, old symbols took on new meanings that both reinforced traditional understandings and motivations and made innovation culturally acceptable.

An understanding of the symbolization process helps to make sense of the contradictions inherent in published accounts and BIA correspondence concerning the Arapahoes. One of the puzzling facts about the Arapahoes has been that intermediaries frequently and convincingly maintained to whites that the Arapahoes wanted to "be like the white man," yet they did not renounce their religion, cease speaking their native language, or replace native with white patterns of social interaction. Observers often erroneously predicted the demise of traditional culture on the basis of the intermediaries' behavior; but in point of fact, intermediaries carefully acted and spoke in ways that had one meaning for whites and another for Arapahoes. Studies of Arapahoe life that have failed to consider the relationship between systems of meaning and systems of behavior have distorted Arapahoe history. For example, in 1947 Feliks Gross found that Arapahoes gradually were losing their "traditional" cultural values. He based his conclusions on observations of behavioral innovations; young people, for example, spoke English more often and "better" than they spoke Arapahoe.[8] Contrary to Gross's predictions, the elderly Arapahoes of today (the youths referred to in Gross's study) speak Arapahoe often and, in the opinion of Arapahoes, expertly. Gross failed to inquire into the *meaning* of the use of Arapahoe as opposed to English in particular social contexts: in the Arapahoe view, Arapahoe was becoming culturally appropriate only in particular social contexts and most appropriate for speakers of particular age categories. Other scholars have described the Arapahoes as "conservative" and unable to adapt to their changing world. They have observed superficial behavior and have attached to it their own meanings rather than looking at what that behavior meant to Arapahoes. From Henry Elkin's 1936 description of Arapahoe society, which pointed to the central role of elders in native ritual, Ralph Linton concluded that the authority of elders was a force for conservatism because the elderly were "the least adapted to coping with new conditions."[9] The Arapahoes, who deferred to elders, were described as poorly adjusted to modern times. In fact, however, through their revamping of religious rituals and their interpretations of political events, the elders played an important role in legitimizing and channeling social and cultural change. While at times appearing "conservative," the Arapahoes have in fact made innovative adaptations to changes in their environment.

CRISES OF AUTHORITY: ENCAPSULATION
AND THE LEADERSHIP PROCESS

Within a few generations after their first contact with whites, the Arapahoes' political system was encapsulated, that is, partly regulated by and subordinated to the national political system while at the same time remaining somewhat independent.[10] Arapahoes dealt with Americans through "chiefs" and later through councilmen, who served as political middlemen in a world increasingly dominated by whites inimical to Indian interests. As contact between Indians and whites became more intense, the incongruities between their political cultures aroused serious conflict. The confrontation between federal agents and Arapahoes produced a series of crises of authority in Arapahoe society; the crises centered on intergenerational relations, the ceremonial order, and the role of political middlemen.

From the time of the first formal contacts between United States officials and the Arapahoes, federal representatives were perturbed by the type of leadership they found among the Arapahoes. Whereas in Euro-American political tradition decisions were made according to majority rule, Arapahoes decided by consensus or apparent unanimity; that is, overt conflict was avoided by compromise and reconciliation of divergent views. Leaders among whites exerted directive, initiatory authority; Arapahoe leaders were expected to articulate group consensus and to persuade other Arapahoes to cooperate and compromise. White observers were also bothered by the fact that elderly ritual authorities played a predominant role in Arapahoe political life.[11]

Edwin James and John Bell of the S. H. Long expedition were the first to write specifically about Arapahoe political behavior. In the summer of 1820 the two men visited a large intertribal camp of Kiowas, Comanches, Cheyennes, and Arapahoes on the Arkansas River. The

Arapahoe "principal chief," Bear Tooth, reportedly was the tribe's main intermediary in relations with whites and very influential among the tribes in the Platte, Arkansas, and Red River region. James was struck by the fact that the Indian headmen or chiefs "seemed to possess only the dignity of office, without the power of command." He noted that the nomadic Plains Indians appeared "to have no laws, except such as grow out of habitual usages, or such as are sanctioned by common consent." In order to maintain his position and retain the support of the influential men, a leader was "compelled to admit them to participate in the authority with which he is invested, and to bestow upon them any effects of which he may be possessed."[12] Bell observed that the presents the expedition gave to chiefs were distributed to their male peers.[13] Chiefs were the most generous of men; in giving to others they ensured their followers' loyalty and appeased the disaffected, and the principal chief won position by "the resources of his own mind, aided by his reputation for generosity and valour."[14] The role of elderly ritual leaders was another source of amazement to the white visitors. James observed that decisions were made through the deliberations of a council of elders who had previously solicited opinions from other respected men. Criers urged people to support the decisions. "Haranguing" in the stillness of morning or evening, they endeavored "to inculcate correct principles and sentiments," so that the people were "swayed to almost any purpose that their elders, for such are their men of medicine (or as the term imports, magic wisdom), think proper to execute."[15] In a few instances the decisions of the elders were executed by younger "chiefs and warriors" or "soldiers," who were given authority to use force if necessary, but in normal circumstances respect for the old "men of medicine" was sufficient motivation to conform.

The political behavior that appeared so peculiar to James and Bell was a source of great consternation to federal officials who subsequently dealt with the Arapahoes. When the Arapahoes became more politically subordinate and economically dependent on the United States, federal officials put pressure on them to modify their political institutions so as to conform to Euro-American concepts of authority relations.

Challenges to the Age Hierarchy

The Arapahoes view aging as a supernatural blessing and a sign of social accomplishment; it is welcomed, not feared. The life course involves a progression through four general age categories, the "four stages" (or "hills") of life:[16] child, youth, mature adult, elder. In general, youths range in age from about twenty to forty; adults, from forty to sixty; elders, sixty or more years. People who behave in ways that are regarded as inappropriate to their stage in life, however, are not accorded the status normally due a person of those years. Specific social roles (including authority roles) and, to some degree, certain attitudes and values are particular to each of the four age categories (and, of course, to gender).

These concepts about age categories were articulated in an age-set–age-grade organization.[17] In the nineteenth century (and probably well before then) Arapahoe males were organized into age sets (peer groups) and as members of a set progressively passed through a series of seven graded ceremonial statuses. There was one grade for male elders; there were four for adult males and two for youths. In essence, as men aged, their progression through the grades (or lodges) as members of an age set bestowed upon them increasing sacred knowledge. Elders (who had achieved the seventh grade or lodge) were ultimate authorities in matters of religion, but in Arapahoe society, with its basically hunting-gathering ethos, they were not necessarily better situated economically than their juniors and did not monopolize political offices. When a member of an age set made a religious vow to complete a lodge ceremony, the vow initiated the transition of his set from one grade to a higher one. Nonetheless, the age-group system functioned as a hierarchy because the participation of younger men in a lodge ceremony was contingent on the supervision and instruction of men of the senior age grades. Social responsibilities and honors were assigned to men of the age grades largely upon the approval of males in senior grades. But while age-group relations were hierarchical in ceremonial matters, the authority of senior over junior was tempered by the requirement of mutual "respect." Seniors were given deference and, in their capacity as ritual instructors, were entitled to receive gifts (but also in turn were obligated to distribute food and goods on certain occasions) and in some instances could compel obedience from their juniors (in settlement of disputes, for example). Yet the elder who possessed ritual authority had a sacred obligation to meet any formal request made by his junior and was expected to help and encourage him. By all accounts, men did not feel threatened by their juniors, for when an age set completed a lodge ceremony, these men did not dispossess the older men who already had achieved the lodge status. Once an age set acquired a particular age grade, the members retained for life the sacred knowledge associated with the grade. Outside of the sphere of ritual relationships, elderly persons were expected to instruct their younger relatives, on the one hand, and to indulge them, on the other. Arapahoes were taught to help and to defer to the elderly. The bond between grand-child and grandparent was particularly strong.[18] Eventually the age-set–age-grade system ceased to function. Nonetheless, even in reservation society one's status and role greatly depended on one's place in the related age-category framework.

As Arapahoes experienced the rapid changes—trading, wars, reserva-tion status—that accompanied contact with Euro-Americans, the influence of elders sometimes was challenged. During the Indian wars of the 1860s and 1870s, youths active in warfare enhanced their status and occasionally attempted to initiate actions of which their elders did not approve. Settlement on reservations brought with it repressive measures that threatened the age hierarchy and the stability of Arapa-hoe society. Federal officials, regarding elders as vessels of tradition who obstructed federal programs of directed change, felt that all leadership positions should be held by young men. They attempted to undermine the elders' authority by prohibiting the ceremonies they directed and worked to discredit them further by encouraging young alumni of government and church schools to act as tribal spokesmen and by employing such youths in agency jobs.

Scholars have viewed the problems of intergenerational conflict that accompanied encapsulation in the Plains area as insoluble. In this view, elders form a traditional or conservative interest group in opposi-tion to younger, more "progressive" cohorts. The elders' role in com-munity affairs is seen to have diminished progressively and their status to have declined.[19] But in fact the age-grading principle minimized the problems of intergenerational conflict among the Arapahoes because it served as both a means of continuity and a stimulus to innovation. The younger generations were expected to learn new social skills and to introduce new ideas but also to use the innovations at the behest and with the blessing of the elders. Arapahoe elders, while by and large receptive to change, interpreted and screened innovations, and through their role in validating change reaffirmed their superordinate position in Arapahoe society. The complementary nature of age categories actu-ally facilitated innovation while reassuring the Arapahoes of cultural continuity because by tradition each age group had definite areas of responsibility and each was morally obligated to support the other.

The Arapahoes weathered a succession of crises in relations between the generations. We cannot understand how they managed to do so without analyzing the meanings of symbols of age. Symbols newly as well as traditionally associated with being "elderly" were used many times by Arapahoes in legitimizing political change and in containing conflict. Simultaneously, the status of the elderly in the age hierarchy was reaffirmed.

The Secularization of Authority

Superordinate to all Arapahoes through most of the nineteenth century were the "water-pouring old men," seven elderly priests who had earned a requisite number of "degrees" through personal ordeals and sacrifices and who had ultimate responsibility for directing all-tribal rituals (including the age-grade ceremonies). This priesthood had custody of seven tribal "medicine bags." In addition to these seven priests, the keeper of the Sacred Pipe (custodian of the most sacred tribal "medicine bundle") mediated between the Arapahoes, both individually and as a people, and the Great Mystery Above.[20] Arapahoes could also obtain personal "medicine power" to accomplish special feats from older men or from a vision quest. Youths were discouraged from attempting to acquire medicine power independently or before they attained maturity. Instead, they were encouraged to apprentice themselves to elders. For the Arapahoes, success in social pursuits, including leadership achievements, was dependent on rapport with or aid from the supernatural, particularly aid obtained through the mediation of elders.

When the federal government's overwhelming military force effectively put an end to Indian–white and Indian–Indian warfare, personal medicine power became less relevant to individuals and gradually ceased to be sought. The tribal religious ceremonies over which priests presided were often suppressed by the government; the ceremonies were difficult to hold because many of the knowledgeable elders did not survive the physical hazards of intensive contact with whites; or the ceremonies were abandoned because they seemed to have lost their relevance to the contemporary concerns of the tribe. Skills were acquired in government and church schools without the necessity of petitioning the supernatural, and some youths who learned these skills believed they could cope with reservation life without apprenticing themselves to elders or appealing for their aid. In addition, religious leaders faced challenges from younger men who participated in such revitalization movements as the Ghost Dance and the "peyote church." In short, the potential for secular authority to exist apart from the ceremonial order developed. These developments periodically brought about crises of authority that threatened to undermine the status of the elders who occupied the high sacred offices in the ceremonial hierarchy and thereby to weaken their influence, which competed with that of government and church officials.

Studies of Plains peoples make it appear inevitable that native religion increasingly became irrelevant to contemporary conditions and was replaced by Christianity, or was superseded by various revitalization movements, or became competitive with Christian or other religious organizations. The thrust of these arguments is that after intensive contact, secular and native sacred authority were inevitably at odds or were incapable of interpenetration.[21]

Yet Arapahoe leaders in the native religion have had the primary responsibility of directing and interpreting the reformulation of political culture. Under the direction of the tribal priests, the ritual symbols of native religion became at once vehicles for mobilization of support for headmen and intermediaries, instruments of political innovation, and means of checking the abuse of secular authority. Sacred symbols frequently served to legitimize political change, and in the process were recharged with meanings relevant to new realities. At the same time that the priests validated new intermediary roles, they perpetuated their influence and reaffirmed the relevance of the native religion.

The Political Middleman's Dilemma

Arapahoe middlemen existed before Indian–white contact, although their importance probably grew as encapsulation proceeded. Before contact with whites, trade between the tribes often was conducted through band or tribal leaders. Later, Euro-American traders negotiated prices and obtained protection and hospitality under the auspices of these leaders. In the 1830s and 1840s, federal officials also tended to deal with the Arapahoes through intermediaries. In 1851 the United States requested that the Arapahoes officially select several intermediary "chiefs" to act as spokesmen for the entire tribe.[22]

Intermediary positions were filled by headmen, men who were acknowledged by the Arapahoes to be brave, accomplished warriors and "good men." A "good man" was generous, even-tempered, conciliatory, respectful toward elders, and devout. Headmen were mature adults, usually selected from the sixth grade (the last lodge completed by the mature adult males before they entered the lodge of the elders). Headmen did not exercise directive, initiatory authority. They were persuasive and conciliatory, not assertive. During group meetings in which decisions were reached about band or tribal movements, subsistence strategies, and ritual activities, matters were discussed until one opinion prevailed. If dissenters could not be won over, they could at least withdraw their objections to the viewpoints of others, and were expected to do so. If one opinion could not be reached, a decision could not be made.

In dealings with whites or other non-Arapahoes the intermediary or middleman served as a go-between or spokesman for his band or several bands and sometimes for all of the Northern Arapahoe people. The Arapahoes expected their intermediaries to act as advocates, defending their people's interests or actions, and as intercessors, pleading their needs and concerns to the dominant white society. They also expected their intermediaries to articulate the consensus of their constituency; intermediaries were not supposed to make decisions independently of their constituents.

At the same time, federal officials sought to induce tribal intermediaries to make decisions on behalf of their constituents and worked to erode the custom of decision making by consensus. They promoted directive, initiatory leadership among Arapahoe middlemen. As the strength of the Plains tribes declined, particularly after the hostilities of the 1860s and 1870s, the Arapahoes were faced with the possibility of virtual extinction if federal officials found them to be "militant" or dangerous. In these circumstances, advocacy became a very delicate matter; yet the Arapahoes expected their intermediaries to demonstrate bravery and to refuse to be intimidated. Finally, intermediaries were expected to work for solutions for a range of problems—fulfillment of treaty agreements, minimization of repressive measures, relief from poverty, for example. Yet federal policies and poor implementation of policies or agreements often made it impossible for intermediaries to be completely successful.

In short, federal officials expected Arapahoe intermediaries to be "good Indians,"[23] to reject tribal values, to be docile and cooperative. The Arapahoes expected these same intermediaries to be "good men"— to conform to the values of tribal life, to resist intimidation by whites, and to try to undermine repressive or undesirable policies and programs. Any "good man," and even more a headman or a man seeking social prestige or a leadership position, was expected to be generous and normally would make frequent public display of his generosity. The display of generosity became increasingly difficult with continued erosion of the subsistence base and persistent federal efforts to enforce a shift from a communally oriented economy to an individualistic one based on the nuclear family.

Many scholars of Plains anthropology have viewed the introduction of the intermediary role as the *inevitable* cause of social disruption and bitter political factionalism. In fact, however, the Arapahoe case shows that disruption was not inevitable. Federal imposition of the majority-vote electoral system, political centralization (with a few spokesmen representing multiple band groupings), and directive, initiatory leadership did not alienate the Arapahoes (as it did people in many other tribes) from the political process. On some Plains reservations the intermediaries who served on elected tribal councils were often individuals who had the educational and language skills to deal easily with Anglo-Americans but were alienated from many of the constituents they purported to represent. As a result, the people who wished to perpetuate native forms of political organization and concepts of authority relations were often pitted against the people who accepted the introduction of Anglo-American concepts and institutions.[24] The Arapahoes, however, reconciled their consensus-oriented political system with the political innovations initiated by the federal government.

Intermediaries on all reservations had to cope with powerlessness in the face of federal domination. In 1934, when Congress passed the Indian Reorganization Act (IRA), which offered tribes recovery from economic stagnation and decline and greater self-determination through the adoption of constitutional governments, the Arapahoes rejected the reforms. Opposition to the IRA was led by Arapahoe elders and ritual leaders. Government officials predicted that the intermediaries would become ineffective and lose the support of their constituents, yet today most Arapahoes regard their tribal government as legitimate and effective and view their status as an "unorganized tribe" as an asset. In contrast, the IRA governments of other tribes—many of them formed over the objections of traditionalists—frequently are bitterly contested and regarded as ineffective by their constituents.[25] Despite the pessimism of federal officials, the Arapahoes have managed to attain greater control over tribal affairs—and have done so without rejecting the authority of the elders.

Among the Arapahoes, traditional concepts of authority relations were accommodated to the new realities precipitated by encapsulation because the behavior of intermediaries, while usually viewed by whites as acceptable, could be interpreted by Arapahoes as the behavior of "good men."

EARLY CONTACTS BETWEEN WHITES AND ARAPAHOES

The Arapahoes lived on the Plains by hunting and gathering, relying primarily on the bison for food, shelter, clothing, and materials with which to make tools. The hunting-gathering life was contingent on the sharing of food and the communal control of hunting territory, and a high value was placed on generosity with respect to property as well as food. The Arapahoes were a nomadic people organized into bands comprised of unrelated individuals as well as kinsmen. The composition, size, and movements of the bands changed with the seasonal requirements of big game hunting and the need to provide pasturage and protection for the group's horses, which probably had been used with great efficiency in the hunt since the early eighteenth century. The tribe spent the late fall, all the long winter, and most of the spring hunting in bands or smaller groups. The bands convened in the summer for communal hunts and all-tribal ceremonies. Band composition might also change if serious conflicts arose or if band members became dissatisfied, and marriages took place between members of different bands. Kinship was recognized bilaterally, and widely extended on the basis of generation. Both parallel and cross-cousins were classified as siblings as far as they could be traced. This wide network facilitated cooperation in hunting and warfare and made possible a flexible band organization. Each band had its own headman, who, as we have seen, led by example and persuasion. But with the development of the age-grade organization and the tribal priesthood (possibly sometime in the eighteenth century), there was an overarching political structure that served to unify the bands during the times such unity was advantageous or necessary.

Little information on Arapahoe political relations before the mid-nineteenth century is available, but documentary sources indicate that the tribe increasingly lost political autonomy and strength because of the incursion of tribes from the east and a decline in population as a result of diseases contracted from whites. These factors, as well as the seemingly miraculous powers of the whites, probably played a large part in the Arapahoes' conciliatory response to whites later in the century.

When the Arapahoes encountered them at the end of the eighteenth century, and for a time thereafter, white people appeared mysterious and awesome to the Arapahoes, who both courted them and were perplexed by them. In fact, after Arapahoes encountered whites, *nih'ôôOoo*—the name of the culture hero (a mythological being who performed miraculous deeds)—came to have the historically secondary meaning "white man." In 1820, Edwin James of the Long expedition reported that Bear Tooth, the "principal chief" (perhaps only of the southern bands of Arapahoes), eagerly pursued peaceful relations and trade with Americans. In 1821 Jacob Fowler also noted the friendliness of Arapahoes toward white fur traders, who cultivated good relations with the tribe. The Arapahoe chief, who was presented with a medal and gifts, told Fowler's trading party that he had been helped to recover from an illness by the whites' medicine.[26] Eventually Arapahoes came to have a more realistic view of white people. Even then, they found the Americans' firearms intimidating and their trade goods enticing, so they sought to remain on good terms with them despite occasional conflict with small groups of trappers or traders during the early nineteenth century.

The Arapahoes apparently moved onto the Plains from the northeast, although just when the move was made is unknown. Their presence west of the Missouri was not noted conclusively until the late eighteenth century (and no record of their life east of the Missouri exists). In 1795 Jean Baptiste Trudeau placed the Caminabiches (later identified as the Arapahoes) on the branches of the Cheyenne River.[27] For the next ten years, traders and travelers noted the presence of the Arapahoes (known also as Tocaninamviches, Kananawesh, Caninanbiches, Canenavich, Caveninavish, Gens de Vaches or Buffalo People, Blue Bead Nation, and Big Bead Indians) in present-day northwestern and central Montana, northeastern Wyoming, western South Dakota, western Nebraska, and the Platte River country in central Colorado, and by 1806 as far south as the Arkansas River in Colorado.[28]

The range of the Arapahoes gradually began to shift south of the Cheyenne River in response to a number of factors. In the seventeenth century, intertribal wars in the upper Mississippi Valley, which in large part were the result of French and English rivalry, caused the westward movement of several tribes. By the mid-eighteenth century, the Cheyennes, then later the Teton Sioux, crossed the Missouri and entered present-day South Dakota, where the Arapahoes and other tribes were hunting year-round.[29] The Arapahoes and Cheyennes formed an alliance, in part to resist the domination of the Sioux and to push other tribes out of the region around the headwaters of the Cheyenne River, and partly for reasons of trade.[30] The Cheyennes began serving as middlemen in the Missouri River Indian trade. From the Arapahoes, who made frequent trips to the Southern Plains to replenish their stock, they obtained horses and traded them to the Arikara, Mandan, and Hidatsa villagers on the Missouri, who gave corn and European trade goods in return. By 1811 the Arapahoes (probably the Northern division) were encountered by explorers and traders in the Platte-Arkansas region; the more northeastern territory is generally assigned to the Cheyennes, who attempted to defend their interests in the face of Sioux in-migration.[31] The most southerly division of Arapahoes, referred to as Chariticas or Dogeaters by their Comanche allies, resided since about 1813 in Comanche and Kiowa-Apache country in Texas. During the summers they reportedly traveled northward to Kansas and Colorado for trade and raiding. This group of 250 families made peace with the Comanches just before they moved south.[32] The Northern Arapahoes probably ranged north from the parks of the Rocky Mountains, in western Colorado, and the Southern Arapahos to the south, congregating periodically in central Colorado.

The tribes converging in the western South Dakota area repeatedly came into conflict. At the turn of the century and in the early 1800s alliances were formed, then dissolved, as the groups fought intermittently over access to hunting territory and to the white fur traders. With help from the Sioux, the Cheyennes and Arapahoes drove the Kiowas southward into Colorado and the Crows farther westward. In the Platte region, they fought the Pawnees.[33] In the mid-1820s, when the numerous Sioux began to dominate the Central Plains north of the Platte, the Cheyennes increasingly joined the Arapahoes in fighting the Kiowas and Comanches on the Central and Southern Plains, eventually driving both tribes south of the Arkansas River.[34] The Arapahoes also fought the Utes in western Colorado. Even between the Arapahoes and Cheyennes, a large portion of whom had left the Cheyenne River area and permanently joined the Arapahoes in the South Platte country, conflicts erupted sporadically. John Bell mentioned that during his visit in 1820 the Arapahoes were on an expedition to avenge the killing of an Arapahoe and the theft of Arapahoe horses by Cheyennes.[35]

In less than a generation after Trudeau noted their occupation of western South Dakota, the Arapahoes had left that area and gone south and southwest. The move was precipitated by hostile pressure from the Sioux, desire for easier access to horses, and the lure of plunder in the New Mexico settlements. In 1829 the secretary of war, relying on information supplied by William Clark of the Indian Office, located the Cheyennes (numbering 2,000) in present-day eastern Wyoming and western South Dakota, and 4,000 "Arripahas" and 2,000 "Kaninaboich" (probably two tribal divisions) in northwest and central Wyoming and in Colorado.[36] Intertribal warfare increasingly had made it necessary for the Arapahoes to rely on their alliance with the Cheyennes in order to hold their hunting grounds.[37] After trading posts were established between 1834 and 1839—Bent's Fort on the Arkansas, Fort William (later Fort Laramie) on the North Platte, and Fort St. Vrain on the South Platte—the remainder of the Cheyennes followed the example of the Arapahoes and relocated to southeast Wyoming and Colorado. In the late 1820s the Arapahoes also joined forces briefly with a portion of the Gros Ventres from Montana and a group of

Blackfeet. When it was to their advantage, the Arapahoes cultivated ties through marriage and trade with Kiowas and Comanches and sometimes served as mediators or emissaries between different tribes. In short, survival became increasingly difficult given conditions on the Plains in the early nineteenth century. The Arapahoes had to be resourceful and flexible, not only in their dealings with other tribes but also with the whites from the United States with whom they came into contact.

The intertribal wars and the Indian raids on the frontier settlements and trade routes were disturbing to the American government, and efforts were made to persuade and/or intimidate the Indians to cease their attacks. In 1835 Colonel Henry Dodge led his dragoons into Arapahoe country between the Platte and Arkansas and made an agreement of friendship with six Arapahoe and two Gros Ventre "chiefs" at Bent's Fort. The chiefs represented a population of 3,600 Arapahoes and 350 Gros Ventres who were still residing with the Arapahoes.[38] But by the 1840s the repercussions of a growing dependence on trade goods, the disastrous introduction of diseases, and the increasing competition among the tribes had begun to put a serious strain on Arapahoe–white relations. Now dealings with the growing white population and the representatives of the United States government became of central importance in the political life of the Arapahoes.

PART I

POLITICAL HISTORY, 1851–1964

1

"They Held Up Their Hands": War Chiefs and Friendly Chiefs, 1851–77

Before extensive contact with whites, battle exploits were the most usual means by which a man earned prestige in Arapahoe society. Band headmen were middle-aged men with reputations for success in battle or raids against the tribe's enemies and for generosity and an even temper. During the western expansion of white Americans in the mid-nineteenth century, incursions into the Arapahoe homeland resulted in the addition of other criteria of authority.

Arapahoes increasingly depended on and sought American trade goods and foodstuffs, and access to these goods necessitated accommodation rather than resistance to whites. Intermediaries were needed who could gain the confidence of the whites and at the same time retain the cooperation and confidence of Arapahoes by earning reputations as "good men." In the 1840s and 1850s whites acknowledged "friendly chiefs," and through these men offered payments of one sort or another for the concessions made by tribal members. But Indian–white relations rapidly deteriorated in the 1860s and 1870s, and so did the influence of the friendly chiefs. Desperate for a safe place to settle in the aftermath of Indian–white hostilities, the Arapahoes were faced with a serious dilemma.

CONFRONTATION AND CONCILIATION, 1842-68

The need to establish friendly relations was precipitated by a set of interrelated conditions, all of which threatened the Arapahoes' survival. Although buffalo were once plentiful in the Plains area, white emigrants traveling across the Plains frightened away the game and destroyed

21

grazing lands. By the 1840s the bison's impending disappearance was noted by many observers. Lieutenant John C. Frémont wrote that in the 1820s and 1830s "a traveler might start from any given point south or north in the Rocky Mountain range, journeying by the most direct route to the Missouri River, and during the whole distance, his road would be always among large bands of buffalo, which would never be out of his view until he arrived almost within sight of the abodes of civilization." Writing in 1843, Frémont pointed to the contrast with the earlier situation: "The buffalo occupy but a very limited space, principally along the eastern base of the Rocky Mountains, sometimes extending at their southern extremity to a considerable distance into the plains between the Platte and Arkansas rivers and along the eastern frontier of New Mexico as far south as Texas." In the winter of 1846-47, when Lieutenant J. W. Abert traveled through Arapahoe country, he noted that the buffalo had almost deserted the Arkansas River since the grass had been worn away by wagon trains; already Indians had difficulty subsisting here in winter and spring. That same year, George Ruxton observed that the prairies, from the mountains to 100 miles down the Arkansas, had been abandoned by the buffalo, and where they were found they were rarely in large herds.[1]

The plight of the Arapahoes was aggravated by the fact that the Cheyennes and Sioux were pushing into the country of the Upper Platte, where they could still find sizable herds, and these groups competed with Arapahoe hunters. Rufus Sage found Oglalas and Brules on the Upper Platte in 1842; he noted that the North Platte was then "Sioux country." Both Charles Preuss of Frémont's party and Theodore Talbot encountered Oglalas on Horse Creek, and Talbot reported as many as 1,500 Oglalas on the North Platte in 1843. Talbot met a large camp of Sioux in July, when they were on the South Platte trading for horses with Arapahoes camped on the opposite side of the river. The two parties were mutually suspicious, "crossing and recrossing during the day, but returning to their respective villages at night, each keeping a sharp lookout on the other's motions." Sage noted in 1842 that the Cheyennes occupied a portion of the Arapahoe lands on the South Platte and its affluents. These Cheyennes had been driven south by the Sioux from the Cheyenne and White rivers. Agent Thomas Fitzpatrick stated in 1848 that the Arapahoes resented the intrusion of Sioux along the south fork of the Platte to the main river and on Lodgepole Creek. The agent noted that more than 2,000 Sioux were on the headwaters of the Platte, where a few years ago there had been none, and the main body of Cheyennes often congregated on the South Platte. The Arapahoes engaged in joint military ventures with the

Cheyennes but the tie was apparently loose at this time. Fitzpatrick observed that in 1847 Arapahoes had killed a Cheyenne and two Arapahoes were killed in revenge by Cheyennes. He pointed out that the Cheyennes' claim to the Upper Arkansas River country and northward was a recent one, disputed by the Arapahoes. But, according to Frémont, by mid-century the Arapahoes were able to hold for themselves only the parks at the foot of the Rockies.[2]

The Plains tribes placed the blame for the reduction and dispersal of bison herds on the white migrants. In the summer of 1843 Frémont observed that the wagons en route to Oregon along the North Platte and Sweetwater rivers had worn a road, destroying grass along the way. Colonel Stephen Watts Kearny estimated that on his summer expedition in 1845 he encountered 2,325 people, 460 wagons, 7,000 cattle, and 400 horses and mules along the Platte road. By 1846, the Indian agent noted that the Indians often complained that the Oregon immigrants had driven the game from this route. Lewis Garrard was told by Arapahoes in 1847 that "white man was bad, that he ran the buffalo out of the country, and starved the Arapahoes." The ranks of migrants swelled, and by 1849 D. D. Mitchell of the St. Louis Superintendency reported that Upper Platte tribes considered raids on travelers through hunting territory the just "retaliation for the destruction of their buffalo, timber, and grass, etc. caused by the vast numbers of whites passing through their country without their consent."[3]

In the face of these problems, the Arapahoes became increasingly dependent on goods and foodstuffs that they bought or otherwise obtained from New Mexican settlements or traders. They particularly sought firearms with which to hunt small game to supplement meat from bison and for use in clashes with other tribes. After the collapse of the fur trade in the 1830s, large numbers of buffalo robes were traded for food and merchandise, so that the remaining herds were further diminished. Agent Fitzpatrick noted in 1847, "The buffalo robe, which is the principal and I might say the only article of trade now left in this part of the country, is becoming so scarce that, in the course of a few years, the Indians will have great difficulty in procuring sufficient for their own clothing and food." With the buffalo dispersed, the Indians had greater need of horses in order to pursue game and transport it to their camps. Horses also could be sold or traded for ammunition and other trade goods. Garrard noted that to obtain a large supply of horses and mules, Arapahoe men conducted raids along the Santa Fe Trail and on settlements in New Mexico.[4]

Raids gradually became less feasible when the United States government, eager to promote the settlement of the western frontier, began to send troops to suppress Indian hostilities along the routes to the west and southwest. The Arapahoes and other tribes found it more practical to try to exact payments or "presents" from travelers, presenting themselves as friendly. Sage noted that the Arapahoes he met in the South Platte and Arkansas country in the fall of 1842 were "considered friendly but expected reward." In the summer of 1846, Francis Parkman remarked that whites were expected to provide feasts and tribute, and he made presents to the Arapahoes with whom he came in contact. Fitzpatrick reported in 1848 that travelers routinely gave Arapahoes and other tribes sugar, coffee, and bread. Augustus Heslep, a member of a California-bound wagon train that encountered Arapahoes on the Arkansas River near Fort Mann in 1849 wrote: "It was certainly an imposing sight. On the one side of the river, in line and well mounted, were about 160 well armed Indians." Charles Pancoast, another member of the wagon train, noted that the Arapahoes, on their way to fight the Pawnees, traded handiwork for trinkets, tobacco, whiskey, and paints, gambled on races, and unsuccessfully sought to trade horses and steers for arms and ammunition.[5]

In the summer of 1845 Colonel Kearny and his troops marched through Arapahoe country and intimidated the tribes with a display of weaponry. Earlier Lieutenant Frémont had noted the Arapahoes' reluctance to face his party's artillery. Kearny and his dragoons, determined to prevent Indians from hindering the settlement of the American West, fired howitzers to warn the Arapahoes and other tribes that the travelers were not to be attacked. Parkman observed that when Kearny swept through the Platte country to South Pass, he called a council at Fort Laramie, and when Arapahoes arrived in large numbers, he threatened to annihilate them in retaliation for recent attacks on white hunters. He fired a howitzer and a rocket, and the Arapahoes "ran away screaming with amazement and terror" to the mountains, where they remained for several months. After encountering Kearny, they were especially eager to avoid confrontations with troops, and they worked instead to negotiate for payments to compensate them for the damages inflicted on them by whites. When the United States declared war on Mexico in 1846, the dragoons again came into contact with Arapahoes, and one soldier, John Hughes, reported that an Arapahoe chief entered the dragoons' camp near Bent's Fort and admired the "big guns." In the past the Arapahoes had dealt primarily with small groups of traders and travelers; now they learned to be cautious.[6]

The Friendly Chief

White travelers drew a clear distinction between Arapahoe war chiefs and friendly chiefs. They cultivated ties with friendly chiefs and gave them presents; the war chiefs, who raided travelers, were avoided. Lewis Garrard observed in 1846 that Coho (Game Leg) was the leader of the "worst" (most warlike) band of Southern Arapahos, and that parties that came in contact with Southern Arapahos asked to deal through a "more friendly chief," Warratoria (presumably the Wattoyea or Two Mountains mentioned below).[7]

In return for allowing travelers to pass unmolested, leaders demanded presents from United States citizens, and they expected gifts from government agents as a reward for curtailing their raids. Arapahoe headmen worked to display themselves to whites as friendly chiefs. In his journal Parkman reported that in 1846 Indians always rehearsed their speeches to whites before meeting with them. He had seen some Sioux rehearsing the speech they were to make to Colonel Kearny on his expected visit that summer: one Indian impersonated Kearny during the rehearsal. In 1849 Agent Thomas Fitzpatrick informed the commissioner of Indian affairs that Arapahoes came to him expecting presents, tobacco, and a feast of coffee and bread. He pointed out that peaceful relations depended on such gifts. Fitzpatrick pointedly commented that if the Indian agent for the Upper Platte tribes failed to bestow gifts generously, the Indians would question his authority to speak for the Great Father (the president of the United States). The friendly chiefs skillfully solicited letters from emigrants testifying to acts of kindness, which they then presented to the agent in anticipation of a peace council and its accompanying rewards. Conversely, intermediaries used credentials obtained from federal agents in their efforts to solicit provisions and testimonials to their good conduct from emigrants. In 1849 Heslep and Pancoast noted that the Arapahoes and Kiowas who approached their wagons were careful to display themselves as "friendlies." One leader bore a white flag and presented a letter from Fitzpatrick certifying to the peaceful character of the bearer, Buffalo Heart.[8]

A headman's skill in establishing himself as a friendly chief affected his ability to attract and retain followers. The symbols of friendship received from whites, such as letters and medals, helped to persuade Arapahoes that a leader was in good standing with whites. Men identified as war chiefs eventually tried to alter whites' perceptions of them, because without the provisions and goodwill of whites, a headman was not considered to be successful. After raiding on the Santa Fe Trail became impractical, war chiefs were less able than friendly chiefs to make the generous distributions expected of headmen. Fitzpatrick observed that Arapahoes and Cheyennes near Bent's Fort were competing to see whose conduct was more pleasing to the agent. Headmen identified as war chiefs, such as the renowned Coho, gradually lost influence. Garrard noted that travelers avoided Coho and sought instead to give coffee and bread to Warratoria or Two Mountains, best known of the friendly chiefs in the Arkansas country. Coho became the leader of only a small band that lived primarily with the Comanches. By 1848 he apparently was attempting to alter his reputation: he insisted to Agent Fitzpatrick that rather than raid for horses, he bought them. Similarly, although Garrard identified Beardy as a prominent Southern Arapaho war chief in 1843, when Lieutenant Abert encountered "Long Beard" (presumably Beardy) four years later, he had obtained at Bent's Fort a gilded epaulette and a paper signed by the trader William Bent identifying him as a friendly chief. The most sought-after symbol of intermediary leadership soon came to be a trip east to meet with United States officials. As early as 1849, friendly chief Two Mountains asked to travel with Fitzpatrick to St. Louis and there to meet with Superintendent D. D. Mitchell. Mitchell not only granted the elderly man's request but also recognized him as the "principal chief" of the Arapahoes.[9]

In attaining success in battle, in dealing with whites, and in virtually all other important endeavors, Arapahoes needed the support of elders. Among the responsibilities of elders was the supervision of the ceremonies of the men's age grades or lodges. Ritually reinforced bonds between age-set members facilitated the formation of well-integrated fighting units. According to A. L. Kroeber, during the nineteenth century there were only seven age sets at any one time, so that all of the men in a particular grade were also of the same age set. Hence the bonds between men of one grade were particularly strong because they all experienced induction into the lodges at the same time. In the struggle for hunting territory the Arapahoes occasionally allied themselves with Oglalas, Brules, and Cheyennes to attack the Crows and Shoshones and keep them from the Yellowstone and its tributaries. On the headwaters of the Kansas River and the forks of the Platte, the Arapahoes and their allies attempted to wipe out the Pawnees. Fitzpatrick reported that by 1848 the Sioux, Cheyennes, and Arapahoes regularly hunted in what was once Pawnee country. And the Arapahoes went westward into the parks and foothills of the Rockies in an attempt to drive out the Utes who hunted in those regions.[10]

Battle exploits helped a man to acquire a reputation for bravery against the tribe's enemies, might help him to gain a leadership position within a lodge, and also indicated his ability to attain supernatural aid. When a man vowed to participate in one of the four adult men's lodge ceremonies in return for supernatural aid, his age set's "elder brothers" (selected from the third grade when the age set entered the first lodge as youths) chose several particularly brave individuals as "honored dancers" to carry special regalia during the lodge ceremony. The age-set members also sought "grandfathers"—men who had already completed the grade that the pledger's age set was preparing to enter—to instruct them during the ceremony. A shield painted with designs received from supernatural forces by the warrior himself or by an elder was symbolic of a man's personal medicine power. Theodore Talbot noted that when he visited an Arapahoe camp in 1843, "on the outside and near the entrance of each lodge [tipi] there is a tripod upon which the warrior's shield, lances, battle axe, and other implements of war are tastefully disposed." Elders who formerly had been successful warriors often were asked for assistance in obtaining war medicine. One of the Arapahoe warriors who earned recognition in the raids and wars of the mid-nineteenth century, Sitting Eagle, described how he acquired his shield: it was given to him by a man who had "fasted on a lone mountain top" until he had a vision in which he was instructed how to make and care for a shield. When the sacred object was transferred, Sitting Eagle was required to fast and pray, receive instructions about behavior taboos, and learn how to care for the shield properly. During this period he also received advice on how to live a good life. The designs on Sitting Eagle's "bear shield" (see Plate 1) symbolized the elements of the vision associated with the shield. The fore and hind legs of the bear are portrayed in the center of the shield; the buckskin pendants denote the bear's ears. The black feathers with the pendants represent the owner of the shield. As Sitting Eagle explained, "The representation of a bear on the shield is to show that the bear is very brave when attacking its foes; just so with a man. The owner of the shield when fighting the enemies he has the courage of the bear." The painted vertical lines at the bottom of the shield denote the sun's rays. When the shield was made, rawhide from the neck of a buffalo bull was dried in the sun. As the sun hardened and strengthened the bear shield, possession of the shield hardened and strengthened the warrior. The Above or supernatural world is symbolized by the blue paint on the top of the shield and the eagle feathers attached to the buckskin pendants. An elder, then, through his mediation with the supernatural, helped a younger man to earn a reputation as a successful warrior and, through his role in the age-grade ceremonies, contributed to tribal military organization.[11]

Elders' orations urged and supported the intermediary strategies of friendly chiefs as well. Their efforts bolstered the ability of the friendly chiefs to influence other Arapahoes and to obtain their cooperation.

Rufus Sage gave this rendition of the speech of an influential Arapahoe elder in admonishing his young men: "My people must not deceive themselves. . . . Those [pointing to pistols] would have laid many of my warriors low, after the medicine-irons had spoken their death words. The Great Spirit has taught the paleface how to fight." In their capacity as ritual leaders, elders worked to resolve conflicts and mobilize consensus. Travelers observed that when whites visited Arapahoe camps, they were met by a group of headmen who acted in concert in dealing with their visitors. Among the Northern Arapahoes, Talbot reported that the "two principal chiefs" or intermediaries in 1843 were Roman Nose and Cut Nose, who met jointly with whites, using the bilingual Arapahoe known as Friday as their interpreter. When Two Mountains of the Southern Arapahos was approached by Garrard's party, he insisted that the other important contemporary friendly chief also be consulted. Although we have few accounts of life in the Arapahoe camps during the 1840s, it does appear that the pattern of intense rivalry that Parkman reported among Sioux headmen was not common among the Arapahoes. For them, the age hierarchy and the influence of the priests contributed to social solidarity. When the bands moved their camps or made a communal hunt or when a serious conflict or emergency arose, headmen chose one of the age sets—usually the one occupying the second or the third grade—to police the camps and compel obedience.[12]

The intermediaries needed the elders' help to generate cooperation, for their authority was greatly circumscribed. As Fitzpatrick expressed it, "The name of Chief . . . is nothing more than nominal, as they have no power whatever to enforce law or order." Intermediaries also gained the loyalty of their people when they received presents from whites and to the elders' praise distributed these gifts generously among their people. Talbot gave an account of sharing among some Southern Arapahos when their headman was given whiskey: "When it is growing scarce you will frequently see a man take a sup of the liquor, and after holding it in his mouth a few moments empty it into the mouth of his next neighbor and so on for a dozen others as long as any of the precious liquid remains. Those who have had it in their mouths will breathe upon the less fortunate ones, that they may at least share its delightful fragrance."[13]

The Fort Laramie Treaty, 1851: The Selection of a Tribal Chief

The importance of intermediary leadership increased after 1849, when the Indian Office sought to treat with tribal representatives in order to establish well-defined areas of occupation for Indians. In this way federal officials hoped to minimize conflict between Indians and whites as well as the intertribal conflicts that threatened the safe passage of whites along the routes to Oregon, California, Utah, and New Mexico.

In 1849 the commissioner of Indian affairs instructed Superintendent D. D. Mitchell to negotiate a treaty with the Indians who ranged the country south of the Missouri River, east of the Rocky Mountains, and north of the lines of Texas and New Mexico. In 1850 Agent Fitzpatrick traveled from tribe to tribe, distributing presents and holding councils, and in the spring of 1851 dispatches were sent to the tribes in this region in an effort to attract all of the important bands to the treaty council. When Mitchell and Fitzpatrick arrived on August 31 at the designated campground, they found more than 9,000 Indians, including Arapahoes, Cheyennes, several Sioux bands, and small numbers of Arikaras, Mandans, Gros Ventres (Hidatsas), and Assiniboines. Crows and Shoshones arrived subsequently.[14]

Negotiations were held on Horse Creek, thirty-five miles east of Fort Laramie, which had been purchased by the federal government from the American Fur Company in 1849. The commissioners succeeded in getting the tribes' agreement to keep peace with each other and with United States citizens, to allow the United States to establish roads and posts through Indian territory, to make restitution for depredations committed by bands or individuals on people of the United States lawfully residing or passing through Indian country, and to accept the United States' protection from the depredations of citizens. The tribes also agreed to recognize the right of specific tribes to control specific tracts, but hunting and travel over all of the tracts were to be permitted to all tribes friendly to each other. Depredations committed by Indians within any of the tracts were the responsibility of the tribe in control of that tract. The tribes also consented to select principal or head chiefs, through whom all business with the United States was thereafter to be conducted, and to sustain those chiefs and their successors during good behavior. The United States agreed to pay compensation for prior damage to hunting grounds: $50,000 per year for fifty years, to be divided proportionally among the Indians (who numbered an estimated 50,000) and to be expended on provisions and merchandise, domestic animals, and agricultural implements. The annuities were to be forfeited by any tribe that violated the terms of the agreement. The treaty was read, interpreted, and signed on September 17. It was ratified by Congress in 1852 but amended to state that the amount

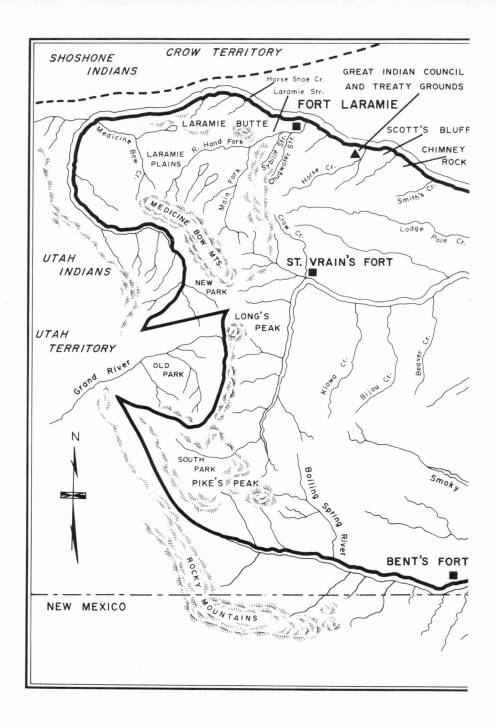

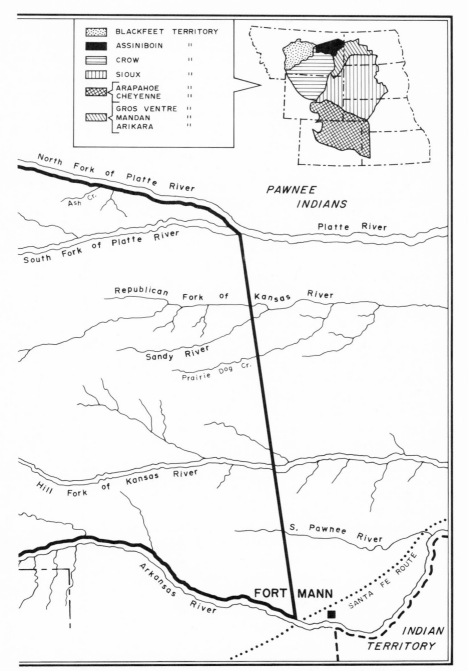

Map 1. Arapahoe and Cheyenne Territory, 1851. Redrawn from the map presented to D. D. Mitchell by P. T. DeSmet in 1851 (map 251, Central Map File, Records of the Bureau of Indian Affairs, Record Group 75, Cartographic Branch, National Archives).

paid was to be $50,000 for ten years, or for fifteen years if the president so desired.[15]

The Arapahoes made the best bargain they could; along with the Cheyennes, they were assigned territory that included most of Colorado west to the foothills of the Rockies, the northwestern part of Kansas, the southwest corner of Nebraska, and the southeast corner of Wyoming (see Map 1). Black Hawk, an Oglala Sioux, protested:

> You have split the country and I don't like it. What we live upon, we hunt for, and we hunt from the Platte to the Arkansas, and from here up to the Red Butte and the Sweetwater. The Cheyennes and Arapahoes agree to live together and be one people, that is very well. But they want to hunt on this side of the river. These lands once belonged to the Kiowas and the Crows, but we whipped these nations out of them, and in this we did what the white men do when they want the lands of the Indians. We met the Kiowas and the Crows and whipped them at the Kiowa Creek, just below where we now are. We met them and whipped them again, and the last time at Crow Creek. This last battle was fought by the Cheyennes, Arapahoes and Oglalas combined, and the Oglalas claim their share of the country.

Despite the objections of the Sioux, however, the Arapahoes retained rights to (though not exclusive use of) the country between the North Platte and the Arkansas, and they acquired official recognition of their rights to the area wrested from the Pawnees.[16]

The council at Horse Creek also initiated the selection of federally recognized tribal "chiefs" who represented the Arapahoes in their dealings with the government. Each tribe was asked to agree on the selection of its chiefs, who then made their marks on the treaty document. Arapahoes and Cheyennes selected chiefs, and finally, after much reluctance and conflict, so did the various Sioux peoples. The Arapahoes' deliberations are not recorded, but after discussing the matter among themselves, they presented Beah-at-sah-ah-tch-che (*bééOei hókechii*) or Little Owl, Beh-kah-jay-beth-sah-es (sometimes written Beka chebetha) or Cut Nose, and Neh-ni-bah-seh-it or Big Man to sign the 1851 treaty and the later amended version. Little Owl was chosen as head chief. After the selection, an Arapahoe elder, Authonishah (who was probably an important religious leader), spoke directly to his tribe, validating the authority of the men chosen: "The whites want to be good to us; let us not be fools and refuse what they ask." He stressed that the Arapahoes were morally obligated to keep their promises to the whites, for "the Great Spirit is over us, and sees us all."[17]

The involvement of elders in the legitimation of the authority of the new chiefs was not observed to occur among the other tribes. The white observers believed that all of the Arapahoes' selections were unanimously agreed to, but Frightening Bear, the Sioux chief finally chosen, seemed uncertain that he would be supported: "I must be a Big Chief or I will be dead." He finally agreed to accept the position, remarking that he was not afraid to die. The Cheyennes also apparently had difficulty agreeing on a chief. They selected one of their priests (the keeper of the arrows), a man named He Who Walks with Toes Turned Out, hoping that the people would unite behind his ritual office. The Cheyennes noted that He Who Walks with Toes Turned Out was not particularly well known for leadership ability, nor was he skilled in dealings with whites. The Arapahoes appear to have selected a man already recognized as a friendly chief. Little Owl, a Northern Arapahoe, was a middle-aged man, "well spoken of by the whites who know him." The fact that elders supported Little Owl as chief would have obligated or at least encouraged the Arapahoes to cooperate with him. The Arapahoes were skilled in the intermediary role; their behavior and their orations were designed to make a favorable impression on the whites at the council. In contrast to the more bellicose style of the Sioux, whose demands whites characterized derisively as "begging speeches," the remarks of Little Owl, Cut Nose, and the other Arapahoes were conciliatory in tone.[18]

The federal representatives gave each chief a "full major-general's uniform from head to foot," and other influential men were given similar but less impressive presents. Percival Lowe, one of the soldiers present, described a chief: "Wearing a saber, [and] medal with the head of the President on one side and clasped hands on the other, he carries a document with an immense seal and ribbon thereon—enclosed in a large envelope, that he may show all comers what the Great Father thinks of him—what rank and power he wields among his fellow men." The chiefs were delegated to distribute the goods issued to the tribes by the federal government—a task that helped their efforts to mobilize support. Five thousand dollars in presents—tobacco, serge, vermilion, blankets, knives, beads, sugar, and coffee—were distributed on September 23, each head chief directing the distribution to his own tribesmen. Cut Nose emphasized that it was particularly important for the government to make the annuity payments faithfully so that the intermediary chiefs could retain the support of their tribesmen: "Whatever he [the chief] does, we will support him in it, and we expect Father [the agent] that the whites will support him." Government officials were aware of the chiefs' need to make distributions and recognized the importance of symbols of intermediary authority, such as medals and special clothing—"the dignity business," as Lowe put it. A medal was particularly valued; it aided a chief's efforts to provide generously for his followers as it generally gave him entry to emigrant camps and, according to Lowe, obligated the travelers to provide a feast and presents.[19]

At the Fort Laramie treaty council each tribe also selected delegates to go east with the treaty commissioners to visit the cities and view the might of white society. The Arapahoes chose two Northern Arapahoes, Ne-hu-nu-tha (*nii'éhii níiOe'eè*) or Eagle Head and Friday, and one Southern Arapaho, No-co-bo-thu or Storm. The president gave the delegates flags and silver medals, and on their return these men were considered important intermediaries.[20]

Breaking the Peace

Despite the treaty, the Arapahoes' predicament worsened. After the defeat of Mexico in 1848 the Southwest was open to settlement by Americans, and with the onset of the gold rush to California the next year, there was a large increase in the number of emigrants passing through Arapahoe country. As early as 1853 Agent Fitzpatrick warned that the Arapahoes, Cheyennes, and many Sioux were in a "starving state," in want of food for half the year. Travelers on the roads drove off the buffalo and the tribes were forced to compete with each other for a dwindling supply of game. Six years later, when whites already had begun to settle permanently on Arapahoe lands, Agent Thomas Twiss noted that the buffalo "no longer covers the valleys of the North Platte and its tributaries, . . . but is found in small bands only, on the Republican and Loup Fork, L'Eau Qui Court, White river, Cheyenne water, and the Yellowstone." Even in the most favorable seasons, the buffalo by then provided a meager supply of food. In April 1860, at a general council of the entire Arapahoe nation on the South Platte, Arapahoe leaders asked French-Canadian trader and government interpreter John Poisal (the husband of Arapahoe chief Left Hand's sister and the father of Fitzpatrick's widow, Margaret) to write to the commissioner to complain that the settlement of whites on Arapahoe lands had driven off the game so that, surrounded by hostile tribes, the Arapahoes were destitute. Moreover, they did not have confidence in the integrity of their agents. But the requests for aid went unheeded and conditions continued to deteriorate.[21]

The annuities—blankets, clothing, dress goods, metal utensils and tools, guns and ammunition—promised in the 1851 treaty were desperately needed, particularly in seasons when there was little game and the men could not trade buffalo robes. But after Fitzpatrick's death in 1854, subsequent agents distributed these provisions at a few central points (in 1855 at Bent's Fort, for example) instead of bringing them to the camps, a practice that created great hardship. Often the distance was too far to warrant the trip, and few Arapahoes received the shares due them. Twiss, agent from 1855 to 1861, married a Sioux woman, and his loyalties apparently lay with his wife's people, for the Arapahoes accused him of diverting their goods to the Sioux. An additional problem was that throughout the 1850s and 1860s the agents appropriated a large part of the annuity goods for their own use. The Arapahoes and other tribes constantly complained that the agents or their business associates stole Indian goods and then sold them back to the Indians or to other whites. When Indian–white hostilities broke out briefly in 1854 and again during the 1860s, annuities were withheld altogether from the Northern Arapahoes and other "hostile" tribes. The government also restricted or prohibited trade during hostilities, thus severely limiting the Arapahoes' ability to sell their robes and obtain the guns and ammunition they needed in order to hunt the small game on which they relied when buffalo were scarce.[22]

At first the Arapahoes responded to their increasing deprivation by surreptitiously butchering stray stock belonging to whites; then in 1855 reports began to circulate of Arapahoe raids to steal stock from emigrants and settlers. Arapahoe intermediaries explained to their agent that they were ill from smallpox and unable to hunt; without stealing from whites they would have starved. By 1859 the discovery of gold in Colorado sparked a huge increase in traffic along the routes through Arapahoe country and led to the establishment of towns along the Arkansas and South Platte. One of Agent Twiss's Sioux contacts commented that the wave of emigrants had stripped the Arapahoes and Cheyennes of their remaining hunting territory. Throughout the 1860s professional buffalo hunters set upon the little game that remained in Colorado and southeastern Wyoming. When gold was discovered in Montana and the Homestead Act of 1862 drew thousands more whites westward, towns sprang up and wagon trails penetrated the Powder River country and the tributaries of the Yellowstone, the last remaining good buffalo ground (see Map 2). In desperation the Arapahoes now attacked whites who trespassed and settled permanently in areas set aside in 1851 for the use of Indians. The attacks grew into a major war in which Arapahoes, Cheyennes, and many Sioux united against whites to resist the destruction of their way of life.[23]

Throughout the 1860s the Arapahoes alternated between friendly overtures toward whites in attempts to obtain the provisions, arms, and

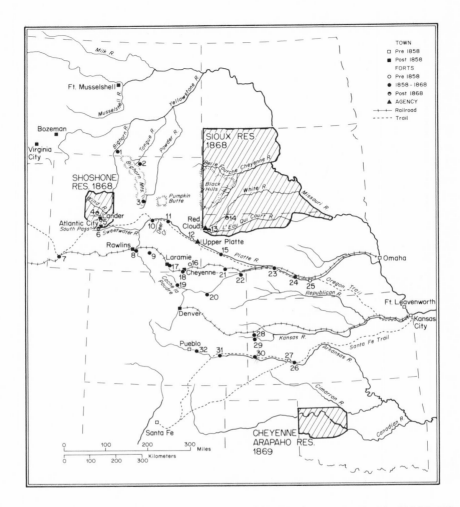

Map 2. Incursions: routes, forts, towns, 1840–77. Forts: 1, Smith (1866–68); 2, P. Kearny (1866–68); 3, Reno (1865–68); 4, Washakie (1871–1909); 5, Camp Brown (1869–71); 6, Camp Stambaugh (1870–78); 7, Bridger (1858–90); 8, Steele (1868–86); 9, Halleck (1862–66); 10, Caspar (1864–67); 11, Fetterman (1967–82); 12, Laramie (1849–90); 13, Robinson (1874–); 14, Camp Sheridan (1874–81); 15, Mitchell (1864–67); 16, Camp Walbach (1858–59); 17, Sanders (1866–82); 18, Russell (1867–); 19, Collins (1863–67); 20, Morgan (1865–68); 21, Sidney (1867–94); 22, Sedgwick (1864–71); 23, North Platte Station (1867–77); 24, McPherson (1863–80); 25, Kearny (1848–71); 26, Dodge (1865–82); 27, Atkinson (1850–54) (Fort Mann, 1845–50); 28, Monument (1865–68); 29, Wallace (1865–82); 30, Aubrey (1865–66); 31, Lyon (or Wise) (1860–89); 32, Reynolds (1867–72). Source: U.S. Department of the Interior, National Park Service, *Soldier and Brave* (Washington, D.C., 1971); Francis Paul Prucha, *A Guide to the Military Posts of the United States, 1789–1895* (Madison: State Historical Society of Wisconsin, 1964).

ammunition that they needed and attacks on whites who trespassed or initiated hostilities. When Albert Richardson visited an Arapahoe camp in 1859 he noted that while the men came forward to shake hands and declare themselves "Good Indians," only a day earlier they had threatened to kill and scalp a station keeper unless he left their country. Lieutenant Caspar Collins, on duty at Sweetwater Bridge in the heart of Arapahoe country during the winter and spring of 1865, wrote that Arapahoes visited him often to smoke, talk, and be feasted. He found them "a friendly tribe if they can make anything by it. Every day or two the chief would send in reports from the hostile tribes and then ask for 'grub,' old clothes, etc., and want to trade for my horse or steal him—either, I think." When the Sawyers expedition set out in 1865 to carve a new route to the Montana gold mines across the Powder River hunting territory, closed to white settlement by treaty, it was attacked by the main body of Northern Arapahoes, who James Sawyers believed had been given provisions the previous winter at Fort Halleck. Albert Holman, one of the teamsters with the Sawyers party, wrote that because the Arapahoes were short of powder, their attack was ineffectual, and for a while they contented themselves with killing and butchering stock. When Sawyers's men shelled the Arapahoe camp with a howitzer, they attacked in earnest, but again with little effect. Finally on September 2 seven headmen carrying a white flag came to solicit a council, claiming that they mistook Sawyers's group for a detachment of soldiers. They were given provisions and entertained for a few days, until they learned of the approach of army troops; then they departed.[24]

These were disturbing times for the Arapahoes; they were aware that they could not hope to prevent white encroachments and that they could not survive without aid from whites. Perhaps Friday expressed their distress most poignantly when he told Ferdinand Hayden in 1860 that the Great Spirit must have turned himself white and given white people powers equal to his own.[25]

Arapahoe leaders, recognizing that attacks on whites were futile, tried to persuade the tribe to battle instead against the Pawnees for control of the Republican River and other easterly territories, the Crows and Shoshones in the Powder River and Bighorn country, and the Utes (Utahs) in western Colorado. Beginning in the mid-1860s the Northern Arapahoes increasingly roamed the area north of the Platte. Sherman Sage, an Arapahoe born in the early 1840s, told an interviewer of his exploits, which took place primarily in central Wyoming and Montana:

> The first fight I was in was when I was about twenty-five years old. We were camped near Fort Casper, and our band went towards Black Mountain to hunt.

The Shoshones attacked us and we killed one of them. I scalped him. There were no Arapahoes killed in that fight. The next fight I was in was a horse stealing trip against the Crows. There were thirty-four Arapahoes, all on foot. Near the Little Horn canyon, on what is now the Crow reservation, we ran into a band of Crows. While our people and the Crows were fighting I went to a brush corral where there were a lot of Crow horses and I got away with twenty-seven head of them. The Crows shot at me, but I got away. One Crow and one Arapahoe were killed in this fight. Another fight we had was on Poison Creek, south of where Moneta, Wyoming, is now. The Cheyennes had some of their horses stolen by the Crows, so we joined the Cheyennes to fight the Crows. We got the horses back. I shot one Crow in the knee, but his people carried him off. I heard that he died the next day. One time we were on Powder River and the Shoshones raided us and stole some of our horses. Twenty young Arapahoes went after them and I was one of the party. We overtook the Shoshones and killed four of them. We got some of our horses back. The Shoshones hid out, but we knew that their camp was not very far away, so after a while we raided them and stole forty more of their horses and killed five Shoshones. At another fight on Nowood Creek we ran into a band of Shoshones who were hunting. Both tribes were at war with each other then. One Arapahoe was killed and we killed two Shoshones and a Sioux who was staying with them at the time. Near Denver, one time, we came upon a band of Utes who were hunting. The Utes scattered and hid in some heavy timber. Six Arapahoes stole a lot of their horses. I got twelve of them myself. One Arapahoe was killed in this fight, but no Utes. The next day, the Utes overtook us and killed all of the stolen horses but six. Where the Crow Agency is now, eight Arapahoes once ran into a band of Crows. One Arapahoe became separated from the rest and the Crows took after him. We killed eight of the Crows and [he] made his get away.

Youths still sought to earn reputations for bravery in battle, but the deterioration of Arapahoe–white relations posed a serious problem for headmen attempting to serve as intermediaries.[26]

As the threat of Indian–white conflict in Colorado escalated, Agent Twiss called a council of Northern Arapahoes on September 18, 1859. Twiss urged them to agree to confine themselves to a significantly smaller area, while the Arapahoe intermediary chief and headman Medicine Man urged the government to provide the winter provisions promised in the 1851 treaty. Medicine Man spoke thus:

Our country for hunting game has become very small. We see the white men everywhere. Their rifles kill some of the game, and the smoke of their camp fires scares the rest away, and we are no longer able to find any game. . . . It is but a few years ago when we encamped here, in this valley of Deer Creek, and remained many moons, for the buffalo were plenty, and made the prairie look black all around us. Now none are to be seen. . . . Our old people and little children are hungry for many days, and some die: for, our hunters can get no meat. Our sufferings are increasing every winter. Our horses are dying, because we ride them so far to get a little game for our lodges. We wish to live. Our Great Father, and you, too, our Father, for these five winters, think for our good, and speak always kind and encouraging words which [will] make our hearts glad.

Intermediaries continued to ask to send tribal representatives to meet officials in Washington and to request presidential medals and other trappings of intermediary status to validate and reinforce their authority. The intermittent hostilities, however, impaired the Arapahoe spokesmen's credibility with government agents, and the government's failure to fulfill its treaty commitments weakened the intermediaries' influence with their tribesmen.[27]

The Friendly Chiefs' Dilemma

After the Indian–white hostilities began, the friendly chiefs of the 1850s, unable to retain the confidence of either whites or Arapahoes, were eclipsed by men who had earned reputations in warfare against whites as well as other tribes and who could not be held responsible for the broken treaty agreements. At the council held in 1859, the Arapahoes presented headmen Little Owl, Cut Nose, Friday, Medicine Man, and Black Bear as their spokesmen. But Little Owl—the tribal intermediary chief chosen at the 1851 treaty council—was not selected as spokesman; instead the Arapahoes named Medicine Man, whose ability to succeed in dealings with whites was still untested. Cut Nose, one of the friendly chiefs chosen as a tribal intermediary in 1851, had ceased to present himself as a friendly chief; he had allied himself with the Cheyennes and camped with them at the head of the Republican for several months of the year. When a group of whites attacked a peaceful Cheyenne-Arapahoe camp on Sand Creek, in Colorado Territory, on November 29, 1864, most Arapahoes abandoned their conciliatory strategy. At Sand Creek the large Cheyenne camp of Black Kettle and a small band of Southern Arapahos led by Left Hand were brutally massacred without provocation. Word of the Sand Creek atrocities spread and incited the Northern Arapahoes, Cheyennes, and many Sioux to wage a major war against the whites in Colorado, Kansas, and Wyoming. After the Sand Creek incident, the agent commented, "friendly Indians lost their influence." Arapahoe leaders during the remainder of the 1860s were identified by federal officials as "war chiefs."[28]

One of the best known of the Arapahoe friendly chiefs was Friday, called by his tribesmen the "Arapahoe American." Friday's career reflected the problems faced by all Arapahoe intermediaries during the 1850s and 1860s. In 1831, Friday and two other Arapahoe boys had become separated from their tribe when a fight started at a large inter-tribal gathering. Thomas Fitzpatrick, who was returning to St. Louis from the Rocky Mountains, found the children on the plains. According to Fitzpatrick's friend Theodore Talbot, Fitzpatrick became so fond of one of the boys, who was called Warshinun (Black Spot) by his people, that he took him back to St. Louis and sent him to school there. Fitzpatrick named the boy Friday. In 1877 John Bourke, an army officer, interviewed Friday about his meeting with Fitzpatrick: "Once on the Cimarron (in what is now southeastern Colorado) a great quarrel arose among the Blackfeets, Arapahoes, and Gros Ventres [Atsina] and several influential men were killed on each side. The bands separated. Friday, then a very small boy, became very much frightened and ran off to the mountains, losing the trail of his people. He was found on a Friday by a party of white men who sent him to St. Louis, Missouri, to be educated." Friday told Bourke that he spent two years in school in St. Louis and that he stayed among the whites seven years altogether. He became very articulate in English and this skill subsequently proved invaluable to his tribe.[29]

As a boy Friday accompanied Fitzpatrick (known to Indians as Bad Arm or Broken Hand) on several of his trips west. William Anderson was present on one of those journeys in 1834. "Fitzpatrick's little foundling Friday," he wrote in his journal, "is becoming every day an object of greater and greater interest to me, his astonishing memory, his minute observation and amusing inquiries, interest me exceedingly. He has been from his band and kindred three or four years, yet some scenes and incidents he describes with wonderful accuracy." On one of Fitzpatrick's trading expeditions, he and Friday came upon a Northern Arapahoe camp, and a woman there recognized Friday and claimed him as her son. He was induced to remain with the Arapahoes, and he took up the old life with enthusiasm. Sun Road, an Arapahoe, described the return of Friday to his people thus:

> They were making a tipi of deer, elk, and antelope when the white man brought the boy back. They were traveling. They saw white people. They had white horses with black ears. They were trading them. It was winter. They heard the Indian boy was going to come. The man had wagons with cows. That was the first time the Arapahoes saw clothing of cloth, flour, sugar, coffee, bacon. The Indians thought the bacon came from a large animal in the river. They met with the whites. They had a big dinner. The hair of the old Arapahoes was tied in a bunch over the forehead. Bad Arm said he gave presents, foods, calico,

so that when ever they saw whitemen traveling they would not hurt them. So the Arapahoes quit fighting with the whites. This white man was there to ask them to stop.[30]

As a youth Friday hunted for his family and attempted to earn a reputation for bravery. Rufus Sage, who met him in 1844, commented, "Few Indians or whites can compete with Friday as a buffalo-hunter, either in the use of the bow or rifle. I have seen him kill five of these animals at a single chase, and am informed that he has not infrequently exceeded that number." Sage said that Friday's bravery in war commanded the respect of his tribe. When Bourke interviewed Friday, he recorded his exploits:

When Friday came back to his people from St. Louis, he wanted to be a big warrior; his first achievement was in a fight with the Pawnees when he shot a Pawnee's pony from under him in the thickest of the fight. For this he changed his name Black Coal Ashes and took one of his father's names—White Crow, while his own cousin, out of compliment to him assumed Friday's cast off name. In a fight with a party of Shoshones, he again behaved with great gallantry and this time took a second name, which had been born by his late lamented paternal progenitor—Thunder—and was again honored by having a step son assume the name White Crow. Finally, being one of the prominent warriors in a detachment which destroyed a village of seven lodges of Utes on Bear River, near where it debouches from the Wah-satch mountains, he took the designation 'The Man Who Sits in the Corner and Keeps His Mouth Shut.' He says that he and a Ute warrior became engaged at close quarters; the Ute leveled his gun at Friday's breast, but the cap snapped and in a second Friday had shot him through the body and snatched the loaded gun out of his dying hand.[31]

In Sun Road's recollections, Friday was an especially important intermediary during the 1840s and 1850s: "The boy became the interpreter. The boy with two chiefs to Washington went. This was the first delegation that went from the Arapahoes to Washington. They started in the fall on horseback. Took all winter and summer to go to Washington and come back." In July 1843 Friday aided the Frémont expedition's efforts to hold a council with the Arapahoes, and in April 1844 gave similar assistance to Rufus Sage's party on the Arkansas River. In 1845 he entered Philip St. George Cooke's camp of dragoons with some Northern Arapahoes from Lodgepole Creek and attempted to assure the soldiers of the tribe's peaceful intent. Friday was at the Fort Laramie treaty council of 1851 and went east with the other Indian delegates. Later he served as interpreter for Little Owl. In 1857, when he was with a war party of forty Arapahoes led by Black Bear, he served as the group's intermediary at a Mormon settlement at Fort

Bridger. Friday accompanied Little Owl and his band of 180 lodges to visit the surveying party of Captain W. R. Raynolds and Ferdinand Hayden in September 1859, bringing messages from Agent Twiss (see Plate 2). Hayden remarked that Friday was the most prominent of the Arapahoe intermediaries and that he was very influential with whites.[32]

When Indian–white hostilities intensified in the 1860s, Friday continued to urge his tribesmen to avoid military conflict with whites. His conciliatory approach lost him the support of many Arapahoes. Friday led only a small band on the Cache la Poudre from 1863 to 1868; after 1863 he became physically and socially isolated from the main body of Northern Arapahoes because he steadfastly refused to fight against whites despite tribal consensus on the issue. Friday took his small band, which varied in size but probably never consisted of more than 175 persons, to camp near the protection of the troops at Camp Collins during the Indian wars of 1864. In August 1865 the agent reported that "Friday and his family" were the only "loyal" Arapahoes. They were sent to Denver, where they remained throughout the rest of the fighting. In 1868, when peace was restored, Governor Alexander C. Hunt of Colorado pressed Friday and his eighty-five remaining followers (mostly elderly people and children) to rejoin the Northern Arapahoes north of the Platte. Late that year he was attached to Medicine Man's band as an interpreter, but he no longer had headman or intermediary status.[33]

Exodus to the North

Partly to avoid becoming embroiled in the fighting in Colorado, the Northern Arapahoes withdrew to the region north of the Platte, where they closely allied themselves with the more numerous and powerful Sioux. They were also drawn northward by the presence of buffalo in Wyoming and Montana. In Colorado it was no longer possible to survive by hunting alone. Colonel Richard Dodge noted that before 1872 the southern bison herd had crossed the Arkansas each spring in columns extending from twenty to one hundred miles wide and then scattered to feed during the summer before going south in the fall. By 1872 the buffalo region had been penetrated by three railroads. Professional hunters shipped hides east by the millions. Dodge observed that between the South Platte and the Arkansas, "where there were myriads of buffalo the year before, there were now myriads of carcasses. . . . The air was foul with sickening stench," and "the buffalo melted away like snow before a summer's sun." The Indians were "reduced to the condition of paupers." Even in the north, where the Northern Arapahoes had established themselves, subsistence was threatened by the construction of Forts Reno, Smith, and Phil Kearny between 1865 and 1868 in the Powder River country.[34]

The Northern Arapahoes, Cheyennes, and several Sioux bands joined together to expel the whites from the Powder River country. Red Cloud, an Oglala Sioux, mobilized the tribes to attack the troops at Platte Bridge in July 1865, Fort Phil Kearny in December 1866, and Fort Smith in August 1867, and for a time travel dwindled in the region. The Arapahoes who would serve as intermediaries during the late 1860s and 1870s made their reputations in these fights; one of the most prominent was Black Coal.[35]

During the late 1860s, the interests of the Northern and Southern Arapahoes diverged. The northern division, who referred to themselves as *nookhóose'inénno'* or Sage People, numbered approximately 180 lodges, according to Friday. Before the troubles of the 1860s they ranged the sources of the South Platte north to Red Buttes, on the North Platte, and hunted as far as the foot of the Bighorn Mountains. The several bands wintered in the parks and on the branches of the Powder River. There were three main bands, ranging from south to north: one, led by Friday, most often roamed on the Cache la Poudre; Medicine Man's band ranged the North Platte and Sweetwater; and Black Bear's band (probably somewhat intermarried with the Sioux) roamed from the North Platte to the Black Hills (see Map 2). The size of the bands varied; during the Indian–white hostilities most of Friday's people joined the other two bands. In an interview in 1940, an Arapahoe elder, Sage, mentioned that there had once been a fourth band, called the Beavers. The others were the Dirty Faces (also known as Greasy Faces), the Antelopes, and the Long Legs (the latter was Sage's band and, by his account, that of Medicine Man). The Southern Arapaho division ranged on the headwaters of the South Platte and south on the Arkansas and its tributaries. The Northern Arapahoes called their southern kinsmen *noowunénno'*, or Southern Men. According to Friday, they numbered approximately 200 lodges and were a "mixture of different kinds of people"; possibly Friday's comment reflected extensive intermarriage among the peoples of the southern plains. Although the northern and southern divisions resided in different areas for most of the year, during the time set aside for the Sacrifice Lodge they customarily came together, and the Sacred Flat Pipe served as the tribal medicine bundle for both groups.[36]

With the onset of the Indian–white hostilities, the Northern Arapahoes withdrew to their northern range, but the southern division had little choice but to accommodate themselves to the whites' determination to settle north-central Colorado. The Southern Arapahos were driven away from the mountains to the lower waters of the Arkansas and were pressured into ceding most of their Colorado lands in 1861. The Northern Arapahoes had not agreed to this giving up of territory and bitterly resented it. In 1865 the Southern Arapahos accepted a small reservation in Indian Territory and in 1867 agreed to a reduction in the area of the reservation, ceding their rights to lands beyond those boundaries. In 1869 they accepted (and eventually settled on) a smaller reservation on the Canadian River, in present-day Oklahoma. The Northern Arapahoes, however, insisted on negotiating with the federal government independently.[37]

Times were difficult for the Northern Arapahoes; they suffered reversals during the Powder River hostilities and their alliance with the Sioux was an uneasy one. Black Bear's band of about five hundred persons was surprised and attacked by General Patrick Connor with the aid of Pawnee and Omaha scouts on August 29, 1865. Thirty-five Arapahoe warriors were killed, several women and children were taken prisoner (and later released), five hundred horses and mules were captured, and most of the lodges and provisions were destroyed. The plight of Black Bear's people put a strain on the resources of the other Arapahoes. At this time the Arapahoes had already suffered a considerable loss of population from smallpox and cholera. According to the Arapahoe elder Sherman Sage, they could no longer raise large war parties, as the Sioux and Cheyennes still did; the small parties they could muster joined the war parties of the other tribes. Their dependence on the Sioux became onerous; by 1867 the Arapahoe headmen were seeking ways to end their war with the whites, separate themselves from the Sioux and Cheyennes, and again obtain provisions and supplies from the government.[38]

In 1867 Medicine Man, as the principal intermediary of the Northern Arapahoes, began conciliatory overtures to reestablish peaceful relations with the whites. At Fort Fetterman he told the commander that Arapahoes did not want to be involved in the Sioux and Cheyenne raids, but neither did they want to go to the Sioux reservation on the Missouri or to Indian Territory in the south; they wanted to stay in the north (in Wyoming and Montana). To his Arapahoe constituents he reportedly said, "So far as we Arapahoes are concerned, we are like the ants. There are a lot of us, but the white men are like the blades of grass on the prairie. We would have no chance if we started to fight them."[39]

Much of the support for conciliation apparently came from elders, who sought to persuade the young warriors to agree to a peace. During the mid-1860s several young men who favored armed resistance to whites had left the Arapahoe camps and joined the Cheyenne Dog Soldier band. Now the elders began to reassert their influence. Although there are no detailed reports of life in the Arapahoe camps at this time, there are indications that the age hierarchy still played an important role in political affairs, even though the warriors were probably more influential than usual. John Hallam characterized the Arapahoe view of leadership thus: "The great war chiefs, in all important offices, always consulted and deferred to 'the medicine men.'" Religious authority was still accorded more respect than an impressive military record, and ritual authority was acquired gradually with age, by degrees. The priests presided over the Sacrifice Lodge, which was held almost annually. Ferdinand Hayden notes that the age-graded men's lodges were functioning, although he gives no information about the role they performed. Hayden names the Dog Society (A-tha-hú-ha), Crazy Society Men (A-há-kai-nin), and Hide Scraper Men (Bi-taí-hi-nin) as groups of "men of the same age" who had dances peculiar to themselves. He also mentions the women's society, the Buffalo Lodge (Ben-a-ti-sin).[40]

In their public speeches, Arapahoe intermediaries appear to have reiterated their deference to and respect for the elders. When the federal government called for a treaty council with the tribes involved in the hostilities, the Arapahoes sent a delegation to make arrangements for a meeting to be held in the spring of 1868. Littleshield, who had been active in the fighting, sent Sorrel Horse and Black Coal, two warriors—probably leaders in their age sets—from his camp in the Bighorn country to meet with the peace commission at Fort Laramie. Friday accompanied them as interpreter. The main spokesman, Sorrel Horse, who presented himself as Littleshield's deputy, addressed the peace commissioners in a speech that revealed the great involvement of the elders in political matters: "My old men told me they would be looking for me, so that they could hear good news from you. I am living with the Sioux on the other side of the North Platte, but I am afraid." He stressed that the tribe wished to live peacefully. He was to report to "our old men," he said, and he added, "Our old people will also ask me for tobacco when I return." When a young man presented tobacco to an old man, the gift was an acknowledgement of the younger man's respect and deference; Sorrel Horse's speech expressed acceptance of the age hierarchy. Among the Cheyennes and Sioux, in contrast, serious conflicts were breaking out at this time between young men who wanted to fight and their elders, who counseled peace.[41]

INTERMEDIARY CHIEFTAINSHIP, 1868–77:
THE SEARCH FOR A RESERVATION

When military reprisals proved costly and ineffectual and public outrage mounted over the Sand Creek massacre and the plight of the Indians, peace commissioners were sent to negotiate with the hostile Plains tribes. The task of the Indian Peace Commission of 1867 was to settle the Indian tribes in areas where they would not interfere with the settlement of the West and to obtain their consent to a program of "civilization." Agricultural instruction was to be the focal point of the civilization effort; the hunting way of life, which was no longer possible, was to be replaced by farming. The Northern Arapahoes, well aware of their predicament, struggled to secure a home for themselves in Wyoming and resisted government efforts to place them elsewhere. As the tribe's economic and political position continued to weaken, intermediaries became less effective in dealings with whites. Tribal cohesiveness began to be eroded as various bands tried in different ways to find some measure of security.

The Treaty of 1868

Friday was paid $315 to cover his expenses in contacting the Northern Arapahoe bands and arranging for their attendance at the peace council at Fort Laramie. Federal officials had clearly stated what the repercussions would be if the Indians failed to sign a treaty: no more provisions. When the 150 lodges of Northern Arapahoes and the Northern Cheyennes met the peace commissioners on May 10, 1868, they had little choice but to agree to the government's terms.[42]

The Indians consented to maintain peaceful relations and to accept responsibility for depredations of Indians against whites, and they agreed to settle on a reservation within one year, either on the Missouri near Fort Randall with the Sioux, in Indian Territory with the Southern Arapahos and Cheyennes, or with the Crows on the Yellowstone, reserving the right to hunt outside of those territories. The government promised agricultural and educational assistance, annuity goods for thirty years, and rations for Indians who settled permanently. Forts Phil Kearny, Smith, and Reno were to be closed and whites were to be excluded from the country north of the North Platte and east of the Bighorn Mountains. Northern Arapahoe intermediary chiefs Black Bear or Wah-tah-nah (*wo'otéénox*), Medicine Man or Bah-ta-che (*bééteet*), Little Wolf or Oh-cum-ga-che (*hóóxei-hokechii*), Littleshield or A-che-kan-koo-eni (*heechexóokéhi'néét*), and Sorrel Horse or Non-ne-se-be signed the treaty.[43]

The reaction of white settlers to the 1868 treaty was reflected in the *Cheyenne Leader* of April 3, 1868: "Though the Government proposes, the pioneer disposes." The hostility of whites made it extremely difficult for the tribes to live and hunt unmolested; nonetheless, the Arapahoes subsisted north of the Platte by hunting the headwaters of the Powder River, trading robes, and soliciting provisions from the military posts. In 1868 Medicine Man's band of sixty-nine lodges accumulated 2,000 robes to trade with the Fort Fetterman trader, and received a credit at the trading post of $25 for each stolen or lost army animal they returned to the post.[44]

The requirement that they locate on a reservation was of immense concern to the Arapahoes. Their intermediaries worked to cultivate good relations with army officers, explored the various alternatives open to them, and warded off federal agents who pressured them to go to the Missouri or to Indian Territory. The Arapahoes were particularly anxious to separate themselves from the Sioux and Cheyennes, who from time to time were involved in hostilities, and they were determined not to become absorbed by larger and stronger tribes. To gain assistance in the struggle to locate in Wyoming, in the fall of 1868 Medicine Man desperately sent for Friday, who was on the Cache la Poudre. Friday traveled north with his band to join Medicine Man on the Powder River that winter, and with Friday as their interpreter the Arapahoes then began to urge the army officers to help them settle in Shoshone country in west-central Wyoming.[45]

Abortive Efforts at Reservation Settlement

In 1869 Medicine Man and Black Bear visited the commanding officer at Fort Fetterman to solicit assistance in settling the Arapahoes on land that had been set aside in 1868 as a reservation for the Shoshones, traditional enemies of the Arapahoes. Friday, Black Coal, and other Arapahoes helped the troops to investigate depredations by other tribes and locate lost stock, and tried in every other way they could to assure the army that they would live at peace with the Shoshones and whites in Wyoming. Eventually, in May 1869, General Christopher Augur agreed to try to secure the help of Governor J. A. Campbell of Wyoming Territory in arranging a council with the Shoshones' principal chief, Washakie. Campbell organized a meeting to be held in October, and General Augur sent Medicine Man, Sorrel Horse, Friday (who was an acquaintance of Washakie), Little Wolf, and Cut Foot under Lieutenant P. H. Breslin's charge. By the time the Arapahoes arrived, however, the Shoshones had left, and the meeting did not take place.

Another effort was made in February 1870. Washakie still was wary, but this time Medicine Man, Black Bear, Sorrel Horse, Little Wolf, Knock Knees, and Little Robe obtained a peace with the Shoshones and their agreement that the Arapahoes might reside temporarily in their country.[46]

The Arapahoes' stay in Shoshone country was short. Whites trespassing on the Shoshone reservation interfered with hunting and came into conflict with Indians. In 1867 and 1868 settlers had entered the Sweetwater and Popoagie area in large numbers to prospect for gold. Several white towns (Miner's Delight, Atlantic City, Lander) and sawmills were constructed along the rivers, and such ranchers as cattleman William Boyd and sheepman William Tweed appropriated the range for grazing land. Farmers began to arrive in the Popoagie and Little Wind valleys in 1869. Soon 5,000 whites were living illegally on the Shoshones' reservation. The Shoshones accommodated themselves to the trespass, but soon after the Arapahoes settled near Lander, settlers blamed them for a raid on three miners on March 31, 1870. In early April a mob of more than 250 vigilantes, assisted by some Shoshones, retaliated by attacking two peaceful parties of Arapahoes journeying from their camp on Wind River toward Lander to trade. In one of those parties was the now aged Black Bear, who was murdered along with several other Arapahoe men (the Arapahoes claimed that eight were killed; white officials counted fourteen). The whites also captured several women and children from Black Bear's and probably Little Wolf's groups. This attack precipitated other hostile encounters between Arapahoes and whites (in which the Arapahoes lost provisions and horses) and aggravated the strained relations between the Arapahoes and Shoshones. In consequence, the Arapahoes left Shoshone country. Medicine Man traveled to Fort Fetterman and, with the assistance of a white trader named Hardwick, convinced the commander and also Governor Campbell that the Arapahoes were innocent of the depredations.[47]

Now Medicine Man and other intermediary chiefs, including Sorrel Horse, Black Coal, and Friday, tried again unsuccessfully to arrange for the Arapahoes to settle in the vicinity of Fort Caspar. Federal officials urged them instead either to go north and join the Gros Ventres on Milk River or to join the Sioux at Red Cloud Agency, on the North Platte near Fort Laramie. For three years the Arapahoes had been exploring the possibility of settling with their Gros Ventre kinsmen. Peter Koch, the trader at Fort Musselshell, was visited by parties of Arapahoes who had come to trade in September 1869. The agent for the Gros Ventres noted that 160 lodges of Arapahoes moved to his vicinity in the winter of 1869, but a smallpox outbreak soon sent them on their way again. In August 1870, after they were forced to leave Shoshone country, the Arapahoes journeyed to Milk River from their main camp on the Bighorn. Medicine Man, accompanied by the trader Hardwick and Black Son (son of the late Black Bear), with Friday as interpreter, visited Koch at Fort Musselshell and informed him they would winter nearby. An epidemic of smallpox among the Gros Ventres and Assiniboines, as well as the Arapahoes' desire to remain in their own country, aborted the government's efforts to place the tribe in Montana. The Arapahoes attempted to keep whites out of the Caspar area and continued to hunt in Powder River country. Provisions obtained at Fort Fetterman and Fort Laramie helped them through the winter of 1870–71. At Fort Fetterman 800 Arapahoes were issued 10,000 pounds of flour, 4,500 pounds of bacon, and small amounts of coffee and sugar. In December each lodge received a blanket, two shirts, one knife, two tin cups, and five pieces each of blue and red cloth. But the scarcity of game increasingly forced the tribe to go to Red Cloud Agency for provisions.[48]

The Arapahoes' experience at Red Cloud was not pleasant. In March 1871 Medicine Man, Friday, Littleshield, and Sharp Nose agreed to affiliate themselves and their followers with the Sioux at Red Cloud Agency, on the North Platte. There Medicine Man died—from bad agency food, the Arapahoes angrily charged—and was succeeded by Black Coal, who gradually gained stature as tribal intermediary. The Arapahoes had frequent conflicts with Chief Red Cloud's Sioux, who overtly attempted to dominate them. Red Cloud commented, "The Cheyennes and Arapahoes are like lost children; they will agree with me at any time." The Arapahoes stayed away from the agency as much as they could, coming in to receive their rations and then returning to the headwaters of the Powder River. During 1872 and the spring and summer of 1873, while they were attempting to hunt, they repeatedly clashed with surveying parties sent out by the Northern Pacific Railroad and with white settlers in Wyoming. In June 1873 a group of whites attacked and killed four Arapahoes near Rawlins. Because of the difficulty of subsisting without agency and military provisions, the Arapahoes were forced to continue their affiliation with Red Cloud's Sioux. When the Red Cloud Agency was moved to the White River in 1874, some Arapahoes went south to Indian Territory, but 963 Arapahoes continued to frequent the agency. Black Coal worked both to improve conditions there and to perpetuate the Arapahoes' ties with military authorities. Black Coal visited the officers at Fort Fetterman, and five Arapahoe warriors (Little Hawk or Cho-tah-sun, Spotted Eagle or Oca-ton-ne, White Bird or Na-cu-vash-ni, Little Dog or Ah-tho-achee, and Wish) served as scouts in the spring of 1874.[49]

While the Arapahoes were hunting on the headwaters of Nowood Creek in the summer of 1874, they were attacked by Shoshones and soldiers from Camp Brown. This attack, known as Bates Battle, effectively undermined the tribe's efforts to avoid residing permanently with the Sioux. The medical officer at Camp Brown recorded in his journal on July 1, "This day dawned upon a day of unusual activity at this post. Indeed, commencing as it did with the presence of Lieut. Gen. Sheridan, Brig. Gen. E. O. C. Ord, commanding the Department, and their respective staff officers, and the welcome tidings that there was a village of hostile Indians within striking distance, it may be considered one of Camp Brown's great days." Having been apprised of the presence of the Arapahoes by two Shoshone youths who had stolen two horses from the Arapahoes a few days earlier, the soldiers made preparations for battle. On General Philip Sheridan's orders, thirty Shoshones were enlisted as Indian scouts for ninety days. The Shoshone scouts (under the command of Lieutenant R. H. Young), Captain Alfred E. Bates with 60 cavalry, the post surgeon, and several citizens joined by Chief Washakie with 160 Shoshone warriors left at sunset, moving northeast toward the Arapahoes, more than sixty miles away. Washakie sent his son Bishop and two other Shoshones to scout for the location of the Arapahoe camp. When the scouts returned and announced that the village was in a gorge just below the troops, the assault began (see Figure 1):

> Now all was activity, the Shoshones donning their war dresses and mounting war ponies. Galloping to the immediate vicinity, the cavalry dismounted, numbers four holding the horses. The tumult was now getting beyond all bounds and in order not to lose the advantage, a charge on the run was ordered. In the fated village all was silent as death, the inhabitants quietly sleeping, the ponies lying lariated at the doors of the tepees. The Shoshones now raised their yells, thus alarming the enemy, before the charging column was fairly within range. Many Indians, rushing from the tepees with their arms, rushed up the face of a cliff, admirably calculated for defense, and a position which the Shoshones were directed to take possession of, but failed. Many of the hostile Arapahoes took to a gorge in which the fight was sharp and effective, the foe falling in every direction in large numbers.

The Arapahoe camp was heavily under seige and much of the large pony herd was captured. Then Arapahoe men climbed the cliffs that hung over the camp and gained the advantage by firing down on the soldiers. "These disastrous results of a fire from an inaccessible enemy rendered necessary a hurried withdrawal from what had now become a

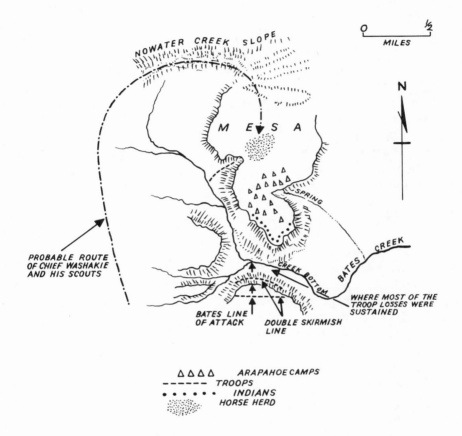

Figure 1. Sketch of battleground from Captain Bates and Chief Washakie. Redrawn from a sketch in "Medical History of Camp Brown," in Fort Washakie file, Western History Research Center, University of Wyoming.

slaughter pen," wrote the medical officer. The troops under Captain Bates withdrew. In the ensuing minutes Bates, observing Arapahoes sending smoke signals, presumably to Sioux allies camped several miles away, and noting that the troops' ammunition was low and that the Shoshones under Norkok's leadership were preparing to leave, ordered the troops to withdraw to Camp Brown.[50]

Although the advantage of surprise was not enough to rout the Arapahoes militarily, the loss of life, the destruction of lodges, and the theft of 200 or so horses were disastrous for the Arapahoes. The medical officer counted 112 lodges in the camp, many of which were burned. According to Arapahoes interviewed in 1924, the village had from 600 to 700 people. The army report estimated the dead at upwards of twenty-four. Arapahoes Goes in Lodge, Henry Lee Tyler, Shot Gun, and Rex Amos noted eighteen casualties and several wounded. Arapahoes living today recall that some families fled south and did not return north till a few years later: "When the cavalry and the Shoshones attacked Arapahoes down here on the Bates land, they took off that afternoon after they started fighting. They took off and these Arapahoes went as far as they could and then they camped over here. . . . That summer, I don't know how many of them went to Oklahoma. My grandmother and her husband went along. My dad was about five years old, I guess. And he had a sister. She was about three or four years old. And they stayed there two years, I think." Bates Battle was a turning point for the Arapahoes. In fact, the Cheyennes thereafter called that time "The Year They Killed the Arapahoes." Goes in Lodge said to his friend E. Farlow that after this fight "they held up their hands; gave up their guns; gave up all their rights to home, liberty, country and independence; put their thumb on a piece of paper (signed the peace treaty); and agreed to fight the white man no more."[51]

The Peace Tribe

As a result of the heavy losses at Bates Battle, the Arapahoes had to struggle to survive over the next two years. Success at hunting was uncertain because of the shortage of horses and the danger of attack. They lived primarily on agency rations. In the tribe's weakened condition they were threatened with loss of their identity as a political entity and absorption into the ranks of other tribes. Intermediaries were faced with the difficult challenge of trying to extract concessions from federal officials who were aware of the Arapahoes' economic and political dependency.

At Red Cloud Agency, the administration of Indian affairs was so scandalously poor that in the summer of 1875 Congress sent a commission to investigate conditions there. Speaking for the Arapahoes, Black Coal told the commissioners through his interpreter, Friday, "When we were on the Platte we used to get a great deal; but since they have moved the agency we have suffered for something to eat.

We don't get enough. . . . We draw rations every ten days, and we eat it all up in four days, and then it's all gone." The rations were of such poor quality that they often had to sell the government issue to whites and purchase food from traders: the flour was occasionally so poor that it could not be made into bread and Indians sold it for horse feed. Arapahoes occasionally received help from Fort Fetterman, but even so, many children starved to death at the agency. The officers at Fort Fetterman reported that Arapahoes killed and ate their ponies and begged for food at the post. Deaths from exposure and disease were high also, in large part because of the poor condition of the tribe's lodges. In the winter of 1874 the agent counted 963 Arapahoes in 96 lodges, many with worn-out covers—two to four families in every lodge. The trader Jules Ecoffee told the commissioners that the Arapahoes did not have adequate shelter: "In the old time they used to count them five [people per lodge], but now, since they don't hunt buffaloes much, they average about eight. . . . In the old time they used to make their tipis out of buffalo-skins, but since then they make their tents out of the canvas used by the government, and they make them larger than they used to." William Rowland, the Cheyennes' interpreter, noted that the Cheyennes usually had eight persons to a lodge, but the Arapahoes had more: "Some of their lodges have two or three families in one lodge. At the little fight they had with the Snake [Shoshone] Indians and some others they lost many of their lodges, and had to double up several families in a lodge."[52]

During the years following the treaty of 1868, the Arapahoes appear to have been united in their response to the pressures of Indian–white contact. There are no detailed descriptions of the age hierarchy or band organization at this time, but the bare outlines of the political organization are visible. Elders were instrumental in the well-being of individual Arapahoes from the time of birth. According to Friday, "In naming children, Arapahoe parents call in the oldest men and women of the band, to secure a 'lucky' appellation for the infant, thinking that people who have had so much experience in the world ought to know what designation is most likely to start the youngster on its travels." At times of stress or challenge adults sought the prayers of the elderly by inviting them to feast. The existence of the four age categories (the "hills of life") as an organizing principle of Arapahoe life is apparent in Ada Vogdes's description of tribal ceremonies. In 1871 Ada Vogdes, the wife of one of the officers at Fort Fetterman, observed that on annuity distribution days the elderly men sat in a circle apart from the rest while the middle-aged men (from whose ranks the headmen were chosen) distributed the goods. The youths also sat apart in a circle, as did little boys. (Females sat together, separated from the males.) It is clear from Mrs. Vogdes's account that the elders sanctioned the proceedings and validated the authority of the headmen distributing the goods; the elders "kept up a constant hollowing, which meant for all the tribe to gather and compose themselves for the gifts they were to receive." The elders also directed the Sacrifice Lodge and other religious rituals held during those years. Colonel Richard Dodge observed the Sacred Flat Pipe in a large Arapahoe camp: "What constitutes the medicine of the Arapahoes is known to no man except the initiated few. The 'parfleche' in which it is kept is paraded on all occasions of ceremony. It is hung up, where all may see the elaborately painted outside, but to touch or look into it would be a sacrilege." Elders also presided over the age-graded lodge ceremonies. Lieutenant William Philo Clark recorded the names of the men's lodges as told to him by the elderly Wolf Moccasin: Young Men's, Medicine Rattle, Image, Medicine Lance, Dog, Crazy, and Old Bulls (or Old Men). Clark also points out that Arapahoe men were especially known for their friendships with men of their own tribe; these friendships cut across kin divisions and may have been formed upon induction into a lodge.[53]

The Arapahoes seem to have been able to induce conformity and avoid dissension and rivalries. Headmen mobilized support in large part by generous distribution of the provisions to which they had access. When the issue cattle arrived at the agency, headmen insisted that they be turned loose to be run down by hunters directed by the headmen or their delegated aides (possibly the members of one of the age sets). Annuity goods also were delivered to the chiefs for distribution. After the issue cattle were killed, the headmen or the intermediaries received the hides, which they sold to the traders. They used the money to provide feasts for the adult males and the elders and to assist the needy. For these acts of generosity they received public praise from the elders. The Arapahoes were insistent that all influential males must be in agreement on treaty matters; the headmen persuaded all to give their names to the agent as an expression of their consent to the 1868 treaty. Headmen were also able to insist that all Arapahoes cooperate with federal agents when the well-being of the band was at stake. Soon after the signing of the 1868 treaty, for example, several stolen army mules were reported to be in Medicine Man's camp. The commander at Fort Laramie requested the return of the stock as a token of the tribe's sincerity. The mules were in the possession of three brothers who did not want to surrender them. Medicine Man attempted to evade a confrontation with the army by moving camp, but the commander warned him that failure to turn over the mules would be taken as an indication that the

Arapahoes wanted war. Medicine Man had little choice: when the brothers continued to defy him, he mobilized band consensus and, possibly calling on one of the men's age sets, cut up the three men's lodges, burned the contents, and drove the occupants out of the camp.[54]

Though some headmen acted as intermediary chiefs in their dealings with Indian Office and army officials, they had no independent authority; they could not initiate any action without popular support. From 1868 to 1875 there were several headmen—including Medicine Man, Black Bear, Sorrel Horse, Friday, Littleshield, Little Wolf, Black Coal, and Plenty Bear—whose bands, which ranged from about ten to seventy lodges, were dispersed throughout Wyoming. In dealings with whites, however, the Arapahoes united behind a few headmen, who, with Friday as their interpreter, served as intermediary chiefs. In 1869 Friday told the officers at Fort Fetterman that the 1,030 Arapahoes had four principal chiefs: Medicine Man, Sorrel Horse, himself, and Brave [Black?] Bear. Later that year, Governor Campbell noted that the "head chief" of all 900 Arapahoes (180 lodges) was Medicine Man, and that Sorrel Horse was second in rank, followed by Little Wolf, Friday ("an Indian of some education and considerable intelligence"), and Cut Foot. In the next few years Black Coal emerged as the main intermediary or head chief.[55]

The troubles of the 1870s created serious problems for Arapahoe leaders and made the task of the intermediaries extremely difficult. Because the tribe needed the protection and rations that came with reservation settlement yet the majority of Arapahoes rejected the specific reservations proposed by the government, bands began to drift away from the main body of Northern Arapahoes. John Bourke was aware of the Arapahoes' predicament: "This tribe is the Jewish trading element of the aborigines of the Plains. Having no well defined territory of their own they are always to be found in association with other bands [tribes]." Medicine Man was adamant in his talks with the officers at Fort Fetterman: his people did not want to reside on the Sioux reservation or in Indian Territory "for fear of mixing themselves up with other tribes." When Black Coal met with the investigating commission in 1875, with Friday serving as interpreter, he expressed the tribe's fears, noting that already many familes had gone south to Indian Territory, thus undermining the position of the northern division in Wyoming: "My people belong to the Northern Arapahoes; some of my people have gone south, and I want them to come back." He also stressed the tribe's resentment of government efforts to remove them from southeast Wyoming, which they considered their native country, and to place them with and subordinate to the Sioux: "The Great Spirit gave us this place here. Look at me and my people and the clothes they have. I have never got anything yet for my land [the Black Hills in eastern Wyoming and western South Dakota]. It is part mine, and part the Sioux. I like them [the Sioux]. They are what I call 'big friends'; they are a big tribe. In the first place, they came from the Missouri River and reached this place, and now they have got up this far, and they claim *all* [italics mine] this land." Black Coal's fears were realistic, for the investigating commission in 1874 encouraged the government to merge the Northern Arapahoes and the Sioux precisely because the commissioners believed the Arapahoes then would be "lost as a tribe" and therefore easier to manipulate. While the Arapahoes were at Red Cloud Agency in 1874–75, Black Coal concentrated his efforts on persuading the army officers who then were influential in Washington to intervene on behalf of the tribe.[56]

The Arapahoes attempted to convince the whites that they would not join the Sioux and Cheyenne hostiles. When in 1875 and 1876 commissions were appointed to negotiate the cession of the Black Hills, where gold had been found, the Arapahoes adopted a conciliatory position. Although leaders of other tribes warned whites to stay away from the Black Hills country, in his speeches to whites Black Coal constantly referred to the Arapahoes as the "peace tribe." According to Bourke, Black Coal and other Arapahoe headmen also offered aid to the officers at Fort Fetterman. During General George Crook's spring 1876 campaign against the hostiles, Black Coal went to Fort Fetterman to tell him where Sitting Bull's hostile Sioux were camped. In those times relations between the Arapahoes and the hostiles were strained; one Arapahoe told Inez Hilger: "At that time we didn't have any celebration because we were afraid some enemy might come. We were moving around. It was at the time of Custer's battle. We were afraid of the Sioux and Cheyennes. The Sioux fought Custer. The Arapahoes took up the cause of Custer." After Bates Battle there were no more clashes between United States troops and the Northern Arapahoes. Arapahoes were conspicuously absent from Custer's battle on the Little Bighorn in the summer of 1876. (According to Arapahoes, four Northern Arapahoe youths—Waterman, Left Hand, Yellow Eagle, and Yellow Fly—and one Southern Arapaho took part in the fight against Custer because they were restrained from leaving a Sioux camp.) Although many white settlers in Wyoming were not convinced that the Arapahoes were the peace tribe, army officers consistently contrasted the friendly Arapahoes with the hostile Sioux and Cheyennes.[57]

The 1876 Agreement

The commission of September–October 1875 could not obtain the consent of the Sioux, Cheyennes, and Arapahoes to cede the Black Hills area. Black Coal and other Indian leaders who met with the commissioners insisted that in return for the Black Hills the tribes be given subsistence for an indefinite time. Another effort was made the following year. The commission of 1876 was instructed by the commissioner of Indian affairs to hold a council with the 4,900 Sioux, Northern Arapahoes, and Northern Cheyennes at Red Cloud Agency. Foremost in the aims of the government were the removal of Indians from the Black Hills and the safeguarding of the routes to that region. An agreement was signed on September 19 and 20, 1876. The tribes had little option but to sign, for if they refused they would receive no provisions from the government. After 1871, Congress no longer viewed Indian tribes as sovereign nations whose willing consent was required before the government could take their homelands; land-cession transactions were referred to as "agreements," not "treaties." Battered by the campaigns against the soldiers and suffering the effects of a drastically diminishing supply of game, the tribes agreed to give up all claims and hunting privileges in the land outside of the reservations defined in the 1868 treaty, and to forfeit additionally the tract between the north and south forks of the Cheyenne River (the Black Hills). They promised to accept one of two options: settlement on a reservation along the Missouri River near Fort Randall or in Indian Territory, to the south. The tribes agreed to three roads through the reservation on the Missouri, and they also agreed to remain at peace and to select men from each band to maintain order. Apparently the Indians were misled into thinking that their demands for perpetual subsistence had been met. Actually, the tribes were promised annuities and weekly rations in the amount of one and one-half pounds of beef or one-half pound of bacon, one-half pound of flour, and one-half pound of corn per person and four pounds of coffee, eight pounds of sugar, and three pounds of beans per hundred persons until they were self-supporting. In order to qualify for rations, parents were required to send their children to school and to work their land if it were cultivable. The government would provide a school, a teacher, and agency employees.

The spokesman for the Arapahoes was Black Coal, who guaranteed the good behavior of his tribesmen but argued for the Northern Arapahoes' right to the northern country, and particularly to the Black Hills. He was intent on dissociating the Northern Arapahoes from the country of the southern division (the Arkansas and Canadian River region), where they had not lived for some time, and where they did not wish to go:

> My friends, you that have come here to counsel with the Indians at this agency, I remember the same thing that took place with my father at the Treaty at Horse Creek, when the Arapahoes, Cheyennes, Oglalas, and Brules were all represented. You have come here to speak to us about the Black Hills, and, without disguising anything that we say, and without changing anything that we say, we wish you to tell the Great Father when you get back that this is the country in which we were brought up, and it has also been given to us by treaty by the Great Father. And I am here to take care of the country, and therefore, not only the Dakota [Sioux] Indians, but my people have an interest in the Black Hills that we have come to speak about today.

Six Arapahoes signed the agreement on behalf of the tribe: Chief Black Coal (*wo'óoseinee'*), Little Wolf (who had also signed the 1868 Treaty), Sharp Nose (*heeniibeet*; literally Long Nose), Crazy Bull, Six Feathers (*neniitootoxúuneet*), and White Horse (*wóxhoox-nookéhit*). The latter three were apparently prominent warriors rather than headmen. In fact, in the 1870s Arapahoe intermediaries were younger than they had been earlier; some were men in their thirties. Military officials expected to treat with well-known warriors, and, moreover, young warriors were especially influential in the Arapahoe camps during times of Indian–white hostilities. After the council, a delegation of Sioux, Cheyennes, and Arapahoes (including Black Coal) left for Indian Territory to inspect the country the commissioners were urging on them.[58]

Arapahoe Scouts: Making the Bargain

The Arapahoes suffered a crisis of authority that peaked in the years between 1874 and 1876. The tribe's economic and political status had deteriorated so seriously that the intermediary chiefs had difficulty generating support. At the same time, they were unable to persuade federal agents to grant the Arapahoes a reservation in Wyoming. During the 1875 investigation of Red Cloud Agency, the commissioners' conclusion that there was no "permanent, responsible" leadership among the tribes at the agency reflected the fact that the intermediaries were not effective.[59] The Arapahoes resolved the dilemma of the intermediaries by seizing the opportunity to provide scouting services to the army. The role of "scout chief" enabled a man to build a reputation as a "good man" and at the same time to obtain provisions and concessions from federal officials.

While Black Coal was visiting Indian Territory, Indian scouts were being recruited by General George Crook for the winter campaign against the hostile Northern Cheyennes and some of the Sioux, who refused to settle at an agency. Crook organized a "peace council" among his scouts, who were from several tribes, some of whom were enemies. Arapahoe scouts were enlisted at Camp Robinson in the fall of 1876 and reenlisted in the winter and spring of 1877. The decision to help Crook was apparently reached by tribal consensus, for during those several months, 155 Arapahoes—virtually all of the younger men—scouted for the army. Prominent older men acted as leaders for the several companies of Arapahoe scouts, who ranged in age from seventeen to forty. Among the prominent Arapahoe warriors who became army scouts were Black Coal, Sharp Nose, Six Feathers, White Horse, Old Eagle, and Yellow Bear. The roster for October–December 1876 lists seventy-three Arapahoe scouts. Thirty-nine were on the roll for December–March; they were led by "sergeant" Plenty Bear (see Table 1). During April–June 1877, Black Coal, Sharp Nose, Old Eagle, and Six Feathers led the scouts, who included White Breast, House (presumably Goes in Lodge or *chiitei,* "dwelling enterer"), Bill Friday (Friday's son), and Sherman Sage.[60]

As scouts, Arapahoe men were able to construct or enhance reputations for bravery and generosity. John Bourke noted that before their enlistment Old Eagle, Six Feathers, White Horse, Yellow Bear, Black Coal, and Sharp Nose were "able men to whom Arapahoes looked up"; Black Coal and Sharp Nose were headmen of equal rank and influence. When Bourke visited in the Arapahoe camp he was entertained in Sharp Nose's lodge, where he saw "on the side nearest the canvas" a "piece of cotton sheeting covered with rude drawings of horses and mounted men," a record of the exploits that attested to Sharp Nose's reputation and success. As scouts Arapahoes performed deeds of bravery that bolstered their standing among their fellows. With the uniforms furnished by the army the scouts wore feathered headdresses that testified to feats of courage, and they also wore personal "medicine" symbolic of supernatural aid. Scouts received a soldier's pay, clothing, provisions, rations, guns, and ammunition, and could keep property seized from hostiles. General Crook told the scouts, "When I first talked with you, I told you if you became soldiers you would be the principal men of the tribe. If you get the horses of the hostiles of course you will be the rich men. You can keep your guns as long as you are soldiers." The scouts urged the army to give their rations to their families in their absence, and used their wealth to provide for the needy and make generous distributions during tribal gatherings. In this way they acted as "good men." The scouts also were asked to assume social responsibilities

Table 1
Arapahoe Scouts, Camp Robinson, 1876–77

Fall 1876

Bears Back Bone	Fat Belly	Old Man	Sleeping Bear
Bear Wolf	Flint Breaker	Old Man[2]	Sleeping Wolf
Big Man	Foot	Painted Man	Spoonhunter
Big Man[2]	Foot[2]	(Arrow) Quiver	Spotted Crow
Big Ridge	Friday, Bill	Red Beaver	Strong Bear
Black Coat	Goodman	Red Man	Walk Around
Black Man	Ground Bear	Red Man[2]	(Walking) Waterman
Blind Man	Head	Sage	White Bow
Broken Horn	Head Warrior	Sharp Nose	White Horn
Bull Robe	Hungry Man	Shaved Head	White Horse
Butcher	Last Warrior	Shaved Head[2]	White Plume
Coal	Left Hand	Shaved Head[3]	Whole Robe
Crazy	Little Fox	Shaved Head[4]	Wolf
Crying Dog	Little Owl	Shell on Neck	Wolf Moccasin
Drives Down Hill	Long Hair	Shuffling Foot	Wrinkled Forehead
Eagle Chief	Medicine Man	Singing Beaver	Yellow Bear
Fast Wolf	Medicine Man[2]	Sitting Bull	Yellow Bull
Fast Wolf[2]	Old Eagle	Six Feathers	Yellow Owl
			Young Chief

December–March 1877

Big Moccasin	Fire Wolf	No Use of Himself	Rope
Black Horse	First Man	One Eye	Roman Nose
Black Man	Flying Bird	One Old Man	Seven Bulls
Black Wolf	Gun	Otter Horn	Sitting Eagle
Blind Bear	Lone Bear	Pine	Sorrel Horse
Blue Mountain	Medicine Man	Plenty Bear	War Bonnet
Brave Bear	Mule	Poor Man	Warms His Ears
Curly	Negro	Red Man	White Antelope
Eagle Head	Nightman	Rides Bear	Wolf
		Ridge Bear	Wolf Wants Meat
			Yellow Rabbit

Source: Camp Robinson records, boxes 2262 and 2363, in Regular Army Muster Rolls, Indian Scouts, 1883–1900, Records of the Adjutant General, Record Group 94, National Archives.

befitting their rank. The scout Sharp Nose's wife, Winnie, explained that when she was fifteen her brother and father arranged for her to marry the thirty-year-old "General" Sharp Nose; he could provide for his in-laws. Salt also married the scout Bill Friday at the insistence of her family.[61]

The scout chiefs took on intermediary roles as well. Through their performance in battle and their personal contacts among the officers they attempted to influence the military authorities to befriend the Arapahoes. Army officers recognized the accomplishments of the Arapahoe scouts in two specific actions: the attack on Dull Knife's Cheyennes on Willow Creek, which effectively destroyed Cheyenne resistance, and the defeat of Crazy Horse and his Sioux followers. On November 26, 1876, Sioux scouts found Dull Knife's village of 200 lodges, and Sharp Nose brought word to Crook. The Arapahoe, Sioux, Pawnee, and Shoshone scouts under Colonel R. S. Mackenzie's command charged the village in advance of the troops and captured most of the pony herd. Unlike the Pawnees and Shoshones (enemies of the Cheyennes), the Arapahoe and Sioux scouts took no scalps. Most of the lodges and provisions were destroyed. When the Cheyennes were refused aid a few days later by Crazy Horse, they surrendered to Crook and enlisted to help the army crush Crazy Horse. The Arapahoe warriors were praised by the officers for their courage and skill in the fight with Dull Knife's people. Bourke wrote that Sharp Nose "was the inspiration of the battle field. . . . He handled men with rare judgment and coolness, and was as modest as he was brave." Crook pressed Crazy Horse until he surrendered in May 1877. The Arapahoe scout Sherman Sage participated in the effort to subdue the hostile Sioux: "I was at Fort Robinson when Crazy Horse came in and surrendered with his warriors. I helped to escort them to the campground which had been set aside for them on the west side of a small tributary of White River." Crazy Horse broke away from the agency on September 3, and to capture him Crook enlisted the aid of "all able-bodied" Arapahoes under Black Coal, Sharp Nose, White Horse, and Yellow Bear and the Sioux under Red Cloud, Young Man Afraid of His Horse, American Horse, and Little Wound.[62]

In their efforts to further the Arapahoe cause the scout chiefs often visited the officers and entertained them in the Arapahoe camp. Sharp Nose, White Horse, and Old Eagle agreed to Bourke's request to teach him Arapahoe words, and Old Eagle assumed the name Washington in token of his desire to "walk in the new road." Friday gave Bourke much ethnographic information and other assistance. Six Feathers became Crook's "brother" (thus, according to Bourke, becoming entitled to tobacco and other gifts). Bourke concluded that when he came to know Indians in their "family relations," they appeared to "better advantage" than when he studied them as enemies. Sharp Nose, he remarked, had "a face inspiring confidence in his ability and determination. His manners are dignified and commanding, coming nearer to the Fenimore Cooper style of Indian than any I have seen since my visit to Cocheis [Cochise]." From time to time the Arapahoes met in council with the officers; they selected Sharp Nose or Black Coal as their spokesman, and after deliberating among themselves presented a united front to their audience. Sharp Nose was particularly successful: "A deputation of Arapahoes, headed by their Chief Sharp Nose, stalked into the room and squatted against the walls, wrapped in black and blue blankets and puffing clay pipes. . . ." As an orator, Sharp Nose, standing erect with his red blanket, "impresses his listeners much more than did Three Bears and Fast Thunder [Sioux Indians] who spoke sitting down," wrote Bourke. Bourke recorded Sharp Nose's address to Crook and the other officers on November 8, 1876, before the troops left to pursue the Cheyennes. Sharp Nose skillfully contrasted the Arapahoes, whom he presented as self-sacrificing and devoted allies, with the Sioux, whom he portrayed as self-serving:

> These are Arapahoes; they are all my people. They are all your friends. Where you go they follow. When you told us you wanted us to help fight the northern Indians, we said, 'all right, we'll go.' When you told the Sioux, they said 'Let's talk about it.' We did not want to talk about it. We said at once we'd go. The Sioux said, 'Better wait until spring, when the grass is green. The winters are very cold in this country and the roads turn into ice.' But we did not want to wait for spring. We said, 'we'll go now. We have come out to fight the northern Sioux and we shall remain with you until you have got through with them.' We are your friends. You must be our friends. As you say, two sticks together are harder to break than two sticks separate. We are your friends. We want to be like white men. We want plenty of ammunition to fight with and good fast horses to ride on. We want to scout in our own way. . . . This country where this post [Fetterman] stands is our country. We have never received any pay for this post and don't want any. We are your friends and intend to be your friends always.[63]

The scout chiefs revitalized intermediary authority. Through their efforts the Arapahoes ultimately succeeded in attaining a home in Wyoming and improved their economic circumstances and their position in intertribal relations. The scout chiefs proudly wore their uniforms even after they were discharged. To the Arapahoes, the uniform symbolized at once the leader's bravery and generosity and his influence with whites; to whites it symbolized the wearer's trustworthiness and loyalty to the federal government. The provisions acquired by the scouts supplemented agency rations and the horses, guns, and ammunition facilitated hunting efforts. Bourke noted that there were at least 200 lodges in the Arapahoe camp, more than twice the number of two years earlier. In addition, Crook (called Three Stars by the Indians) promised the tribes who aided the army that they could settle in the Yellowstone and Tongue River area. According to Arapahoes, Crook agreed to help place them on a reservation on the Tongue River (in the vicinity of Sheridan, Wyoming). Goes in Lodge explained:

> The General asked us, "which land do you like best?" Ground Bear, a Northern Arapahoe, got up and said, "This is the best land, right here on Tongue River Reservation," and another Arapahoe, White Horse, said, "This is the land we like best." Then the General said we will set up a stake as a sign that we picked this land for our reservation. And we set up the stake and we said we want an agency and a school and a ration house and shops here. The General said, "It is right that you get these things because you have helped to fight the bad Indians." But no definite time was set when we should get this Reservation.

Although Crook was not able to fulfill his promise to place them on the Tongue River, their scouting activities brought the Arapahoes special recognition from the army. Correspondence with the War Department in the spring of 1877 documents the army's strong support for the tribe's effort to remain in Wyoming rather than go to Indian Territory. At the request of the Arapahoe principal chiefs, Colonel Mackenzie of the 4th Cavalry at Camp Robinson persuaded the secretary of war not to oppose the Arapahoes' request to settle north of the Platte "in view of their steady loyalty to the government through all the troubles with the Sioux and Cheyennes." He wrote, "The Arapahoes would be of assistance to the troops in keeping the Sioux out of the Big Horn Mountains." The Arapahoes' scouting activities aided their efforts to remain in the north in still another respect. Under Crook, Arapahoe scouts and Washakie's Shoshone scouts were required to establish friendly relations, and it was at this time that they "patched up some sort of peace with the Shoshone." This accommodation paved the way for the placement of the Arapahoes at the Shoshone Agency.[64]

The Delegation of 1877

In response to the urgings of the Indians at Red Cloud Agency, a visit to Washington and other eastern cities by a delegation of Sioux and Northern Arapahoes was approved. Lieutenant William Philo Clark, who was in command of the Arapahoe and Sioux Indian scouts at Fort

Robinson, made the arrangements for the trip. The Arapahoes selected Black Coal, Sharp Nose, and Friday, who acted as interpreter, to speak for them (see Plate 3). Red Cloud, Big Road, Little Wound, Little Big Man, Iron Crow, Three Bears, American Horse, Young Man Afraid of His Horse, Yellow Bear, Spotted Tail, Swift Bear, Touch the Clouds, Red Bear, White Tail, He Dog, and Little Bad Man represented the Sioux groups. According to Crook, the delegates were given instructions by their people as to what issues should be raised. The primary goal of the trip was to persuade the government not to settle them on the Missouri or in Indian Territory. The Arapahoes particularly were anxious not to be sent south because the 1876 delegation to Indian Territory had reported that the area was not a suitable place to live. The tribes also urged an increase in the beef ration and a continuation of the distribution of cattle "on the hoof" rather than "on the block" (that is, already slaughtered) so that the chiefs could continue to supervise the beef issue.

The delegates met with President Rutherford B. Hayes and Secretary of the Interior Carl Schurz during the last week in September and the first week in October. After the speeches of the Sioux, Black Coal addressed the president and the other officials, giving an account of Arapahoe–federal relations that was calculated to impress them with the Arapahoes' loyalty to the government and their willingness to cooperate with the "civilization" program. He argued against placing the Northern Arapahoes with their southern kin in Indian Territory:

> I have been good since I became acquainted with the white man. I have been a friend of the white man. At first I was a little foolish but I have learned better since. Whenever you have sent us advice our people have listened to it; and whenever your commissioners have come out to see us we have always shaken hands with them—I have not two hearts and always shake hands with them as I do with you today. Last summer I went to see the country at the south—the Indian Territory—I visited many tribes. Southern Arapahoes, they told me it was sickly in that country. They say they cannot raise everything in that country, and that it is sickly; they said a good many had died since that they had been there. I listened to what they said, and when I came home I told my people what I heard; and they said 'that is good; now you must push and talk for us for we want to stay in this country. If you will give us a little piece of land, where the soil is good, we can raise corn. You must try to talk about that. The first time you see the Great Father tell him all about that.' My people have always listened to the words of the Great Father.

Black Coal then argued that the Sioux reservation on the Missouri also would be unsuitable. The Arapahoes, he said, having made peace with the Shoshones, would be "good Indians" if they were placed in Wyoming, on the Shoshone reservation:

> I told them about this country to the north—the Missouri—that they must go either to the south or to the Missouri, and these two things are against them; we do not want to go to either of these places. Our tribe held three councils before I came away and we all agreed that if you would give us good land—we are a small tribe—we will be happy. We want a good place in which to live. We are a small tribe; our village is 170 lodges; we would like to join the Snakes. The Snakes are a small tribe. The old people of the two tribes are dying off. A long time ago we used to travel together and were at peace; and I guess now the young people around me would like the Snakes. I think we will get along all right. I am good and I guess they are good. The way Dr. Irwin told me. He used to be agent for the Snakes. The Dr. knows all about it. We cannot talk their language but make ourselves understood by signs; after a while we will learn to talk their language a little; and we will get along very well. There was a time when we had trouble—the last two or three years. I used to go up in their country near the Sweetwater. I used to go there to hunt and I had a little trouble there—some of my friends went there and had trouble with the Snakes. The whites would go through our camp and that is the way they always gave me trouble; and now if you will let us join the Snakes we will get along first rate, and will have no further trouble.

Black Coal also reminded the president that the Arapahoes had given the government valuable assistance in subduing the hostiles. Now the government should help the Arapahoes:

> Last summer General Crook, Lieutenant Clark, and Mackenzie—we worked together, and were trying to stop the trouble, and we were promised whenever everything was quiet, and the difficulty settled, we would come down to see our Great Father. These two men sitting here—General Crook and Lieutenant Clark—will remember what we were promised. It was settled quietly and it is all over and this day I have [come] down to talk about it. You ought to take pity upon us and give us good land, so that we can remain upon it and call it our home. If you will give us a good place to stay where we can farm—we want wagons and farming implements of all kinds; provisions and annuities of all kinds—all to be given to us as we want them.

Black Coal's speech reveals much about Arapahoe politics. He makes it clear that the Arapahoes authorized him only to express tribal consensus. In his description of the way he came to enlist as a scout and to be selected as a leader of scouts, he acknowledges the influence of a more experienced man and indicates his receptivity to group sentiment: "When General Crook, Lieutenant Clark and myself worked together I wanted to enlist as a soldier—I did not do so at once; I thought over it and made up my mind in a few days and said yes. I spoke to my friend, and said, 'You are a war chief—what best is to be done? Well, just as you say, I will do.' So they made me chief [a leader of scouts] and we went out after the Northern Indians, not to fight them, but to bring them in." He recognized that Sharp Nose, who was from another band, also was an intermediary chief; the two leaders supported each other during the council: "My friend Sharp Nose was head man that time [in the campaign against the Sioux]. He did well and will have something to say, and you ought to listen to him."[65]

The next day, September 27, the remarks of Sharp Nose followed those of Spotted Tail, Swift Bear, Touch the Clouds, Red Bear, White Tail, Red Cloud, and Little Bad Man. Sharp Nose distinguished himself from the Sioux delegates by presenting a pipe to the president. Sharp Nose reiterated Black Coal's request to send the Arapahoes to Shoshone country and asked for annuities and assistance in taking up a sedentary agricultural life. On October 1 the delegates wore "white men's clothes" as an indication of their willingness to adjust to reservation life. Before the conference ended, government officials agreed that the Arapahoes could settle in Wyoming near the Shoshones. In his final remarks, Sharp Nose requested a wagon painted black for himself and one for Black Coal: the wagons could be used to transport provisions; the black paint would serve to symbolize victory in an encounter with an enemy. Before they left, members of the delegation were given suits of clothing and presidential medals. They returned to Red Cloud Agency on October 11, after a brief visit to New York City.[66]

As a result of the council (and probably of the pressure of the Kansas state legislature, which protested the placement of "northern hostiles" in the nearby Indian Territory), the Arapahoes were authorized to move to the Sweetwater country. They were also to be issued supplies for the winter. At the time of the surrounding of Crazy Horse's band, the Arapahoes were noted to have 104 carbines and 38 pistols; the president promised that ammunition for the winter hunt and annuity goods (blankets, duck, calico, and blue cloth) would be waiting for them when they reached Fort Fetterman. The secretary of the interior sent Agent James Irwin of Red Cloud Agency to the Shoshone reservation to obtain the Shoshones' consent to the arrival of the Arapahoes. Irwin wrote the commissioner on October 27, 1877: "They [the Arapahoes] and the Shoshones both understand that the Arapahoes are to hunt this winter and be located on or near the Sweetwater in the spring."[67]

2

"Others Tell Me What I Am to Say": Chieftainship in the Reservation Context, 1878–1907

While preparations were under way to receive them near the Shoshone Agency, the Arapahoes set out on October 31, 1877, from their camp along the White River, six miles west of Red Cloud Agency. They were escorted by Lieutenant H. R. Lemly. By the time they arrived at Fort Fetterman, on November 13, the 155 head of cattle they had been issued had been eaten, and they camped for several days while the tribe was issued annuities and the men hunted with arms and ammunition lent to them by General Crook. Moving on, they reached the Sweetwater country and on November 27 stopped in the vicinity of Independence Rock, about fifty miles west of Fort Caspar, several miles short of their designated winter camp. They passed the winter there, then in early spring divided into several groups and moved on.[1]

On March 18, 1878, twenty-one lodges under the leadership of Black Coal arrived at the Shoshone reservation and camped two days' ride from the agency headquarters. Black Coal, accompanied by ten other Arapahoes, met with Agent James Patten, who reluctantly issued rations for Black Coal's people. Patten protested to the Indian Office that the Arapahoes should not have been placed at the Shoshones' agency. But by May, most of the remainder of the tribe, including those under Sharp Nose's leadership, who had been several miles to the northeast, had congregated on the reservation.[2]

Then began a struggle to subsist on short rations, to counter the Shoshones' efforts to have the Arapahoes removed, and to resist the government's attempts to undermine tribal institutions. Arapahoe leaders worked over the next three decades to cope with these problems and to buttress their authority in the face of ever mounting opposition on the part of federal officials to the role of "chiefs" in reservation society. In the reservation context, as in earlier years, the age hierarchy underlay Arapahoe concepts of authority and the patterns of their political behavior. The intermediary authority of the council chiefs, who were mature adult males, and the ritual leaders, who were elders, was mutually reinforcing. Despite the problems encountered at the Shoshone Agency, the Arapahoes coped successfully with crises of authority and grappled resourcefully with the privations and frustrations of reservation life.

CHIEFS, COUNCIL CHIEFS, AND OLD MEN:
LEADERSHIP AND AGE-GROUP RELATIONS

A man's political role and status depended largely on his age category: child, youth, mature adult, elder. At St. Stephen's, a Catholic mission established among the Arapahoes in 1884, the records reflect Arapahoe concepts of age and leadership. Males over the age of eighteen are classified in one of four ways: "old men," "council chiefs," "chiefs," and "sons of" one of the above.[3]

Men classified as "sons of" were youths. As they had been children during the hostilities of the 1870s, they had not earned a reputation for bravery in battle, and so were allowed little part in the decision-making process.

One earned "chieftainship" by building a reputation for exploits in battle (including scouting), and many youths and adult males could claim this status in varying degrees. Black Coal's daughter Anne Wolf told ethnologist Inez Hilger that "an Indian who was known to have killed and scalped a number of men of any tribe with which the Arapahoes were at war" could be "proclaimed a chief." Sharp Nose's grandson expressed it this way: "Especially when you learn how to fight and how to attack and how to get around and kill him and how to stay away from getting hurt and getting killed, scouting around like that, and pretty soon you have made it and then they call him 'chief.' That's where the name 'chief' come from—*nééchee*."[4]

"Staying away from getting hurt" involved medicine power, or *béétee*. Special accomplishments resulted from a successful relationship with supernatural forces, and all warriors had their personal medicine, which they often carried or displayed on their persons in some fashion. *Béétee* was associated with such chiefs. It is said that Six Feathers had the ability to prophesy: "He was kind of like these fellows they call scientists that know some of the future. And they used to call them prophets. He was something like that. He was telling the people,

'Someday you're going see wagons running around without team hitched up.' And he meant these cars. 'And later on you're going to see something flying around up in the sky, making a lot of noise.' And that's the airplanes. He must have dreamed that or something." More often, *béétee* was linked with war exploits. Wallowing Bull, according to his grandson, had "some kind of a power. . . . A heat wave come from hill. . . . Somehow this old man used to use this hot wave to get the enemy away. He'd be right midst of the enemy. They shoot him. They couldn't hit him."[5]

Chiefs could participate when Arapahoes met to discuss matters affecting the tribe, but they had no particular obligation to do so. They had considerable prestige in reservation society, however. Parents selected them to pierce their children's ears (to facilitate the maturation process) at such ceremonies as the Sun Dance, and they were praised by elders during tribal celebrations.

Recognition as a council chief depended not only on war exploits but also on demonstrated qualities of level-headedness and generosity and on the ability to establish one's credentials with government representatives. The council chiefs—men in their forties and fifties—presented themselves to army officers at Fort Washakie and to the agents as warriors capable of inspiring the confidence and cooperation of other warriors. Concomitantly, to earn recognition and support from Arapahoes, a man had to be able to influence federal representatives so as to obtain provisions and special consideration of one sort or another. Council chiefs were regarded as mediators and spokesmen in Indian-white relations, but had no coercive powers among their own people. They often consulted other subchiefs, men who contributed to decision making but did not usually speak to federal officials themselves.

"Old men" (in their sixties or older) were given more deference than the younger chiefs and council chiefs. Their longevity was viewed as a sign of supernatural blessing, and they held the positions of greatest authority in tribal religious ritual. Old men who were ritual authorities were particularly effective agents of social control because they mediated between the Arapahoes and the supernatural. Their approval also was essential in the council chiefs' efforts to earn a reputation for successful mediation with whites. When I speak hereafter of "ceremonial elders," it is these ritual authorities I shall be referring to.

INTERMEDIARY STRATEGIES OF COUNCIL CHIEFS, 1878–1907

The council chiefs were expected to meet two sets of expectations: those of the white federal officials and those of their constituents.

The Arapahoes expected their council chiefs to obtain concessions and benefits from whites and also to exhibit the qualities of "good men"—generosity, bravery, respect for elders, and responsiveness to group consensus. These two aspects of the intermediary role were at times in conflict because "good men" were likely to make a negative impression on federal agents, and council chiefs could protect tribal interests and obtain provisions only by gaining the confidence of the agent and his superiors. The council chiefs had to act and speak in ways that indicated to whites that they were reliable allies of the government, and which at the same time indicated to their fellow tribesmen that they were effective intermediaries and dutiful headmen. During the years 1878 to 1887 an important task of the intermediaries was to convince whites that the Arapahoes were "good" or peaceful Indians and therefore deserving of assistance. After 1887 the Arapahoes' predicament worsened as a result of intensified government efforts to obliterate tribalism and to stress economic and political individualism. These new policies presented additional challenges to the intermediaries.

Council Chiefs, 1878–87

For the first few years after their arrival at the Shoshone Agency, the council chiefs worked to ensure that the tribe's location in Wyoming was secure, first by pressing the government to resettle the Arapahoes in northern Wyoming and then, when that effort failed, by resisting the Shoshones' attempts to have them removed from the Wind River area. The council chiefs tried to convince federal agents that it was to the government's advantage to have the Arapahoes as allies against potentially hostile tribes. They realized that their efforts would be strengthened if the Arapahoes appeared to be united behind them. In working to convince their constituents that they were brave, humble, and generous—that is, worthy of respect and support—the council chiefs hoped to prevent overt dissension among the tribe. They behaved in ways that reaffirmed their constituents' expectations yet at the same time persuaded whites that Arapahoe leaders were firmly committed to defeating Indian hostiles, mobilizing the tribe to cooperate with the agent's programs, and rejecting the hunting way of life in favor of "white man's work."

"Once I Was Wild": Relations between
Intermediaries and Federal Officials

After settlement on the Shoshones' reservation, the Arapahoe council chiefs continued to press the government to settle the tribe in either the Powder River or the Sweetwater country, as had been agreed upon during the Crook campaign. Their arrival in Wyoming aroused alarm among white settlers and some army officers, who feared a resumption of the hostilities that had bloodied the 1860s and 1870s. Eager to convince the government of their loyalty, the council chiefs protested their peaceful and cooperative intent in their meetings with federal representatives. The image they presented of themselves was calculated to inspire confidence so that the government would place them on their own reservation in the north.

In July 1878, Governor John W. Hoyt of Wyoming Territory met with the council chiefs in Sharp Nose's lodge. At their request, he recorded the proceedings and later forwarded them to the president and the secretary of the interior. With Friday as interpreter, he recorded Black Coal's speech as follows:

This was the country of my fathers, now dead and dying. When, last fall, we saw the Great Father, we asked for either this place, the country along the Sweetwater, or that about Fort Laramie. It was agreed we should come here.... We promised the Great Father several things and we have kept our word. We have come to the place given us and have behaved like good Indians. We have made friends with the Snakes and the Utes, and we shall see the Crows and make peace with them. But the government has been slow in fulfilling its promises to us. The government promised us a separate agency; but we are still under the Shoshone agent. . . . He may be a good man, but he talks crooked and does not understand the Indian business. We fear he keeps for himself what belongs to us. Washakie saw him about food. Agent said, 'Nothing for Arapahoes yet. You must give them a part of yours until supplies come.' We have not much game unless we go far away, and we have not cattle as the Shoshones have. My people are much hungry and must sell furs and even their ponies for food that was promised us. This is not right. We were promised a separate trader but we are forced to trade with the Snakes' trader, who pays very little for our furs and makes us pay a great price for what we buy from him. If there were two traders both the Snakes and ourselves would be better off. We were to have farming tools and be taught how to till the land; but we have almost no implements at all, and there is no one to teach us how to work. When we came from Washington, General Crook told us he would come out in the spring and see that everything was made right. But he has not come, and many things, you see, are not right. We have many children. We love our children. We very much want a good school house, and a good man to teach our children to read your language, that they may grow up to be intelligent men and women, like the children of the white man. And then, when Sunday comes, we would be glad of some good man to teach our people about the Great Spirit. Once I was wild. Then at last I found the white man's trail. It is better than the red man's. I hope my people will all find it and stay in it.

Though Black Coal stressed the tribe's willingness to cooperate with government efforts to introduce social change, in practice the Arapahoes firmly resisted some aspects of the agents' civilization program. But in formal councils with federal representatives they were careful to present an image that they hoped would bring about policy decisions favorable to Arapahoe interests.[6]

The council chiefs were particularly adept at manipulating white fears of Indian depredations, specifically the dread of a renewed outbreak of the Sioux. Even in 1889, the *Cheyenne Daily Leader* expressed alarm at the occasional Sioux visits to Wyoming: "It is hoped that Col. Jones [the agent] will succeed in keeping the troublesome marauding Sioux off the reservation. They are a dangerous disturbing element and have several times caused trouble with the Arapahoes." In council with influential whites, Arapahoe leaders emphasized the role of the Arapahoes as allies, warriors who were potentially dangerous but who were now peacefully disposed toward whites. Black Coal, accounting to the agent for past hostilities, pointedly informed Agent Patten in 1878 that the Arapahoes had wanted an agent and a reservation of their own for several years, but that the Sioux "abused" them and would not let them have peace. Black Coal told the prominent and influential Episcopal missionary John Roberts that Chief Red Cloud of the Oglala Sioux had tried to induce him and his tribesmen to remain with the Sioux at Red Cloud Agency and fight the white soldiers, but that he had refused. When a judicial hearing was held in 1879 in the case of an Arapahoe who had murdered a fellow tribesman, teacher Ellis Ballou recorded the following speech (translated by Friday) by an elder kinsman of the murderer:

> I said to Waterman, "My friend, you did a bad thing in killing Fast Wolf—he has many friends; but don't you get scared and run away. The best thing for you to do is to give up your soul, and overtake Fast Wolf. You know when the Arapahoes made treaty with the government we promised to do right. You have not done right. Today you act fool—did very wrong to kill this man. Now don't be a bigger fool, and try to run away. Open your heart—give yourself up like a man. You heard how Crazy Horse [the Oglala] died. . . . When whites tried to arrest him he took his horse and 'skinned' out—he was a coward. But he was caught and delivered over to the soldiers. Now don't you be fool and coward."[7]

Crazy Horse was one of the government's most formidable foes in its efforts to subdue the Teton Sioux. By thus capitalizing on the whites' fear of Sioux hostilities and verbally dissociating themselves from the Sioux, the chiefs tried to influence the agent's perception of the Arapahoes. In fact, however, for two decades after their arrival at the agency the Arapahoes continued to receive, entertain, and participate in rituals (including the public recounting and dramatization of war exploits in "war dances") with the Teton Sioux.[8]

The Arapahoes also demonstrated that they were "good Indians" when they helped the agent deal with a small band of Cheyennes, led by Big Heart and White Hawk, who had come to the Shoshone Agency with the Arapahoes. As the Cheyennes impressed the agent as being intractable, their presence threatened Arapahoe efforts to reassure federal officials that they had been right in settling the Northern Arapahoes in Wyoming. When some of the Cheyennes slipped away from the reservation in 1878, Arapahoes under the supervision of officers at Camp Brown followed them and forced them to return. And in the fall Arapahoes enlisted as scouts to help the army in its campaign against the Bannocks.[9]

In 1884, when the government still had not granted the Arapahoes an agency apart from the Shoshones, the council chiefs wrote to "President Washington," urging that they be moved to the Tongue River country, as General Crook had promised his Arapahoe scouts. The letter stressed that the Shoshones were violence-prone, and thus a bad influence on the Arapahoes, who wished to remain "good" toward the whites.[10]

The speeches of the council chiefs during those early years stressed the personal ties between individual Arapahoes and influential whites, particularly General Crook. The help given the government by the scouts, the chiefs argued, entitled the tribe to special aid and consideration. When Crook's promises were not fulfilled, the council chiefs attempted to renew old bonds and initiate new ones. Their efforts centered on obtaining permission for a delegation to Washington. In formal councils they requested that some of their children be sent to Carlisle Indian School in Pennsylvania. At Black Coal's urging, the Arapahoes' teacher, Ellis Ballou, obtained admittance to Carlisle for thirteen children.[11]

When their children departed in 1881, the council chiefs, in a meeting with James Patten (the proceedings of which they requested be forwarded to Washington), affirmed the reciprocal obligations of the chiefs and the officials in Washington. This relationship, they stressed, was formalized by the presentation of a pipe, carried by the children, from each of the council chiefs and subchiefs to an official. Sharp Nose remarked for the record, "We give our children to the government to do as they think best in teaching them the right way, hoping that the officers will, after a while, permit us go and see them. . . . I send by my son Dickens a pipe for the President of the United States." And White

Horse stated, "I send by my son Cyrus a pipe of peace to be given to Secretary of War. We don't want fight white men anymore. . . ." Black Coal wished the government in Washington to know that Arapahoes "have given our children, whom we love, into their hands. We wish also to assure you by this that we never more want to go on warpath, but always live in peace." The Arapahoes hoped that the pipes would be acknowledged by the white officials and that they would infuse the children's trip east with a special solemnity and importance. For the Arapahoes, a pipe was symbolic of peaceful intent, truthfulness, and mutual obligation. Chief Black Coal sent his fourteen-year-old son, Sumner Black Coal; Chief Sharp Nose, his fourteen-year-old son, Dickens; Friday, his two grandsons Hayes (the son of Bill Friday) and Grant (the son of Iron); Chief Little Wolf, his son Lincoln; Chief Washington, his son Horace; Old Man Scarface, his son William Shakespeare; Chief White Horse, his son Cyrus; Chief Littleshield, his daughter Mollie; Subchief Grasshopper, his son Peter; Subchief Wolf Moccasin, his son Garfield; Subchief New Lodge, his son Raleigh; and Subchief White Breast, his daughter Libbie. Several of the children subsequently died or developed chronic illnesses. Only the sons of Black Coal, Little Wolf, White Horse, Scarface, and Wolf Moccasin returned alive and in good health, and these boys served as scribes for the council chiefs.[12]

The council chiefs' efforts to present themselves as "good Indians" and allies were rewarded. Governor Hoyt secured a trader, teacher, and farmer for the Arapahoes, and his visit resulted in an investigation of the unpopular Agent Patten (1878–79). During Agent Charles Hatton's term (1880–82) the chiefs obtained permission for a five-member delegation to visit their children at Carlisle and for a meeting in Washington in February 1882, but the delegation's efforts to ameliorate conditions were unsuccessful. The tribe requested further meetings in 1885 and 1886 in the hope of persuading the government to let them move to the Tongue or Powder River country (the Sweetwater region was by then heavily settled by whites), but the federal government was unwilling to take further action in the Arapahoe case. Agent Sanderson Martin (1884–85) bluntly informed the council chiefs, "The big council [Congress] at Washington has said to the President that never again as long as the sun shines shall he make another treaty with an Indian. You can not go to Powder River. Here you must stay and die. So must your children. . . ."[13] As the Shoshones were unwilling to have the Arapahoes stay, the council chiefs turned their efforts toward convincing the agents that they would cooperate with the civilization program. At the same time, the traditional duties of headmen fell to the council chiefs.

Plate 1. Sitting Eagle's shield. Model, collected by Cleaver Warden, 1900; diameter is 56.6 cm. The designs symbolize the owner's relationship with a supernatural helper from whom the owner acquired the medicine powers that enabled him to become a chief. Courtesy of the Field Museum of Natural History, Chicago.

Plate 2. Arapahoe chiefs near the Rocky Mountains, ca. 1859. Friday is at the far right; the man to Friday's right is probably Little Owl. At this time the Arapahoes were still able to hunt buffalo for a major part of their subsistence; note the buffalo robes worn by the chiefs. Courtesy of the National Anthropological Archives, Smithsonian Institution.

Plate 3. Delegation of 1877 to Washington, D.C. Front row, left to right: Touch the Clouds (Miniconjou Sioux), Sharp Nose (Arapahoe), Black Coal (Arapahoe), Friday (Arapahoe); back row: all unidentified. Black Coal and Sharp Nose are shown wearing the formal dress of intermediary chiefs. Courtesy of the National Anthropological Archives, Smithsonian Institution.

Plate 4. Arapahoe camp on the Shoshone Reservation, 1881–82. These Arapahoes were camped on the bank of the Little Wind River, a short distance above the hot springs. By this time the buffalo were scarce and the tribe relied on canvas for their tipis and cloth goods for their clothing. Courtesy of the National Anthropological Archives, Smithsonian Institution.

Plate 5. Arapahoe and Shoshone chiefs on the occasion of President Arthur's visit to the reservation, August 1883. The Shoshone chiefs shown are: (1) Jim Washakie, (3) Aah-an-golta's son, (4) Mat-koi-ta, (5) Mud-sat-sie, (6) Mam-a-van-a-zah, (7) Com-an-ch. The Arapahoe chiefs are (9) Wallowing Bull, (10) Ground Bear, (11) Sage, (12) Black Coal. Charles Washakie (13) and George Washakie (2) are Shoshone youths; the person indicated by the number (8) is unidentified. The Shoshone chiefs are positioned more prestigiously than the Arapahoes, reflecting the status of the Arapahoes at the agency during the early years of settlement on the reservation. Courtesy of the Western History Research Center, University of Wyoming.

Plate 6. Arapahoes and Shoshones signing the cession agreement, April 1904. The Shoshones are: (2) Tigee, (3) George Terry, (5) Dick Washakie, (6) George Harris, (8) Charlie Lahoe, (14) Charlie Washakie, (19) Charlie Meyers. The Arapahoes are: (9) Morris White Plume, age 32; (17) Crook Sharp Nose (Crook Norse), age 31; (18) Yellow Calf, age 44; (20) Edward Wanstall, age 35; (21) Reverend Sherman Coolidge, age 44; (22) Bad Teeth (Byron Trosper), age 44; (23) Seth Mule, age 49. The white men are: (4) Clerk Churchill, (7) Ed Martinez, (10) Captain H. G. Nickerson, (12) Major James McLaughlin, (13) F. G. Burnett, (15) H. E. Wadsworth, (16) Dr. S. H. Welty. None of the Arapahoes shown here were council chiefs at the time of the agreement. Courtesy of the Western History Research Center, University of Wyoming.

Plate 7. Sharp Nose and Captain William C. Brown at Fort Washakie, 1899. Sharp Nose, who served as scout at the fort, and other council chiefs cultivated friendships with army officers at the fort. Courtesy of the National Archives.

Plate 8. Arapahoe delegation to Washington, D.C., March 1908. Left to right: councilmen Little Wolf, Lone Bear, Yellow Calf; interpreter Tom Crispin, standing. The councilmen, wearing "white men's clothes," met with officials in the Indian Office and the Bureau of Catholic Indian Missions. Courtesy of the National Anthropological Archives, Smithsonian Institution.

"People Depending on Him":
Relations with Arapahoe Constituents

After the military threat of the Plains Indians subsided, Congress was increasingly less liberal in appropriating funds for the support of the tribes. The government's failure to provide adequate rations aggravated the existing tensions between the two tribes. Violence was narrowly averted on ration-issue days.[14] The council chiefs had to struggle to perform their roles as advocates and intercessors. So as to prevent the agent from capitalizing on social divisions in the tribe in order to implement controversial policies and programs, they sought to present a united front, yet they had to be careful not to appear to be acting on their own authority. The council chiefs also worked to convince their constituents that they would not be intimidated by the whites or the Shoshones, that they could obtain provisions from government and nongovernment sources, and that they could distribute tribal resources equitably in the face of the mounting pressures brought about by conditions of poverty.

The council chiefs, aware of their precarious political position at the Shoshone Agency, sought to prevent disputes among members of the tribe which the agent could exploit in his efforts to resist tribal demands. Their task was especially difficult because the Arapahoes were used to living in dispersed bands for most of the year and resolving serious conflicts by social fission. Settlement on the reservation threw the bands into permanent proximity and increased the likelihood of quarrels and rivalries. In order to increase their effectiveness with the agent, Arapahoe leaders sought to unify their people behind the council chiefs.

The tribe first settled in two large encampments about ten miles apart and in one smaller camp nearer the agency headquarters (see Plate 4). In the late summer of 1879, Friday's small band was camped at the mouth of Trout Creek and Sharp Nose's group was between Friday's camp and the large following of Black Coal, at the Forks of the Wind and Popoagie rivers. When Friday died, in May 1881, he left no clear successor. Both Bill Friday, his son, and Iron, his son-in-law, had some influence, but apparently not enough to hold the support of the people settled in the Trout Creek area.[15]

By 1882 several families were camping together along the Little Wind River from Trout Creek to the Forks; a few families camped east of the Forks and others on the Wind River. In attempting to cooperate with the agent and raise hay for sale to replace income lost from the trade in hides, the large camps dispersed into several smaller encampments along the rivers and constructed irrigation ditches, the men from each band using a borrowed plow. Henry Lee Tyler, from Little Wolf's camp, described the building of irrigation ditches thus: "One year after arriving on this reservation, our agent induced us to try to farm. . . . In farming, we cannot get results without water, so these people . . . tried to make their own ditches. A little further down, another bunch of Indians tried to construct their own ditches as best they knew how. Still further down, another ditch was constructed by the Indians. My friends, I can show you the marks of those old ditches, before they were cut up. Each year, more Indians tried to farm, and eleven or twelve ditches must have been made by these Indians."[16]

The camps of extended families were settled along the rivers in at least six main clusters from east to west: *hotei-niichihehe'* or Wind Riverers (literally, "bighorn sheep creekers"), *nischêhiinenno'* or Antelope People, *heeyóôneehiiho'* or Long Leggers, *cheinowuuhuno'* or Quick to Angerers, *tee'i'eiOi'* or Greasy Facers, and *chóo'ou'éiinenno'* or Lump on Forehead People. Several Big Lodge People (*bêesôowú'unenno'*), formerly a tribal division distinct from the main body of Arapahoes, were living among these groups (a large number among the Antelope People). They still spoke a distinct dialect and held an acknowledged place as the custodians of the tribal medicine bundle, the Sacred Pipe.[17]

Each family camp acknowledged one or more senior males as headmen. These men were often council chiefs or subchiefs, as well. Conflict and ill feeling sometimes existed between the various camps, but federal officials were not made aware of social divisions. Black Coal's and Sharp Nose's followings had been antagonistic to each other just before they settled on the reservation. According to Arapahoes living today, the tension was due to a quarrel in which Black Coal wounded a man in Sharp Nose's band. But once they came to the Shoshone Agency, both Black Coal's group (numbering about 700) and Sharp Nose's people (approximately 250) acknowledged both men as council chiefs. Black Coal, who was recognized by the agent as head chief, and Sharp Nose, who was second in rank, were never observed to clash in the presence of whites. In the formal councils, Sharp Nose always waited until Black Coal spoke, then expressed agreement. When Black Coal died, in 1893, Sharp Nose was accepted by all as head chief. Other Arapahoes who were accorded the status of council chief by both the tribe and federal representatives were Friday, Little Wolf, Washington (also known as *nii'êhii-beh'iih*, "old eagle"), White Horse, Eagle Head, and Eagle Dress (*nii'êhii-biixuut*, literally "eagle shirt"). These men spoke in the meetings with government agents but always in support of the position taken by Black Coal and Sharp Nose. Several subchiefs acted as advisers and counselors, but they did not speak officially in the meetings between Arapahoes and whites: Six Feathers, Willow, Young Chief, Wolf Moccasin, Scarface, New Lodge, Crooked Legs, Curly Hair, Blind Warrior, Plenty Bear, Spotted Crow, Weasel Horn, Shoulder Blade, Black Horse, Iron Man, Little Owl, Grasshopper, Sun Road, and Littleshield (who died soon after he arrived with his followers, several months after most Arapahoes had settled on the reservation).[18]

By 1890 James Mooney reported that Arapahoe bands were consolidated into three main groups: Forks of the River Men, Bad Pipes, and Greasy Faces. Mooney gives only the English translation of these band names, but Arapahoes today recall the native terms: Black Coal's people were referred to as *nóonó'owú'unénno'*, "forks people," and the family groups under Sharp Nose were called *woxúuchó'ono'*, "bad pipers." Mooney states that the Greasy Faces (*tee'i'eiOi'*) were under the leadership of Spotted Horse, but I can find no record or recollection of a leader with this name living on the reservation at that time. Throughout the 1880s and 1890s, the Arapahoes supported several council chiefs who acted as spokesmen, articulating tribal consensus and presenting the Arapahoes to federal officials as a unified people.[19]

In eliciting the appearance (if not always the reality) of tribal consensus, council chiefs relied on the support of the elders, who admonished the people to "get along" with each other. The council chiefs made use of regalia—symbols of leadership—which the Arapahoes associated with old age and supernatural blessing. A. L. Kroeber makes clear how one council chief's regalia evoked strong sentiments that encouraged tribal members to work toward consensus and to avoid disruptive behavior. According to Kroeber's account, the council chief was a commanding figure at formal tribal meetings. At the sight of the scepter carried by the chief as a mark of his office (see Figure 2), the people fell silent out of respect. Attached to the top of the wooden staff were several dark crow feathers, representing the hair of old men, and an eagle plume, representing the headdress of old men. At the base of the staff were four buffalo-hair pendants, signifying scalps, that is, the war exploits of successful long-lived men. The scepter, an emblem of the council chief's acceptance by the tribe's elders, validated his authority in the eyes of the Arapahoes. Kroeber also observed that this particular chief's headdress called attention to his personal exploits and his access to supernatural power. Although the original vision experience that provided instructions for the making of the headdress is not known, Kroeber noted that the "horse medicine" gave the owner the ability to accomplish extraordinary feats with horses. The "buffalo medicine"

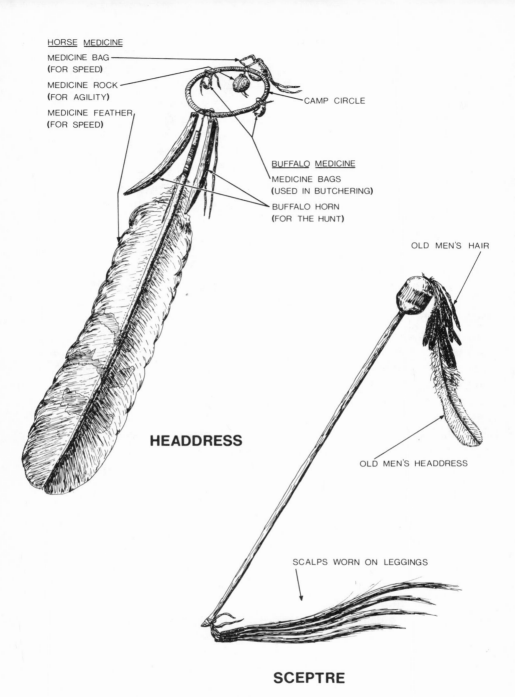

HORSE MEDICINE

MEDICINE BAG (FOR SPEED)

MEDICINE ROCK (FOR AGILITY)

MEDICINE FEATHER (FOR SPEED)

CAMP CIRCLE

BUFFALO MEDICINE

MEDICINE BAGS (USED IN BUTCHERING)

BUFFALO HORN (FOR THE HUNT)

HEADDRESS

OLD MEN'S HAIR

OLD MEN'S HEADDRESS

SCALPS WORN ON LEGGINGS

SCEPTRE

Figure 2. Head chief's scepter and headdress. Collected by A. L. Kroeber, 1900. American Museum of Natural History: 1073, 1074. Scepter length is 72 cm.; headdress diameter is 7.5 cm., length 39.5 cm. (The large medicine bag on the headdress is a partial reconstruction.)

facilitated hunting. The personal medicine, or *béétee*, of the owner was attached to a circular headpiece symbolizing the camp circle and signifying that the feats accomplished in battle and in the hunt benefited all Arapahoes.[20]

Council chiefs won the backing of their constituents also by their display of bravery in confrontations with whites and Shoshones and demonstrations of the regard in which they were held by federal officials. Black Coal and Sharp Nose were particularly adept at conveying the impression, through dress and other forms of display, that they were formidable. A visit to Washington signified to the Arapahoes that the government was impressed by a council chief's reputation and his ability to influence his people's behavior. Council chiefs brought back from these visits gifts that in the Indian view signified the special relationship between the president and the chief. Medals were routinely presented at such conferences. On several occasions during 1878–87 both Black Coal and Sharp Nose, claiming that their medals had been stolen, successfully petitioned the agent for ceremonies in which new medals were presented. In this way they periodically impressed the tribe with the high esteem in which they were apparently held by the government. Black Coal had a special outfit that he wore when he confronted federal representatives on behalf of the tribe—a broadcloth suit and watch and chain presented him by the secretary of the interior, a white felt hat with an eagle feather stuck in the crown, and his medicine on one of his fur-wrapped braids. Sharp Nose, who had the distinction of being Crook's head "soldier," often wore his army uniform. As an indication of his close tie with the general, Sharp Nose named one of his sons General Crook. When Sharp Nose spoke to his people about reservation conditions, he inspired confidence by his display of the symbols of his successes in military encounters as well as by his oratory. His grandson remembers: "He used to go out of the tipi in the morning after sunup and then he had army cap, and he put war bonnet on and had a sword and gun. A lot of people camped around there. He'd talk to them, wise them up. Things that coming, what the government was going to do with us, learn us and all that. He'd sing war songs and he'd talk to his people."[21]

Mary Jackson, daughter of an officer at Fort Washakie, gives an account of a confrontation between Black Coal and the Shoshone chief Washakie in the 1880s which demonstrates how council chiefs attempted to exhibit bravery against the whites and Shoshones before their constituents on the reservation:

> The Shoshone chiefs, Washakie and Otoi, had been invited by the officers' mess to luncheon, and with them were included their arch enemies, the two

Arapahoe chiefs, Black Coal and Sharp Nose. . . . All had gone smoothly, the Indians seeming to enjoy themselves extremely, while story after story was told, in regard to different fights in which both officers and Indians had been engaged during the previous years. . . . After a time the conversation drifted into lighter, merrier channels, although an Indian never unbends to any great extent from his dignity and reserve. One of the younger officers at the table, hoping to liven things up a bit, had secretly filled Black Coal's glass, with the contents of a fresh bottle of Worcestershire sauce, then holding his own glass aloft, and calling out "How" he drank the Indian's health; the Arapahoe took up his glass, and at the first taste realized a joke had been played on him, but he kept on and drained the "joke" to the end, then looking straight at the lieutenant, said, "Young man give heap good firewater." The other officers, realizing something had happened, and fearing the silly joke might prove serious especially if only one chief was fooled, hastily mixed another glass of the same burning concoction for Washakie, Black Coal keenly watching their preparations. The wise Washakie knew there was something afoot, but he took his glass, and gazing steadily at the Arapahoe asked: "Why do the tears come to Black Coal's eyes when he drinks the firewater of the soldiers?" Black Coal looked at him seriously a moment and replied: "Because Black Coal is thinking of his dead grandmother." Washakie then stood up and said "How" and drank his Worcestershire with steady hand and smiling face. The Arapahoe watched him shrewdly, and when he had finished, turned to him and said: "Why do the tears come to Washakie's eyes when he takes the white man's drink?" Then splendid old Washakie quietly replied, "Because Black Coal did not die when his grandmother did." Such a shout went up from all present, which of course saved the situation. . . .[22]

Through humor, Black Coal maintained dignity in an awkward situation. He and Washakie expressed and acknowledged their ambivalent feelings toward each other, but also subtly indicated their contempt for the officers.

If a council chief's authority was to be regarded as legitimate, he had to exhibit some success in helping people obtain food and other necessities. This task was especially difficult because of the government's failure to provide what the tribe had been promised. Game became increasingly scarce: there were 2,400 buffalo killed in 1882, 1,500 in 1883, 500 in 1884, and none in 1885. Yet despite the shortage of game, only half rations were authorized by the Indian Office. In the 1883–84 fiscal year Agent James Irwin (1882–84) was authorized to issue a weekly ration per person of 4 pounds of beef, 16/10 pounds of flour, 3 ounces of bacon, 1 1/3 ounces of beans, 2 1/4 ounces of coffee, 2 3/4 ounces of sugar, and 3/5 ounce of baking powder. In 1885 the beef ration was reduced to 2 1/2 pounds, and only beef and flour were issued regularly. The tribes were expected to purchase food supplies, despite the scarcity of buffalo and the sharp drop in prices for hides. They sometimes resorted to selling their annuity goods to whites in order to buy food.[23]

The problem of short rations was compounded by agency graft and the intrusion of white settlers in the vicinity of Wind River. Rations were stolen before they could be issued, and much of the equipment and supplies purchased for Indians as prescribed by treaty was appropriated by whites. In 1886, when Arapahoes were farming at a minimal level, the agent took half their hay crop in return for permission to use the mowing machines that had been purchased for the agency. Encroachment on reservation resources by cattlemen and adventurers was rampant. Trespassing stock grazed freely on the reservation; much of the Indian-owned government-issue cattle was stolen, as was reservation timber.[24]

The council chiefs struggled to convince the whites that they supported civilization efforts and at the same time to demonstrate to their constituents their ability to distribute provisions equitably and provide for the needy. By supporting the Indian Office's efforts to encourage farming, wage work, and receptivity to Christianity, the council chiefs pleased the agents, and they managed to do so in ways that convinced the Arapahoes of their fairness and generosity.

The council chiefs vigorously pressed requests for larger issues and for control over the distribution process. One of their most important duties was to supervise the issue of supplies received from the federal government, including the butchering and distribution of cattle delivered on the hoof. The men ran the cattle down on horseback and butchered them as they had formerly butchered buffalo after a communal hunt. Sharp Nose emphasized the importance with which the council chiefs viewed this custom: "The game has all gone and we want the President to put cattle on the range so that we can shoot them." The chiefs not only decided how the meat was to be distributed but also sold the hides and used the money to meet their obligations. When rations were issued, the council chiefs and many of the headmen also received larger shares than the norm. At the issue of December 30, 1877, at Fort Fetterman, just before the tribe moved to the Shoshone Agency, the chiefs received a portion of the goods "tied up in bundles and delivered to them separately." This act signified to the Arapahoes that the government accorded special status to the council chiefs. On the reservation the council chiefs received special issues, often in the form of extra rations (for example, almost 100 pounds of flour per week). With their extra share of issue goods, they provided for persons in need, fed visitors, and feasted the people at tribal gatherings.[25]

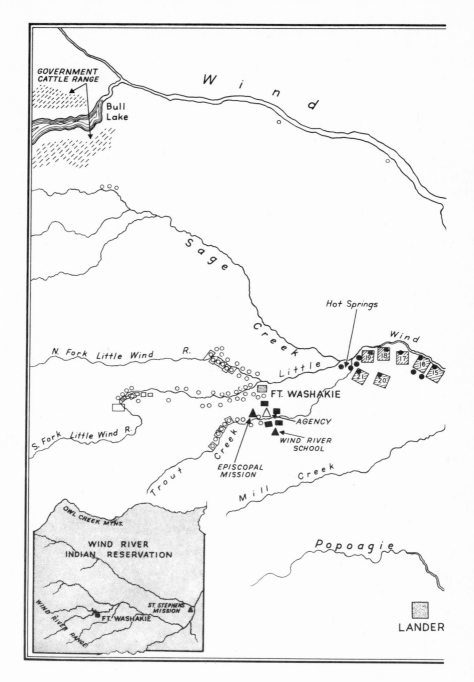

Map 3. Camps and farms, 1886–89. Redrawn from "Sketch of Indian Farms and Ranches, Shoshone Agency, Wyoming," in File 5764-1886, Letters Received by the Commissioner of Indian Affairs, 1881–1907; sketch in Shoshone file 13678–

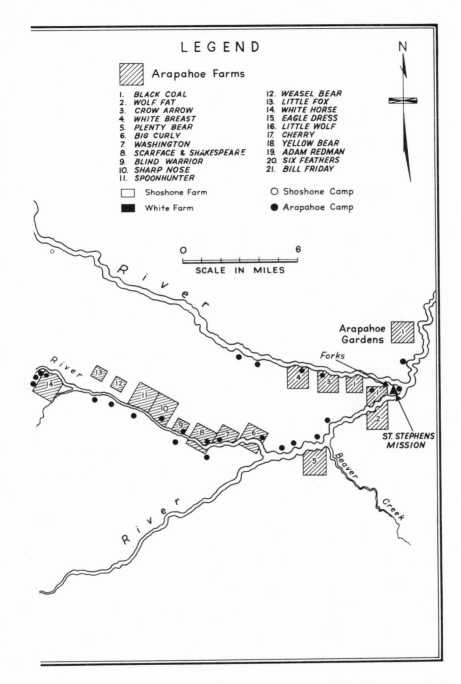

LEGEND

▨ Arapahoe Farms

1. BLACK COAL
2. WOLF FAT
3. CROW ARROW
4. WHITE BREAST
5. PLENTY BEAR
6. BIG CURLY
7. WASHINGTON
8. SCARFACE & SHAKESPEARE
9. BLIND WARRIOR
10. SHARP NOSE
11. SPOONHUNTER

12. WEASEL BEAR
13. LITTLE FOX
14. WHITE HORSE
15. EAGLE DRESS
16. LITTLE WOLF
17. CHERRY
18. YELLOW BEAR
19. ADAM REDMAN
20. SIX FEATHERS
21. BILL FRIDAY

▢ Shoshone Farm   ○ Shoshone Camp
■ White Farm   ● Arapahoe Camp

N

0 ———————— 6
SCALE IN MILES

River

River

River

Arapahoe
Gardens

Forks

ST. STEPHENS
MISSION

Beaver Creek

1887, Special Cases 143; "Outline Map of Shoshone Indian Reservation," map CA 473, Cartographic Branch, Central Map File, all in Records of the Bureau of Indian Affairs, Record Group 75, National Archives.

The council chiefs and headmen also made periodic public distributions of produce from their farms. By 1886, Chiefs Black Coal, Sharp Nose, and White Horse had large hay fields and vegetable gardens in which most of their followers worked, pooling labor and sharing the produce (see Map 3). Sometimes agency or mission personnel gave assistance. Agent Thomas Jones (1885–88) reported that large extended-family camps were situated along the Wind and Little Wind. The fields or farms, which were under the control of council chiefs and other headmen, were centers for the production of hay for sale and the cultivation of some vegetables. The farms under Black Coal's and Sharp Nose's control provided income for band members (see Figure 3) and food for the band, for intertribal feasts, and for any needy Arapahoes. One large garden ("Arapahoe Gardens") was a major source of Black Coal's supply of provisions for his chiefly obligations. White Horse probably had the largest group of followers on the western sector of the Arapahoe settlement area, but he apparently did not have as much influence as Black Coal or Sharp Nose. Shoshone farms at this time appear to have been operated by single nuclear or extended families.[26]

When the council chiefs entertained visiting tribes or white dignitaries, their hospitality brought them prestige and bolstered their standing as intermediaries. One of the priests at St. Stephen's wrote of Black Coal's actions when a party of Oglala Sioux paid a visit: "You must think how shrewd our Chief Black Coal acted on the occasion, the day previous; he sent two lieutenants, with a squaw and boy in a spring wagon, from the camp ground of the Sun and War dance to act

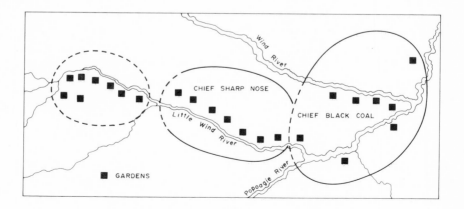

Figure 3. Centers of redistribution.

as guides for the Sioux and keep the whole band away from his tibby (tent) as they would have cleared out all his provisions and ours too as well. All the vegetables (cabbages, turnips, melons, and etc.) growing in his garden, the greater part of which he pulled same day and brought in his wagon on the next to the dance camp and feast[ed] all the Indians in attendance." And when President Chester Arthur visited the reservation on his way to Yellowstone Park in the summer of 1883, he was met by the council chiefs and Sharp Nose presented him with a horse at an assembly of the Indians at the agency (see Plate 5).[27]

Wage work at the agency, Fort Washakie, and the missions offered Arapahoes an opportunity to earn money to purchase food and supplies. Chiefs were often selected for government employment because federal officials recognized that chiefs could better control their people if they could help them subsist; they used their salaries and other benefits to provide for their followers. Until his death, Friday earned $25 monthly as agency interpreter. Sharp Nose was employed as a scout at Fort Washakie from 1881 to 1890. In complaining of his tribe's need for more government help, he explained to the commander that his scout's ration was sufficient if he were "selfish enough to use it himself," but he was obligated to use it to "feed all his family and other people depending upon him." Sharp Nose reportedly also did some "cattle rustling" (probably the shooting of trespassing stock) in order to provide for his people. Local rancher John Hunton noted that Sharp Nose had married one of his daughters to Frank Brand, a "rustler"— presumably another means of obtaining beef to distribute. Agents reported that council chiefs pressed for employment for other Arapahoes, as well. Monthly salaries for policemen, scouts, and laborers ranged from $5 to $30. The jobs were evenly divided between the Shoshones and Arapahoes, except that the Shoshones at first resisted serving as Indian police. In the 1880s the council chiefs were allowed to choose or influence the agent's choice of agency employees. It appears that the Arapahoe council chiefs were careful that men were chosen from each band; they did not attempt to allocate jobs only to their own followers. For example, serving as Indian police at one time or another were Yellow Owl, Washington, and Six Feathers, who were affiliated with Black Coal's band; Eagle Head, who was associated with Sharp Nose; Wallowing Bull and White Horse, from the large camp west of Sharp Nose's settlement; and Yellow Bear, from Friday's band. And at the government boarding school in 1885–86, jobs that paid $15 a month went to Carlisle alumni Sumner Black Coal and William Shakespeare, of the Forks People, and Adam Redman, of Sharp Nose's band. Several men from each band were hired to haul freight from the railroad at

Rawlins. And in the 1880s, Black Coal arranged for Arapahoe work groups to cut wood and do other work for the Catholic mission in return for several hundred dollars in payment, which he personally distributed to the workers.[28]

Council chiefs also sought to take advantage of the resources of the two missions on the reservation, St. Stephen's and the Episcopal mission located near the agency headquarters. Friendly contacts between Arapahoe leaders and white missionaries persuaded the whites that the Arapahoes welcomed Christianity. St. Stephen's regularly feasted Arapahoes with beans, hominy, coffee, and bread, and on special occasions the food was delivered directly to Black Coal's tipi. One year the mission purchased 2,400 pounds of beef per week, most of which was distributed to the Arapahoe community in one form or another. Black Coal welcomed Father John Jutz, who established the mission in 1884, and the Sisters of Charity, who briefly operated a school there. Father Jutz had been asked by Black Coal to make several payments in return for permission to build and plant in the Forks area. After Father Jutz returned east in 1885, the priests who followed him attempted to construct buildings on at least three occasions, each time making a payment, only later to be told to move. Black Coal appropriated the improvements on the land, thus providing several of his followers with garden plots. Agent Thomas Jones reported in ire that Black Coal pursued the mission from place to place and solicited money by claiming rights to the land. The agent estimated that the Catholics gave the Arapahoes approximately $15,000 in cash, provisions, and improvements during this time. In fact, the Bureau of Catholic Indian Missions, which recognized the importance of gaining the goodwill of the chief, instructed the priests at St. Stephen's to grant Black Coal's requests whenever possible. The Episcopal mission near the agency also gave them provisions. Both Black Coal and Sharp Nose made a point of greeting the bishop and other church officials on their visits.[29]

Council Chiefs, 1888–1907

After 1887 the Arapahoes and their council chiefs faced new kinds of problems created by policy changes in Washington. They were threatened with the loss of a large portion of reservation land, and the agents were instructed to destroy the institution of chieftainship. In addition, the government's contribution to Indian subsistence was further reduced. The intermediaries continued to present themselves as allies of the government's civilization program while striving at the same time to live up to Arapahoe ideals of intermediary leadership. The council chiefs assumed the responsibility of approving leases of reservation lands and used the funds to provide for the people in the same way they had used the government issues. And during the negotiations for land cession, they forcefully countered Shoshone charges that the Arapahoes had no right to live on the reservation.

"A Mark at the Four Corners":
Relations with Federal Officials

With the passage of the General Allotment Act and subsequent legislation, the government accelerated its efforts to "civilize" the Indians. The new policy was intended to destroy tribal organization by dealing with Indians as individuals rather than *en bloc*. As individuals, Indians were to be assimilated as rapidly as possible. The Allotment Act of February 8, 1887, designed to encourage assimilation through individual ownership of property and the destruction of the tribal land base, provided that each Indian was to be allotted land, which was to be held in trust for twenty-five years. During that time it could not be sold or the title encumbered. After twenty-five years, a patent in fee (negotiable title) could be issued and in land matters the native owner would become subject to the laws of the state in which the land was located. Citizenship was offered allottees. The act also provided that after each individual had been allotted land, the remaining acreage could be purchased by the federal government and the purchase money spent on behalf of the tribe by Congress. Later, on March 2, 1887, Congress gave the secretary of the interior the authority to use tribal funds from the lease or sale of land in any manner he determined best for the tribe. Legislation of February 28, 1891 and August 15, 1894 provided that individual allotments could be leased under the supervision of the secretary if individuals did not make productive use of their lands and that tribal "council" leaders could lease tribal land for farming, grazing, or mining purposes. In these ways the federal government sought to abdicate responsibility for the support of Indian peoples and also to apply sanctions so as to encourage assimilation into white society.[30]

Commissioners instituted stern measures to make Indians self-supporting and to destroy Indian customs. Commissioner Thomas J. Morgan (1889–93) instructed the agents that beef was to be issued only "on the block" (already butchered). The amount of rations authorized was drastically reduced, as well. Commissioner William Jones (1897–1904) issued instructions that able-bodied Indians were to be given rations only if they were employed in some capacity. The reduction of the ration rolls was described as a "humane act" to stimulate "self-help." Although the agents at the Shoshone Agency varied in their dedication and ability to implement the new policies, these measures wrought severe hardship on the Arapahoes and Shoshones, and threatened to undermine the authority of their leaders.[31]

When the rations were reduced, the suffering of the Arapahoes was intense. Mooney visited the tribe in 1892 and recorded this Ghost Dance song, which was sung to a plaintive tune, sometimes with tears rolling down the cheeks of the dancers as the words brought to mind thoughts of their predicament:

> Father, have pity on me,
> Father, have pity on me.
> I am crying for thirst,
> I am crying for thirst.
> All is gone—I have nothing to eat,
> All is gone—I have nothing to eat.

By 1889 each person entitled to rations received only about one pound of beef and ten ounces of flour once a week. Captain William Quinton reported to the secretary of war that the tribes were in "a state of semi-starvation." By 1890 the ration was fourteen ounces of beef and eight ounces of flour. That year the agent allowed rations to only about half of the Arapahoes; and as it was the Arapahoes' custom to share among themselves, the food received by each individual was less than the actual ration allowed. As the years passed, the ration rolls were reduced further. Black Coal also complained about the necessity for most Arapahoes to travel over sixty miles on issue days. "They have not enough to eat, and what they do get they have to lose too much time in going for. We are a long distance from the agency. It takes three days to go and return for a small piece of meat and a little flour. Then the horses and people are tired, rest one day; by this time the rations are all eaten. Only three days more and my people must travel to the agency again." The tribes were not able to supplement their diet sufficiently by hunting because game was very scarce on the reservation; trespassing stock of whites used most of the pasturage. In addition, Wyoming (which became a state in 1890) prohibited Indians from hunting outside the reservation, and rations were withheld from Indians who were caught doing so. Sharp Nose remarked to the commander at Fort Washakie that now the Arapahoe was "a beggar upon his own land."[32]

The Arapahoes struggled mightily to earn money by cutting and selling wood, hauling coal, laboring on government irrigation ditches,

and raising hay, grains, and vegetables for sale. The school superintendent wrote in *The Indian Guide* in 1897, "We are not perfect and the
battle has only begun. We have plenty of tepees and blankets yet in
sight, horse racing and gambling and Indian customs still hold sway, but
the blanket is laid aside long enough to plow, harrow, build fences and
houses, cut wood, make hay, etc." He reported that the agency mill had
ground more than 250,000 pounds of flour from wheat grown by the
Indians, the larger part of it by the Arapahoes. A good part of the
Arapahoes' flour was turned over to the traders to pay debts. Arapahoes and Shoshones also sold wheat to the agency, the government
boarding school, and Fort Washakie, and fulfilled contracts for hay, oats,
and potatoes. More than 100,000 pounds of oats were grown in 1897.
In 1901 the Arapahoes sold half of their oat crop to Fort Washakie—for
ten cents less per hundred pounds than the price paid to whites. Arapahoe leaders—including Chiefs Black Coal, Sharp Nose, Lone Bear, Littleshield, Wallowing Bull, and the priest Weasel Bear (who was custodian
of the Sacred Pipe)—as well as such prominent warriors as Poor Flesh,
Shot Gun, Stonebreaker, Goes in Lodge, Mountain Sheep, and White
Breast, encouraged farming by working their own farms.[33]

The Arapahoes were aware that while they suffered, whites were
profiting from the presence of the agency. As one inspector from
Washington admitted, "There is never at any time enough cattle slaughtered to supply these Indians with more than half the rations they are
entitled to," yet "the agency employees and school people get whatever amount they require, and this of course is the best part of the
meat." Neighboring whites (sometimes in partnership with the agent)
blatantly stole lumber, agency cattle, rations, and supplies, and allowed
their stock to graze on the reservation. Indians who killed the stray
animals could be arrested and prosecuted in Wyoming courts. The most
determined effort to stop stock trespass was made by Captain P. H.
Ray, agent from 1893 to 1895. Ray collected fees from stockmen and
was fairly effective in removing trespassers. His dedication to duty
antagonized state officials and the Wyoming press, which was dominated by cattle interests. Wyoming officials indicted him for theft of
the trespassing stock, but the charges were proved false. The *Cheyenne
Leader* accused him of attempting to incite the Indians to attack
whites; the newspaper warned, "If the Indians once taste human blood,
God only knows where it will end." In the spring of 1895 Ray was replaced by Captain Richard Wilson (1895–98), who was less diligent in
fulfilling his responsibilities. The council chiefs complained that he did
not remove trespassing stock and that he short-weighed the wheat that
they brought to sell at the agency.[34]

The deprivation took its toll among the Arapahoes. After their arrival, the Arapahoe population had increased slightly, from 938 in the fall of 1878 to 972 in 1885, probably because Arapahoe families traveled from the Indian Territory and elsewhere to join the tribe in Wyoming. A deficient diet, exposure, and disease resulted in high infant mortality and a high overall death rate. Agent John Fosher (1889–93) reported that by 1893 the Arapahoe population had fallen to 823. Deaths outnumbered births every year until 1901, when the population slowly began to increase (see Fig. 4).[35]

Even though the Indians had great difficulty in supporting themselves, federal agents and local whites vigorously pressed for the cession and leasing of farming, grazing, and timber lands. The Arapahoes felt threatened with removal from the reservation altogether. The

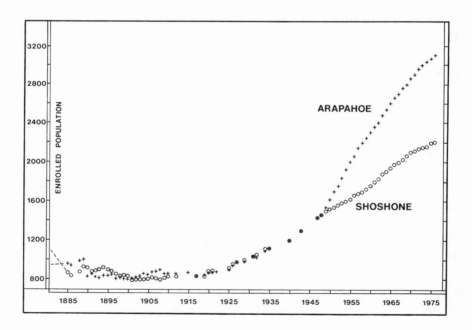

Figure 4. Arapahoe and Shoshone populations on Wind River Reservation, 1885–1975. Source: Monthly Narrative Reports of the Superintendent, Shoshone Agency, in Letters Received by the Commissioner of Indian Affairs, 1881–1907, and Superintendents' Annual Statistical Reports, 1907–38, Shoshone Agency, both in Records of the Bureau of Indian Affairs, Record Group 75, National Archives; Records of the Office of the Bureau of Indian Affairs, 1939–1975, Fort Washakie, Wyoming.

Arapahoe council chiefs had the difficult task, first, of presenting a cooperative and conciliatory stance during council meetings, so that the government would not move the tribe or curtail the issue of rations, and second, of minimizing the amount of land lost to the tribe. In the course of agreeing to allotment, leasing, and cessions, the council chiefs attempted to obtain as many benefits for the tribe as they could.

Although the concept of individual ownership of land was alien to the Arapahoes, Black Coal, Sharp Nose, White Horse, and Eagle Head bargained for more provisions by offering in 1888 to agree to cooperate with the allotment of the reservation in return for cattle and a cash payment to the tribe. Whites were gratified but surprised at the tribe's reaction; before the favorable response, however, the Arapahoes were aware that the Shoshone chief Washakie was attempting to persuade the government to remove them and they were very anxious. Their agreement to the allotment of reservation land would make their removal more difficult. In 1895 Sharp Nose (head chief at this time) and fifty prominent Arapahoes again agreed to allotment on the condition that stone markers be placed at "the four corners" of the reservation to establish the Arapahoes' title to the lands they had settled on. The following year they offered to accept allotment if they were permitted to send a delegation to Washington to discuss their difficulties. The alloting of the land eventually began in earnest in 1900; their seeming willingness to accept allotment in the preceding years had won them a reputation for being cooperative and therefore deserving of aid.[36]

The reservation lands north of the Wind River were particularly attractive to white stockmen. Beginning in 1898 Agent H. G. Nickerson worked to solve the problem of trespassing stock and to increase tribal income by insisting that the cattlemen apply for leases and pay the amount agreed upon in the lease. With the consent of the council chiefs, Nickerson arranged five-year leases of two cents per acre for grazing land and he also leased lands for coal mining. Although the fees were very low, the leases did bring money to the tribe. The Arapahoes were well aware that reservation lands could produce much-needed income. In fact, they sometimes sought out lessees: in a letter to the commissioner in 1905, a group of prominent Arapahoes urged, "Please send out a good friend of Indians to find them mines. We give him fifteen cents for every dollar." The council chiefs not only approved of the leasing of land but had the responsibility of consulting with other Arapahoes and then recommending to the agent how the lease income should be spent—so much for a per capita payment in cash, so much to purchase seed for the tribe, and so on. Apparently the Indian Office accepted the chiefs' recommendations fairly consistently. Gradually lease money replaced rations as a major source of subsistence.[37]

The main arena of Indian–white political relations during the post-1887 era was the cession council. In these meetings, held in 1891, 1893, 1896, and 1904, the council chiefs maneuvered to provide for economic relief and to improve the status of the Arapahoes at the Shoshone Agency. Though the Arapahoe council chiefs recognized the base intentions and methods of the commissioners, the sale of land had come to seem a means to secure the funds and services they needed and recognition of their joint title to the reservation. As early as September 1889, Black Coal and Sharp Nose (and the Shoshone chief Washakie, as well) had expressed willingness to sell some land. In the 1891 cession council Arapahoe leaders had to confront directly a Shoshone challenge to their permanent occupancy. Until 1890 the Arapahoes had clung to the hope that General Crook would fulfill his promise of a reservation in Tongue River country, but now he was dead. Just before the 1891 cession council, Washakie and twelve of his subchiefs sent this message to the Indian Office: "We understand that the Arapahoes have made application to have an agency or sub-agency established for them on the east side of this reservation. Now we do not object to the Arapahoes having an agency of their own, near to us, but we do seriously object to them having an agency or anything else built on our land that will give them any right to any land on this reservation." The main spokesman for the Shoshones at the council, George Terry—a white man enrolled as one-eighth Shoshone—pointedly objected to the presence of the Arapahoes at the meeting.[38]

The first cession council was held in October 1891 with Commissioners J. D. Woodruff, C. H. Merillat, and J. H. Brigham. Here the tribes agreed to cede about half of the reservation (although Woodruff, a Lander resident, felt this was too small a tract) for $600,000. The commissioners told the Indians that the Arapahoes' treaty annuities were to expire in 1899 and the Shoshones' in 1900; thereafter they would receive no more rations or provisions. The tribes were also threatened with the possibility of being pushed off the reservation by the expanding white population. The commissioners assured the Indian Office that the tribes had much more agricultural, timber, grazing, and coal lands than they could ever use, and that if Indian holdings were reduced from approximately 2 million to 700,000 acres, the stock of white ranchers could be prevented from trespassing. Repeatedly the three men assured the chiefs that the cession would make the Indians wealthy: "They will be rich, and will have all they want to eat. Any of us will be glad to help them in any way." With these tactics the commission obtained the signatures of 283 of the 393 men over eighteen years, a majority of each tribe; but Congress failed to ratify the 1891 agreement, primarily because the senators felt that the tribes were ceding too little.[39]

A second group of commissioners (Frank Sterling of Montana, John Meldrum of Wyoming, and Napoleon Crump of Arkansas) met with the tribes in January and February 1893 and urged a new agreement that would leave the Indians even less land (300,000 acres). Lander interests were particularly eager for the cession of the "southern strip," the land south of Mill Creek. The tribes, however, were angry at Congress's rejection of the 1891 agreement and rejected the new provisions, primarily because of strong Arapahoe resistance to the loss of so much land. The Indians needed the land south of Mill Creek for pasture, a wood supply, and, as Black Coal pointed out, a home for future generations.[40]

In 1896 pressure was brought on the tribes to cede the natural hot springs in the northeast corner of the reservation and ten square miles of surrounding land (see Map 4). On April 21, 1896, of 457 men over the age of eighteen, 180 Shoshones and 93 Arapahoes signed the agreement presented to them by James McLaughlin. In return the Indians were to be paid $60,000, $10,000 of which was to provide cattle for the Arapahoes and either cattle or per capita payments for the Shoshones. The remainder was to be spent in five annual installments at the discretion of the secretary of the interior for the benefit of the Indians; the distribution of small amounts of rations was to be extended for five years. Congress amended the agreement (Act of June 7, 1897, 30 Stat. 93), and on July 10 the tribes approved the changes. In the following spring, $5,000 worth of cattle were issued to the Arapahoes. But the remainder of the payments were not forthcoming, and the tribes bitterly protested.[41]

In April 1904 James McLaughlin was sent to renegotiate the cession of a major portion of the reservation. He informed the tribes that as a result of a Supreme Court decision, the government did not need to secure the tribes' consent to open up "surplus lands" to white settlement, and that the government was therefore extending them a courtesy in discussing the matter at all. Large reservations, he explained, were impossible in view of the whites' clamor for land. He pressed for the cession of 1.48 million acres north of the Wind River, which would leave 808,500 acres in the "diminished portion," and he advised the tribes that the sale of the land would realize more than $1 million. The Arapahoes opposed the sale of that much acreage, however, and they particularly objected to ceding everything north of the Wind River

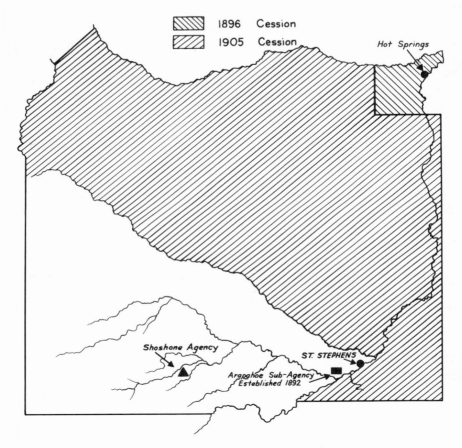

Map 4. Land cessions, 1896–1906, Wind River Reservation. Source: Office of the Bureau of Indian Affairs, Fort Washakie, Wyo.

because several Arapahoe families were then living in that area. Lone Bear—considered the successor to Black Coal, who had died in 1893, and the head council chief since Sharp Nose's death in 1901—also argued that the price was too low: the land was worth twice the amount proposed by McLaughlin. Lone Bear's subchiefs from the eastern end of the reservation concurred with him. Plenty Bear, Broken Horn, Medicine

Eagle, Sun Road, Buffalo Fat, Goes in Lodge, Coal, Sleeping Bear, Sitting Eagle, Stone Breaker, Gun, Sitting Bear, Big Head, Mountain Sheep, Painted Wolf—all stressed their support of Lone Bear's position. Little Wolf and Tallow, council chiefs from the western settlement area, expressed the hope that the land north of the Wind River would be "saved." Yellow Calf, a younger man coming into prominence but not yet considered a council chief, commented, "The Bill is good, but want change a few things." The Reverend Sherman Coolidge, an Arapahoe interpreter at the council (at the government's, not the tribe's, request) and Episcopal missionary from the western settlement area, spoke in favor of accepting McLaughlin's terms, as did the Shoshone spokesmen.

Before the discussions concluded, Lone Bear's wife was taken ill, and he left the council to attend her. After his departure the Arapahoes' resistance was less effective. Although many Arapahoe leaders withdrew from the council with Lone Bear, McLaughlin obtained 282 signatures, a majority of men over the age of eighteen (see Plate 6). Of 247 Shoshone men, 202 signed, but only 80 of 237 Arapahoes; 33 of these Arapahoes were under the age of thirty, hardly adult from the Arapahoe point of view.[42]

The agreement was amended and ratified by Congress on March 3, 1905, and all land north of the Wind River to the junction of the Popoagie and from the mouth of the north fork of the Popoagie to the southern boundary of the reservation was ceded to the government (see Map 4). In return the government promised that individuals settled on the ceded portion would be paid for their land, and that the government would purchase at $1.25 an acre two 320-acre sections and pay the Arapahoes and Shoshones $50 per capita within sixty days after the lands were opened for sale or "as soon after as possible." Proceeds of leases on the "ceded portion" were also to go to the tribes, and from the proceeds of sales the government was to secure water rights for the irrigation of Indian lands.

According to the 1904 agreement the government was to attempt to dispose of the ceded lands, but in the amended 1905 agreement they were not bound to do so. Under the provisions of the laws governing homesteads, town sites, and coal and mineral lands, land was to be sold for $1.50 an acre during the first two years, for $1.25 during the next three years, for the highest bid not less than $1.00 during the next three years, and subsequently to the highest bidder. Proceeds were to go to the tribes' accounts after the government had been reimbursed $85,000 for the initial per capita payment, $35,000 appropriated for a survey of ceded lands, and $25,000 for irrigation work. For ten years the money in the tribes' accounts was to be applied by the secretary of the interior to irrigation, the purchase of livestock in amounts up to $50,000, schools in amounts up to $50,000, and the General Welfare Fund (which could be used for rations). An accounting of the funds was to be made in July of each year. After ten years the expenditure of the proceeds was to be renegotiated.[43]

The Arapahoes objected to the amended version of the agreement, and Lone Bear sent this message on March 6, 1905: "We think treaty ratified by Congress not agree with original treaty signed by tribe." Then, in a letter dated December 17, 1906, elders Runs across River and Stone Breaker and council chiefs Lone Bear, Little Wolf, Tallow, and Yellow Calf, with the assistance of their two young interpreters, William Shakespeare and John Jesus Lewis, protested bitterly that they still had received no per capita payments and that against their wishes parts of the ceded portion were town sites (Riverton), for which they received no payment. When the $50 per capita payment finally was made, children's money was withheld from many families. The tribes were furious. Agent H. E. Wadsworth wrote in support of completing the payment: "Even Mr. Roberts, the missionary who has lived so long among them [the Shoshones], was afraid of the lives of himself and family. . . ." But the Indian Office's attitude was that Indians were too "indolent and imprudent" to manage their own affairs, much less those of their children, and the children's money was kept in the tribes' account in Washington. Tribal leaders met with McLaughlin in 1907 and expressed their dismay over the violation of the 1904 agreement. The elderly Little Wolf (a ritual leader as well as a council chief) tried to persuade government representatives to release the children's money: "When you came out here to make the treaty of April 21, 1904, I did not jump around and try to get away and pay no attention to what you had to say. I was in favor of the treaty and am glad you made it. I knew we were going to deprive the future generations of land; still I signed it. When you promised us that we were all going to get fifty dollars apiece, we were glad and signed the treaty. . . . Try and get us this money for the children." Two years later the Indian Office finally agreed to give the tribes the children's per capita payments.[44]

"All Pull Together and All Agree on One Thing": Relations with Arapahoe Constituents

The difficulties encountered by the council chiefs during the cession councils threatened to undermine their authority as intermediaries. Their problems were compounded by a series of attacks on "tribalism" implemented by the agents. Severe sanctions were applied against polygyny, dancing, and the use of the native language in the government school. The agents also sought to destroy what they perceived to be the undue influence of the chiefs in the Arapahoe community. In their capacity as advocates the council chiefs could be troublesome to the agents, particularly to those who did not conduct agency business honestly or competently. Agent Richard Wilson, one of the latter, complained that the Arapahoe leaders "are continually worrying me in one way or another. It is quite a common occurrence for twenty or thirty of them to call at my office and spend all day in making interminable harangues to me on their grievances."[45]

Agent P. H. Ray (1893–95) was a career army officer who before his appointment as agent had led a company of Arapahoe infantry at Fort Washakie. He was as diligent about following Indian Office orders to eradicate native traditions as he was about obeying instructions to expel trespassing stock. Indians who entered into polygynous marriages were imprisoned and tribal gatherings were discouraged by threats of punitive measures. Ray also tried to undercut the chiefs' skill at "fostering and perpetuating the influence acquired in war." He struck forcefully at the chiefs' ability to retain their people's respect and loyalty by enforcing the commissioner's order to issue beef on the block. He attempted to deliver each household's share to the senior male in the family, thereby eliminating the chiefs' role in the distribution process. Determined to stop the council chiefs from "feasting an idle and dissolute following," Ray sought to make it impossible for chiefs to sponsor tribal or intertribal feasts and giveaways. He attempted to stop council chiefs from collecting part of their followers' income or crops, as well as occasional tribute from white owners of trespassing stock.[46]

Agent Herman G. Nickerson (1898–1902) was one of the pioneers who settled in the Sweetwater area in the 1860s. As Indian agent he continued the policy of eradicating tribal customs. It was during Nickerson's administration that Indian names on the agency rolls were changed from approximate English translations of native terms to more "civilized"-sounding ones: Lone Bear, for example, became Lon Brown; Yellow Calf became George Caldwell. When Nickerson found the council chiefs less pliable than he had hoped, he discontinued the practice of issuing them extra rations, took away their power to influence the selection of Indian police, and ordered the policemen to take instructions from him alone. When the police resigned in protest, they were replaced by younger, inexperienced alumni of the government boarding school. Until then the leader of the Arapahoe police had been Sage, the leader of the Dogmen Lodge.[47]

Nickerson's successor, H. E. Wadsworth, dismissed the chiefs who were employed as judges in the Court of Indian Offenses and continued Nickerson's practice of selecting policemen from among youths loyal to the agent. He was forced to admit that under these circumstances the police positions were very difficult to fill: "A member of the force is looked upon with suspicion and dislike by the members of his tribe, for he is often called upon to carry into effect orders of the agent, which are in direct opposition to the wishes and traditions of his tribe. They think that in carrying out the orders of the agent and the department a policeman is taking sides with the white man against his own people, and hence are always continually trying to 'get even' with him by running off his stock, tearing down his fences, breaking his ditches or flumes and headgates."[48]

At the same time that the Indian Office attempted to undermine the chiefs' authority by withdrawing the economic supports for their role, it tried to weaken their position further by introducing a "representative" tribal council that it considered more compatible with the civilization program. When Congress enacted legislation in February 1891 and August 1894 to supplement the Allotment Act so as to permit the leasing of trust land, the act provided that a tribal business council could make decisions on behalf of the tribe in transactions involving tribal or nonallotted lands. The business councilmen were to be selected by majority vote, a type of selection process was designed to end the influence of the "self-proclaimed" chiefs, as government agents termed them. The existence of a business council would also relieve the government of the customary burden of meeting with and providing a feast for the entire tribe when an important decision had to be made. Moreover, a small group of business councilmen would presumably be easier to manipulate than the tribe as a whole.[49]

The tribes at the Shoshone Agency accepted the idea of a business council, but the councilmen did not then behave in the way the government had anticipated. In December 1893, 200 members of both the Arapahoe and Shoshone tribes met and, with Sharp Nose and Washakie as their main spokesmen, authorized a representative council for the purpose of approving leases. Each tribe chose six council members, who served from 1893 to 1897. Two other business councils subsequently were chosen, one in 1898 and the other in 1903 (see Table 2). No record exists of how the selections were made. These councilmen were in fact the council chiefs who had been serving as intermediaries all along, and they continued to serve as their tribe's advocates, to articulate tribal values, and to intercede with white officials to obtain economic assistance for their people.[50]

Although by the late 1890s the government no longer needed the

Table 2
Members of Arapahoe Business (Chiefs') Council, 1893–1907

1893–97	1898–1902	1903–7
Sharp Nose	Sharp Nose*	Lone Bear
Plenty Bear	Lone Bear	Tallow
Eagle Head	Plenty Bear	Little Wolf
Tallow	Tallow	Wallowing Bull* / Yellow Calf†
Old Man Elk	Little Wolf	William Shakespeare
Bull Gun	Wallowing Bull	John Jesus Lewis
	Sherman Sage	
	William Shakespeare	

*Died in office.

†Replacement.

Source: Correspondence in Shoshone files, Special Cases 191, 1893–1907, and Letters Received by the Commissioner of Indian Affairs, 1881–1907, both in Records of the Bureau of Indian Affairs, Record Group 75, National Archives.

help of warrior chiefs to suppress hostile Indians and therefore disparaged the importance of chieftainship, the Arapahoes still expected their intermediaries to be brave and formidable. Though their battles now were waged with words, the symbols of traditional chieftainship reassured the Arapahoes that a man could not be intimidated. All of the men selected for the Business Council in 1893 were warriors with well-established reputations for bravery. Their ages ranged from forty-two to fifty-eight; all had participated in the intertribal wars and had probably also been scouts. Sharp Nose, Plenty Bear, and Eagle Head were acknowledged as council chiefs before 1893. On the council of 1898–1902, only the young interpreter William Shakespeare was not a chief. On the 1903–7 council, only Yellow Calf, who replaced his half brother Wallowing Bull on the council, lacked battle exploits—and even he went to some lengths to establish his credentials as a warrior. Although he had been too young to enlist as a scout at Fort Washakie, he said, he had accompanied the Arapahoe scouts when they went out to subdue the Bannocks in 1878: "During that time we battled with the Bannocks, only one was killed and [we] took seven prisoners and brought them here at the post. I was sixteen years old when I was the only one [boy who] went with the soldiers here at the post." Despite

the government's efforts to minimize the chiefs' influence by establishing a representative business council, the Arapahoes continued to
refer to their intermediaries as council chiefs; in fact, the Business
Council was actually called the Chiefs' Council by the Arapahoes.[51]

From the Arapahoe viewpoint, the most important occasions of
interaction between Arapahoes and federal officials were the council
meetings on the cession and leasing of land: the proceedings were carefully recorded and sent to Washington, and the lands themselves were
of immense value to the tribe. In these meetings intermediaries attempted to influence federal officials' impressions of the Arapahoes
so that the officials in Washington would be more kindly disposed
toward the tribe. Often the council chiefs were more concerned with
the reactions of whites in Washington to what was recorded in the
minutes than they were with the reactions of their white audience. In
informal encounters with the agent, when no minutes were taken, the
council chiefs were more intent on pressing the agent to grant specific
requests than on making a favorable impression on him. The cession
and leasing council meetings were also important because on those
occasions Arapahoe and Shoshone leaders met face to face; under
ordinary circumstances they seldom saw each other. In their confrontations with Shoshone chiefs, the Arapahoe council chiefs tried to be
publicly assertive, to impress their constituents with their bravery in the
face of Shoshone hostility.

During the 1891 cession council, Black Coal greatly enhanced his
reputation as a brave man and an effective advocate by deflecting the
Shoshones' efforts to dominate the proceedings. Although Arapahoe
leaders who customarily deferred in council meetings to Washakie,
whom they respectfully termed "the old chief," in the 1891 meeting
Black Coal and the other Arapahoe spokesmen took an independent
stance. They requested a "divided reservation" and a separate meeting
with each tribe on the cession issue. When Washakie acquiesced to the
commissioners' demands that lands be ceded on the southern boundary
of the reservation, Black Coal and Sharp Nose refused to agree. The
disagreement between Black Coal and Washakie was bitter. Washakie
complained angrily, "Twenty-two years ago I first came here. I thought
this land was mine. I always thought I owned it, or had an interest in
it until today. Now the people who came here to stay with me quarrel
with me, and with the men the Great Father has sent out here to treat
with us." Black Coal replied that the Arapahoes, far from being quarrel-
some, actually obeyed the government's instructions when they came
to the reservation, and that they had learned how to work like whites
in an effort to cooperate with the government. He protested Washakie's

change of heart over the sale of the southern lands. In his opening sentence he made clear that Washakie's status was no higher than his own: "Washakie is an Indian, and so am I. The government sent us here to live here with the Shoshones, and when I brought my Indians here I told them to work, and it would give them a better name. And I told them they would have to live here all their lives. Washakie told me he would only sell that part of the reservation north of Wind River. I heard him with my own ears." By their refusal to cede all of the land requested, the Arapahoes laid claim to a future at the Shoshone Agency and asserted their equality with the Shoshones. Black Coal insisted, "The Arapahoes were sent here by the government, and we now claim that we have as much right here as the Shoshones. We are willing to sell that land north and east of Wind River but don't want to sell any more. If the Indians [Arapahoes] were not going to live here always they would do it [sell a larger tract]." Black Coal's performance at the cession council was long remembered and alluded to by Arapahoes as an example of his bravery.[52]

During the negotiations for land cessions between 1891 and 1904, the council chiefs—with first Black Coal, then Sharp Nose, and finally, in 1904, Lone Bear as their main spokesmen—referred to the agreements as "treaties," and managed to give a new interpretation to the treaty relationship, as well. A dominant theme in the Arapahoes' speeches was that of the "broken treaty." The chiefs both expressed the nature of Arapahoe–white relations in these new times and worked to shape those relations toward an outcome favorable to the tribe. At the 1891 council Black Coal passionately presented his views on the treaties of 1851 and 1868 and the agreement of 1876: "The treaty we had on Horse Creek forty years ago, then the president didn't keep his word with us. . . . Then there was a treaty twenty-three years ago; that was broken in the same way. . . . There was another treaty at the Black Hills. . . . I think these three [commissioners] are good men, and I want them to help get all these treaties back. . . ." Black Coal requested for the tribe the money that he felt had not been spent on the "clothes and rations" promised in the "treaties." No longer considered a "nation" or a military force with which the federal government had to reckon, the Arapahoes were now dependent on the federal government—politically, in that they had no treaty rights to the Shoshone reservation and needed the government's support to remain there, and economically, in that their subsistence depended directly or indirectly on the government. By stressing the "broken treaties" they hoped to move government officials toward a more charitable position. The intermediaries no longer proclaimed their friendship and loyalty to government interests (as they had in the 1870s) in order to forestall fears of war with whites. Now their loyalty was presented as a quality that morally obligated the government to help the people it had wronged. If the Arapahoes were wronged, then there could be dignity in the tribe's dependence. As advocates, the council chiefs also portrayed the contemporary negotiations for land cession as "treaty councils," asserting the government's obligation to furnish provisions to those in attendance. In the 1896 council the commissioners were pressured into participating in a smoking ceremony with the council chiefs and sponsoring a feast for the tribes. The council chiefs considered it their duty to gain tangible benefits from the meetings, as well as to negotiate the cessions. In 1891 they succeeded in attaining government consent for an Arapahoe subagency at the eastern end of the reservation, which offered Arapahoes in that area relief from the long journey to receive their rations at the main agency (see Map 4).[53]

The council chiefs, who initiated friendly ties with army officers at nearby Fort Washakie, also defended the tribe against suspicions of militancy during the time when the Ghost Dance was introduced among the Plains tribes. The new religion offered believers a future world where there would be no whites. Federal officials were fearful that this aspect of the religious movement might lead to an Indian uprising. Although the Ghost Dance religion was well established among the Arapahoes from about 1889 to 1893, the council chiefs repeatedly visited the officers at Fort Washakie to reassure them. When Sioux from Pine Ridge came to visit the Arapahoes and discuss the news of the Ghost Dance rituals, the Arapahoes assured the officers that the Sioux were more knowledgeable than they about farming and were at the Shoshone Agency to help them with their advice. In the summer of 1890, although the military authorities knew that at least some Arapahoes participated in the Ghost Dance, they reported that the new religion did not "seem to have produced any impression upon" the Arapahoes. That winter the Arapahoes convinced the post commander, who informed the war department, that they intended to remain peaceful and that they would not "harbor malcontents" among the Pine Ridge Sioux, who had a reputation for militancy and who had recently been involved in an armed conflict with whites at Wounded Knee. The council chiefs, and particularly Sharp Nose, who was serving as a scout at the fort, frequently visited and cultivated good relations with the army officers, whose reports could influence the way the tribe was dealt with by federal officials (see Plate 7).[54]

The government's introduction of a business council was an effort to undermine the Arapahoes' practice of discussing important matters in a tribal meeting until consensus was reached. Federal agents supposed that the individuals selected to represent the tribe would make their own decisions. In actuality, the council chiefs continued to do as they had always done: they reiterated positions taken and decisions reached by all prominent men. This fact is abundantly clear in the records of the cession councils. During the negotiations of 1891, when the commissioners pressed Black Coal to concur with Washakie's decision to sell the southern tract, he repeatedly said that he could do nothing until the matter had been thoroughly discussed in a tribal meeting. He told the commissioners, "I am only one Indian; there are but a few Arapahoes here. I want all the Indians to talk it over first. It is not with our tribe as it is with some others. If I should sign a treaty without the consent of the other Indians, some of them would kill me." An eloquent speaker, Black Coal urged his fellow tribesmen to come to a unanimous decision and maintain good feeling toward one another: "I want every Arapahoe to know all that is in the treaty and to say that it is all right, then they cannot say that I have signed a treaty that was wrong. I do not want to walk on nails, but on a smooth, broad road. I want the Arapahoes to all pull together, and all agree on one thing. I do not want them to go in every direction like a balky team—one pull ahead and one back, or off to one side." Black Coal clearly expressed his commitment to nondirective, noninitiatory authority for himself and the other council chiefs: "I only say what others tell me to. I don't know all these things myself, but others tell me to say what I do. . . . I only say what I am told to say. I don't say these things myself."

At the 1896 cession council, Sharp Nose was the main spokesman for the Arapahoes, Lone Bear was second in rank, and Tallow was third. Several days before they met with the commissioners the Arapahoes held meetings and eventually reached agreement to cede the hot springs area. When Sharp Nose (who was interpreted by school alumni Henry Lee Tyler and Thomas Crispin) spoke before the commissioners, he reaffirmed that he was there only to articulate the consensus of the tribe. He signed his name on the agreement and remarked, "I wish that the other Arapahoes will sign it too." Each of the other Arapahoe council chiefs then voiced his assent to what Sharp Nose had said. When the 1904 cession council met, the tribe had already decided what its position on the proposed cession would be in an all-tribal meeting. Lone Bear, an effective advocate and accomplished orator, articulated the tribe's decision. In the words of Buffalo Fat, an elder, "We made up our minds before coming here." Similarly, in 1904 and 1907 the agent pointed out that when leases were made, the council chiefs received specific instructions from a general council of Arapahoes on how they

wanted their lease income spent. Regardless of their personal incli-
nations, the chiefs felt bound to follow the course set by the tribe as a
whole.[55]

At this time Shoshone tribal politics worked quite differently. Chief
Washakie apparently had such great personal influence that he had the
authority to make decisions on behalf of his tribe. After Washakie
died, in 1900, 120 Shoshones petitioned the commissioner to select a
new chief or chiefs: "We are now left without a head to look to. It is
now with us like a man with many tongues all talking at once." Without
Washakie's strong leadership, the several Shoshone bands and factions
were reportedly having "pitched battles."[56]

While council chiefs were careful not to behave in ways that other
Arapahoes could interpret as too assertive, they still tried to demonstrate that they could make sure that provisions were distributed
equitably, and that they could obtain the maximum from the government. Lease money was the primary means available to the council
chiefs in this effort. The tribe as a whole, not the chiefs, decided how
the lease money should be spent, and the chiefs tried to persuade the
agent to concur. The head council chief kept in his possession and
carried with him on public occasions a record book of land leases:
"Now it was agreed that the leading chief of the Arapahoes was to have
a little memorandum book about half as big as the palm of my hand,
made purposely for notations of that kind. And each and every time
that a lessor paid in, so much for oil leases, so much for sheep leases,
so much for horse grazing permits, and each month this chief brought
his little book in and he was being told how much of tribal funds they
had." Periodically each tribe met to decide how the available funds
should be spent. The council chiefs' lease book was in its time a symbol
of their ability to provide for their people. In that sense, it was comparable to the document of "good conduct" given to friendly chiefs by
emigrants and to the army regalia worn by the scout chiefs of the
1870s. The council chiefs also made personal sacrifices in order to give
financial help to their tribesmen. Agent Nickerson noted that as a result
they were always impoverished.[57]

Land leasing and allotment and cession negotiations proceeded un-
eventfully in the 1890s, with the agents and council chiefs reaching
mutual accommodation. But by the middle of Agent Nickerson's term,
serious friction developed between him and the Arapahoes. Nickerson
was dissatisfied with the tribe's progress toward a more "civilized" or
Westernized type of political organization (and probably by the chiefs'
opposition to some of his policies). He attempted to augment the authority of men he considered "progressive" and to erode the authority of

those he termed "old kickers"—that is, men who did not conform to his wishes. He tried to gain support for his programs by offering special benefits in return for cooperation. In this atmosphere a struggle began between the Arapahoes—particularly the elders and adult males—and the agent over control of the Chiefs' Council and the political process in general. Nickerson appointed delegates to go to Washington on behalf of their tribes, instead of permitting the tribes to select their own delegates; he circulated a petition among the tribes to determine how lease money should be spent, rather than dealing directly with the council chiefs; he attempted to create a breach between the Upper Arapahoes (those in the western, elevated country of Arapahoe settlement) and the Lower Arapahoes (those on the eastern end) so that much of the people's energy would be expended in fighting among themselves rather than resisting the agent's plans.[58]

Nickerson was aided in his efforts by Sherman Coolidge, who advocated the eradication of traditional Arapahoe customs and beliefs. As a young boy Coolidge had been taken captive in the attack on the Arapahoes in 1870 and subsequently reared by whites. Educated as an Episcopal minister, he graduated from Seabury Divinity School and was ordained in 1884, then briefly attended Hobart College, in Geneva, New York. He came to the Shoshone Reservation to assist the Reverend John Roberts at the Episcopal mission. In 1902 he married a well-to-do white woman from New York and lived with her on the reservation. He spent most of the years between 1884 and 1910 at the Shoshone Agency, where he served as a part-time issue clerk as well as missionary.[59]

When the Indian Office authorized a delegation to Washington in 1899, Nickerson selected the delegates. The Arapahoes were outraged because they wanted to be certain that the tribe's true feelings would be conveyed to Washington. Nickerson had chosen Sharp Nose (an Upper Arapahoe), Plenty Bear (a Lower Arapahoe), and the young interpreter William Shakespeare. The Upper Arapahoes (Bad Pipe People and Greasy Face People) apparently were agreeable to Sharp Nose's selection, but the Lower Arapahoes (Forks People) were displeased with the selection of Plenty Bear and William Shakespeare. Lone Bear, successor to Black Coal as main council chief of the Lower Arapahoes, had Carlisle graduate Garfield Wolf ("class of 1885") write in protest to the commissioner: "Nickerson selected Plenty Bear and William Shakespeare. We Indians did not choose them as they do what he said. We disapprove of them except Sharp Nose. Nickerson force William Shakespeare as interpreter so I declined to go. Signed, Lone Bear, Chief-successor to my brother Black Coal." The protest was to no avail.[60]

In 1900 Nickerson tried to undermine the authority of the council chiefs by circulating a petition among Arapahoes of all ages and statuses to obtain their views on how their lease money should be spent. Nickerson and Coolidge also tried to set the Upper and Lower Arapahoes against each other. In 1901 Coolidge tried to provoke a confrontation between the two groups when he insisted to the Indian Office that thirty-five "principal men" of the Upper Arapahoes and "the council speaking for this part of the Arapahoe tribe" disavowed the authority of the Lower Arapahoe chiefs. It is also likely that Coolidge hoped to minimize the Upper Arapahoes' contacts with the Catholic mission at the eastern end of the reservation. In response, the Lower Arapahoes demanded that the Upper Arapahoes be moved eastward, closer to the Lower Arapahoe settlement area. To the Indian Office, Nickerson portrayed the Upper Arapahoes as "progressive" and the Lower Arapahoes as "old kickers." About this time the government was beginning to try to survey and allot the reservation; in protest against Nickerson, the Arapahoes now opposed allotment.[61]

When a delegation was authorized again in 1902, Nickerson again chose the delegates. His choices this time were Sherman Coolidge and Henry Lee Tyler, a youth who had been serving as an interpreter. A third delegate, Wallowing Bull, was chosen by the Upper Arapahoes. All three were Upper Arapahoes and only Wallowing Bull was a council chief. Wallowing Bull at first refused to go in protest against Nickerson's actions, but later changed his mind. The Lower Arapahoes steadfastly opposed Nickerson's choices, and enlisted the aid of the priests at St. Stephen's. At the priests' instigation, officials of the Bureau of Catholic Indian Missions in Washington complained to the Indian Office about Nickerson, charging that he had chosen three Shoshones who were his personal friends and that he ignored the Arapahoes' wishes in selecting their representatives. Church officials forwarded a letter from the Arapahoe chiefs, written for them by Garfield Wolf: "I have been speaking to the agent about the men that are to go to Washington. We gave him the name of five men that we would like to go to Washington. Of these five he could choose whom he like best, but on condition that two of them could speak English and one [only] Indian. Now he does not want that, but he wants to choose other men different from those we proposed to him, some friends of his that went already to Washington with him and did nothing for us or rather did us harm for they could not speak our heart. We do not want that the agent should have his own way in this matter." Nickerson caused such resentment that Upper and Lower Arapahoes met and agreed to oppose his reappointment. The Catholic leaders also urged Nickerson's removal: "His term of office is marked by turbulence and friction. The Indians are opposed to him." The Indian Office did not intervene in the selection of delegates, but soon afterward Nickerson was replaced by H. E. Wadsworth.[62]

Once Nickerson was out of office, the council chiefs resumed their customary activities. A few of those who had been allies of Nickerson left the reservation or kept low profiles. Sherman Coolidge, who increasingly lost the goodwill of his tribesmen and eventually the confidence of his superiors, finally became disheartened and left the reservation in 1910. Those Upper Arapahoes who had opposed Nickerson subsequently were well regarded by all of the Arapahoes. Wadsworth was a much less aggressive agent of directed social change than Nickerson had been. He constantly complained that he had no control over the Arapahoe council, which he viewed as "unprogressive."[63]

"DEVOTEES AND PROPHETS": POLITICS AND RELIGION

The Arapahoes understood that the council chiefs' success in dealing with whites and retaining the respect of their people ultimately depended on supernatural aid. The intense religiosity of the Northern Arapahoes figured importantly in political behavior, for personal and public goals were undertaken only after petition to the supernatural and failures or reversals were often interpreted as supernatural sanctions. When James Mooney visited the Arapahoes in Wyoming in 1892, he observed, "In religious matters it may be said briefly that the Arapahoes are devotees and prophets, continually seeing signs and wonders." He pointedly contrasted this intense religiosity with the ethos of other tribes, such as the more skeptical Cheyennes. Obtaining supernatural aid was an Arapahoe preoccupation, and success in this endeavor required the mediation of elders, particularly the ceremonial elders, the priests who directed the tribe's religious rituals. As they, too, worked to contain conflict and shape group consensus, they had a central though indirect role in tribal politics. When the pressures of the reservation experience caused the authority of the ceremonial elders to be challenged, the political order and the entire fabric of Arapahoe society were threatened.[64]

The Political Role of Ceremonial Elders and Lesser Ritual Authorities

In Arapahoe belief, tribal members stand in a special relationship to the Creator; the relationship is symbolized in the Arapahoe custodianship of the Sacred Pipe (*sé'iichóo,* "flat pipe"). The Arapahoe origin myth (which could be told only privately and to persons participating in specific rituals) has never been recorded from an individual with the training and the right to relate it. Accounts of the myth obtained from Arapahoes are fragmentary and varied. The earliest recorded version was written down by Sherman Coolidge in 1890 and is actually a synopsis. A. L. Kroeber recorded another version in 1900. What follows is the 1890 account, with bracketed interpolations where the account varies from Kroeber's version.

> Long ago, before there were any animals, the earth was covered with water, with the exception of one mountain, and seated on this mountain was an Arapahoe, crying and poor and in distress [Kroeber's account indicates that the person was seated on the Sacred Pipe, which floated on the water; in George Dorsey's account, the person was Father, who was also the pipe]. The gods [Creator] looked at him and pitied him, and they created three ducks and sent them to him [Kroeber indicates that the person called for the water birds]. The Arapahoe told the ducks [water birds] to dive down in the waters and find some dirt. One went down in the deep waters and was gone a long time, but failed. The second went down and was gone a still longer time, and he also came up, having failed. The third [the duck] then tried it; he was gone a long time. The waters where he went down had become still and quiet, and the Arapahoe believed him to be dead, when he arose to the surface and had a little dirt in his mouth [other accounts provide for a fourth and more successful attempt on the part of turtle, who brings earth under each of his legs]. Suddenly the waters subsided and disappeared, and left the Arapahoe the sole possessor of the land [the person put the dry earth on the pipe and then blew it from his fingers in the four directions, then spread out the dried mud to make the earth]. The water had gone so far that it could not be seen from the highest mountains, but it still surrounded the earth, and does so to this day. Then the Arapahoe made the rivers and the woods, placing a great deal near the streams. [From the earth the person made two Arapahoes and two whites; he also gave them genitals and instructed them in sexuality.] The whites were made beyond the ocean. There were then all different people, the same as at the present day. Then the Arapahoe created buffaloes, elks, deer, antelopes, wolves, foxes, all the animals that are on the earth, all the birds of the air, all the fishes in the streams, the grasses, fruit, trees, bushes, all that is grown by planting seeds in the ground. This Arapahoe was a god. He had a pipe and he gave it to the people. He showed them how to make bows and arrows, how to make fire by rubbing two sticks, how to talk with their hands, in fact, how to live.[65]

(Note that Kroeber's version accounts for the creation of whites as well as Arapahoes.)

The Sacred Pipe, then, is the embodiment of the Creator, the Great

Mystery. Possession of the Sacred Pipe from the beginning of time directly links the Arapahoe people and the Creator, and the proper care of the Sacred Pipe is synonymous with maintenance of a harmonious relationship with humans, nature, and the Creator. Anthropologist George Dorsey explained that as the Sacred Flat Pipe was the instrument of creation, "if it should be destroyed or stolen an earthquake would follow, and there would be a flood." Thus the care of the *sé'iichóo* (also referred to as the Old Man) was viewed by the people as a sacred trust, central to the well-being of the tribe and of the earth itself. The Sacred Pipe and other sacred objects were contained in a bundle, wrapped in cloth offerings, which was cared for at all times by a priest, the keeper of the Sacred Pipe. After the Arapahoes settled at the Shoshone Agency, they continued to perform the rituals periodically necessary to meet their obligations to the *sé'iichóo*. Seven lesser tribal medicine bundles were in the keeping of seven priests known as *chiinéchii-bhe'iihohó'*, or water-pouring old men. Nothing is known of the content of these medicine bags or their ritual use, nor is it known whether all seven priests were living when the Arapahoes first came to the agency. The water-pouring old men and the keeper of the Sacred Pipe formed a tribal priesthood responsible for mediating between the tribe as a whole and the Creator. They had particularly important duties during the *beeyóóowu'* or lodge ceremonies. These are the men I refer to as the ceremonial elders.[66]

The ceremonial elders had considerable influence over the Arapahoes because they were at the top of a hierarchy of religious offices or statuses. As Cleaver Warden (a bilingual Southern Arapaho employed by the Field Museum to do research on the Arapahoes at the turn of the century) put it, ritual authorities were "promoted by degrees." With each promotion an individual increased his knowledge of spiritual matters and his competence in performing rituals of intercession with supernatural forces. The ceremonial elders had acquired the maximum knowledge and competence. Other Arapahoes depended on them for the success of tribal ceremonies. Individuals who wanted to learn to perform directive functions in such tribal rituals as the Offerings Lodge (Sun Dance) or men's lodges had to apprentice themselves to the ceremonial elders for long periods of time. Under their tutelage the younger men earned their way through a hierarchical series of "offices" (spiritual stages or ritual proficiencies) by completing a set of tasks or ordeals associated with each office. Although ceremonial elders and lesser ritual authorities who were in the process of accumulating degrees probably had *béétee* or medicine power, a man's personal *béétee* did not entitle him to an office in the religious hierarchy. *Béétee* gave an individual the power to cure, to find objects, to predict the future, or to achieve success in battle.[67]

Because of the long apprenticeship required to obtain the degrees of the priesthood, a man normally had reached old age by the time he achieved a significant amount of ritual authority. Kroeber observed in 1900, "It is the old people who most paint themselves for religious motives." The elders applied paint daily—red pigment only, in contrast to the greater variety of paints used by younger Arapahoes. Red paint (made from red earth and tallow) symbolized old age, sacredness, earth (or subsistence), and life—particularly that of the Arapahoe people. The very physical appearance of these elders reminded those around them of their central role in the well-being of the tribe. The Arapahoes viewed their society as comprised of four broad categories of people, each category subdivided by sex: male and female children, male and female youths, male and female mature adults, and male and female elders. In both sacred and secular realms, the amount and kinds of authority permitted an individual were based on that person's age category. In the ceremonial hierarchy, a man's status was in large part determined by his position in the series of men's age grades. As we have seen, Arapahoe males were organized into age sets that progressively passed through the series of grades by successive initiation into seven ceremonial lodges. A man progressed through the lodges as he aged, each lodge more sacred than the last. (The lodge organization is discussed in more detail below.) The age hierarchy was operative more informally in the acquisition of *béétee*. The *bééteet* ("man with medicine power" or medicine man) often acquired his powers by purchasing them (through apprenticeship) from an older man who over a period of time gave instructions in the use of the songs and ritual objects associated with the medicine power. Or he might acquire *béétee* from a spirit helper who appeared to him in a dream. In that case, he would consult an elder as to how the dream should be interpreted. A man could also obtain *béétee* by fasting in isolation to attract the pity of a spirit helper. If he succeeded in having a vision, he would ask an elder to interpret it for him. The vision quest, which was a common pursuit of adolescent males in other Plains tribes, was considered dangerous for one so young and was undertaken usually after a man reached maturity. Similarly, youths were not considered qualified for positions of political authority.[68]

It was important for Arapahoes to cultivate the goodwill of the elders; from the moment of birth throughout an individual's lifetime, old men and women could intervene to help a person achieve a successful life. Parents asked an elder to choose their child's name; the elder had the right to bestow a name that formerly belonged to a successful individual (usually one of the elder's relatives). The Arapahoes believed that the name and the accompanying prayers by the elders would help to ensure the child's future success. The elders prayed for children at various stages of their development. As a youth matured, he sought out elders to help him acquire supernatural aid. When elders chose to express their opinions on matters of public policy, it was difficult for younger Arapahoes not to follow their wishes, since they relied so completely on the elders in all other matters. The elders monitored the behavior of their juniors (including the council chiefs) in many ways, encouraging bravery, equanimity, and generosity through public orations in which they praised individuals who exhibited those qualities. Kroeber observed public giveaways in which the relatives of individuals who sought to improve or validate their status gave property away on that person's behalf: "This public giving-away, which is practiced also in the Sun Dance and on other occasions, is called 'chief gives away' (nantcanahaanti) [*nééchééno'he'eht*]." Kroeber also reported that members of the men's lodges sang before the tents of "four chiefs or other good men," who were then expected to bestow gifts on the singers. After such generosity, old men would honor the "good men" by praising them in public. At social dances old women frequently sang songs that singled out individuals for past deeds of bravery. In this way public displays of generosity, bravery, and other virtuous qualities were linked with political status. Old men also used their influence to promote the council chiefs' efforts to convince federal officials that the Arapahoes had become "good Indians." In public orations they encouraged the Arapahoes to work at farming as well as to fulfill their ceremonial obligations and to avoid quarrels. Thirty-four-year-old William Shakespeare observed in 1897, "The old Indians used to always talk to us about going to war, and now they talk to us different—about farming and how to farm and they tell us young men to work hard at farming."[69]

The influence of old men and old women in the priesthood was felt by all Arapahoes, particularly in times of personal or social crisis. In general, men had responsibility for all-tribal ceremonies, which emphasized social unity; they mediated between the Creator and all Arapahoes. Seven female priests presided over rites that aided particular families or individuals. Some information is available on the political role of the men known as ceremonial elders. What kind of political roles the female priests had is unknown. High ritual status for women was acquired through the ownership of tribal medicine bags, which contained the implements for porcupine-quill work and tipi painting. Sometime before the tribe settled on the reservation, seven such bags were in the custody of female elders. By the turn of the century, few were still in the possession of old women qualified to use them. The owners of medicine bags were petitioned by women who were seeking supernatural aid, usually for a relative. The woman would make a vow to work quills in symbolic designs on cradle boards (if the prayer were for an infant), robes, or tipis. The "prayer" was worked into the design to "drive away the sickness or trouble from the person or persons." A woman who wished to undertake quillwork had to apprentice herself to an old woman who had custody of one of the bags. After earning degrees in the execution of quillwork, she might eventually attain or inherit the medicine bag from its custodian and the right to conduct rituals in which quillwork was supervised. To do quillwork outside of the context of an apprenticeship would have been sacrilege. Firewood, one of the medicine-bag "owners" interviewed by Cleaver Warden, had earned the right to inherit her mother's bundle when the latter died, about 1885. Firewood "reached the remarkable record of sixty baby cradles, fourteen buffalo robes, five ornamented tipis, ten calf robes, and one buffalo leanback cover." On her forehead, her chin, and just in front of each ear she wore a large red spot, and a small dot on her nose. She also had five dots painted on her scalp in the same pattern. These designs symbolized the manner in which Man-with-the-Flat-Pipe distributed the earth in five directions at the time of creation.[70]

The ceremonial elders and lesser ritual authorities played a central, if indirect, role in encouraging the Arapahoes to reach consensus in discussions of problems and in containing or resolving conflict. Such efforts were vitally important to the council chiefs' attempts to present a united front to federal officials. By means of the Sacred Pipe and lodge rituals and the interpersonal bonds engendered between participants in these ceremonies, the ceremonial elders effectively guided the Arapahoes toward social solidarity and discouraged divisiveness.

Weasel Bear (also known as White-Haired Old Man) was the keeper of the Sacred Pipe when the Arapahoes came to the reservation, and he held this position until his death in 1904. As the pipe's keeper, he was the ultimate authority on rituals involving its use. He and the elders who assisted him were responsible for the successful performance of Sacred Pipe rituals. The keeper attended the pipe daily, praying for the well-being of the tribe. He also assisted individuals who vowed to pray through personal sacrifice to the pipe. When an individual made such a vow, the keeper instructed him in the performance of the correct rituals. The vow also was made known to the entire tribe and their prayers and assistance were sought. The rite thus not only involved the individual petitioner but also served to unify all Arapahoes spiritually and socially. Warden noted that individuals who fulfilled vows involving the Sacred Pipe thereafter had a religious obligation to behave with kindness and honesty toward all the people. During Sacred Pipe ceremonies Arapahoes were forbidden to quarrel on pain of supernatural sanction. George Dorsey (drawing on Warden's fieldwork) gave this translation of one individual's vow to "fast with the Pipe":

> On behalf of my child I wish to make it known to you all that I cannot help but decide to fast with the flat-pipe. As you all know the nature of this vow I ask each and all of you to put your mind in accord with mine to the end that my child may recover. It is my wish to endure this hardship, to cleanse the past and establish a bright future for my family and the tribe. Today I ask you all to be kind to one another for we are soon to be purified. It will be our desire that our future days may be lengthened and that we may obtain bright rays of sun into our respective tipis. Can you realize how it is to have a sick child? I do not know whether my child will live or not, so you will please help me in my supplication. Listen to me, friends, I ask your assistance in the way of food and wish you all to be present at the painting of the pipe for we wish to increase and to be preserved.

In the spring, just before the vegetation appeared above the ground, Weasel Bear would publicly "smoke the Sacred Pipe" seven times, passing it four times around a circle of tribesmen from right to left. To symbolize a state of spiritual purity (spiritual rebirth), each person present inhaled four times, then took the smoke in his hands and rubbed it over his body. Prayers were made at this time, and youths as well as elders were allowed to participate. There were other rituals involving the pipe, all central to the well-being of the tribe and to the acquisition of the knowledge that earned degrees for would-be ritual authorities. Ceremonial elders could require individuals to take an oath on the Sacred Pipe as a guarantee of peace or of truth; the oath was a force for social control, since the Arapahoes believed that violation of such an oath would bring disaster.[71]

The *beeyóóowu'*, "all the lodges," which included the *hoséihoowu'* (the Offerings Lodge, also known as the Sacrifice Lodge and the Sun Dance), the series of men's age-graded lodge ceremonies, and the women's *benihtóoowu'* (the Buffalo Lodge), were performed when one or more individuals made a religious vow to sponsor or "put up" the lodge; others then could vow to participate. For the Offerings Lodge and the men's lodges, a votary sought an instructor from among the ranks of those qualified to offer supervision and counsel in the lodge. Supervisors (called grandfathers) in the Offerings Lodge were men who had participated in the lodge several times before. In the men's graded lodges, a man who had completed the lodge ceremony once could then serve as a grandfather. These lodge ceremonies brought the entire tribe together and promoted social harmony, not only during the several days required for the performance of the ritual but also during the preparatory period (which in the case of the Offerings Lodge lasted several months). (The religious symbolism of the lodges is beyond the scope of this discussion; it is ably described in George Dorsey's *The Arapaho Sun Dance* and A. L. Kroeber's *The Arapaho,* Part III.)

The participants in the Offerings Lodge, who fasted and prayed for four days, were fulfilling vows made to the Creator in thanks that their personal supplications had been granted. By taking part in the ordeal they were also thought to be making a sacrifice on behalf of the tribe. The Arapahoes were strongly committed to the Offerings Lodge, and although some agents tried to enforce the Indian Office's ban on the ceremony, particularly in the 1890s, the ritual continued to be held almost annually. In 1889 the "piercing" (self-torture by tearing of the skin) apparently was undergone for the last time when a student at the government boarding school subjected himself to the ordeal. Kroeber states that the lodge (without the piercing rite) was held in 1899 and 1900; he made his observations of the ceremony in 1900. Dorsey documents the holding of the ceremony in 1903, 1904, and 1905. During the 1880s the Arapahoes apparently convinced the Indian agents and military authorities at Fort Washakie that the Offerings Lodge would not interfere with the civilization effort. Boys at the government school, for example, were acknowledged to be good students even though they participated in the lodge. The ceremony was held during Nickerson's tumultuous term. Nickerson complained to the commissioner that he ordered the Arapahoes not to hold the lodge, but their leaders insisted that the ritual would be performed as usual. One agency employee said that the Arapahoes circumvented the Indian Office's prohibition of the Sun Dance by secrecy if the agent was popular and by "flaunting tactics" if he was not. When the agent did succeed in preventing the Offerings Lodge in 1907, several Northern Arapahoes went to Oklahoma to fulfill their vows in the Southern Arapahos' Sun Dance. [72]

The seven men's grades, in the order in which they were entered, were the Kit Foxes, Stars, Tomahawks, Spears, Crazies, Dogs, and Old Men. The last five involved varying degrees of sacred knowledge. The most sacred was called the *hinénniinóowu'* (Old Men's Lodge), followed by the *héOowoowú'* (Dog Lodge), *hohóokóówu'* (Crazy Lodge), *biitohóówu'* (Spear Lodge), and *hiiche'éexóowu'* (Tomahawk Lodge).

Most of the lodges were held several times between 1878 and 1907. Once an age set had completed a lodge ceremony, the members were permitted to perform the ceremony again. The Tomahawks apparently did so from time to time, the other grades more infrequently. The lodge ritual made the tie between men of an age set more emotionally intense and created ties between them and several men from the age set two lodges removed who were selected as "elder brothers" to the initiates. The elder brothers helped with the arrangements for the lodge ceremony. The most significant bonds formed were those between the instructors (grandfathers) and the initiates (called grandsons). The sacred knowledge conveyed to the novices in the lodge ceremonies has not been studied. It is clear, however, that in the age grades the men were socialized and oriented toward service to the tribe and respect for the elders. Cleaver Warden commented that the lodges had "a strong 'will power' to correct past deeds and to teach young people in better attainments." Good behavior was encouraged by the selection of exemplary men for "degrees of rank and honor by presentation of different kinds of regalia." Before boys were old enough to enter the first in the series of grades (the Kit Foxes), they were organized into groups in preparation for their later experiences. In this account of one such group (the Blackbirds) formed soon after the turn of the century, an Arapahoe man explains how he and his fellow Blackbirds were given advice and encouraged to work together harmoniously for the benefit of the tribe:

> Now this society consisted of little boys, age group of about six to about fourteen. Now these little boys . . . didn't technically have a Blackbird age society group. . . . About the only time they would gather would be during the ceremonials such as the Sun Dance. The opening night of the Sun Dance they would perform. They selected an advisor. He was known among the tribe as their big brother. Now it was the big brother that would teach them certain dances and give them advice on what was ahead of them, what life was and they were supposed to sit there and listen and do work together. . . . Back in 1908 [approximately] we selected Chief Littleshield as our advisor, one of the last recognized Arapahoe chiefs. For some reason we were lucky to get this man who was very kind and honest. And he taught us many things, told us the stories of the society. All the little boys used to go around and clean up the camps, go into tipis, take the ashes out and help the old folks. And this was a society which was recognized by the tribe. They would be called upon to do certain work around the camp which was not too heavy for them.[73]

The *beeyóóowu'*, which the ceremonial elders directed, gave supernatural sanction to a network of ties among individuals from different kin groups and bands, which had political repercussions. Most important of these ties was the grandfather-grandson bond. When a man vowed to participate in one of the lodges, he chose as his grandfather someone who was not a kinsman and usually someone who was considerably older. This choice initiated a lifelong relationship of mutual respect and aid, which also extended to a lesser degree to the families of the two men. The bond between families was symbolized by an exchange of food during the lodge ceremony: the family of the grandson fed the family of the grandfather and the grandfather's family reciprocated. Such exchanges meant that the two groups became one "family"; the members of both groups were now obligated to one another. The grandfather and grandson were obligated never to speak badly of each other and to offer each other aid in times of need, and the grandfather continued to serve as his grandson's spiritual adviser even after the conclusion of the lodge ceremony. Unlike such instructors in other tribes, he did not lose possession of his knowledge of sacred things when he shared it with his grandson. Thus the antagonism between instructor and novice that Robert Lowie found in other Plains tribes, in which men of one grade purchased the rights to the secrets of a higher grade, was absent from the age-graded lodges of the Arapahoes. Once an Arapahoe man completed a lodge ceremony, he held its secrets for life. Mutual respect between grandfathers and grandsons had supernatural sanction. As Warden put it, "Much care must be taken to preserve tranquility and respect of the two relations." The Arapahoes believed that if one were insulted by the other, the health of the insulted man would deteriorate; if one failed to aid the other, his neglect could "come back on him"—result in illness or disaster. The grandfather had the authority to defuse his grandson's anger: if the grandson became violent, his grandfather's presence could calm him. In extreme cases, the grandfather calmed his grandson by thrusting a pipe into his hands. When the Arapahoes came to a decision in a tribal meeting, the ceremonial grandfather–grandson relationship aided in the formation of a consensus and helped to contain serious conflict.[74]

On July 21, 1879, when Waterman killed Fast Wolf, he created a serious problem for the Arapahoes. Ordinarily murders resulted in revenge killings or, ideally, in payment of compensation to the victim's relatives. But at this time the Arapahoes were trying to convince federal officials that they were peaceful or "good" Indians. The murder tarnished their image, and more killings would have tarnished it further. Moreover, Waterman was from Black Coal's band and Fast Wolf from Friday's group. A feud between these two bands would have undermined the council chiefs' efforts to present a united front to federal officials. After the killing, Waterman prepared to resist retaliation by

Fast Wolf's relatives. Cherries, one of the ritual authorities, went to the camp of Waterman's kinsman Young Chief (of the Forks People) and said, "This is going to make bad work. Your brother Waterman has killed Fast Wolf. Now something must be done. We don't want war among ourselves." The old man convinced Young Chief that Waterman should surrender to the whites at the agency and that to do otherwise would be "foolish" (that is, *hohooko,* "crazy"). That which is *hohooko* is contrary to the natural order, spiritually and socially chaotic. Such elders as Cherries were the ultimate judges of what was "out of order." Young Chief then went to Waterman and tried to persuade him to give himself up to the whites and to face bravely what they both thought would be certain death: "You have been blind. You did not consider your brothers and their wives and children in the trouble you have brought on them. Fast Wolf has many relatives. So have you. Will you try to run away and be killed and have a war brought on among ourselves?" Waterman agreed to surrender. Then, with the help of the elders, Young Chief set out to convince his tribesmen that Waterman's surrender was an act of sacrifice and selfless service to all the people (and thus that an act of revenge by Fast Wolf's group would be inappropriate). As he explained it to the agent (with Friday interpreting), "So I started with him. Then we passed lodges. I said, 'Here is Waterman. Come and see him. He has given himself up to die.' The squaws all came out and shook hands with him and cried. When we came to Sharp Nose's village, I called them and all came out and shook hands with him. We got to Friday's camp just at daylight; I called out to Friday, 'Get up. We have got Waterman, and want you to go with us to the post.'" Black Coal also went to the agent and stated his support for Young Chief's actions. It is clear that although Black Coal played an important role in the crisis in his capacity as intermediary, he did not have the authority to prevent the threatened interband violence. The moral authority of such elders as Cherries, however, was supernaturally sanctioned and cut across band divisions.[75]

Several years later, when the Arapahoes were worrying about whether they had a future on the reservation, Weasel Bear brought his influence to bear. During the several years of cession negotiations the people were worried about their lack of clear title to the reservation lands. As in times of crisis generally, ritual authorities gave reassurance through recitation of myth, prayer, and oration during tribal gatherings, and in prophesy. During the months of discussion before the 1904 cession, Weasel Bear, keeper of the Sacred Pipe, recounted how the pipe once prophesied that the Arapahoes would one day have a good and a secure place to live. His reassurance calmed the Arapahoes and

helped the council chiefs and other headmen to persuade them to support the chiefs at the cession council. Weasel Bear told of the time the
Northern Arapahoes decided to come to Wyoming rather than accom-
pany the Southern Arapahos to a reservation in Oklahoma:

> When I heard that we were all to be removed to another country, to tell the
> truth, I didn't know what to do, since I had in my possession our Father, the
> Flat Pipe. The people didn't ask me to go south or to go north, to save the Flat
> Pipe from injury and destruction, but they left me to decide what was best for
> the whole tribe. So I would sit alone, to think and pray to the Flat Pipe for its
> guidance and deliverance, and for the people too. One day, as I was fasting on
> the top of a high mountain . . . , I found myself in a trance, . . . with this Flat
> Pipe in front of me, standing in solid position on a tripod. All around me, as
> far as my eyes could see, there was a deep blue water (sea), rolling like moun-
> tains toward me, but I at once knew that there was a true companion with me
> to save me. The Flat Pipe knew that I placed my faith sincerely, also recog-
> nized my tender weeping (crying for mercy), spoke to me, saying that I must
> remain close to the mountains (the northern portion of the United States) and
> take the consequences; that I should think of the Flat Pipe more than ever, to
> care for it and protect it from bad encroachments; that hereafter it would
> naturally be of great comfort and blessing to our kindred, that in years to
> come, there would be a change, when the Arapahoe race, being the race located
> in the center by the Father, would be saved, and delivered into good land; that
> I must be moderate in my ways, be good in my thoughts, control my con-
> science for the good of all, and ask for blessings upon the people from time to
> time, especially in time of famine, plague, etc. So, after having been inspired
> by the Flat Pipe, I took the commandments to fulfill, or teach them to the
> people. The water then subsided, and I found myself again in "usual senses."[76]

Crises of Authority among the Ceremonial Elders

The political influence of the elders, which was a strong force for social
stability in the traumatic decades of the 1880s and 1890s, depended
largely on the perpetuation of the age hierarchy and its reinforcement
by the religious authority of the ceremonial elders. But ritual authorities faced serious difficulties that threatened to undermine their influence and minimize their role in reservation life. As priests died and
agents took repressive measures to curtail the Indian "dances," the
ceremonial elders found it increasingly difficult to pass their knowledge
of tribal ceremonies on to younger men. Christianity was potentially
competitive with the native religion and the government offered incentives and imposed sanctions to pressure the Arapahoes toward conver-
sion. During those years, too, several revitalization movements were

introduced among the Arapahoes. The new faiths had particular appeal to the young people. By offering them a chance to express their individualism and to exercise authority, the new religions threatened the age hierarchy and the position of the ceremonial elders.

Under the hardships of reservation life, many elders and priests died before they could properly train successors; yet the Arapahoes continued to perform their sacred rituals, adapting the requirements of religious office to contemporary circumstances. Weasel Bear, custodian of the Sacred Pipe, died in 1904, apparently without any male heirs or fellow *béesóowú'unenno'* (Big Lodge People) properly trained to succeed him. The care of the Sacred Pipe was entrusted to Collie Judson (*níí'ehíhi'-béétee,* "medicine bird"), who was married to Weasel Bear's daughter Ute Woman. The couple had been given some instruction in pipe ritual, but Judson was only twenty-nine years old and did not have a ritual status comparable to that of Weasel Bear.[77]

By the 1890s almost none of the seven *chiinéchii-bhe'iihohó'* or water-pouring old men were still living. James Mooney indicated that the Arapahoes were shaken by the passing of the priesthood. He recorded this song, which refers to a vision in which the singer has seen the seven priests still performing their rites:

> The seven venerable Chínachichíbat priests,
> The seven venerable Chínachichíbat priests.
> We see them,
> We see them.
> They all wear it on their heads,
> They all wear it on their heads.
> The Thunderbird,
> The Thunderbird.
> Then I wept,
> Then I wept.

The last of the water-pouring old men was Plenty Poles, who died in 1894, at the age of about eighty-three. In the absence of the traditional priesthood, Weasel Bear apparently assumed major responsibility for ceremonial direction until his death. He supervised the Sun Dance in 1900 and some of the men's lodge ceremonies. Other elders also pooled their knowledge and helped to direct tribal ceremonies during this time. Each of the seven priests had custody of a tribal medicine bundle, which was supposed to be transferred to his successor in office. Kroeber noted that in 1900 all of the seven bundles were still in existence, and a few years later, although no water-pouring priests were still living, none of the Arapahoes who had the sacred bundles would sell them. The women's priesthood also had passed out of existence; not all of the seven women's medicine bundles had been passed on, and in fact Kroeber was able to purchase one of the seven bags. Although at least some of the ritual knowledge of the water-pouring old men was passed on to other Arapahoes, the ceremonies of the women's priesthood apparently did not survive.[78]

To the Arapahoes who wanted to hold tribal religious ceremonies, the absence of priests was as troublesome as government opposition. By 1910 some of the elders who were directing the Sacrifice Lodge or Sun Dance had one of the school alumni write to anthropologist George Dorsey: "I am asking you to send me a Sun Dance book so I can look and read for Sun Dance Priests. Because old peoples all died. So we have no Sun Dance Priests now." The ceremonial lodges of the men's age grades were particularly difficult to hold. The most sacred lodge, *hinénniinóowu'* (called the Old Men's Lodge), apparently was not held after the Arapahoes settled on the reservation. Cleaver Warden commented that the elders who directed the lodges he witnessed in 1900 and 1904 "lacked . the requirements of laws governing the Lodges." He noted that when the Dog Lodge ceremony was held on November 22, 1904, the elders disagreed on the procedure for the painting of the participants.[79]

By the turn of the century, then, the Arapahoe priesthood and the complex of tribal religious ceremonies they directed seemed to be about to disappear. Yet the ceremonies went on. Although the elders who directed them were not formally qualified as water-pouring old men, the Arapahoes regarded them as ceremonial elders, quite capable of assuming priestly duties. Some aspects of the tribal rituals were altered or reinterpreted to accommodate the abilities of the men available to direct them. The elders emphasized flexibility in revising specific procedures and criteria for ritual leadership in order to perpetuate native religion in general. And so the rituals survived the crisis of leadership brought about by the deaths of the priests and repressive government policies. Mooney noted Weasel Bear's flexibility in regard to Sacred Pipe ritual. Although the pipe had always been carried on foot with the bundle tied to its bearer's back, Weasel Bear relaxed the rules when he had to and occasionally rode on horseback with the pipe bundle on his back. He never, however, rode with the pipe in a wagon. The ceremonial elders in charge of the Sun Dance decided to eliminate the piercing ceremony in order to placate the federal officials, who found the rite "barbarous." And although not all men participated and the age grades had fewer significani social functions after the Arapahoes settled at the agency, the men's lodge ceremonies continued to be held periodically.[80]

The focus of the age grade members' activity was religious; policing duty and warfare were no longer possible. Participants in *beeyóóowu'* ("all the lodges") prayed for physical and psychological well-being under the difficult conditions of reservation life. The Tomahawk, Spear, Crazy, and Dog lodges took place several times but were studied only at the turn of the century, by Cleaver Warden. In fact, the Arapahoes were assisted by Warden's employer, anthropologist George Dorsey, in seeking the agent's permission to hold the ceremonies. The *hiiche'eexóowu'* or Tomahawk Lodge (also referred to as the Clubboard Lodge) was observed in 1904. The participants included Henry Lee Tyler (a thirty-three-year-old alumnus of government boarding schools, then serving as an interpreter), George Blackburn (twenty-four years old), Peter White Plume (twenty-four years old), and George Wallowing Bull (twenty-five years old). The *biitohóówu'* or Spear Lodge (sometimes referred to as the Thunderbird Lodge) and the *hohóokóówu'* or Crazy Lodge were observed in 1900; the *héOowoowú'* or Dog Lodge was held in 1904. In the Dog Lodge ceremony the initiates were Yellow Calf (who took his deceased half brother's place on the Chiefs' Council that same year), Yellow Bear, Stone Breaker, Runs across Water, Sitting Bear, Red Sun, Wooden Legs, Fast Bird, Eagle Feather, Birds Head, Goodman, Eagle Breath, Nightman, Blow Away, Mule, and Coal. The chosen grandfathers of the initiates were Buffalo Fat, Scarface, Little Owl, Spotted Crow, Crooked Foot, White Breast, and Bear Back Bone. According to Warden, some men later pledged to complete the Spear and Crazy lodges, but it is not clear if in fact they did so. Northern Arapahoes did, however, go to Oklahoma to participate in the Crazy Lodge ceremony held there about 1906.[81]

Youths were particularly active in the lodge ceremonies, and the elders apparently relaxed the rules so that they could participate at younger ages than they could have done in earlier times. The graded lodge ceremonies were the most important all-tribal rituals in the spring and fall. To the participants they were immensely satisfying. As Warden said, the rituals would "vanish away any discrepancy of mind." It appears that after 1900 men were entering the lodge series at very young ages and becoming initiated into the adult male lodges as youths. The Spear Men (*biitohuinénno'*) got progressively younger: Mooney reported they were about thirty in 1892, Kroeber noted the average age as twenty-five in 1900, and Robert Lowie reported that in 1910 they were about eighteen years old. Similarly, Mooney gave the age of Crazy Men (*hohóokeenénno'*) as fifty; Kroeber, forty; Lowie, twenty-five. Most of the men initiated as Dog Men (*heOébnenno'*) in 1904 were in their late thirties and early forties. These were difficult times for youths; federal agents were encouraging them to stop deferring to the elders and to take on responsibilities not permitted them by tribal custom. Yet the opportunities offered by the government often caused the youths to be ostracized or ridiculed by their own people. The elders, by encouraging youths to enter the lodges under their direction, perpetuated the age hierarchy and at the same time offered the young men a chance for prestige in Arapahoe society.[82]

The elders were also flexible about the youths' participation in the new religious movements. The Ghost Dance and peyote rituals, introduced during this era, were not treated as though they competed with the native religion. According to Arapahoes living today, several people had prophesied the coming of the new religious movements and thus helped to sanction them: "They said that Sage had that vision that the Ghost Dance was coming and that peyote was coming. And so did Yellow Calf. And they told their people that . . . this Ghost Dance was coming and that this peyote was coming. That they could take part in it if they wanted to. But not to misuse it or to put it above the [Sacred] Pipe ceremonies. They were told that the pipe was here long before those others were. And they said that the pipe was going to be here long after those others were gone. That's what they predicted." In the prophecies, which were messages from the supernatural, the Arapahoes were warned not to neglect the native religion, but always to keep it first in their hearts, or "above" other faiths.[83]

In 1889, news of Wovoka, the Ghost Dance messiah, was brought to the Wind River area by the Bannocks. That summer Arapahoe elders sent Sage in company with five Shoshones to learn about the new faith. In the fall two Arapahoes, Sitting Bull and Bill Friday, went with Shoshone, Cheyenne, and Sioux delegations to investigate the Ghost Dance movement further. By the end of the year the Northern Arapahoes and many Shoshones were fervent believers in the new revelation that through supernatural means whites would be removed from the Indian homeland, that their deceased relatives would come to life, and that the bounty of former times would recur. The Ghost Dance faith flourished throughout 1890, but when the predicted new world did not materialize in 1891, the Shoshones abandoned the faith and some Arapahoes had second thoughts as well. Black Coal was dubious about the merits of the Ghost Dance, and so he sent another delegation led by Yellow Eagle and including Washington, Goes in Lodge, Black Bear, and Michael Goodman. Upon their return they spoke against the movement, but some Arapahoes, including Sharp Nose and many of his followers, still continued to participate in Ghost Dance rituals.[84]

Mooney observed that the Arapahoe elders were the ultimate

authorities in Ghost Dance matters. Although vision experiences encouraged individual interpretations and motivated some youths to seek leadership positions in the Ghost Dance movement, the elders discouraged individual initiative or tried to incorporate innovations into the ceremonies over which they had authority. Sitting Bull, a Southern Arapaho youth who had lived with the northern group since about 1876, tried to develop a personal following even though he had no status in the traditional ritual hierarchy. His ambitions were thwarted and he was pressed into leaving the reservation in 1891. He traveled to his relatives in the south, settled there, and by the time he was thirty-six years old had become the most influential of the Ghost Dance prophets among the Southern Arapahos.[85]

Yellow Calf had a vision in which supernatural beings taught him a new ceremony called the Crow Dance, or *hoúúnohowóót*. In 1904 Warden recorded the story of Yellow Calf's vision:

A young man named Yellow Calf in Northern Arapahoe was taken sick and had violent hemorages. The story of the messiah was then being agitated among the Northern Arapahoes, for a part of them had visited the western tribes, meeting a man who proclaimed he was a holy messenger from the spirit land. This man after returning from the western Indians told the story of the message, and in his message he told them that there was a time coming soon when the earth would be renewed with its inhabitants. . . . Yellow Calf was very low, all the doctors in the tribe failed to cure him. Hearing of the better world he made up his mind to die and go there, expecting that he would return soon. Anyway in any event he was not conscious for a long time, having had another hemorage of the lungs. His body was cold and stiff. It finally came to its normal temperature. The relatives and friends were in the lodge. Some of them cried, but the man comforted them saying he was in the spiritual world receiving gifts. After Yellow Calf had recovered his senses, he told them he had left them and reached the spiritual world. He assured the people of the dances which were to be the forerunner of the new world. . . . He told the people it was to be a religious dance. The time came when he went to work and made bustles of eagle feathers, whistles and horn spoons, bows and arrows, headdress of feathers. During this ritual that he inaugurated there were songs which were made up by him. There were songs for the opening of the dance, and blessing of the food, and closing of the dance.

According to Kroeber, many of the elements of the Crow Dance were contained in the Omaha Dance, which was brought to the Northern Arapahoes by the Sioux, who obtained it from the Omahas. The Omaha Dance was fused with elements of the Ghost Dance to become the Crow Dance of Yellow Calf's vision. Kroeber reported, "The Arapahoes had the [Omaha] dance until, at the time of the Ghost Dance, the older limitations as to the kind and color of feathers and the accompanying regulations were given up or modified; and the ceremony was called 'Crow Dance'." Under the influence of the elders, some aspects of the new ceremony were made to parallel the lodge ceremonies. Individuals sponsored the dance upon making a vow, and the proper performance of the ritual required coaching from others who had already performed the rites. After the Arapahoes lost interest in the Ghost Dance, the Crow Dance continued to be popular for a time. In 1900 Kroeber remarked of the Crow Dance, "It is chiefly the younger people who take part in it; but the older do not look upon it as in any way an intrusion or innovation, and give it full approval."[86]

Just as the elders attempted to influence the form that the Ghost Dance and the Crow Dance took among the Arapahoes, they also tried to shape the way the new rituals were perceived by whites. The Arapahoes were aware that the Indian Office was anticipating trouble among Sioux followers of the Ghost Dance, and the elders wanted to make sure that the agent did not regard the new ceremony as in any way militaristic. No doubt they encouraged the visits of council chiefs to Fort Washakie. The chiefs and several Arapahoes who were agency employees succeeded in their mission: the agent reported that among the Arapahoes there was "no temper or condition of insubordination." When the Indian Office increased its efforts to curtail the Ghost Dance, the Arapahoes danced in secret. Mooney mentions that on his visit to the tribe in 1892 the agent informed him that there was no Ghost Dance activity on the reservation. When he visited the Arapahoe camp in the company of the agency clerk and Henry Reed, a man of Cheyenne-Arapahoe-white descent who had succeeded Friday as the tribe's interpreter, he was assured that the Arapahoes were no longer interested in the new religion. After the clerk returned to the agency, "satisfied that that part of the country was safe so far as the Ghost Dance was concerned," Mooney and Reed were invited to meet with tribal elders: "By this time it was dark, and the Indians invited the interpreter and myself to come over to a tipi about half a mile away, where we could meet all the old men. We started, and had gone but a short distance when we heard from a neighboring hill the familiar measured cadence of the ghost songs. On turning with a questioning look to my interpreter—who was himself a half-blood—he quietly said: 'Yes; they are dancing the Ghost Dance. That's something I have never reported, and I never will. It is their religion and they have a right to it.'"[87]

The Ghost Dance had scarcely been accommodated before the elders faced the introduction of the peyote ritual. The peyote religion was well established among many of the tribes in Oklahoma, including the Southern Arapahos. The Northern Arapahoes had heard about the healing powers of peyote ritual and some men went to Oklahoma to learn of the new faith. According to one Northern Arapahoe, John Goggles, peyote was introduced to the Arapahoes in Wyoming by William Shakespeare after a visit to Oklahoma:

> There was a man here on this reservation, William Shakespeare, one of the first Indian boys to go to school at Wind River. Then went to Genoa, Nebraska, to high school. Before he got through high school he got sick, so he was released from that school to come back here to reservation. Just at that time the people heard something about this Peyote Worship in Oklahoma. So his father asked him if he would go down to Oklahoma and find that medicine down there. Had sinus trouble and thyroid disturbance, glands all bad. His father thought much of this educated son and didn't want to see him die so soon. So he obeyed his father and said he would try it. His father got another man to go with him (he was about forty) a closely related cousin, White Antelope. . . . [After attending peyote services in Oklahoma,] he felt good and thought he had found something to heal him. After [the peyote] meeting was over chief [the leader of the peyote ritual] told him he would be cured and he could take this meeting to his people and tell them how to worship. When he got back home he was lot better and told what he saw and what they had done for him. . . . He started [peyote] meeting[s] here about 1895 or '96.[88]

The peyote religion gradually gained converts, mostly among youths, who found that in their peyote visions they could have spiritual experiences without apprenticing themselves to elders. Goggles, a peyotist himself, commented, "At that time the people felt two ways about it; they study about it, and they stay back and don't care about it." At first the elders were concerned that the youths would forget their obligations to the Sacred Pipe and would abandon their faith in the native religion. Instead of repudiating the new rituals, however, they held that Arapahoes could participate in peyote meetings without offense to the Sacred Pipe if they also fulfilled their duty to the pipe and kept the native religion first in their minds and hearts. Peyote (*hóh'oyóóx* or "thorny plant") became an additional way of praying; it did not compete with the Arapahoe religion.[89]

Christianity also was nominally accepted but generally did not interfere with the Arapahoes' participation in native religious ceremonies. Among their converts the Catholics named Yellow Calf and two elders, Scarface and Buffalo Fat, among others. Yet these men continued to direct native ceremonies as well. The Arapahoes reportedly were interested in Christian teachings, although it appears that to a considerable extent Christianity was understood and reinterpreted according to Arapahoe concepts of the supernatural. Note this version of the birth of Christ, which was told to other Arapahoes by the priest Weasel Bear:

> A white woman who was with child kept it secret. When she was about to give birth she went to the barn and delivered there, while her husband was away tilling the soil. She left the child there. But the other man (the Indian) was subsisting entirely on game, living at ease. When the white man came back he went to the barn and found the boy running about. This was the son of Above White Man, Hixtcaba Nih'anOaan [the Arapahoe word for the Creator, applied also to the God of Christians]. He was known to be truly the son of Above White Man, for his skin was yellow and his hair long. Other people heard of him and came and killed him and buried him, but he returned to his mother, telling her: "Thus I have returned." Then the people heard of him again, and bound and burned him. He became ashes, but returned to his mother. Again the people heard of him and took him, now a full-grown man, and nailed him on a cross. How he went up is not known, but nevertheless he went up. The Indians had lived in accordance with the teachings of the man (the Creator) until this son of Above White Man was killed. Then among them also death and bloodshed occurred.

The Sisters of Charity observed an interest in Christian rites and stories even among the children:

> Only a short time after school opened and they had assisted at Mass once or twice, they were seen in the yard kneeling in a circle and one boy going around saying something, and this was in imitation of the priest giving holy communion at the railing. When the Stations of the Cross were brought and hung in the Church, Father Kuppens, through Shakespeare, gave an explanation of them to the children. They were all attention, and as soon as it was over and they left the Chapel they hastened away to the riverbank, where stood the old camp which the workmen had used while building the mission-house, and tore off some planks, with which they made a cross. Then some of the larger boys took off their shirts, tore them into strips and tied one of the small boys to it, and started in procession to the house shouting and yelling. The Sisters at first on hearing the noise and seeing the disorderly rabble were terrified, thinking perhaps they had really nailed the child to the cross, but upon instant examination it was found that he was only tied upon it, but that so securely that by himself he could never have broken his bonds.

The missionaries found the Arapahoes friendly and apparently fairly receptive to their teachings; possibly this was one important reason that they came to the aid of the chiefs and of Weasel Bear, Buffalo Fat, and other ceremonial elders in their struggle against Agent Nickerson.[90]

The ceremonial elders weathered several crises of authority during their first three decades on the reservation. In doing so, they ensured the perpetuation—though not without modifications—of the native religion. And they retained influence and considerable control over the members of the tribe without generating a breach between old and young or between those who practiced the native religion and those who practiced new religions. Their flexibility enabled them to continue to motivate tribal unity and to contain social conflict. Their strategies complemented those of the council chiefs. Each group attempted in its own way to present the Arapahoes as cooperative or at least not troublesome to the whites. The elders thus helped to generate support for the council chiefs' efforts to achieve tribal unanimity in their dealings with whites, and the council chiefs aided the ceremonial elders' efforts to prevent the whites from totally suppressing native rituals. When the council chiefs of the nineteenth century were replaced by other leaders, the elders drew on traditional ritual symbols and applied them in new political contexts to validate the authority of the new twentieth-century intermediaries.

3

"Getting Along Well": The Old Council, 1908–36

Sherman Sage—veteran of the Indian wars, scout, and briefly a member of the Chiefs' Council—was asked in 1914 whether he preferred the old life of the warrior or the more peaceful contemporary era. The old man's response crystallized the Arapahoe view of the changes that came about when the Business Council gradually assumed the functions of its predecessor, the Chiefs' Council: "'In those days, a man used to be honored according to the damage he could do the enemy, and so all young men were brave; but now a man gets on well if he is pleasant and kind to other people, and that is the better way.'"[1] In the twentieth century, a reputation for bravery and protestations of peaceful intent no longer moved federal officials to respond favorably to tribal leaders' requests. Now Arapahoe leaders tried to impress them with their commitment to "progress" and their ability to manage reservation business affairs.

NIITOTO-NÉÉCHEENO', "SIX CHIEFS": THE ARAPAHOE BUSINESS COUNCIL

The early twentieth century brought new challenges to the authority of Arapahoe leaders and to the viability of the Arapahoe way of life. The strategies that the council chiefs had used were not adequate for the kinds of problems the Arapahoes faced in the years between 1908 and 1936. Changes in government policies made it more difficult for the tribe to subsist and for its leaders to cope with its problems. The federal government had all but stopped its distribution of rations and supplies. Arapahoe intermediaries struggled to help their people and to maintain their authority by their efforts to manage the reservation's resources and to gain control over the tribe's income.

With the hope of convincing federal officials that they could manage their own affairs, the Arapahoes demonstrated their "progressive" bent by enthusiastically choosing six "business councilmen" rather than "chiefs" as intermediaries. In talking with federal agents, the Arapahoes usually referred to their intermediaries as the Arapahoe Business Council, but among themselves they usually referred to the councilmen as *niitoto-néécheeno'* ("six chiefs"). After 1936, when tribal business councils changed under the impetus of the New Deal, the Arapahoes referred to the *niitoto-néécheeno'* as the "old council." Lone Bear and other leaders who served on the council met with whites in "white men's clothes." The feathers and other marks of chieftainship that had been worn when the council chiefs met with whites were left at home. Federal officials viewed the Arapahoe Business Council as potentially more "progressive" and more tractable than the Chiefs' Council; to the Arapahoes, the business councilmen had the same prerogatives, obligations, and constraints as the old council chiefs.

Economic Problems and Political Goals

On the Shoshone reservation, Indian Office controls over tribal and individual resources and repressive sanctions against traditional economic, political, and religious institutions were continued during the administrations of Commissioners Robert Valentine (1909–13), Cato Sells (1913–21), and Charles Burke (1921–29). The Indian Office policy of assimilation was given new impetus by the Burke Act of 1906, which allowed for individual allottees to be declared competent to manage their own affairs and thereby to receive a patent in fee to their allotments. At the Shoshone Agency, as well as elsewhere, the Burke Act resulted in the loss of Indian land and further impoverishment of Indians. The Indian reform effort of the 1920s exposed the incompetence and fraudulent practices of federal personnel charged with managing Indian lands and income, and investigations of reservation conditions strengthened congressional efforts to improve conditions. But from the Arapahoe perspective, the changes implemented during the more humanitarian, though still paternalistic, administration of Commissioner Charles Rhoads (1929–33) led to little improvement. And when Commissioner John Collier's New Deal programs were introduced on the Shoshone reservation in 1934, the changes sparked a political and social crisis.[2]

In those trying times it was difficult for councilmen to impress their constituents with their ability to protect and provide for them. The superintendents' efforts to undermine traditional authority were facilitated by the fact that officials in Washington were deaf to requests for the distribution of food and supplies. Following the government's policy of detribalization and reduction of financial support for tribal groups, the superintendents denied rations to Arapahoes deemed capable of physical labor. Unlike the Arapahoe leaders in the late nineteenth century, who concentrated on pressing the government to enter into or comply with treaty agreements, the business councilmen had no recourse but to focus their efforts on increasing the tribe's income from leases and gaining control over the expenditure of that income.[3] The use of reservation resources, then, became the focal issue in conferences held in Washington with tribal delegates. While appeals for rations were still occasionally made, they were presented in terms of temporary help for the needy—orphans, old people, the blind and crippled who were not able to work—rather than as a treaty obligation of the government toward the tribe.

The Arapahoes' economic problems were compounded by the government's failure to adhere to the provisions of the 1905 cession agreement. The Shoshone and Arapahoe tribes did not receive full payment for the lands they had ceded, the cattle they were promised, or the irrigation system and the water rights they had been led to expect. Income from the projected land sales was not forthcoming because most of the acreage remained unsold. When the ceded portion was opened to settlement, 10,559 persons applied for 1,600 homesteads. To select homesteaders from the large number of applicants, a lottery was held in Lander in August 1906. The land could not produce without irrigation, and the state gave the Wyoming Central Irrigation Company a contract for two canals. The WCI then offered service to the homesteaders for a fee. The fees were too steep for most settlers, and large numbers of them soon left amid accusations of graft. The government then offered leases on the ceded portion.[4]

The Arapahoes bitterly resented water charges, which they considered a violation of the 1905 agreement. Indian allottees were levied charges for irrigation whether or not they used the ditches, and when they could not pay, they were urged to lease or sell their land. Since the money from the sale of the ceded portion had not materialized, the government hoped to apply money received for water use to the cost of the ditches. Of course, the Indians were having a hard time obtaining the necessities of life; they had no money left to pay the water charges. In anticipation of the sale of allotted lands on the "diminished portion," local whites circulated advertisements in eastern cities to attract buyers. These notices increased the Arapahoes' apprehension and frustration.[5]

With almost no rations coming from the government and with the promises of the 1905 cession unkept, the Arapahoes were forced to sell or lease their allotments and seek wage work. After the passage of the Burke Act (and particularly after 1917), the superintendents at the Shoshone Agency were encouraged to issue patents in fee to "competent" Indians. Persons who were shown on the tribal census roll to have "one-half degree" or less of "Indian blood" were especially likely to be declared competent; the fact that they were illiterate or unaware of the implications of acquiring fee simple title to their land was often ignored. Many individuals who received patents in fee sold their allotments to whites in Riverton and Lander for far less than the land was worth. In 1920 the agent accused "land Shylocks at Riverton" with virtual theft of Indian lands. Land speculators had been given lists of "competent" Indians by agency employees and bought their allotments for a fraction of their value before they were officially put on sale. One Arapahoe woman was paid $5 for land appraised at $1,550; another received $100 for land valued at $1,200.[6]

When individuals leased or sold their allotments, the money was held in a trust account. When and if it was released, it usually was issued only in the form of purchase orders at one of the white-owned stores. The leasing of tribal lands—particularly 58,500 acres of oil, coal, and gas lands—developed into a major scandal. Speculators leased mineral lands for low prices; then, rather than extract the minerals, they subleased the land for a higher price. Agency employees were also paid by oil companies to prepare leases beneficial to the companies.[7]

The government hired Arapahoes and Shoshones for manual labor on various projects, such as irrigation or road work, but graft at the agency cut into the Indians' wages. Arapahoe leaders protested to the commissioner that during Superintendent H. E. Wadsworth's term (1902–12), checks were issued to individuals (some of whom were not actually employed) and part or all of the money retained by agency employees. Indian workers' checks were negotiated by the storekeeper, who paid workers in merchandise rather than cash. Indians (whether literate or not) were required to approve the transaction by "touching the pen" without being allowed to see the figures entered in the account book. Thus an Indian had no record to show how much he had received in relation to the amount he was entitled to. Agency employees were accused of pocketing the difference.[8]

The Arapahoes were very much aware of these exploitive practices and expected their leaders to curb the abuses. Councilmen sought to influence government policy primarily by sending delegations to Washington. Their efforts to attain approval for visits to the commissioner were successful in 1908, 1913, and 1928. On those occasions they insisted that a record be kept of the proceedings of their meetings so that they could show their people what had been said.

The delegation in 1908 consisted of Lone Bear (*wóx-niísehit*), Yellow Calf (*nihoonou'u*), and the elderly Little Wolf (*hóóxei-hokechii*), with Tom Crispin (White Horse's bilingual stepson) as interpreter, as well as three Shoshones (see Plate 8). The Arapahoe delegates complained to the commissioner that the provisions of the 1876 agreement had been violated,[9] and they raised objections to their lack of control over mineral lease money, the amount of the wages paid on government jobs, and the unfulfilled promises of the 1905 cession agreement (including the fact that the $50 per capita payment had been withheld from minors). They expressed alarm that the state of Wyoming was insisting on its right to control the use of water for irrigation on the reservation. And the councilmen made a special appeal that the Indian Office stop its sanctions against the Sun Dance.[10]

After the delegates' visit, the Indian Office agreed to raise the wage from $3.00 to $4.00 per day for a man with a team of horses and from $1.50 to $2.00 for a man without a team. (These wages were less than those offered whites for the same work—since the whites agreed, whites worked harder than Indians.) The Indian Office also agreed to issue the children's per capita payments to their parents. Finally, the commissioner took a more conciliatory position toward the Sun Dance, relaxing the prohibition if "barbarities like the laceration of the body" and "indecencies" were omitted and if the ceremonies were not permitted to interfere with work.[11] Thus the delegates had succeeded in demonstrating the effectiveness of the Business Council.

The delegation of the winter of 1913—Lone Bear, Yellow Calf, and the interpreter Crispin, together with three Shoshones—again expressed opposition to the water charges. The delegates insisted that the 1905 agreement provided for government financing of the irrigation program in return for the cession. Yellow Calf had made this point to an inspector a few months before the delegation left for Washington: "Two head men of the government here raised their hands to God saying they had done everything straight and that there would be no cheating of one another. . . . And we remember what he said about these ditches at that time. There was to be a certain amount of money set aside for [construction of] these ditches and he told us 'you work on them yourselves and get this money back [in wages] and nobody can say anything to you about these ditches,' that is what he told us."[12] The delegates also protested Wyoming's attempt to control water rights on the reservation. Since the title to water for irrigation depended on use, Indians were being pressured to sell as well as lease allotted lands that they were not farming. Of course, they found it virtually impossible to farm all of the allotted lands because of lack of capital. Besides, much of the land was in heirship status; that is, an Indian who had been allotted a parcel of land had since died, and his heirs held only fractional shares in it. The delegation also urged that money from tribal leases be distributed directly to the Indians, who were suffering because of the termination of the general distribution of rations. Only small per capita payments—$6 in 1908 and $5 in 1909, for example—had been made.[13] To the tribe's outrage, the bulk of the lease money was spent at the discretion of the Indian Office—one year for a telephone line to the agency. In a council meeting in 1911, Yellow Calf pointed to the injustice done the tribe: "We made these leases for our children, for the old and helpless and for those who can't work. I know the government is taking care of us, but they ought not to interfere with our lease money. I was shocked when I heard that they had used this lease money. I don't understand why the government did not notify us when this money was going to be used. Probably God has made the Indians just like the white man, and I do not understand why the government did not ask us if they could use this money." Other councilmen also complained that individuals who leased or sold their allotments were forced to accept money orders for specific items not necessarily of their choosing, rather than cash.[14]

The 1913 delegation arrived at a time when a new president was beginning his administration. The newly appointed commissioner granted an extension on water-use requirements until 1916, so settlement of the question of water rights was postponed.[15] The Indian Office took steps to purchase the cattle promised the tribe in the 1905 agreement. With $30,000 the government bought 1,953 heifers and 5 registered bulls. The cattle brought the further advantage that the Arapahoes could raise and sell hay to the government for support of the herd. Lease money was still withheld from the tribe's control, but to the delegates' satisfaction, the Indian Office consented to use the funds to build a flour mill and a sawmill so that the Indians no longer had to deal with local merchants. And Joseph Norris, the replacement for the bitterly resented Superintendent Wadsworth (transferred late in 1912), accompanied the delegation and made further reforms upon their return. His efforts won support among both the Arapahoes and the Shoshones.[16]

Norris (1912–16), with the consent of the secretary of the interior, established new regulations for the leasing of mineral lands on the ceded portion, which President Taft had withdrawn from sale in 1912. Any lessee who produced nothing from the land had to pay 15 cents an acre the first year, 40 cents the second, and 75 cents the third. Up until now the lessee had paid only a royalty after production started. By the new rules, royalties were the same as those paid on federally owned Wyoming land outside the reservation: the coal royalty was 10 cents a ton and the oil royalty was 12.5 percent of the amount produced. Money began to accumulate rapidly in the tribes' accounts after 1914, when the Indian Office began to lease as grazing land the unsold acreage on the ceded portion. In 1915, 1,118,677 of 1,221,000 acres on the ceded portion were being leased. Norris had collected $100,000, much of it from stockmen whose animals had previously trespassed. During World War I, Wyoming shared in the national prosperity, and the reservation economy prospered with it.[17]

During the 1920s a general economic decline in the state adversely affected economic conditions on the reservation. Only a minority of Arapahoes were able to farm, and Indians could obtain wage work only intermittently. In the view of Superintendent E. A. Hutchinson (1917–22), many Indians, having leased their allotments to whites "for a mere bagatelle," were "aimlessly drifting, Micawber like, waiting for something to turn up."[18] A constant source of frustration and annoyance was the government's refusal to distribute tribal income in regular per capita payments. Hutchinson channeled the income—largely from the leasing of unallotted tribal land—into such projects as an Indian hospital and agency salaries. By 1920 he had reduced the number of persons receiving rations to 100. Water charges of $1 an acre were being levied against individual Indians. Most Indians lived in canvas tents and brush shelters.[19] Despite the widespread suffering, the Indian Office allowed only minimal and occasional per capita payments to the Arapahoes: for example, $12 in 1920, $20 in 1921. To the tribe's further dismay, the Arapahoe cattle herd was sold at a loss. There were accusations—never thoroughly investigated—of graft involving agency personnel.[20]

As the dissatisfaction of their constituents grew, the councilmen clamored for a delegation to Washington. The chairman of the Arapahoe Business Council in 1922, Henry Lee Tyler, alarmed by the declining support for the council, made a strong effort to obtain the help of Senator John Kendrick of Wyoming in obtaining the Indian Office's consent for a delegation. Permission was denied, however, so the council resorted to correspondence to urge a settlement of the Black Hills claim and regular per capita payments, as well as an end to the water charges.[21]

But the protests had no effect, and confidence in the Arapahoe Business Council waned. Sporadically during the 1920s, meetings outside the confines of the council were held and petitions sent to Washington by groups of Arapahoes. In the proceedings of one such committee meeting held January 17, 1923, the group demanded accountings of money obtained from the sale of land and from the oil leases on the ceded portion from 1905 to 1922. This particular meeting was chaired by forty-three-year-old Mike Goggles, and twenty-eight-year-old Scott Dewey acted as secretary.[22] The Indian Office ignored the appeals. In desperation, on March 25, 1927, the Arapahoe Business Council voted not to lease any more tribal lands until the tribe's members were permitted to receive the income in per capita payments. Yellow Calf spoke for the council: "We have decided it is time right now for us to stop and not lease any more land until we receive the lease money first, and also to see whether if we don't sign the leases whether we are forced or not."[23]

Finally, in February 1928, the Arapahoes were allowed expense money to send one delegate to Washington. They elected a forty-eight-year-old Carlisle graduate, Robert Friday, as their delegate, then took up a collection to send Yellow Calf as "alternate" delegate.[24] The two men—both of whom were councilmen at this time—pressed concerns in three areas: water charges, per capita payments, and oil well production. But their efforts were of no avail. The Arapahoes were bitter about the continued levying of water charges for lands under irrigation. As Arapahoe councilman Sam Wolfrang put it in a 1927 meeting, "I feel that I own these ditches, as they were constructed by my people. I feel that the Supreme Being has placed these streams coming from the mountains, that my people may use them freely."[25] Despite the protests of Friday and Yellow Calf in Washington, regular per capita payments were again denied the tribes, although a small payment was made in 1929. The delegates asked also that the thirty-five oil wells that were shut down be "unplugged" so that the oil could be marketed and generate more tribal income. The Indian Office refused, arguing that sixty-nine wells were producing all the oil for which there was a market.[26]

"Both Young and Old and Crippled and Well":
Political Strategies and Symbols of Authority

At a tribal meeting in 1913, Yellow Calf expressed the relationship between the councilmen and the superintendent: "Mr. Norris, our father, is at the head of this reservation and in order to obtain a good name for our father we must get to work and help our father and try to lift him up by helping ourselves and, when we get him up high where his name will be known all over the world by our work as to helping ourselves through his advice, we will be glad when his name is as great as some of the men who have good names and we will have a good name as well."[27] Leaders sought to influence the superintendents by presenting the Arapahoe political process and Arapahoe society in general as "progressive" and responsive to government programs. In 1913, when the Arapahoe delegation visited the Indian Office with Superintendent Norris, Yellow Calf attempted to convince the officials that Norris could count on more support than the tribe had given to any earlier superintendent. At the same time, Yellow Calf was addressing his comments to his tribesmen; he spoke in a way that suggested his role as a ritual leader and prophet, one who "saw things" beneficial to the people:

> I look on it and I see that I have something that I have never seen before in my own thoughts; it is very light and very clear—there is some chance of our people, Shoshones and Arapahoes, to get on their feet and be a man some day. I see that chance right now. I look back while we were talking here this morning, and saw the Agents of long way up [ago], saw many years in between. I see that one sleeping there, and that one right there still close here, and this man [Norris] came along and stood alongside where we were and he woke us up, and told us things we didn't know before.[28]

And later in a council meeting Lone Bear proclaimed, "When he [the commissioner] says here is something for you to do, nothing for us to do but to take it up and do it and not consider how poor we are."[29]

It was in this social context that the Arapahoes acquiesced to the government's urgings for new leadership—a "business council" comprised of six "elected" representatives. While officials were encouraged to view the council as elected, in fact a selection process of a different order—selection by the elders—was the pattern.

Tribal leaders also tried to secure aid for their constituents from missionaries. They generally cultivated good relations with both Catholic and Episcopal missions, even at times playing one off against the other, and they discouraged their constituents from conflict over religious activities. Lone Bear's views were typical of other leaders', and were repeatedly stressed in the counseling of other Arapahoes: "I pray according to the way I was taught by the church and when I get through I pray my Indian way. Wherever I go and there is a church and time to go to that church and if I do not belong to that church, it does not make any difference. I go over there and go to that church. It is all for one God. We are all heading for the same God."[30] Arapahoe councilmen courted the favor of Catholic officials in Washington and appealed to them to restrain unpopular priests at St. Stephen's. The 1908 delegation visited William Ketcham, the director of the Bureau of Catholic Indian Missions, gave him gifts, and expressed their desire for the tribe to convert to Catholicism rather than Protestantism. Ketcham was delighted; and when in 1913 the delegates protested the actions of Father P. F. Sialm, Ketcham urged him to make concessions to the Arapahoe leaders. When Father Sialm did not placate the Arapahoes, he was transferred. The councilmen were able to influence the Catholic officials largely because the church feared that the Episcopalians would make gains.[31] In 1910 Bishop Nathaniel Thomas had bought land from Yellow Calf and Seth Willow, and in 1913 he established St. Michael's Episcopal Mission among the Upper Arapahoes. (According to church tradition, when the Arapahoes were told of the plans to establish the mission, they said, "*ïïOeti*," which means "good"; so it was that the St. Michael's area became known as the Ethete community.) One of the St. Michael's workers, who visited Indian homes to bring gifts of food and clothing, noted that the Shoshones usually did not invite them inside, but among the Arapahoes, "we enter the camp at once, and nearly always are received cordially. On account of this seeming friendliness of the Arapahoes, it is harder to determine the true feeling toward us."[32]

Both missions were successfully solicited for communal feasts, clothing, wage work, loans, intervention with federal officials, and other benefits. Typical of the feasts provided was St. Stephen's distribution at Christmas in 1912: 300 pounds of beef, 150 loaves of bread, 300 pounds of potatoes, 30 pounds of sugar, and 15 pounds of coffee.[33]

The Arapahoes also devoted considerable effort to cultivating relationships with local whites. During this time tourism became increasingly important in Wyoming, and the cooperative ventures of Indians and whites probably were related to this development. Arapahoes hired out for performances in the Wild West shows of Wyomingite E. J. Farlow and for film work with Tim McCoy. Farlow took Arapahoes to Casper in 1900 and 1914, to Denver and Cheyenne in 1913, to Hollywood in the 1920s, to several eastern cities, and to Europe. During Fourth of July and Labor Day celebrations, Arapahoes performed in parades in neighboring towns and requested donations for Indian celebrations. Despite cooperation between Indians and whites, local whites generally remained contemptuous of Indians.[34] Prominent and powerful whites from outside the local area were courted more successfully by Arapahoes. Several were "adopted" by tribal leaders at a public ceremony and given Indian names. Those so honored, as well as many individuals invited to witness tribal ceremonies, often feasted the Arapahoes (see Plate 9). More important, they sometimes attempted to intercede for the tribe in Washington, particularly in regard to legalization of the Sun Dance (which had been prevented during Hutchinson's term). Arapahoe leaders also persuaded state congressmen and state officials in the Federated Women's Club and the Red Cross, for example, to intercede for them. In communications with whites, Arapahoes and other Indian leaders referred to the Sun Dance as the Harvest Dance or the Sage Chicken Dance—names suggestive of entertainment rather than a religious event.[35]

Members of the Business Council made consistent efforts to display their success as intermediaries and to maintain their reputation for generosity. Tangible gains for the tribe were important, but so were the symbols of successful intermediation. Councilmen could enhance their reputations with distribution or display of objects that, while of relatively small monetary value, were symbolically associated with intermediary skills.

To generate confidence among their constituents, delegations sought to return from Washington with tokens of their personal influence with federal officials. When the delegates met with President Theodore Roosevelt in 1908, each brought back an autographed photo of the president. On this occasion Little Wolf presented Roosevelt with a pipe and tobacco pouch. In 1913, in making the traditional request for beef for a feast upon the delegation's return, Lone Bear explained that the councilmen needed a physical emblem of their relationship with Washington officials: "Now, my friend, I don't want to go back without anything. . . . They used to bring back good clothes, or a badge, or something. I want to bring back something with me." In 1928, when Yellow Calf met with Assistant Commissioner Edgar B. Meritt, he was given a document to which was affixed an official-looking red seal and ribbon, in which the commissioner noted that Yellow Calf had "taken up various matters in which his tribe is interested and has shown a deep interest in the welfare of his people."[36]

Councilmen had to find new ways of making public distribution. The communal garden produce distributed by the chiefs of a former era was no longer available for distribution, as the men who had formerly worked the gardens had abandoned them when they were forced to go to work for wages on government irrigation ditches. As Yellow Calf explained to an inspector from Washington, "About the building of ditches, if you will remember, Major, when they started to building these ditches, there were some few Indians that were farming at that time and furthermore men were sent out from this agency telling us to quit farming and come and help build the ditches, and some of those who did not like to give up their work on the farm were threatened to be punished if they did not respond to work [on ditches]."[37] Until Hutchinson's term in 1917, the councilmen had received sizable quantities of rations with which they provided for their constituents, and they had been paid sums of money by the superintendent to act as straw bosses on roadwork or other agency projects. With these funds they gave aid to other Arapahoes, sponsored tribal celebrations, and entertained visitors. And it was the custom for white persons interested in obtaining leases to make small payments in cash or goods to Indian leaders. The councilmen used the money to pay for tribal feasts and dances or all-tribal ceremonies.[38]

The fabric of Arapahoe social life was held together by reciprocity and redistribution. The Arapahoes consistently worked in groups, sharing labor as they shared material things. During the late 1920s and 1930s, when the government increased economic aid for agricultural development, groups of men moved from camp to camp so that each man helped the others with a hay crop or building chores. Similarly, when the Upper Arapahoes wanted to erect a community hall, leaders directed each family to haul hay to centrally located stacks, which were then sold and the proceeds used to purchase building supplies. Personal gains were ideally to be shared with the tribe. When a group of Arapahoes performed in Philadelphia in 1926, they used their pay to feast the entire tribe on their return. Councilmen, too, were expected to make a public distribution of any benefits they received.[39]

While Indian Office officials, intent on a policy of individualism, attacked such customs as generalized sharing and gift giving, the councilmen publicly reiterated and reinforced the values that underlay the patterns of sharing. Among the Arapahoes, resources traditionally were allocated on the basis of need, so that the affluent and able-bodied shared with the poor and the weak. The Indian Office's refusal to distribute lease money in per capita payments and its insistence on using some of the funds to finance farming equipment for the few Indians who were trying to operate farms or ranches conflicted with Arapahoe principles. As Lone Bear put it, "They do not understand things, and they undertake to think for a man living here. They think their own way and think they can change the Indians in accordance with their own way of living. They think the Indians can make money and have money like they can, but that is impossible."[40]

Councilmen were skilled orators in their native language and many of them could also speak movingly in English (although they sometimes used an interpreter). In their speeches they commented on the economic issues of the day in a manner calculated not to offend government officials, but did so in ways that reaffirmed the traditional values. Goes in Lodge, speaking publicly through an interpreter in council in 1913, said, "There are orphans and old people who are not able to do anything and if they would get this per capita payment as we asked for it, even though it would only be one dollar or two dollars, it would be quite a help to these people." Lone Bear, in a 1914 council meeting, commented: "The old people do not get much benefit, whereas if they would be given this lease money, that is derived from the leases, in per capita payments, then the old and blind and crippled would have a benefit from this lease money as well as the young ones; and we ask our superintendent to recommend this good and strong to the department." Complaining about the fact that the $60,000 or so derived yearly from leases was being spent on agency expenses without consultation with the Business Council, Littleshield said in the same council meeting:

> When these Indians, the Shoshones and Arapahoes, began to lease the tribal lands, they got a good deal of the money before this land was ceded to the government, and it was all paid in and then the superintendent called in the Indians, asking them what should be done with the money. They would say they want it to be paid to the Indians, want it to buy cattle; want it to buy some other things the Indians got at that time. That was a good time, both young and old and crippled and well got their share up to about four years ago. Then the government back in Washington used the money as they thought best for the Indians.

And in a 1914 meeting Sam Wolfrang argued against expenditure of tribal income to help individuals set up farms and ranches: "There is blind and widows and cripples who do not benefit by it. No one except a few of the able bodied men [benefit] by expending this money in such work. The only way, in justice to the Indians, is to have it in payments and let the cripples and others get it. . . . Let the Indians, each and everybody as a tribe get an equal share of these monies." In portraying and defending Arapahoe notions of the proper organization of economic relations, leaders consistently referred to the needs of the "blind," the "crippled," and "old people." Such individuals actually constituted a tiny minority of the Arapahoe population. The references to the blind, crippled, and old were metaphorical. The orators were reaffirming the sharing principle with powerful images of people in pitiful circumstances who depended on others for their survival. Such symbols were viewed as potentially effective with whites as well, since requests for per capita payments could be phrased in terms of help for those unable to work; the payments could therefore be viewed as only a temporary measure in the tribe's progress on the "white man's road." Among the characteristics that identified an effective and popular councilman, then, was the ability to make public affirmation of Arapahoe cultural values, even in the face of government opposition.[41]

The public display of personal generosity also was crucial to a councilman's status and reputation. Littleshield, successor to Lone Bear as head councilman, was described by missionaries as having "died in poverty because of generosity." A man who was about to be selected for a seat on the council was given advance notice so that on the day the elders publicly picked the new councilmen he would be prepared with gifts to distribute to the crowd.[42]

In return for the support of their constituents, the councilmen also were expected to reflect prevailing opinion on an issue, mobilize public sentiment in support of decisions reached in general council meetings, and avoid sparking dissension. In 1915 Goes in Lodge admonished the men on the Business Council: "Consult your other people who are not members of the council and have it understood outside, and [then] when you come in here and whatever you do there is not any chance for any argument anywhere. There is no chance [then] for anyone to say the council did not do this or had not ought to have done that." Yellow Calf reiterated Goes in Lodge's advice: "It [council business] is a tribal matter and therefore there should be a meeting besides the councilmen, [with councilmen] consulting the outside [non-] members . . . ; we are going to have no quarrels among ourselves." Usually councilmen decided which of several competing bids for mineral leases to accept only after they had consulted their constituents, particularly the elders. As one councilman explained during deliberations on a 1911 lease, a decision was made only after the councilmen "talked it over with the tribe" and received their instructions. Another councilman added, "There are other people smarter than we are." In this instance, a delegation of elders and a few younger men inspected the site of a coal deposit and interviewed representatives of mining companies. The councilmen felt an obligation to implement the group consensus, despite adverse criticism and pressure from the Shoshone Business Council and the superintendent. Old Man Sitting Eagle reaffirmed the council's actions: "I remember a long time ago how the chiefs used to take things slowly and go easy. Take time. I was brought up by some of the chiefs and I know how they used to deal with the government. We Arapahoes will talk it over and try to find out what is the best way to lease this land." Even when a particular decision was a mere formality, councilmen publicly declared their obligation to consult their constituents. The insistence on "talking it over" reaffirmed the councilmen's commitment to decision making by consensus.[43]

The Arapahoes placed great importance on political consensus within the council, as well. In their efforts to generate support among their constituents and to exert influence over federal agents, councilmen spoke with one voice. In fact, a search of all council minutes filed in the National Archives for this period shows that when votes were taken, the Arapahoe Business Council's vote was almost always unanimous. Councilmen's statements frequently show how effectively these shared understandings shaped individual councilmen's actions. In 1932 one councilman remarked in joint council, "Now I am in favor of this paper here. But if I do sign it I am afraid [because] some of the [Arapahoe] councilmen are gone." And another councilman added, "I really have my ideas on this subject myself, all my own, but before I take any steps I would like to have a conference with the other members of the Arapahoe Council."[44]

The superintendents at the Shoshone Agency frequently complained of the Arapahoe councilmen's refusal to act independently. Government officials viewed the Arapahoe leaders' commitment to group consensus as an indication that the individual councilmen lacked initiative and foresight. But to the Arapahoes, the councilmen's conformity was an indication of their trustworthiness. Some agency officials accused councilmen of profiting personally from donations given to the council by whites hopeful of attaining leases; yet all indications from contemporary records and from the recollections of Arapahoes still living are that all such donations were redistributed and that the councilmen were held in high regard by their constituents. In short, the Arapahoes viewed their councilmen not merely as intermediaries, but as headmen.

The Joint Business Council:
Forging an Arapahoe-Shoshone Alliance

Presenting the tribe as progressive and maintaining unanimity among themselves were important strategies in the Arapahoe council's dealings with federal agents. In coping with the government's efforts to detribalize Indian peoples, the councilmen employed an additional tactic. They formed an alliance with the Shoshone councilmen in order to increase their effectiveness as advocates for Indian interests at the Shoshone Agency. In keeping with the detribalization policy, government officials encouraged the development of the joint council. Hence, particularly in the 1920s and 1930s, the superintendents brought most reservation business before the jointly convened tribal councils. In fact, Hutchinson's successor, Reuben P. Haas, attempted in December 1925, January 1931, and again in November 1934 to instigate a constitution and by-laws that made no provision for meetings or responsibilities for separate tribal councils. Though these documents were never formally approved by the Indian Office or subscribed to by the tribes, they nonetheless constituted a threat to the integrity of tribal government. In response, the Arapahoe and Shoshone business councils achieved an accommodation and delegated to each other complementary kinds of advocacy roles.

There were several obstacles to cooperation between the two tribes. Outside of the joint council activities, Arapahoes and Shoshones had little direct contact. A few friendships existed within the context of peyote rituals, but visiting between the Arapahoe and Shoshone communities was hampered by poor roads and harsh winters. Besides, the old resentments lingered on. By 1930 there were only four intermarriages between the two tribes.

During the first half of the twentieth century, large numbers of Shoshones left the reservation area. Out-migration of Arapahoes occurred much less often. In 1933, when there were 1,075 Arapahoes on the tribal roll, 995 were living on the reservation, 22 on other reservations, and 58 elsewhere. In comparison, of 1,245 enrolled Shoshones, 879 were at the Shoshone Agency, 66 on other reservations, and 300 elsewhere.[45] Although enrolled Shoshones outnumbered enrolled Arapahoes, out-migration placed the Shoshones in a weaker position numerically at the agency.

Shoshones were painfully aware of the increasing number of Arapahoes living nearby and were still resentful of the Arapahoes' presence. In fact, during the first half of the twentieth century, the Shoshones worked to institute a legal case against the United States for the settlement of the Arapahoes at the Shoshone Agency. Normally, however, conflict in public council meetings was avoided. One rare occurrence of overt hostility took place in 1911, when the Shoshone council had decided that a mining lease should go to a particular individual. The Arapahoes refused to agree, and there was a bitter confrontation. Shoshone councilman Herman Tigee said, "You Arapahoes, a long time ago you came here, you were poor; the Shoshones took pity on you, helped you out. Now you are against them. You ought to remember what the Shoshones did for you." Yellow Calf replied that Arapahoes shared their annuity goods with the Shoshones: "I was not poor when I came here sixty years ago. There was a treaty about a certain portion of the land belonging to us, that is the state of Wyoming. . . . I came here with [annuities from] that treaty of thirty-six years ago [the 1876 Agreement]. When I came here you had only eight years left of your treaty and when that expired you didn't have anything. My friends, you have been living off of us."[46] To restore order, a decision on the lease was postponed.

The estrangement of the two tribes was complicated by the presence of a significant "mixed-blood" community among the Shoshones. Shoshones had been intermarrying with whites for generations. In 1914 there were 767 full-blood and 107 mixed-blood Arapahoes, compared with 498 full-blood and 342 mixed-blood Shoshones. In 1921 there were 717 on the tribal roll as full-blood Arapahoe and 157 with mixed ancestry. There were 453 Shoshones enrolled as full-bloods and 437 as mixed-bloods at that time. By 1936, when the enrolled populations of Shoshones and Arapahoes were almost equal, 831 Arapahoes were enrolled as full-blood, compared with 433 full-blood Shoshones. And 249 Arapahoes were more than one-half Arapahoe but less than full-blood; 221 Shoshones were in this category. Strikingly, 48 Arapahoes were less than one-half but more than one-fourth Arapahoe, compared with 272 Shoshones. And while no Arapahoes were considered to be of less than one-fourth Arapahoe blood, 207 Shoshones were considered to be of less than one-fourth Shoshone blood. In 1931 the agent reported only 21 non-Arapahoe spouses among the Arapahoes. Six women were married to whites, 2 to Mexicans, and 13 to persons from other Indian tribes (primarily Shoshones, Southern Arapahos, and Gros Ventres). In contrast, there were 82 white, 4 Mexican, and 19 non-Shoshone Indian spouses among the Shoshones at that time.[47]

Both the Arapahoes and the Shoshones defined cultural identity not in terms of "blood," but rather in terms of social behavior. Many of the individuals enrolled as mixed-blood Shoshones actually were considered culturally traditional or full-blood Shoshones. Only a portion of the group with white ancestry was characterized and labeled as mixed-blood. Within the mixed-blood category there were alternative lifestyles. The mixed-blood Shoshones were concentrated at Burris on the Wind River and on the South Fork of the Little Wind. On South Fork the mixed-bloods developed a ranching lifestyle, served effectively as interpreters and intermediaries (and sometimes militant advocates) with whites in the late nineteenth and early twentieth centuries, and sometimes made marital alliances with Shoshone families considered culturally full-blood. Marriage with a full-blood could effect a change in cultural identity from mixed-blood to full-blood. The people at Burris interacted primarily with each other and with local whites. In the 1930s many mixed-bloods (particularly if they had fair skin and dressed like whites) attended white dances at local night spots and otherwise moved freely in white society. They did not participate in Indian ceremonies and were exclusively Christian. Children (especially those from Burris) attended the one-room public schools with whites, rather than the government and mission boarding schools or day schools for Indians. Economically, most of this mixed-blood group was much better off than the rest of the Shoshones; many had fairly sizable herds of cattle or sheep.[48]

As the Shoshone council members, acting as spokesmen for full-blood, mixed-blood, and other interest groups, had differential abilities and interests, they had some flexibility in dealing with whites and considerable leeway in individual innovation. In a council meeting in which individuals were being selected to represent the Shoshones in meetings with white officials, the old Shoshone warrior Heebeecheechee spoke of his need to rely on men who had learned how to deal effectively with whites: "I cannot read or write and I do not feel that I could do justice and I would rather have Charles Lahoe, Joe Lajeunesse [mixed-bloods], or George Washakie [descendant of Chief Washakie] go [to Washington]. There are people here who can do better than I and we are not in two factions; we are all in one and we can hear from our representatives when they come back."[49] Shoshone councilmen, then, realized that some kinds of skills were more effective than others in particular times and places. Sometimes, however, mixed-blood councilmen disagreed with the others on certain issues.[50] This potential for conflict and disagreement could aggravate the apprehension and resentment that the Shoshones already felt because of the presence of the unwelcome Arapahoes, who managed to achieve such striking political unity.

Cooperation between the Shoshone and Arapahoe councilmen also was impeded to some extent by differences in organization, dynamics, and style (see Plate 10). Shoshone councilmen (particularly the mixed-bloods) were impatient with the Arapahoes' reluctance to decide matters on their own, especially when this reluctance made for delays.[51] The Arapahoe councilmen were so well respected that generally they held their positions for life or until retirement. The membership of Shoshone councils, in contrast, changed often, and there were frequent calls for new elections to replace particular councils. Only two members of the 1913–16 Shoshone council had been carried over from the 1908–12 council. On the 1917–20 council, only one councilman was retained from the earlier council. None of the councilmen of 1921–25 were returned to office in the 1926–30 term. And in the 1931–34 term, only one councilman from the previous council was reelected. In contrast, at least three and sometimes all of the Arapahoe councilmen were carried over from one term to the next (see Table 3).[52] The apparent instability in the Shoshone political process was sometimes confusing, worrisome, or annoying to the Arapahoes.

Despite the tension between the two tribes, the Shoshone and Arapahoe council members had common goals: an increase in the

Table 3
Members of Arapahoe Business Council, 1908–36

1908–12	1913–16	1917–20
Lone Bear	Lone Bear	Lone Bear*
Yellow Calf	Yellow Calf	Yellow Calf
Tallow / Henry L. Tyler†	Henry L. Tyler	Henry L. Tyler
Shot Gun	Sam Wolfrang	Sam Wolfrang
Sitting Eagle	Littleshield	Littleshield
William Shakespeare	Goes in Lodge	Goes in Lodge

1921–25	1926–30
Josiah Oldman / Yellow Calf†	Yellow Calf
Henry L. Tyler	Henry L. Tyler
Sam Wolfrang	Sam Wolfrang
Littleshield* / Chester Armstrong†	Chester Armstrong
Little Ant	Little Ant
Robert Friday	Robert Friday

1931–34	1935–36
Henry L. Tyler	Henry L. Tyler
Sam Wolfrang* / Mike Goggles†	Mike Goggles
Robert Friday	Robert Friday
Bruce Groesbeck	Charles Whiteman
Scott Dewey	Alonzo Moss
Paul Hanway	Tom Crispin* / John Goggles†

*Died in office.

†Replacement.

Source: Tribal Relations and Land files, in Central Files, Shoshone Agency, 1907–39, Records of the Bureau of Indian Affairs, Record Group 75, National Archives.

amount of income from tribal leases, the distribution of tribal income in cash per capita payments, and the safeguarding of reservation resources from further encroachment. Councilmen believed that these goals were more likely to be achieved if overt conflict could be prevented during joint meetings. One Shoshone wanted his fellow councilmen to stop "bucking each other." Joe Lajeunesse added that if the councilmen quarreled, "they'll take our privilege of holding council away from us and decide our questions from Washington."[53]

The superintendents' efforts to institute truly joint decision making, and thereby to weaken each tribe's organization, were steadfastly resisted by both the Arapahoes and the Shoshones. Each council allowed the other to decide matters concerning its own tribe without interference. Thus, although the superintendent insisted that the joint council vote on all applications for enrollment in either tribe, council members subverted his intent. When several individuals applied for enrollment in the Shoshone tribe, for example, the Arapahoes asked the Shoshone councilmen's views, then voted with them to deny the applications. Chester Armstrong, an Arapahoe councilman, commented at the time, "The Shoshones are opposing the enrollment of these people and therefore the Arapahoes have the same feelings toward these applicants."[54]

In their attempts to cope with unpopular government policies and programs, the Arapahoe and Shoshone councilmen exploited the differences in ability and style between the members of the two councils. The Arapahoes (and often a few Shoshone councilmen as well) relied on the Shoshone mixed-blood councilmen to perform certain kinds of advocacy roles. Such mixed-bloods as Joe Lajeunesse and later Charles (Dee) Driskell assumed a more militant, assertive stance than the Arapahoes were able or willing to take. These men often dominated council meetings during particularly tense situations. During the 1908 delegation's discussions with officials in Washington, mixed-bloods John Lajeunesse and William Boyd most aggressively voiced the tribes' complaints about the unfulfilled provisions of the 1905 cession and the mismanagement of reservation mineral resources. They bluntly charged that the monopoly held by the Wyoming Central Irrigation Company permitted the company to charge outrageously high fees for irrigation on the ceded portion, thereby discouraging homesteaders and enabling the company to acquire unsold lands very cheaply at public auction.[55] During Wadsworth's term it was the Shoshone mixed-blood leaders, outraged by agency corruption, who persistently harassed and intimidated the superintendent—so much so that Wadsworth left the agency headquarters and took up residence at the government school, where he had the protection of school employees.[56] And in 1932, when Superintendent Reuben Haas—also mistrusted by the tribes—tried to abolish the Shoshone council because of its rebellion, and then tried to remove its mixed-blood chairman, Charles Driskell, on the grounds that he assaulted the clerk at the agency, the joint council refused to vote for Driskell's removal and signed a petition to send a delegation to Washington to complain about affairs at the reservation. This exchange is an example of the kind of verbal harassment the Shoshone mixed-bloods employed against Haas:

> Driskell: No chance of our signatures wearing off [the petition] is there, Mr. Haas?
> Aragon: Any chance of tearing the papers?
> Haas: That goes in as a part of the council![57]

Although the Arapahoes did not engage in confrontations of this sort, they evidently appreciated the mixed-bloods' skill in countering the superintendent's heavy-handed methods.

"NOT A CROSS WORD SPOKEN":
CULTURAL CHANGE AND SOCIAL ORDER

By the creative use of religious symbols, elderly ceremonial leaders helped to legitimize the council's authority and to suppress conflicts that could have lessened its effectiveness. They initiated new leadership roles for young Arapahoes who sought ways to participate in their changing society. In response to the needs of the younger generations, the elders encouraged the formation of new social sodalities and revitalized the Crow Dance. Even Arapahoe cultural identity depended in large part on recognition by influential elders.

The Old People

As in past eras, positions of ritual authority in Sacred Pipe and Sun Dance ceremonies were held by elderly men who had been apprenticed for many years to older men with supernatural knowledge. Most ceremonial elders also were *bééteet* and could cure, prophesy, or invoke a curse. On many levels, then, the elders mediated between the Arapahoes and the supernatural—between life and death, chaos and order. Despite white officials' efforts to minimize their influence, the ceremonial leaders perpetuated their authority in secular as well as spiritual matters.

Councilmen were selected and installed by means of the Drum Ceremony during a gathering of the tribe. A kettledrum was brought to the center of the camp circle or hall by a group of singers, usually of advanced years. Elders with ceremonial authority selected out of the crowd (or had a councilman do so) the men they considered best qualified for council positions. In 1977 one eighty-two-year-old man gave this recollection of the ceremony: "They had a dance; then the head men they select who they want. Two men go—while they's drumming—two men go around and dance. They look around, see this guy and that guy. They pick them out. Dance around in the circle. Then some head chief stand up and step out, tell them about why they been selected. They going lead the people, take care of the affairs with the superintendent. That's why they selected them."[58] Seated around the drum, the singers drummed and sang "chief songs" in honor of those selected; then the chosen men and their families held giveaways for all the people. Later the superintendent was informed of the results of the "election."

The drum was symbolic of the interrelationship of the supernatural, nature, and society, and the Drum Ceremony symbolically affirmed the Arapahoes' covenant with the Creator, the Great Mystery Above. As the drum was a sacred symbol, its use in the ceremony for new councilmen both validated their leadership roles and reinforced their awareness of their social obligations and their subordination to the ceremonial elders. Cleaver Warden secured one of the kettledrums (or double drums; see Figure 5) and recorded these observations of Northern Arapahoes:

> The double drum represents the sun. The [red] paint which it bears represents the heat from the sun, as well as the tribe. Both sides represent heaven and earth. The inside of the drum shows the air and life for people. The strings forming triangles represent tipis at night and day. At the bottom of the triangles are the bows. The five drum sticks are typical of a human hand, because they are bound at the top in buckskin, which represents the skin. The [red] painting which it bears typifies the human race. . . . The forks are stuck in the ground at four places, the same places where the Four-Old-Men are located in the sky. . . . The eagle feather pendant at the top is an eagle.[59]

The drum, then, represents the cosmos: air, a filament, links earth and the heavens or sky world above, just as the hollow of the drum is enclosed by two skins. The four drum supports are positioned at the cardinal points or "four corners" of the universe. The drum's circularity is symbolic of the cycle of life: the rise and setting of the sun and the birth and death of tribespeople. The sacred red-earth paint on the

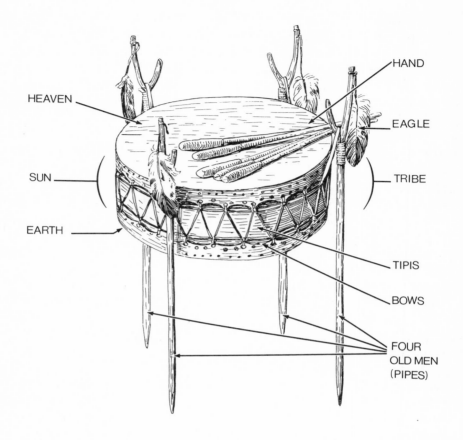

Figure 5. Kettledrum, drum supports, and drumsticks. Collected by George Dorsey, 1902. Diameter, 46.9 cm.; height, 17.8 cm. Source: drawing no. 67739, file A-1, in George Dorsey–Cleaver Warden Collection, Field Museum of Natural History, Chicago.

drum simultaneously represents the earth, the sun, human beings, and the life force (manifestation of the Creator); thus is expressed the oneness of all life forms.

When the drum is played, Arapahoes direct prayers to the Great Mystery Above by an interlocking set of symbols of mediation. Air in one form or another (breath, sound, steam, smoke) effects communication between humans and the supernatural. Prayer takes the form of songs that resound in the atmosphere, penetrating the division between earth and heaven. The "heat" of the drum (represented by red paint) propels the sound upward, as the smoke of the pipes (symbolized by the drum supports) aids the ascension of prayers to the Above. The drumsticks are symbolic of the fingers of the human hand, which are especially potent funnels of energy or "power" from one medium or sphere to another. The drumsticks frequently bore an eagle symbol worked in quills. The eagle, one of the creatures of the firmament (birds), soars highest or closest to the Above and is particularly far-seeing and strong; hence the eagle (symbolized by the feather pendants) is employed as a mediator between humans and the Great Mystery Above. In fact, Arapahoes refer to the singers at the drum as "eagles." The drum supports are referred to as the "four old men" (as well as "pipes"): the mythological four old men represent the former (deceased) keepers of the Sacred Pipe—especially effective petitioners on behalf of the Arapahoe people.[60]

Throughout the Drum Ceremony, the newly selected councilmen were impressed with the importance of their council offices. As the kettledrum was also used at the Sun Dance, it gave to the council selection ritual a particularly sacred tone. The values of social unity and harmony were reaffirmed through the symbolic association of the drum lacings with the tipis of the camp circle and with the bows used to hunt for and protect the tribe. The importance of the elders in mediating between the Creator and the younger generations of Arapahoes was also emphasized. Pipes are closely associated with old men, and red-earth paint with old people. The drum, then, was also a symbolic vehicle for the expression of the ritual authority of the elders, as was the elders' dominance of the selection process. In 1973 a seventy-nine-year-old Arapahoe described the selection of councilmen thus: "The older people, the oldest people, would select them. You got, well, there's Shot Gun, Seth Willow, Drives Down Hill, Old Man Sage—all of them old-timers, old-timers. Warriors, you know. They do a lot of deeds. And they choose them, but they had to know they was qualified."[61] The four elderly men named probably were prominent in the Drum Ceremony after 1916, when they were ritual authorities in their sixties and seventies. The ceremonial elders' public selection of councilmen was comparable to the public naming of individuals by respected elders. When an elder bestowed a name, the recipient obtained both a blessing and a moral obligation to live a good life; the new name both assisted the individual and inspired him to conform to behavioral ideals. Even when election by ballot was instituted in 1930, newly elected councilmen were installed in office by means of the Drum Ceremony.

The individuals selected as councilmen were all devout practitioners of the Arapahoe religion and accepted the authority of the elders.

Between 1908 and 1920, the council was dominated by Lone Bear, from Lower Arapahoe, and Yellow Calf, from Ethete. These two men were exceptionally articulate in the native language and were fluent enough in English not to be completely dependent on interpreters. Both had served as police in the 1880s and on the Chiefs' Council subsequently, and they were well respected by their constituents. Lone Bear (1854–1920), the elder of the two, was recognized as "head man" or head councilman, but he always consulted Yellow Calf. Each leader customarily made a speech expressing the council's consensus on a matter discussed. Lone Bear, like councilmen Shot Gun, Sitting Eagle, Littleshield, and Goes in Lodge, had hunted buffalo, fought against other tribes, and served as a scout. Yellow Calf (1860–1938) was born too late to have been a scout, but he was held in exceptional regard for his religious leadership and his oratorical ability. Yellow Calf's vision precipitated the Crow Dance among the Northern Arapahoes during the 1890s. He was one of the individuals who became Dogmen in 1904. And he revitalized the Crow Dance and other customs during the early twentieth century. After Lone Bear's death, Yellow Calf was head councilman and Littleshield, from Lower Arapahoe, was second in influence.

In the 1920s, Henry Lee Tyler (1871–1936) became particularly prominent on the council, acting as chairman for over a decade. Tyler was a gifted orator in both Arapahoe and English. His father was Night Horse, a famous *bééteet* of the Crow tribe who married Red Robe, an Arapahoe woman, and took up residence with the Arapahoes. Night Horse died about two years after Henry's birth, and the Arapahoe chief Little Wolf, a relative of Night Horse, took care of Henry (named Singing Man Night Horse) and his siblings. As a boy Tyler moved with the Arapahoes to Red Cloud Agency, then Fort Fetterman, Fort Caspar, and finally Shoshone Agency. He was educated by the Reverend John Roberts at the government boarding school at Fort Washakie, where he was an excellent pupil, then attended Genoa Indian School in Nebraska for three years. As a youth he served as interpreter at the cession agreement councils of 1896 and 1904. It was about this time that he was given the name Henry Lee Tyler by the agent. In 1902 he went to Washington as interpreter for the Arapahoe delegation, and he interpreted at the agency for Agent Nickerson. Later he was employed as clerk at the agency during Wadsworth's term. Henry's brother Tallow (Hugh Tyler) was a member of the Chiefs' Council and later the Arapahoe Business Council, and when he retired in 1910, he requested that Henry be chosen to take his place. Henry (like William Shakespeare) served as interpreter and "apprentice" to the older councilmen. He made his home at Mill Creek, but he cultivated ties with Lower Arapahoes. In fact, two of Tyler's daughters were married to sons of Lone Bear. Tyler was also an active participant in the native religion. He became one of the Tomahawkmen at the turn of the century, and he was a noted singer and Sun Dance participant.[62]

Robert Friday (1881–1947), on the council in 1921 until well into the 1940s, was the first man born on the reservation to serve on the council. The son of the scout Bill Friday and his wife, Salt, Robert attended Carlisle and Haskell, briefly returned to the reservation, then left to work at several jobs off the reservation. In 1910 he wrote to an official at Carlisle, "I dread to return on the reservation because there is no encouragement for return students. I am better off here [in Topeka, Kansas], and away from home. Please do not put this in paper." Nevertheless, he returned to the reservation in 1912 and worked at the government boarding school as a baker and interpreted for school officials. He began to interpret for the Arapahoe Business Council in 1921.[63] After years of apprenticeship on the council, his educational attainments began to bring him increasing regard. Despite his achievements in the non-Indian sphere, Friday was a devotee of the traditional religion.

The councilmen were reluctant to boast of their accomplishments, and they often belittled themselves in public. One elderly Arapahoe recalls that Lone Bear was excessively modest about his role as an intermediary. "He used to say, he says, 'My wrists are small,' he said, 'because the white people dragged me into being a leader.' That was his expression of being drafted into the leadership."[64] Councilmen always avoided speaking of personal successes; rather, the elders assumed the task of praising the councilmen on public occasions. In effect, the elders monitored and passed judgment on the actions of councilmen through publicly praising them during giveaways and other tribal ceremonies.

The council members frequently acknowledged their commitment to the goals of the elders. In a council meeting in 1914, Lone Bear explicitly stated the Arapahoe council's duty, as he saw it: ". . . that man sitting over there. He is an old man. He is expecting these young people [councilmen, in their fifties] to make some kind of a deal here that would benefit him, that is what he is expecting." One of the goals of the elders was to gain Indian Office approval of the Sun Dance. The delegation to Washington led by Lone Bear and Yellow Calf in 1908 successfully urged the end of the ban on the Sun Dance, but a few years later the commissioner instructed the superintendent to enforce the prohibition again. In 1921, when the tribe sent the bilingual Tom

Crispin to Washington to discuss its legal claims against the government in the matter of the acquisition of the Black Hills in 1876, Crispin also used the opportunity to protest the ban on the Sun Dance.[65]

Until the early 1930s (when there was some turnover among the youngest of the councilmen), men selected for the council served until they were overtaken by age, illness, or death. During the years from 1908 through 1936, there were 174 council positions (computed annually), and these offices were held by only 22 men. The continuity of membership was in large part the result of the councilmen's success in satisfying the elders.

As in earlier times, elderly Arapahoes, particularly those with ritual authority, had pervasive influence over all Arapahoes, not merely councilmen. Elders intervened in individuals' lives when they bestowed a name at birth or in later life. Old Man Sage told Inez Hilger of an instance in which he intervened on behalf of a youth: "About seven years ago [1933] a young man came to me and asked to take my name so that he could go straight. He was in many difficulties and did not lead a good life. He lied a good deal. I waited until they had a dance and then in public I told that I was giving this boy my name so that he could go straight, be kind to the old people, and to any orphans that there might be, not to steal or lie anymore, to be a good man. And he did live up to it."[66] To succeed in life, to gain acknowledgment and respect from other Arapahoes, an individual needed the support of elders.

Religious experiences were a focal point in the lives of most Arapahoes, and in order to participate in religious rituals an individual needed an instructor and adviser who had already undergone the ceremony and received the training necessary to supervise its performance. Most ritual advisers were of advanced years, particularly those who had major ritual responsibilities. Elders had important roles in the Sun Dance, which in the twentieth century was the most important all-tribal ceremony. As we saw earlier, the Sun Dance was an occasion when Arapahoes were reminded of the importance of cooperation, harmony, and good behavior. Goes in Lodge (a councilman and an important Sun Dance official) said in 1913, "That is four days that there is not a cross word spoken in the Arapahoe tribe during the ceremonies." Superintendents' reports indicate that despite the prohibition of the Sun Dance, it was held each summer until 1913. In that year Superintendent Norris's efforts on behalf of the Shoshones and Arapahoes were to no avail and apparently the tribes were prevented from holding the ceremony. During the next ten years the Arapahoes enlisted the aid of local townspeople and nationally known whites in an attempt to persuade the Indian Office to reverse its policy. Finally, in 1923, the Sun Dance was once again permitted, and it has been performed annually ever since.[67] As in the nineteenth century, the eldest men with the greatest amount of knowledge and experience in the Sun Dance were the most sought-after for the position of grandfather. This relationship not only was important to the conduct of the Sun Dance ceremony, but also had an effect on Arapahoe society in general. The grandfather–grandson relationship obligated the two parties and their families to be helpful and respectful toward one another throughout the year. Thus the ritual tie between the Sun Dance participants served to promote peace and cooperation among unrelated persons.

Elderly ritual authorities also supervised rites involving the Sacred Pipe. Individuals could earn ritual status (acquire degrees of supernatural knowledge) by completing religious vows to fast with the pipe or to "cover" the pipe (with gifts). Such ceremonies also were of benefit to the spiritual state of all Arapahoes and helped to promote social unity. In the Covering the Pipe Ceremony observed in 1936 by John Carter of the Bureau of American Ethnology, after the bundle containing the pipe was opened, all Arapahoes who wished to do so were permitted to touch the pipe. Food given to the keeper of the Sacred Pipe and his assistants by the individual who pledged the ceremony was blessed and offered to the four directions, the Above, the earth, and the Sacred Pipe. Carter reported that "whoever eats this food is blessed, and receives health, long life, and good luck." The food was taken home and shared throughout the community.[68]

In rare instances when an individual behaved in an extremely disruptive fashion, male ceremonial elders were important agents of social sanction. They could interpret the cause of unfortunate events, and in this way could single out and associate the actions of disruptive individuals with supernatural retribution. Elderly women were also important in curbing antisocial behavior. After the turn of the century, women's roles as ritual specialists declined: they did not continue to apprentice themselves to the quill workers, and their participation in the Sun Dance was curtailed. The elderly women were still effective in deterring misconduct, however, because any man who behaved in an unseemly manner could be sure of being ridiculed and publicly embarrassed by them. Even the business councilmen were sensitive to their criticism. Yellow Calf's realization that the council's failure to gain regular per capita payments reflected badly on the council's reputation is revealed by his extreme distress at occasionally being criticized for this failure by the women: "We get the whole blame from the tribe. Even women say something, 'Why what are those councilmen for. They sign a lot of leases. Where is the money; we never get anything.'"[69]

Elders also worked to mitigate dissension and social schism by preventing one band or residential community from dominating tribal leadership positions. Work on irrigation ditches during the early twentieth century permitted the Arapahoes to move onto allotted lands that could now be irrigated. Extended families usually lived together on one person's allotment. But in the winter, when the water was shut off, the people moved back to the rivers and lived together in large winter camps. There were three residential areas: Lower Arapahoe, Mill Creek, and Ethete (see Map 5). Those who settled at Lower Arapahoe continued to be known as Forks of the River People, as they had been called in the 1880s and 1890s. To the west, among the Upper Arapahoes, there were two areas of settlement. A community formed under the leadership of Henry Lee Tyler and others was designated *wosóuhuno'* by Tyler, which was reportedly the name of a well-organized and active sodality of Southern Arapahos in Oklahoma. The opening of St. Michael's School at Ethete in September 1917 helped to shape the identity of the Upper Arapahoes who lived in the Ethete area. St. Michael's Mission encouraged the perpetuation of Arapahoe cultural traditions and customs. The school complex was designed in the form of a camp circle. Pupils dressed in beaded Indian dress on special occasions, and teachers occasionally also wore Indian-style clothing given them by their students' families. To the government employees' horror, the mission staff was lenient toward peyote and sanctioned the Sun Dance; the director, the Reverend Royal Balcom, even offered prayers on the latter occasion. Farming and vocational training were encouraged, but not as a means to destroy the Arapahoe lifestyle. Soon St. Michael's had drawn all Upper Arapahoe students away from the government boarding school at Fort Washakie, and because of the Episcopalians' greater tolerance of native ritual and the potential economic benefits from a mission, many of the Upper Arapahoes—including Yellow Calf— gradually participated less in the activities of the Catholic St. Stephen's Mission and more in those of the Episcopal St. Michael's. The Ethete Arapahoes, still adhering to old ceremonial and social patterns yet oriented toward the "progressive" agricultural training offered by the mission, were called *konóutoséiOi'*, "those without shawls [or blankets]." As one old woman recalls, they danced traditional Indian dances wearing the clothing of the whites.[70]

Tribal leadership positions were allocated fairly evenly between Lower and Upper Arapahoes. Almost always three men from each area

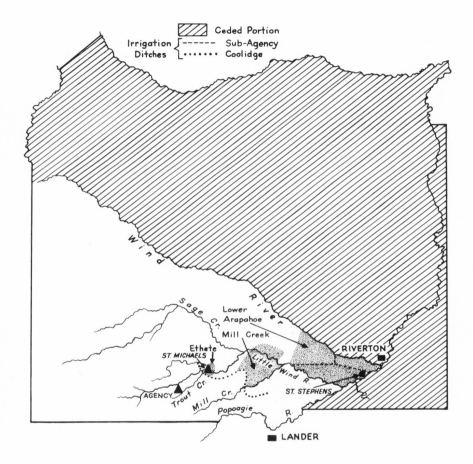

Map 5. Wind River Reservation Arapahoe settlements, 1914–36. Redrawn from "Map of Wind River Reservation, Irrigation History," map 4-16-c-146, folder 1, Wyoming, Irrigation Division, in Records of the Bureau of Indian Affairs, Record Group 75, Cartographic Branch, National Archives.

were selected by the elders to serve on the council. When councilmen were elected by ballot, the Arapahoes voted on a slate of candidates at large, always electing men from each of the three residential areas. In both the 1930 election and the 1935 election (see Table 4), the winning candidates generally drew large votes from both upper and lower districts.

Table 4
Votes received by winning candidates
from Upper and Lower Arapahoe
for seats on Arapahoe Business Council, 1930 and 1935

Year and candidate	Lower Arapahoe	Upper Arapahoe	Total
1930			
Henry Lee Tyler	62	40	102
Robert Friday	58	43	101
Bruce Groesbeck	42	37	79
Sam Wolfrang	51	17	68
Scott Dewey	30	31	61
Paul Hanway	37	20	57
1935			
Robert Friday	60	63	123
Mike Goggles	36	68	104
Alonzo Moss	52	48	100
Henry Lee Tyler	48	51	99
Charles Whiteman	30	42	72
Tom Crispin	41	19	60

Source: Tribal Councils 064, 1930, in Box 196, Archives Branch, and Tribal Elections 065, File 347446, Records Center, in Wind River Files, Record Group 75, Federal Archives and Records Center, Denver.

The elders stressed that each Arapahoe should support and cooperate with all of the councilmen, not just those from his own residential area. The selection of delegates for trips to Washington also followed this principle.[71]

The ceremonial elders or "old men" also attempted to diffuse ritual authority so as to mitigate potential conflict between Upper and Lower Arapahoes. During this era, the two highest ritual authorities—those who directed the Sun Dance—were selected so that each of the two districts was represented. For much of the 1908–36 era, Coal Bearing from Lower Arapahoe and Sam Shot Gun from Upper Arapahoe were the senior old men. Coal Bearing was born about 1852 and died in 1934, and Shot Gun was born about 1855 and died in 1941. In decision making, both had to agree. In fact, all of the ceremonial elders were supposed to concur before any action was taken.

Ritual leaders were very receptive toward innovation. Their flexibility helped to prevent resistance to the authority of the elders and lessened conflict over access to positions of authority in the native religious organization. When no individuals had been formally trained to perform particular rituals, other devout men were chosen to carry on the ceremonies. To some degree, rituals were adapted to the level of knowledge and training (the "degree") held by the person or persons selected to direct them. Collie Judson, son-in-law of the deceased keeper Weasel Bear, was keeper of the Sacred Pipe throughout the 1908–36 era. He had received instruction in the care of the pipe, but it was considered to have passed from Weasel Bear to his daughter, a "blood" relative and one of the *béesóowú'uenno'*. Collie's wife, Ute Woman, died in 1921, but Collie still cared for the pipe, and he continued to do so even after he remarried. The Sacred Wheel, which had been cared for by the keeper of the pipe, was taken by Beaver Dog Chief (Beaver Dodge), one of the "old men" who directed the Sun Dance Lodge and had the right to pray with the wheel during the Sun Dance. Here again there occurred a diffusion of ritual responsibilities. One elderly man recalls the separation of the pipe and wheel thus: "This wheel used to stay with this pipe. This Collie Judson used to keep it all the time. Used to be together all the time. There was such a time, during the Sun Dance, he [Beaver Dodge] didn't take it back. He was telling these old people he was going to fix it up, going to repair it, replace it. Then take it back. But he never did. He just kept it and kept it." The old people did not intervene. By allowing the wheel to stay with Beaver Dodge, they gave tacit approval to the change.[72]

The old men's continued tolerance of nontraditional religions also helped to prevent social schism. Such noted peyote leaders as John Goggles and enthusiastic supporters of the missions also participated in the Sun Dance. One missionary noted, "Practically all the Arapahoes are now Christians, yet they revere their Sacred Pipe. As they say, 'It comforted and strengthened our forefathers in their wanderings, in troublous times past, and cheered their dying moments.'" Young Arapahoes attended peyote meetings or Christian services, and often both. The Episcopal missionaries noted that Herbert Welsh, one of their aides, also was a peyotist, and that he saw peyote as "integrated with Christianity."[73]

In the early twentieth century, the prestige and authority of many councilmen was enhanced by their possession of personal medicine power. Shot Gun, Sitting Eagle, Goes in Lodge, and Yellow Calf were *bééteet*: they had authority in the sacred as well as the secular sphere of Arapahoe life. The councilmen who gained their offices in the

1920–36 era, however, were not medicine men. By the 1930s few *bééteet* were still living, and in most cases their medicine power had not been passed on to someone else. The Arapahoes viewed supernatural power as inherently dangerous; perhaps the elders did not wish to entrust their medicine power to the youths educated by the whites. Interestingly, when William Wildschut visited the reservation in 1923, he obtained a medicine mirror that had originally formed part of Weasel Bear's personal medicine and had been used to avert danger, cure illness, and prevent bad luck. In the twentieth century, this medicine had become Sun Dance medicine, used exclusively in the Sun Dance Lodge under the supervision of ceremonial elders.[74] The reservation hospital now attracted patients who would earlier have sought a native cure, and the *bééteet* role thus lost its attractiveness to young men. As candidates grew scarce, the elders encouraged both mature and young men to participate in Sun Dance and Sacred Pipe rituals instead. In short, by the 1930s elders ceased to pass their personal medicine power on to their juniors, but ritual status and personal well-being were still attainable primarily by apprenticeship to a hierarchy of ceremonial elders. The native priesthood was open to Arapahoe men, but usually not the role of shaman. In this way, with the passage of time the authority of the ceremonial elders was probably augmented.

The growing influence of the ceremonial elders was particularly apparent in the way the use of individually owned pipes changed among the Arapahoes. At the time the tribe settled on the reservation, virtually all adult males had pipes, which they used in praying and in cementing social bonds and agreements. Elders assisted younger men to obtain and use their pipes properly. In their relations with whites, leaders often insisted on smoking in order to sanctify the proceedings, and they frequently presented pipes to prominent whites as a sign to their people of the special bond that existed between the donor and the recipient. By the early twentieth century, elders discouraged pipe rituals except in the Sun Dance, where the ceremonial elders supervised each dancer's handling of his pipe. Pipes, as sacred objects, were thought to be potentially dangerous; thus to misuse them would bring misfortune. Leaders who were not *bééteet* or priests were considered unqualified to handle pipes. Whereas the sacred and secular spheres of leadership once were intertwined and the linkage symbolized in the ways a leader used his pipe, by the 1930s sacred and secular authority was compartmentalized: only ceremonial elders were trusted with pipes, and this privilege bolstered their authority.

The Organization of Sodalities
and the Revitalization of the Crow Society

The men's age-graded lodges ceased to be active in the 1908–36 era. Repressive measures against Indian dances and the new interests of people born after the tribe settled on the reservation made the continuation of the lodge organization impractical. In its place another type of association, the sodality, developed. Sodality activities paralleled in many respects the secular functions of the lodges. Elderly Arapahoes encouraged these new organizations, which offered people a chance to engage in activities that brought them social recognition and benefited the community. The sodalities were composed of people of one sex and of approximately the same age. The groups organized games and dances, raised funds to help the needy, and brought together people from many different kin groups.

Before the organization of sodalities, nonreligious community celebrations apparently had been organized by ad hoc groups:

> It was a social gathering along about the first part of July. The Indian children would be given a penny; so they became a committee by accepting this penny. They were preparing all this during the winter. Their parents would make beadwork—moccasins, beaded vests, . . . what have you. The parents—the father and the mother—would act as a committee to help the child out who had received a penny. So they all worked together and when the summer came, they were ready for these big Indian dances. I do not know whether they had a chairman or secretary or what, but each Indian did his best. Food was donated by the tribe. Each family would bring coffee, bread, and whatever they had so they could have a feast. And those of us that received this penny, when the time came, there was a big giveaway for the visiting tribes.[75]

Sodalities seem to have been organized first among the congregation of St. Stephen's. On March 9, 1912, Jim Grass, a Sioux catechist, arrived at St. Stephen's to take up missionary work. At his first meeting, on March 21, officers for a men's group were selected. A women's sodality formally assumed the responsibility of cooking for communal celebrations. When Grass left in April, the idea of such formal organizations was firmly planted. The Episcopalians also established sodalities among the Upper Arapahoes at this same time.[76]

Another of the earliest sodalities was the Christmas Club. Both missions had been distributing gifts and providing a feast at Christmas. Such generous displays were compatible with the Arapahoe ideals of leadership. The men's sodality began to assume the responsibility for the Christmas celebration at St. Stephen's. Christopher Goggles sponsored the Christmas doings and led the group in executing the program in 1913. He wrote to his teacher at Carlisle (which he attended from 1904 to 1909), "I am preparing Christmas for about 500 people as I am the president of St. Joseph's Society at St. Stephen's, Wyoming. I hope to do well and have a good Christmas." At about the same time, Arapahoe men organized Christmas clubs not affiliated with the churches. They called their organizations the *hoonóúOeihiího'* ("hangers," or "those who hang things on a tree"); one was formed among the Upper Arapahoes and another among the Lower Arapahoes. Any club organized to celebrate Christmas was inoffensive to officials bent on eradicating Indian customs, but to the Arapahoes, these new groups were variations on an old theme. One elderly man recalled the first efforts of the committee at Mill Creek:

> It must have been sometimes in December. The Arapahoes were camped at what is known as Seventeen Mile Crossing. They were building irrigation canals, using picks and shovels. In the dead of winter they built these canals. And we little boys and little girls didn't never heard of Christmas. So some Indian that probably saw Christmas somewheres decided to put on a little Christmas for the children. A big tent was put up. Someone brought benches and a Christmas tree and the tree was all decorated. So they called the little boys and all the younger children into the tent. They told us that they were going to have Christmas. Someone was going to come and bring us candy and toys. So while we were sitting in there, we heard them—bells, horses, and sleigh. We could hear them coming out in field somewheres. We didn't know where they came from. Anyway, the sleigh stopped in front of the tent and here comes Santa Claus. Walked in—red suit on, white beard, and white hair. . . . And that's when we took off. We never saw Santa Claus before in our lives and this was something that came to us all of a sudden so we were frightened. We all took off down into the brush and along the ice and played around there, while they was hollering for us to come back. Santa Claus brought some good things for us. We never did go back. . . . We hid in the bushes practically all night. So whatever they did around there in the Christmas tent, well, I don't know 'cause I wasn't there. But anyway, they had Christmas. It was intended for us, but we left them.[77]

About that time other groups of men took responsibility for organizing social dances, games, and horse races in the summer and early fall. They were called *ko'eikoohuubeehiiho'*, "people who oversee the running in circles." White observers referred to these events by such names as powwows and harvest-home camp meetings.[78] The *ko'eikoohuubeehiiho'*, like the men in the other kinds of sodalities, were youths under the age of about forty; as in the men's lodges, their activities created friendships that cut across kin groups.

Women formed several clubs that raised money for tribal feasts.

They made quilts and other items for sale, then contributed the money for the tribal celebrations. The most long-lasting of these clubs was the Memorial Club. In the spring, the members made paper flowers with which to decorate the graves (in imitation of grave-decorating ceremonies witnessed among agency employees in the early days of the reservation). This group was known as *bébiiOóóbe'iiyeihíího'*, "people who fix up the graves." The Ethete club reportedly was established by Yellow Calf, probably in the late 1920s.[79]

A sacred society and three drum groups organized in the late 1920s provided new opportunities for mature men and youths to acquire prestige through participation in religious ritual. When he became an elder, Yellow Calf revitalized the Crow Dance and organized a drum group that he made responsible for supervising the *hoúúnohowóót* or Crow Dance ceremony. *Hoúúno'*, or Crowmen, who performed the dance, were chosen and supervised by the head of the drum group, the *hiitó'eihi'it*, or keeper of the drum. According to Arapahoes, Yellow Calf purchased the rudiments of the ceremony from a Pine Ridge Sioux named James Black Horse, and then in a vision was instructed by supernatural beings how the ceremony was to be conducted among the Arapahoes. In Yellow Calf's vision, the singers at the drum were to be called Eagles. He himself was to lead the Ethete Eagles as *hiitó'eihi'it* ("he who keeps the drum"). Yellow Calf's vision prompted the organization of drum groups at Mill Creek and Lower Arapahoe, which took responsibility for revitalizing the Crow Dance for their communities. The Crow Dance had four component dances—spear dance, bow-and-arrow dance, spoon dance, and kingfisher or whistle dance. Each drum group selected four youths as *hoúúno'*, each of whom was given the prescribed regalia and instructed in one of the dances. The Crow Dance ceremony was performed when someone made a vow to sponsor the ceremony in return for supernatural aid. As one Arapahoe explained, "So this person makes the pledge and then she [or he] goes—let's say it's a woman that makes the pledge for her dad or something like that—well, she in turn goes to the keeper of the drum, who is in charge of the *hoúúno'*. She tells that man that she made this pledge and for him to get those dancers ready. It's a person outside that makes a vow. But these men are set there to perform these dances and the drum keeper has to tell them what to do 'cuz he's in charge." During the preparations for the dance, a puppy was ceremonially killed as an offering from the supplicant. (The puppy's flesh is traditionally consumed in religious ceremonies; it is a sacred food, and its consumption represents the close bond between dog and man in mythological times, as well as in historical times before the tribe

acquired horses.) One of the men designated to kill the puppy explained this ritual thus:

> When they're ready to kill it, they know where my tent is, so they come over.
> "Well, here's the pup you're going to kill so we can cook it for the Eagles."
> I get my bow and arrow. They roped it tight; they hold it. And I tell the little
> pup, I said, "Now little pup, you're doing a lot of favors to the Indians. They
> kill you so the Eagles could eat. He made a pledge so person that was sick
> could get well." And they do, they do get well. They have to cook, kill this
> pup. "I don't do it to be mean, to kill you, but they eat the pup, eat this, and
> when they was short of meat they had to eat pups, the meat. And it's my duty
> to shoot you and then they can cook you. . . . I'm not mean to kill you," I
> tell that pup. [I] pray to him. I take my bow and arrow and I hit him on the
> ribs, so that little arrow bounce back. "All right, take him back." So this guy
> got the pup and he led him back to his camp and they tie his mouth and choke
> him, hang him. They hang him; he dies and they take him and burn that fur
> out [off].[80]

The Crow Dance ceremony provided youths with an opportunity to
acquire prestige in the sacred sphere, while at the same time it reinforced the age hierarchy. The Crow Dance and the secular sodalities
offered youths unhappy with their meager role in the contemporary
political and ritual order a way to earn the respect of their fellows and
increase their sense of self-importance without threatening the religious
and age hierarchies.

"One-Hundred Percent Arapahoe":
Defining Cultural Identity

In 1935 Councilman Tom Crispin died in office. An Arapahoe discussing his replacement said, "I charge the five Arapahoe councilmen
to pick a man . . . who has the ability to speak English and Arapahoe.
He must be a one-hundred percent Arapahoe in blood, and likewise his
wife and his children, and he must be in sympathy with Arapahoe
ideas."[81] In actuality, "blood" was an insignificant criterion in comparison with behavior, or what the speaker referred to as "sympathy
with Arapahoe ideas." Arapahoe cultural identity was defined by social
behavior, particularly by respectful attention to Arapahoe elders and by
participation in community activities. Yet it was continually being reshaped so as to accommodate changing social relationships and economic contingencies.

At the turn of the century, people who came to visit or marry
Arapahoes were often absorbed into Arapahoe society and listed on the

Indian Census Roll as Arapahoes if they settled on the reservation and conformed to Arapahoe social norms. One elderly Arapahoe explained one such case, the enrollment of his Gros Ventre grandmother and her sister as Northern Arapahoes:

> They come here in 1906, I think. All this place was allotted. Surveyors allotted everything on the reservation. In 1906 [the government] started give allotments. My grandmother was visiting Arapahoes. And they asked the [my] two grandmothers where they was from. They said "Gros Ventre, [from] Montana." "We're giving allotments to Indians, Arapahoes and Shoshones, eighty acres apiece. Now if you going back to Montana, we won't give you allotment. But if you intend to make your living here and stay all the rest of your life, well, we'll give you allotment." She say, "I like this country and I think I'll stay."[82]

Others, such as Mule (a Cheyenne) and Spoonhunter (a Sioux), came to the Shoshone Agency with the Arapahoes in 1878 and were enrolled as Arapahoes then. Years later, when the roll indicated "degree of blood," these originally non-Arapahoe Indians were listed as "full blood Arapahoe." Before 1914, the Arapahoe roll listed the names of persons considered to be members of the tribe but made no attempt to record actual ancestry. In 1914 the superintendent began to record "full blood" or "half blood" beside the names of persons on the roll. Of course the assignment of "degree of blood" was in large part guesswork. Some white captives and adoptees who were culturally indistinguishable from Arapahoes were listed as "half blood" Arapahoes although they had no Arapahoe ancestry.

To maintain recognition as an Arapahoe, one had to participate with other Arapahoes in reciprocity networks. People who claimed Arapahoe identity on the basis of ancestry alone were rejected when they petitioned the tribe to put them "on the roll." In 1927, when the tribe was attempting to win a legal claim against the government for violation of the Black Hills Treaty, many persons of Arapahoe ancestry who lived off the reservation were eager to enroll as members of the tribe. Councilman Little Ant (1861–1939) remarked, "It seems that there is only one object why these people are trying to come in and enroll here on this reservation. Before that they didn't seem to have any relatives, but [they now want to enroll] just because there is a claim pending in the Court of Claims."[83]

Individuals who were involved in the network of social obligations and expectations were considered to be "100 percent" Arapahoe, whatever their ancestry, and encountered no social barrier to service on the Arapahoe Business Council. Councilman Lone Bear (on the roll as "one

half Arapahoe blood") was culturally Arapahoe. His father was reportedly a white man but had not been involved in Lone Bear's life. Lone
Bear, who had some physical traits associated with whites (he was
partially bald), was fond of joking about his white ancestry: "You can
all see for yourselves that I have been baptized. I am bald where I was
baptized."[84] Councilman John Jesus Lewis, who interpreted for the
1903–7 Chiefs' Council, was the son of a Mexican-Indian government
scout, "Casouse" Ruis (also known as Susa Lewis), and a Crow woman.
John, born about 1852, was one of the Crow scouts during 1876–77.
In 1880 he began to live with the Shoshones on the Wind River. He
married a Shoshone woman and appears on the Shoshone roll as John
Casouse until 1895. Then he married an Arapahoe woman, went to
live with the Arapahoes, and was listed on the Arapahoe census as an
Arapahoe. He appears on the 1914 census as "one half Arapahoe."
Able to speak English and fairly sophisticated in the ways of whites
and in farming methods, he was apparently accepted as a useful and
cooperative peer. But his behavior began to be disruptive, and he was
subsequently shunned by the tribe. Eventually Lewis left to live in
Montana.[85]

CRISIS IN THE 1930s

The influence of the elders and the authority of the pre-1930 councilmen did not go unchallenged in the 1930s. Superintendent Reuben P.
Haas was able to capitalize on the frustration and ambition of several
young Arapahoes, and in doing so to pose a serious threat to the
structure of age-group relations among the Arapahoes. Earlier superintendents had viewed the elders' influence with emotions ranging from
bitter opposition to tolerance. Wadsworth urged the Indian Office to
abolish the Business Council: "The election of such a committee is
always more or less of a farce and under the most favorable circumstances the tribes do not seem to be willing to abide by the action of
such committee, but wish to discuss and settle in general meeting all
questions of any importance." Wadsworth was particularly hostile to
the elders, who dominated the selection process: "The rank and file . . .
do not generally concern themselves with the selection of the members
of these committees." Wadsworth argued that the council was not
really representative: "Self-styled 'headmen' and 'chiefs' who have
for years dictated the policies of the tribes . . . manage to secure their
selection . . . and continue in such positions at their pleasure." But
because of the corruption of Wadsworth's administration and an

inspector's report that cited the Arapahoe councilmen's cooperative attitude, Wadsworth's recommendations were ignored. It was not until the later years of Haas's term that a serious effort was made to wrest control from the Arapahoe elders.[86]

Reuben Haas, of part Potawatomi ancestry and married to a white woman, was clerk at the Shoshone Agency before he became superintendent in 1922. He worked to transform the Arapahoe and Shoshone societies into communities more nearly like those of the neighboring whites. In the 1930s particularly he focused his efforts on winning the support of young Arapahoes and "progressive" Shoshones. Haas also attempted to secure the election of Shoshone and Arapahoe councilmen who were sympathetic to his aims. He pressed on the tribes a series of constitutions and by-laws designed to facilitate detribalization, aid the election of persons in their twenties and thirties to the council, and erode the influence of the tribal elders.

In an effort to increase the self-confidence and influence of younger men, the superintendent extended special aid to those who wished to farm and raise livestock. Haas initially had a fair amount of success: in 1926 more than half of the Arapahoe families were operating individual family farms, on which they grew hay, some wheat, oats, potatoes, and garden vegetables. Thirty-six of the ninety families at Lower Arapahoe were farming. The percentage was greater among Upper Arapahoes: fifteen of the thirty-one families at Mill Creek farmed, and thirty-three of fifty-five families at Ethete. By 1933 the number of farms at Lower Arapahoe had decreased, but those at the upper end of the reservation had increased. Haas also organized livestock cooperatives and offered revolving credit: anyone who obtained cattle or sheep through the loan program could repay the debt with calves or lambs that the animals produced. The members of the cooperative contributed labor and grazed their herds in common. In 1930 seven Upper Arapahoes owned 100 head of cattle and eight owned 350 sheep. The program was not very successful at Lower Arapahoe: five Arapahoes owned but six head of cattle.[87]

When Haas initiated the preparation of a constitution and by-laws for the joint council, the Arapahoe councilmen apparently took little part in the project, but with the cooperation of at least the Shoshone mixed-blood councilmen a constitution was completed in December 1925. It provided for both tribes to assemble for a voice-vote election of councilmen, made council decisions binding on all members of the Shoshone and Arapahoe tribes, and empowered two representative councilmen from each tribe (to be elected by the other councilmen) to sign leasing agreements for the tribes. The minimum age for council office was set at thirty and the term of office at four years. The constitution was designed to minimize the role of the elders and the participation of tribespeople in general in tribal government. Haas was attempting to institute initiatory decision making by elected representatives, according to Anglo-American ideals of democratic government. Meetings were to be called by the superintendent, who could remove councilmen at will. At this time the members of the Arapahoe Business Council ranged in age from forty-six to sixty-six; four members were over sixty. The forty-six-year-old Robert Friday was considered to be an apprentice to the older men. Haas's attempt to restructure the council government failed because the Indian Office did not formally approve the constitution and by-laws and the Arapahoe councilmen ignored the proposed changes. Under pressure from Haas, two representative councilmen were elected from each tribe, but the two Arapahoes, Henry Lee Tyler and Sam Wolfrang, generally continued to consult other Arapahoes before acting on council business.[88]

When the 1930 council election was about to be held, Haas insisted that the members of each tribe cast ballots. The Arapahoe elders were suspicious of the electoral process and opposed the replacement of the drum ceremony with balloting. When the election was held, in December 1930, only half of the Arapahoe men and twenty-six women voted. For the six Arapahoe council positions, three men were reelected from the earlier council: Tyler, age sixty; Wolfrang, age sixty-four; Friday, age fifty. The three newcomers were considerably younger; from the Arapahoe point of view, forty-year-old Bruce Groesbeck, forty-year-old Paul Hanway, and thirty-five-year-old Scott Dewey were "youths," and therefore not fully reliable. While the election of the elder three signified the Arapahoes' determination not to break completely with the old ways, the election of three youths was indicative of the tension between the generations. Scott Dewey and Bruce Groesbeck, both Carlisle Indian School alumni, were exceptionally articulate in English and Arapahoe and were sympathetic to Haas's efforts.[89]

In January 1931, when the newly elected council assumed office, Haas initiated another effort to establish a constitution and by-laws. In the 1931 document youthful tribespeople were further encouraged to run for council office. Both men and women over the age of twenty-one were eligible for election. The council members were encouraged to be less responsive to the opinions of their constituents: they were empowered to elect replacements for members who resigned or died in office and to change the constitution by a two-thirds vote of the members of both tribal councils. The 1931 constitution also encouraged council members toward independence by providing that meetings were to be called by them rather than by the superintendent (as was formerly the custom). The provisions delegating some measure of authority to the council were seemingly unacceptable to the commissioner's office, which insisted that the council was merely an "advisory body," with no authority to call meetings or transact any business without the consent of the Indian Office. The 1931 constitution, like the 1925 document, was not approved in Washington.[90]

Haas persisted, however, and in November 1934 the council made a third attempt to draft a document that would win the Indian Office's approval. Perhaps encouraged by Commissioner John Collier's proposed reforms in federal–Indian relations, the councilmen prepared a document that reflected their desire for more independence from Indian Office supervision and greater control over tribal funds. There were fourteen articles, signed by Shoshones Driskell and McAdams and by Arapahoes Dewey, Friday, Goggles, Hanway, and Groesbeck. The document provided that the joint council was to transact business and protect the interests and rights of the tribes and of individuals having tribal business. Election was to be by secret ballot of tribe members twenty-one and older; candidates—twelve individuals nominated in public meetings—were to be at least thirty years old, reservation residents, and able to speak, read, and write English; council members were to serve four-year terms, with half of the terms expiring every two years; voting was to be held separately in the Lower and Upper Arapahoe communities and in the three Shoshone districts; judges in Indian Court were to be appointed by the joint council. The council could remove for cause a member by majority vote and could fill vacancies. A quorum of eight members must be established in order to transact business that affected both tribes. The superintendent was to be deterred from "harassment" of council members. The council was to approve purchases from tribal funds, as well as sales and leases of tribal property. And finally, this constitution and the by-laws could be amended or repealed by a two-thirds vote of the council members. But like the two earlier proposals, this document was not approved by the Indian Office (also known at this time as the Bureau of Indian Affairs, or BIA).[91]

The 1931–34 council was no more successful than earlier councils, and at the next election the three younger councilmen, Groesbeck, Dewey, and Hanway, were not returned to office. They had had no more success than their elders in securing per capita payments or gaining control over the leasing of tribal lands. Voters—who now accepted the balloting process—elected men to the 1935 council who ranged in age from fifty-five to sixty-six years.

The men who had accepted the superintendent's support in their attempts at farming and ranching had had little success, and therefore could not generate support for agency programs or respect for their personal abilities among their fellow Arapahoes. Federal policies fluctuated and agency programs were poorly implemented. When the young Arapahoes failed to prosper, they were ridiculed. Tom Crispin, who had worked enthusiastically for agricultural development and for the organization of "community chapters," or associations to encourage agriculturalists, complained to Haas:

> It hurts one's feelings to have all that locality [his residential community] know he is failed and his [chapter] members and his own tribe say "The Chapter organization is not what I thought it was, I want to resign." Pretty soon there is no one. Pretty soon there is only five or six of us. When this office don't help us along lines suggested we will have failure. . . . For instance, each and every one of us had council [discussion] at the Chapter meetings and it was the idea to purchase half a dozen chickens and a rooster for every member. They [the BIA] didn't do that. They said to build chicken coops. I and two other of the boys here, and one man who was vice-president in my district, we built chicken houses and didn't get the chickens. . . . When they organized that Chapter work, why did they come out and tell us that they would help. They did not do it; that is not right.[92]

Several individuals who had more than the average amount of schooling on the reservation had also supported Haas's programs, and in fact had requested patent in fee status for their allotments. When the taxes on the lands and the other problems of competency put these people in difficulty, they were in the embarrassing position of having to request help from the older, experienced councilmen. In short, the young people's support for the superintendent was short-lived, in part because of the BIA's inability to implement the programs it advocated, and in part because of the elders' disapproval of the agent's efforts.

The Old Man with Medicine in His Hair:
Intervention by the Elders

Throughout the early 1930s, the ceremonial elders did not look on idly when there was dissension within the Arapahoe community. They were not opposed to education or to farming and ranching as long as young people did not abandon the values held by the older generations. The elders did not discount the usefulness of a "white man's education" in dealings with whites, particularly when the educated individuals acknowledged the superior wisdom of the elderly. They approved the

Plate 9. Councilman Henry Lee Tyler greeting a white visitor at the Tomahawk Dance, March 1930. The dancers behind Tyler are holding the ceremonial clubs of the lodge. The two women at the far right assisted their male relatives who participated; they are Mary Agnes Goggles, on the left, and Mrs. White Plume, on the right. The Tomahawk Dance, as well as the annual Sun Dance, was attended by white spectators and received coverage in local newspapers. The white community's interest was partly a product of the emphasis on tourism in Wyoming and also due in part to the tribe's efforts to persuade whites to intercede with federal officials on behalf of the tribe. Courtesy of the National Anthropological Archives, Smithsonian Institution.

Plate 14. The Eagles and the women singers sitting at Drum Number One, 1975. These ceremonial elders are seated in the center of the Blue Sky community hall at Ethete. The women sit separately from the men (cf. Plate 11). During the social dancing, the Arapahoes circle the drum. Old Man West Shakespeare is on the far right and the keeper of the drum, Robert Sun Rhodes, is the second man from Shakespeare's right. The women, left to right, are Helen Cedartree, Winnie Big Road, Regina Arthur, Josephine White. Photo by Sara Hunter-Wiles.

Plate 15. Ceremonial elder Inez Oldman receiving gifts at memorial giveaway for Ben Goggles, July 1979. Elders are the first to be given gifts, which may include dress goods and shawls, as shown here. The giveaway for Goggles was held at the Ethete powwow. Photo by Sara Hunter-Wiles.

Plate 16. Ben Friday, one of the "four old men," seated at Drum Number One, July 1979. Photo by Sara Hunter-Wiles.

selection of youths who were particularly good at communicating in English to sit on the Arapahoe Business Council and read and interpret for the other council members when necessary. In 1932 and 1933, St. Michael's Mission held adult education classes for elderly Arapahoes. Aged people came to learn to read and write and "do figures." Among the graduates were several leaders, including Yellow Calf, who thereafter signed his name to documents instead of making his mark. At the same time, elderly men and women ridiculed educated youths who in their opinion tried to behave like whites. This is what the superintendent referred to when he wrote of the school graduates, "Those who stay on the reservation, as nearly all do, must face the ridicule of the older people if they try to progress."[93]

The ceremonial elders also used their ritual authority to try to lessen the tension between the youths and their elders. In 1931, just a few weeks after the disruptive ballot election of 1930, the old men decided to revive the Tomahawk Lodge, which had not been held for a quarter of a century (see Plate 11). In their role as grandfathers, the elders initiated "respect" relationships with the novices. Some thirty youths were pressed into participating, and significantly, many were among the enthusiastic agriculturalists aided by the superintendent. Among the "elder brothers" selected by the novices was Henry Lee Tyler, at that time head councilman and the most experienced council member. The Tomahawk Lodge ceremony was pledged by Lester Pine in return for the recovery of his ailing sister. There were no age sets at this time, but at the suggestion of the elders, some other youths decided to participate, and they encouraged others to do so. The lodge was held March 16–20, 1931, a few miles east of Ethete. At least one tent was provided for "imitation" Tomahawk men—those who had completed the lodge in earlier years but had not gone on to enter the Spear Lodge. For four days the old men supervised the making of the regalia. The dancing took place in the evening. At the conclusion of the ceremony, the dancers or novices were divided into two groups— "short men" and "tall men"—for a foot race.[94] Participation in the lodge ceremony gave the youths a sacred obligation to be respectful of the elderly men who supervised the ceremony and who helped with the arrangements during the ritual. The ceremonial elders who directed the rite were grandfathers in the same sense that the elderly advisers in the Sun Dance served as grandfathers to their Sun Dance grandsons. Although youths still were eager to increase their participation in tribal government, their reluctance to offend the ceremonial authorities was reinforced.

In cases of blatant disrespect and defiance among youths, an elder with *béétee* might retaliate by supernatural means. One such case is recorded: "There was an old man one time who had a small piece of medicine tied to his hair on the back of his head. . . . A man who had gone to Carlisle and had come back, thought he was smart, and snapped his fingers at that thing in this old man's hair. This old man used power, and that fellow got worms in his nose and he died of it. He tried to get the old man to take them out, but the old man wouldn't do it. That was about ten years ago [1930]."[95] The old man with the medicine in his hair effectively made an example of the scoffer.

Reorganization, 1934–35: The Wheeler-Howard Act

As pressures for change grew among the tribes at the Shoshone Agency, a movement was afoot in Washington to reorganize federal–Indian relations. In 1933, when John Collier took office as commissioner, he and his staff began to develop a reform program designed to permit the Indian tribes as much freedom as possible to regulate their internal affairs and to assist the political and economic rehabilitation of Indian communities through loan programs and the acquisition and consolidation of landholdings. His aides drafted the necessary legislation and Collier visited Indian communities to enlist support for it. During the summer of 1934, when Collier's reforms were being attacked in Congress, he intensified his efforts to mobilize support among the Indians. In the face of congressional opposition to many facets of the Collier plan, a weakened version of the bill was passed on June 18, 1934.[96]

The passage of the Indian Reorganization Act (IRA), also known as the Wheeler-Howard Act, was a major departure from previous government policies in regard to Indians. The bill provided for measures to conserve and develop Indian lands and resources, to extend to Indians the right to form business and other organizations, to establish a credit system for Indians, to grant them certain rights of home rule, and to provide for vocational education for Indians. No more land was to be allotted to individuals and the trust status of reservation lands was to be continued until Congress directed otherwise. The bill would apply to those tribes that chose by majority vote to accept its provisions. Later, Congress set June 1935 as the deadline for the tribes' acceptance of the IRA. By the end of 1936, however, the new legislation and the resultant BIA policies and programs had begun to affect all tribes, whether they accepted the act or not. In future years, the changes introduced during the Collier era came to provide new opportunities and challenges for Indian leadership.[97]

BIA officials met several times with Shoshone and Arapahoe groups at the Shoshone reservation early in 1934. Then a general council was held on February 23, 1934, bringing together "the Arapahoes, the breeds [Shoshone mixed-bloods], and the Shoshones," as one old Shoshone observed. The proposed changes were considered carefully. Tribespeople were alarmed by suggestions that the allotment policy would be reversed, and lands consolidated and placed under tribal control. This provision was understood to mean that individuals could no longer call their allotments their own. The two tribes feared they would lose land as they had done in the past, and that a general social disorganization would follow. John Timbana, a Shoshone, remarked, "Turn our lands all back to the government as a tribal land, we would be just like a coyote—we would be trotting around from place to place. We would probably commit a depredation on our neighbors—the white people." Shoshone leader Driskell commented that *real* self-government would mean that Indians selected Indians to go to Washington to legislate. The tribes were finally polled separately by Collier's representatives. The Shoshones unanimously rejected the suggested reforms, 90 votes to none.[98]

The Arapahoes took a similar stance. Elderly Arapahoes were the main spokesmen, and the session was opened with a prayer by a cere-monial authority. During the course of the discussion it became clear that the old people felt particularly threatened by the impending change. The Arapahoes voted 52–0 against the reforms, giving four reasons for their decision: (1) because "the care of our aged and infirm is a sacred duty to the whole tribe," some provision was needed to ensure the fulfillment of that responsibility; (2) the government was not to be trusted, particularly in view of its failure to act on the Arapahoes' Black Hills claim; (3) the people wished to keep the ownership and use of their land unchanged; and (4) the people disapproved of any drastic change. Yellow Calf pointed to the unkept promises of the 1905 cession agreement and the need for assignment of land to the children born after the allotments were made. Forty-one-year-old Dominick Harris stressed the tribe's distrust of government proposals and promises, comparing government actions with those of a wolf stalking its prey: "We are just like a feared people that there is some big wolf circling around to see its way to take what we have got." The elder Sage, after reviewing the long history of treaties and agreements on which the Arapahoes based their right to Wind River lands, said, "I think that we ought to be left alone just where we are." Obviously viewing the proposed reforms as one more federal scheme to appropriate Arapahoe lands and renege on commitments to the people, he said:

Friends, I recall back many years when our forefathers agreed upon the land questions with the government. That is the Treaty of 1851. The substance of that treaty at that time was that the time will come when you are well enough fixed and well enough off in wealth—your children and your grandchildren and their grandchildren may not be the ones and they may be the ones, it all depends upon such a time when you have reached the stage of life of a well-to-do person—then the change will take place. The treaty that was agreed upon between the government and this man's father (indicating Henry Lee Tyler) at that same place—Fort Laramie in 1868—the treaty was very similar to 1851. It was also in the treaty of Black Hills [1876 Agreement], it was agreed upon for any change towards civilized life would have to take seven hundred years, that was understood and the time is not yet here.[99]

The government persisted, however, and invited Indians to send representatives to the Plains Congress to be held in Rapid City, South Dakota, on March 5, 1934. There Collier's proposals were explained and clarified and BIA officials attempted to allay the Indians' fears and win their support for the IRA. All of the Arapahoe councilmen attended the session. Bruce Groesbeck and Scott Dewey again voiced the tribe's resentment over the "unfulfilled treaty" of 1905 and the threat to water rights. Groesbeck said that the tribe wanted the unsold ceded portion back. Expressing the Arapahoes' distrust of government aims, he admonished: "I am asking the Honorable Commissioner Collier to see about the other agreements that have not been fulfilled. Look to that."[100]

Later, in a joint business council meeting at the agency, Driskell pointed out that if the tribes approved the bill, it could still be amended by Congress: "It is like buying a pig in a poke." Dewey said, "The policy of the government has been to rob and to cheat and to beat the Indian [out] of his property." Yellow Calf, officially retired from the council but in attendance, also spoke against the bill, expressing his fear that the IRA would result in the theft of Arapahoe lands: "I am a little bit afraid of this idea for this reason—that there has been nothing said from that bill directing the disposal of our valuable oil, mines or anything of that kind. The white people are smart and they can foresee things a long ways ahead and there might be a time when I will be lifted clear off this reservation and put somewhere else." More group meetings were held, but when the tribes were polled again on April 7, 1934, the Arapahoes voted 115 to 1 against the bill, stating for the record that they felt that the change would not be good for the old and indigent and that they did not want any land transfer. In their own tribal meeting, the Shoshones also voted against the bill, 153 to 5.[101]

After the Indian Reorganization Act (a revised version of Collier's draft) was officially passed by Congress on June 18, 1934, the Shoshones and Arapahoes were asked to vote formally to accept or reject its provisions. First, a Shoshone and Arapahoe delegation was sent to Washington in April 1935 to meet with Collier. There was controversy over the selection of the delegates, who (despite the reservations of Arapahoe councilmen) had been chosen by the joint business council rather than the tribespeople themselves. By this time Driskell had changed his position on reorganization, and to the superintendent's dismay, all of the Arapahoe councilmen and two of the Shoshones voted not to send Driskell to Washington. "It is difficult to control the whims of an Indian Council when they decide to give you a surprise," complained Superintendent Forrest Stone. Robert Friday and Tom Crispin were selected to represent the Arapahoes, and Irene Meade and Wallace St. Clair the Shoshones. In Washington, Collier could give no assurance about elimination of the water charges, dismissed the complaints about unfulfilled treaties, and ignored complaints about the oil leases.[102]

At this time the tribes were still pressing for per capita payments. After 1931 Congress authorized only occasional small payments from oil and gas royalties, and in May 1935 the BIA refused to make the small payments in cash. Five dollars in cash and $40 in store orders were authorized for each Arapahoe. One Arapahoe commented, "The government won't trust us with forty-five dollars so why should we accept [the IRA]; the government don't trust us to even handle our own money."[103]

The official vote on the IRA was taken, this time by ballot, on June 15, 1935. There was a record turnout of about 80 percent of eligible voters. Despite considerable harassment from federal officials, the Arapahoes voted heavily against the bill, 238 to 117. The Shoshones, among whom a large turnout of mixed-bloods favored the bill, voted by a one-vote margin for the IRA, 175 to 174. When the absentee ballots were counted, the final vote total was 339 for and 467 against acceptance of the IRA. The BIA ruled that both tribes would have to accept the act if it were to be put in effect at the Shoshone reservation. Hence, unlike the majority of the Plains tribes, neither the Arapahoes nor the Shoshones were ever subject to political reorganization under the provisions of the IRA.[104]

Former councilman Scott Dewey offered this comment to Superintendent Stone: "From what I can see or have been able to learn, the Arapahoes rejected the Act because the majority of the old Indians were against it, and the children of these older Indians, naturally, fell in with them." Stone was depressed: "I have the feeling that somehow we have been passed by, just as a big car will go roaring along the road and you find yourself in a little two-wheel cart, with the harness broken, and sitting off by the side of the road, as you see them go by."[105]

4

"The Old Indians and the Schoolboys": The New Council, 1937–64

Although the Arapahoes refused to reorganize their tribal government under the provisions of the Indian Reorganization Act, they were subjected to intense pressure from Superintendent Forrest Stone to make extensive changes in their political process. This was a time of confusion and apprehension, not only because of the superintendent's insistence on change, but also because the Arapahoes themselves, while recognizing a need for new kinds of leadership, were wary of the individuals who could provide the new skills required. Yet a "new" business council gradually took form. Personal qualifications that would have been inappropriate or irrelevant to council leadership in earlier eras came to be essential after 1937. And as the members of the Arapahoe Business Council gradually succeeded in obtaining sizable monthly per capita payments and more independence in relation to federal agencies, they increased their political leverage within Arapahoe society.

The rise of "educated" councilmen was encouraged by the BIA, in part to minimize the influence of the elders. Councilmen were offered the chance for more extensive power in return for support of the BIA's efforts to introduce political institutions that were at odds with contemporary Arapahoe political culture. Despite these pressures, the elders retained their directive influence in Arapahoe politics. The new council's authority was tempered and its powers were held in check. Responsibility for restraining the council and containing social conflict in general lay with the elders, who succeeded in their task in large part by sanctioning a general compartmentalization of spheres of leadership. Authority was further circumscribed by the proliferation of sodalities and a greater diffusion of ritual prerogatives.

"THE FASHION OF NEW DAYS":
INTERMEDIARY LEADERSHIP

In 1937 Superintendent Forrest Stone (1935–45) insisted on a new election of Business Council members, although two years remained of the incumbents' four-year terms. Stone wanted not only a new election, but changes in the electoral procedures as well. His proposed changes profoundly disturbed the Arapahoes. At a well-attended council meeting on January 8, 1937, George Wallowing Bull voiced his and other elders' opposition to the proposals: "There are two parties, the old Indians and the schoolboy[s], and they won't agree with one another about the election of councilmen. I know they will not agree with me in selecting the council, these schoolboys; and the schoolboy who knows and understands his English, will select whatever he wants for his council, but as an Indian, the old custom of selecting the council was—like I would pick out from the crowd in this room, the people I am in favor of."[1] The images in the old man's speech—"the old Indians" and "the schoolboys"—were important symbols in the years to come and served to crystallize the relationship between tribal political tradition and the unwelcome innovations pressed by the Bureau of Indian Affairs. "Educated" Indians—characterized by the Arapahoes as knowledgeable about white society but basically loyal to Arapahoe traditions and to the influential elders—could serve the ends of the tribe in its dealings with whites. But "schoolboys," who had internalized the cultural values of non-Indian society, were unpredictable. In labeling youthful dissidents "schoolboys" the elders emphasized their inexperience, unreliability, and lack of sound judgment.

Superintendent Stone had begun urging a new election and electoral reforms as early as 1936: "Ever since I have been at Shoshone [Agency], and it is only fair to tell you, there have been continued complaints against the members of both councils; people who have maintained that the council didn't rightfully represent the people of the tribes; that the council had resorted to many methods to keep the people in darkness as to their affairs; that the majority of the people didn't want the present council." Stone objected to the "old custom" whereby "groups will get together and say you can vote on these men and on these men only"—that is, the influence of the elders in the electoral process. At the January 8 meeting the interpreter Mike Goggles spoke for Tom Spoonhunter, an Arapahoe elder: "It was a law that the election was to be held at a certain time for the new council and he thinks it was no time to change council now and wonders who set up this law to have a new election at present." Another Arapahoe, Nell

Scott, said that she and Luke Smith had been asked to urge Stone to retain the old system of nomination, but that Stone had refused. In short, the Arapahoes refuted Stone's contention that the Business Council was unpopular. In a February 24 meeting, Ben Friday, a spokesman from Ethete, remarked, "The majority of the people around seemed to want the council to remain. Just two or three made a kick."[2]

Relentlessly Stone pressed for a new election, an end to the elders' influence over nominations, and the introduction of "districting." He urged that the Shoshones in the Burris area organize as a district and nominate and vote on a slate of candidates, one of whom would gain a seat on the Shoshone Business Council. The Shoshones in the more heavily populated Fort Washakie area were to nominate candidates and vote for five individuals to serve on the council. The Arapahoes were advised to vote in two districts, Lower Arapahoe and Ethete, each of which would elect three members of the Arapahoe Business Council. (Robert Friday pointed out to Stone that the Arapahoes considered Ethete and Mill Creek to be two districts, not one.) This arrangement would have been a great change from the old system, in which votes were cast for all Arapahoe candidates by all members of the tribe, regardless of place of residence. The Arapahoes rejected the proposed innovations, but the new election did take place, on March 30, 1937, under the supervision of the Bureau of Indian Affairs.[3]

During the latter part of 1936 and the first few months of 1937, the Arapahoes discussed the merits and shortcomings of the "old council" and the possible advantages of electing younger, better educated people to the Business Council. Robert Friday was a vigorous proponent of reorganization of tribal government. At a meeting on December 1, 1936, he spoke in favor of change and the educated leader: "The past two years there has been agitation, dissatisfaction against the present council. The main reason is that the younger type, some that has been to school and learned a little more progressive ways, they know more than the older people. That is where the trouble lies. Old people feel they have different ideas. They have their ideas on the old ways. . . . We should think in the new fashion, the fashion of new days." Friday suggested that the "old Indians" were disrupting efforts to implement federal reforms that would benefit the tribe, particularly programs to aid individual enterprise and the introduction of constitutional, majority-rule government. He advocated changes in Business Council government even though the tribe had rejected the IRA: "I am willing to change hands to elect a new council, but when we do that, they must draw up by-laws and after these by-laws are approved by the Indian Office, the superintendent and the council must be governed by these by-laws. The agitators have their minds on the old ways. They must have no agitation but must be governed by these by-laws."[4]

Henry Lee Tyler, who at the age of sixty-four had served on the Business Council for twenty-six years, defended his performance as a councilman and criticized the attack on the leadership of the "old council." Tyler did not acknowledge the existence of "new days" that called for major political reorganization. The current conflict was the work of a few malcontents: "All of the time I have been on the council, always has this criticism and agitation been going on against the council." Mentioning that he had worked with Friday's father, Tyler called the people's attention to the youth of the council's critics and to his own long experience in tribal government: "Since I have been elected to the council I have worked with many different agents and different people. I worked with Lone Bear and Yellow Calf and Friday, this man's father (pointing to Robert Friday), and Wallowing Bull and Sherman Coolidge." He compared the turmoil of 1936-37 with the conflict during Agent Nickerson's term, suggesting that agitators or "kickers" were persons who thought only of themselves and who had not worked for the tribe, as the councilmen had done: "We had worst trouble just like now, and lots of kick. They called us to a meeting and we tracked it up and brought everything out and it was just a few men had started it. Men that was never on the council. They are the worst kickers." Tyler stressed his longevity, which was an indication of supernatural blessing: "Ever since I am on the council I have been working with different people; some changed; some died and some quit but I am still on the council all the time. Men I used to work with are most all dead, they have died off. They changed council but elected me all the time since 1916 [1910]." Tyler also drew attention to his family's good reputation and to his own receptivity to the counsel of his tribesmen (thus reaffirming his commitment to nondirective, non-initiatory leadership): "Arapahoe Indians claim just like this. My father has been a great chief. He helped make the treaty by the government in 1868. It was shown on the minutes he helped open up this country. They used to have long trains of covered wagons. My father helped open up the West side. He was a great friend of the white people. The Indians tell me, 'Your father was a great chief; a good man. You do just like your father used to do.' I have tried to do the same thing as my father." Then, in a rare show of direct criticism, Tyler described the youthful critics of the council as people who sought to "explode something," people who threatened the social order and, implicitly, the spiritual state of the tribe: "If we change council, it will be the same thing, someone will come up and criticize. There is no way we can stop it. They are just a small part of the people but they think they are strong. They think they can explode something." He concluded by commenting that because of ill health he did not want to continue to serve on the Business Council, but he reaffirmed the value of his many years of experience on the council.[5]

At subsequent tribal meetings Tyler admitted that the old council had not always been successful in its efforts to influence federal officials, but he stressed that it had tried to use the money to which it had access to benefit all Arapahoes—"to help every man, woman and child on the reservation." He acknowledged that mistakes had been made: "Since that time we have found out they have found clauses in the leases that do not permit immediate production or sale of this oil and we found that the leases ran indefinitely and then we could not make them produce or market this oil."[6]

Robert Friday knew that people were impatient for the distribution of tribal income in per capita payments and that the Business Council had failed to persuade the government to release tribal funds to the tribe. Friday charged that the chiefs—many of whom served on the old council—were unable to comprehend contemporary financial matters: "Just think what our former chiefs have done; for example our chiefs would have done better if they had leased the Thermopolis area [Hot Springs], but they sold it for sixty thousand dollars, and in less than five years they eat it up." He also charged that the Chiefs' Council encouraged the government to retain control over the expenditure of the 1905 cession money. In the words of another Arapahoe, "The old fellows' agreement to Congress was that they wasn't able to take care of their money; they were just like babies. They wasn't able to take care of their money so they turned it over to Congress. It seems to me that that law has got everything tied up, money that we get from oil fields goes to the treasury and it is locked up and we can't get no use of it."[7]

Before the new election, Charles Whiteman, an "old Indian," expressed the predominant tribal sentiment that younger, "educated" Arapahoes should be given a chance to prove that they could be effective in working for Arapahoe interests: "Recent years things has changed. The council seems to be changing. Things seem to be getting harder and the Indians seem to feel now when they ask the agent or the government for a thing they should get it right then. They don't seem to have patience. That is the reason why they don't like the council. . . . Probably these people that want to change the council probably they are smarter or wiser than the present council. Probably if they get in they will do a great service for us." Speakers in the tribal meetings urged moderation and compromise by presenting as "agitators" the persons they viewed as inflexible (Tyler used the label in reference to the youths and Friday used it to refer to the elders). Spokesmen from Lower Arapahoe, Ethete, and Mill Creek expressed confidence in the council—in the worth of the old order—although they agreed with the superintendent's wish for a new election in order to allow formal resolution of the conflict generated by the people who were restless with the status quo. All but one of the incumbent councilmen agreed to the new election.[8]

In a community meeting before the election, the Arapahoes nominated all of the 1935–36 councilmen and several former councilmen (Henry Lee Tyler, Alonzo Moss, Charles Whiteman, Robert Friday, Mike Goggles, John Goggles, Yellow Calf, Scott Dewey, Bruce Groesbeck, Paul Hanway, Josiah Oldman), but also some newcomers: Tom Joe Duran, Otto Hungary, John Little, Jerome Oldman, Aaron Willow, and the first woman to run for election, Nell Scott. Three hundred twenty-three Arapahoes (at least two-thirds of the eligible voters) elected Robert Friday (199 votes), Nell Scott (who received the second highest number of votes—the exact total is not recorded), John Goggles (180 votes), Bruce Groesbeck (146 votes), Mike Goggles (136 votes), and Charles Whiteman (129 votes). All but John Goggles and Charles Whiteman were considered "educated" Indians. Four members of the 1935–36 Business Council were reelected, despite Stone's claim that constituents were dissatisfied. The critically ill Henry Lee Tyler and Alonzo Moss were the only two councilmen replaced. Elected in their stead were Bruce Groesbeck and Nell Scott.[9] This trend continued in the years to come: younger, "educated" leaders were elected to the Business Council along with more experienced elder leaders.

Nell Scott, "Council Lady"

The Arapahoes recognized a need for a new kind of aggressive leadership in relations with the federal government. The young leaders selected for council positions were not the "schoolboys" held in disdain by the elders, but rather individuals who, while they could assert tribal interests in a non-Indian social context more effectively than the "old Indians," accepted the ultimate authority of the elders. Councilmen who alienated the elders were ultimately unable to generate support from their constituents. The individual most successful in the councilman role during the 1937–64 era was Nell Scott (see Plate 12).

The career of Nell Scott, who served thirty years in all and was often chairman of the Arapahoe Business Council, is particularly interesting in view of her apparent marginality to tribal life. She lived on the Shoshone portion of the reservation as the wife of a white man, was unable to speak the Arapahoe language, and was unfamiliar with much of Arapahoe custom. Anthropologist Henry Elkin briefly visited Wind River in 1937 and concluded that Nell Scott's election was indicative of the Arapahoes' submission to the outlook and values of the dominant society: "The great majority, unable to attain within its [traditional cultural] scope a full and satisfactory organization of their lives, display no conviction in the ultimate value of the cultural forms or real interest in their perpetuation. They elect to the council a half-breed woman, long married to a white, who neither speaks Arapahoe nor has any firm connection with the society."[10] What Elkin failed to perceive was that Scott's selection, at the instigation of the elders, was not a rejection of "cultural forms," but a clever means of helping to preserve those forms and the values that underlay them. Scott's efforts on behalf of tribal goals and her receptivity to the elders throughout her thirty-year career on the council have vindicated the elders' choice of the young woman for council leadership.

Before the 1937 election, Nell Scott had earned the elders' appreciation on many occasions by aiding individual Arapahoes in their personal dealings with agency personnel.[11] Just before the election, several elderly Arapahoe men, including Henry Lee Tyler, conferred and decided that Nell Scott would be useful in achieving the long-sought goals. Scott recalled her meeting with the elders this way: "We was there one day, and there was five Arapahoes came over—Shot Gun, Yellow Calf, and Henry Lee Tyler, Sr., and two other Arapahoes I don't recall. They came up to see me and invited me down to their general council the next day. . . . So I went down and Henry Lee Tyler wanted to know whether I was enrolled on the Arapahoe roll and I told him yes. And he said, 'I'm going to put you on as a council lady.' . . . They nominated me and I got on." Despite her marginality, Henry Lee Tyler, in Scott's recollection, remarked, "Well, we want her; she's been away from the reservation, probably knows. She's got a good education. So I nominate her to run as council lady."[12] The political position of a council member depended in large part on how ably he or she could interact with whites to achieve benefits for the tribe. Scott was noted for her forceful personality and her ability to intimidate verbally both Indians and non-Indians. One of her colleagues on the council remarked of Scott's performance on the council, "Some rough words! Well, she was a good fighter against the whites. Good politician."

Nell Scott was born in 1888 in Evanston, Wyoming. Her mother, Julia, had long ago been found alone after a battle between Arapahoes and Shoshones and had been adopted by a white man named John Felter. She was then about six years old.[13] When Julia grew up she married a white man by the name of John Burns. They had two children, John and Charles, who were also adopted by Felter. She divorced Burns and married another white man, Anton Weilaudt, and Nell and her sister Teresa were born. When Julia divorced Weilaudt, she resumed the name Felter and went to the Shoshone Agency at the time allotments were being given. Nell Scott recalled:

> My mother was living down in Evanston and Senator C. D. Clark told her she was to come over and get her inheritance by getting her land and enrolling, enrolling us kids. Now, we came by wagon. We met with the General Council [the entire tribe], the Arapahoes. My brother was big enough to remember so he went to the meeting with my mother. And Yellow Calf turned us down because he said he didn't know what tribe we belonged to. . . . Then Washakie, Chief Washakie, sent for us and put us on the Shoshone roll. Then we got our land out there at Crowheart. Then we had to go to school in order to obtain our inheritance. So we went to the government school. . . . And it was the Shoshones and Arapahoes, both tribes, going to school there. The Shoshone kids were good to us but the Arapahoes were mean to us. We was "white kids from Evanston."[14]

In 1898 Nell and her sister and half brothers were enrolled and eventually allotted land with the Shoshones, possibly because Washakie was eager to increase the number of his followers at that time.[15] Julia married a Shoshone, John Hereford, and resided with the Shoshones for the rest of her life. Nell returned to Evanston because of ill health and went to high school there. While she was away the superintendent removed her name from the Shoshone roll. Apparently Julia's Arapahoe ancestry was established after the family settled on the reservation, because in 1909 Julia again asked the Arapahoe tribe to enroll Nell and her brothers and sister as Arapahoes, and they did. For several years Nell lived in Evanston, and there she married William T. Scott, originally from Boston. In 1927 the Scotts bought land on the reservation and built a house: "We came over here; we didn't intend to live here at the time. We never did get away."[16]

Despite her upbringing among whites, Scott worked most of her adult life to protect Indian rights and to improve living conditions for the Arapahoes, particularly the aged and the children. Her dedication stemmed from an empathy for persons deprived and abused. In her reminiscences of the things she had heard from her relatives, this event seemed to have left a particularly vivid impression: "My mother was left after the battle. They found her hid under sagebrush, so I've been told. Now this is all hearsay. And they said that my mother was captured by a Mexican. And he took her up to South Pass, where . . . Pa and Ma [Felter] was working. And [the Mexican] wanted to take and adopt her over. Pa said no. He [the Mexican] said, 'Well, I'll trade her for the gun. If you don't, I'm going to kill her 'cause I've got no place to keep her and I don't want her.' That's what Pa told me. Pa felt sorry for her."[17]

Perhaps Nell Scott's awareness of her mother's predicament was a significant factor in her commitment to the Indian people. Her sympathy for the plight of the Indians at Wind River, whom she found suffering from hunger, exposure, and disease, and her irritation at the heavy-handed BIA policies were strong motivating forces in her fight against oppressive governmental actions. Childless, Nell Scott had a long and successful career on the council before she retired at the age of eighty, in 1968.

"My New Name": Shared Understandings about Leadership

The success of the "new" business council is reflected in its extraordinary stability and continuity in membership. No election protests were ever made, and the 84 two-year terms from 1937 to 1964 were filled by only 32 individuals (see Table 5).

Reassuring their peers was particularly problematic for the young "educated" council members. They found it difficult to behave submissively toward their elders while at the same time assuming increased responsibility and authority in reservation affairs. One leader expressed the dilemma of the new breed of councilman when he related to ethnologist Inez Hilger his difficulties in attempting to enhance his reputation in the Arapahoe community. He had begun to use the name of a prominent ancestor in order to signify to others that his personal accomplishments were comparable to those of the ancestor. He told Hilger: "Although the Arapahoe have not yet accepted my new name (a prominent uncle's name) many call me by it. If I maintain my good character and reputation, I will eventually have the name because that is the custom of our people. Those that object to my having this name say that I have not yet earned it. But I tell them that I think I have, for I have done much for my tribe. I have been in Washington many times in the interests of the Arapahoe, and I have represented our people in court cases."[18]

In this 1937–64 era, as in earlier times, the authority of councilmen

Table 5
Members of Arapahoe Business Council, 1937–64

1937–38	1939–40	1941–42
Nell Scott	Nell Scott	Nell Scott
Robert Friday	Robert Friday	Joe Duran
Mike Goggles	Charles Whiteman	Ben Friday
Charles Whiteman	Bruce Groesbeck	Orlando Antelope
John Goggles	Alonzo Moss	Dave Headley
Bruce Groesbeck	Jerome Oldman	John Blackman

1943–44	1945–46	1947–48
Nell Scott	Nell Scott	Nell Scott
Ben Friday	Ben Friday	Ben Friday
Dave Headley	Dave Headley	Scott Dewey
Robert Friday	Scott Dewey	Elk Redman
Charles Whiteman	Elk Redman	Paul Hanway
Scott Dewey	Tom Shakespeare	Issac Bell

1949–50	1951–52	1953–54
Nell Scott	Nell Scott	Ben Friday
Ben Friday	Ben Friday	Bruce Groesbeck
Scott Dewey	Scott Dewey	Joe Duran
Dave Headley	Henry Tyler	Alice Quiver
Henry Tyler	Paul Hanway	Leonard Warren
Steven Duran	Ernest Posey / William Hanway[*]	Ralph Antelope

1955–56	1957–58	1959–60
Nell Scott	Nell Scott	Scott Dewey
Ben Friday	Ben Friday	Steven Duran
Scott Dewey	Scott Dewey	Lloyd Goggles
Henry Tyler	Henry Tyler	Joe Duran
Otto Hungary	Steven Duran	Martin Underwood
Martin Underwood	Lloyd Goggles	Jess Miller

1961–62	1963–64	
Nell Scott	Nell Scott	
Ben Friday	Ben Friday	
Martin Underwood	Jess Miller	
Jess Miller	Lloyd Goggles	
Arnold Headley	Arnold Headley	
Herman J. Moss	Martin Underwood / Eugene Ridgley[*]	

[*]Replacement.

Source: Records of the Office of the Bureau of Indian Affairs, Fort Washakie, Wyo.

was not viewed as legitimately directive—despite the fact that in principle the BIA allowed the council to make some decisions binding on or affecting all members of the tribe. Council members were expected to be attuned to the feelings and attitudes of their constituents and to reflect their views in Business Council policies and programs. Any important matters were expected to be discussed among adults in the community, either informally or in all-tribal meetings (in General Council). Councilmen, then, were conscious of the importance of behaving so as to appear modest and unassuming, generally cooperative and responsive to group consensus, and respectful of the needs and judgments of the elders. Charles Whiteman expressed the nature of Business Council leadership thus: "My people, you Arapahoes elected us as councilmen by your votes and you look upon us to help you and now it is up to you people to do anything you want to with the council members if we should ever make a mistake, and you don't have to be afraid to do whatever you want to do with us, the councilmen." Superintendent Forrest Stone, who transferred to Wind River from the Crow Agency, noted in dismay, "There has not been the usual evidence of courage on the part of the councilmen here . . . in taking responsibility that is to be observed at some other jurisdictions."[19]

There was a short-lived effort to "modernize" the Joint Business Council by instituting a constitution and by-laws that gave the council new powers. In June 1937 Stone named Bruce Groesbeck, Robert Friday, and Shoshones Irene Meade and Lynn St. Clair to a committee to prepare a constitution and by-laws, with the assistance of the superintendent and some of his staff. The committee submitted the draft in April 1938, and after making some changes the Joint Business Council approved the document on September 27. The Arapahoe and Shoshone general councils gave their approval but the BIA informed the tribes' delegation of March 1939 that several provisions were unacceptable. The Bureau suggested revisions and recommended that the delegates approve the revised constitution, but Arapahoe councilman Jerome Oldman insisted that the changes be referred back to the elders. After the delegates' return, the tribes refused to approve the document, but several of its provisions were customarily followed by the joint council all the same. After 1939, the business council of each tribe conducted a November election every two years. The councils appointed judges and clerks for the election. The Arapahoes voted for six Arapahoe councilmen at large and the Shoshones voted for six Shoshone councilmen. When the six winning candidates from each tribe were formally installed in January by the chairmen of the incumbent councils, they comprised the Joint Business Council. The councilmen from each tribe voted for their respective chairmen. The chairman of the Arapahoe Business Council alternated with the Shoshone chairman in presiding over joint council meetings. Meetings were conducted according to parliamentary rules and minutes were recorded. In order to be eligible to run for election or to vote in council elections, an individual had to be an enrolled member of the tribe and twenty-one years of age. The Business Council was authorized to develop and carry out programs to protect Indian tribal customs and religious freedom, guard tribal rights and property, conserve natural resources and direct their use along lines of development for the greatest good, retain tribal lands in tribal ownership, and make recommendations on government programs. Tribal resources were to be divided equally between the two tribes.[20]

Several provisions in the proposed constitution were ignored. First, the constitution stipulated that candidates for office run in a primary election to be held in October and publicly state their qualifications for office. The twelve candidates who won the most votes in the primary were to be placed on the November ballot. This provision (probably suggested by Stone, who opposed the "nomination meetings" where candidates for the November election were generally selected by the elders) was not followed. In the Arapahoe view, persons who sought seats on the council and who spoke on their own behalf demonstrated immodesty and self-centeredness, and thereby revealed their unsuitability for the positions. Second, the draft constitution provided for a tribal referendum in the form of a petition signed by 25 percent of the eligible voters in order to revoke a council decision. The referendum was favored by the BIA as a more "progressive" way of exerting a check on council powers than the traditional intervention of influential elders. The Arapahoes ignored this provision, as well. The tribe's displeasure was keenly felt by the council members, who depended on the goodwill of other Arapahoes for personal economic and social support, as well as political support; the tribe viewed petitions as superfluous. Third, the 1938 document gave the joint council authority to dismiss by a majority vote a council member who missed three consecutive meetings without an acceptable excuse or who was guilty of "misconduct"; the council was empowered to appoint a replacement in such a case or in the event of a council member's death or resignation. This provision, too, was ignored. The occasional councilman who behaved inappropriately by Arapahoe standards was counseled by elders, usually kinsmen or a ceremonial grandfather, or in rare cases was pressured into resigning. A dismissal by the council members themselves would have

been seen as excessively assertive. Council replacements were elected
by their tribe in a special election.

At election time there was no campaigning. Such behavior would
have been frowned upon. Groups of elders often decided that a particular individual showed leadership promise and, after seeking the individual's consent, placed his or her name in nomination at a general council
preceding the election. If the elders had sufficient influence, the candidate's election was virtually assured. Individuals overtly ambitious for a
seat on the Business Council were rare. Such a person might make his
interest known to some elders indirectly, through a friend or relative.
The confidant would then mention to others that the individual "might
be good on council." Frequently Arapahoe leaders would portray their
selection as a draft in response to public pressure. As Mike Goggles put
it, "I haven't worked, myself, to be one of the Arapahoe leaders. The
Arapahoes have chosen me themselves."[21]

The individuals elected to the "new" business council increasingly
tended to be mature men; the elders did not usually serve on the council, as they had done before 1937. When the tribe held meetings to consider Stone's proposals for electoral change, Tom Shakespeare, a youth
by Arapahoe standards, told the superintendent that "the majority of
the younger people think they should leave one member [on the coun-
cil] who is well posted as to present council's actions."[22] Hence, during
1937–40 and 1943–44, Charles Whiteman (in his late sixties) held a
Business Council position. He was rarely vocal in the meetings, and
apparently was elected to "oversee" the actions of the others. By 1945,
council seats were held by people in their late forties and fifties. In fact,
the median age of the 1963–64 councilmen was forty-five, compared
to fifty-six for the 1937–38 councilmen.

It is clear that, although elders did not usually sit on the Business
Council, councilmen held themselves accountable to them. When
the renewal of oil leases was discussed in June 1937, Nell Scott commented, "We are looking out for the older Indians. I don't feel like
signing the lease unless we get a per capita payment through for these
older people in distress." When the Business Council drafted a constitution and by-laws, Jerome Oldman insisted that any changes instigated
by the commissioner's office be submitted to the tribe for the *old
people's* approval: "Present it back to the old people first."[23]

The elders carefully monitored the actions of the "younger generation," made more confident by the increased responsibility and opportunities offered by the BIA. They publicly expressed concern that
"the younger generation are getting a long foot now," that young
Arapahoes would take on more responsibility and authority than was

appropriate for their stage in life. In 1940 a councilman who had been singled out for praise by the superintendent was frequently seen drinking at tribal ceremonies and behaving in a rowdy and pugnacious manner toward other Arapahoes. Although he was chastised by some elders, he made no gesture of atonement toward those he had offended. In fact, another councilman insisted that he had been threatened by the man in question. With the encouragement of constituents, the offended councilman brought his charges before the Joint Business Council and urged the members to oust the troublemaker from his council seat. The Shoshone Business Council, however, was reluctant to vote to oust an Arapahoe, and Superintendent Stone resisted the dismissal of this particular councilman, so he was retained. But at the next election the man lost his council seat. Despite years of service on several previous councils, he had lost the elders' confidence. Councilmen could not retain their positions if they went against group sentiment. Two members of the 1935–36 council had spoken in favor of accepting the IRA. According to Stone, these "schoolboys" subsequently were "discredited and thrown in the discard as councilmen." Nell Scott commented about one of these men: "When they voted for him he only got three or four votes. . . . He was a regular sucker. . . . He was a smart man but he was too smart. He was for the government."[24]

Similar inattention to the people's expectations caused Nell Scott's council seat to be briefly in jeopardy. In 1930 she started proceedings to rectify the unauthorized action of agency personnel in removing her from the Shoshone rolls when she was a child. She charged that the action had been part of the agency staff's attempts to suppress her mother's criticisms of agency management. In 1939 the Shoshones were awarded a sum of money in the settlement of a suit against the United States, and at that time local newspapers publicized Scott's long-standing appeal to the Shoshone General Council for transferral to the Shoshone rolls—an appeal that had been denied. The publicity precipitated an effort on the part of Arapahoe councilmen—some of whom resented her rise to the position of main spokesperson in meetings with Washington officials—to remove her from the council.

At a General Council meeting held July 30, 1939, the "chairman of the day," Andrew Brown, charged that Scott "made a mistake by putting in an application to enroll with the Shoshone tribe and the Arapahoe Indians wants to get her off the council on account of this mistake and [because] she was going to quit the Arapahoe tribe." The General Council decided to circulate a petition to remove her and submit the document to the Arapahoe Business Council. In a Business Council meeting on August 8, Stone directed the council to vote on the matter, and five councilmen voted to remove her, citing three reasons: (1) "We know that she is Arapahoe, but she claims to be a Shoshone woman, and tried to get on the rolls of the Shoshone tribe"; (2) "We know the reason she wanted to get on the Shoshone rolls is because of the money involved"; (3) "The Arapahoe people feel that under the circumstances they cannot depend on her and ask that she be dropped from the Arapahoe council, but still remain on the Arapahoe roll." At Stone's urging the council allowed her thirty days to appeal to the tribe before the removal became official.

The attack on Scott was skillfully led by Robert Friday (at times jokingly referred to as Nell Scott's "campaign manager"), who announced at the General Council that Scott was not loyal to the Arapahoes and that her sympathies were with the Shoshones.

> Friday: I can prove that Shoshones have told me that Mrs. Scott said if she was elected to the council she would not help the Arapahoes but would help the Shoshones.
> Scott: That is a lie. Bring that Shoshone to me. . . . My work disproves any of that. Why, Andrew Brown, himself, and others have come to me, and I have taken things up with the office for them. . . . I say my work shows I have worked for the Arapahoes. I also heard, Robert, that you told Gilbert Day and Robert Harris that I was a white woman and should be put off, and now is your chance, and you are going to try to put me off.

Friday's attack was facilitated by Scott's lifestyle, which approximated that of the rural white population. She and her husband, for example, did not participate extensively in the giveaway custom. Friday charged, "Not only myself, but most all of my people says it appears that Nellie Scott is trying to get on the Shoshone rolls because of the money involved and very likely she wants to get her share of it. Now in the Arapahoes' minds, they think this is dangerous to the Arapahoes. They feel that in the future she might be bought, and they can't depend on her today."

Charles Whiteman spoke: "I want to say that I don't want Mrs. Scott to feel hurt about it, but it is in the people's minds that she tried to desert her people. She should have come and asked her people if she could get enrolled with the Shoshones; that would have been the sportsman-like way. But she didn't. She tried to desert her people without their knowledge and it looks very bad." And Friday charged, "My people feel that it would have been all right if she wanted to enroll with the Shoshones, if she had told them. Maybe they would have said all right for her to go on, or they might say for her to resign, but she didn't give her people any consideration whatever."

Scott's position was shaken by the controversy, but her aggressive defense in the face of her hostile colleagues reinforced people's perception of her as a formidable advocate, and she did devote much time to pursuing the grievances of individuals against the Bureau of Indian Affairs. Even her fellow council member Jerome Oldman had to admit, "I think a lot of her, but through her mistake there is too much pressure from the people and we are trying to put her off, but I know from time to time I will go to her for advice."

After the Business Council meeting, a petition was circulated on her behalf and many of the adult Arapahoes signed. And so she was able to ride out the crisis. She made no more "mistakes." She acted as the tribe's most assertive spokesperson in several clashes with the federal government, and she attended tribal celebrations.[25]

Scott was able to retaliate against Friday in later years, when she charged that he benefited personally from a council position. Friday, while a member of a tribal delegation to Washington, was given a set of false teeth at federal expense. Commenting on the incident several years later, Scott said that at first she had not intended to use the false-teeth issue to discredit Friday: "He said, 'Don't tell nobody.' I said, 'I'm not a stool pigeon.'" But at a General Council meeting some time after the delegation's return, Friday again tried to discredit Scott, saying that her background and lifestyle made her unpredictable and unreliable. It was then that she began to use the incident in Washington as a means of casting doubt on Friday's selflessness and his commitment to tribal goals:

> He got up and read me off about . . . [how] I didn't know the Indian ways, and all that stuff. I laid him down then. I told them, "All right now. You people paid us fare to go back there. Got him a set of false teeth, sixty-five-dollar purchase order." So I said Mr. Friday had done nothing to help the tribe. I was the guy that done all the talking, going here and going there, all by myself, while he was looking for teeth. . . . He got up and called me a white woman; he called me everything in General Council down at [Lower] Arapahoe, see. And the chairman of the day come over and whispered to me, "Nell," he said, "he's talking after you being a white woman, you didn't know Indian ways and that we ought not consider you on the council because you's a white woman and you've never been among the Indians." . . . And I said, "Fine. I've got him now."[26]

Nell Scott had sufficient perceptiveness and oratorical skill to manipulate the Arapahoes' impressions of an individual's degree of conformity to their behavioral ideals. She also was aggressive and fearless in personal confrontations. Her assertiveness tended to sway the timid or undecided toward her point of view.

After World War II, several veterans who were active in community projects and attentive to the elders were singled out to serve on the Business Council. To the Arapahoes, success in the military service indicated both supernatural protection and ability to get along and stand up for oneself in white society. In the 1950s a few veterans between the ages of thirty and forty were elected along with older councilmen: Henry Tyler (son of Henry Lee Tyler), Lloyd Goggles (son of John Goggles), and Martin Underwood. In the 1960s other former servicemen attained council positions. Military service increasingly began to be a major asset to an individual who sought to convince other Arapahoes of his potential as an advocate in dealings with whites. By the 1963-64 term, four of the six council members were veterans.

The new breed of councilman had to behave in ways that reaffirmed Arapahoe ideals and expectations of leadership. They also used their skills in interacting with white society to broaden their authority. Councilmen assumed responsibility for aiding individuals who needed assistance in dealing with local BIA personnel and other whites. Alonzo Moss expressed the view that the Arapahoes expected their councilmen to act as advisers and counselors: "They want advice from time to time, as to what they should [do] in their personal affairs as [well as] tribal affairs." Bruce Groesbeck concurred: "There are certain things that the council must look into—two or three minor things, little petty things, or individual little grievances that may come up among the people or among ourselves or between the councils or Indian Service officials." The councilmen also sought to obtain more jobs for Arapahoes on several federal work projects (WPA, CCC) by opposing the federal policy of hiring large numbers of "foreign" Indians for these jobs. In interceding with local federal agents and in aiding people with their personal business, councilmen made reputations for themselves as effective advocates.[27] The new councilmen's greatest success, however, came in a series of victories in clashes with federal officials in Washington.

"The Song of the Reservation, 'Can't Get It'": Economic Problems and Political Strategies

During the 1937-64 era, the new council established itself as an effective advocate by cooperating with the Shoshone Business Council in a series of successful attempts to thwart the implementation of unpopular federal policies, to defeat Indian Bureau efforts to retain control over the tribes' income, and to obtain redress for past wrongs. As a result of a successful lawsuit brought by the Shoshones against the United States to recover damages for the settlement of the Arapahoe tribe at Wind River, the federal government recognized joint Arapahoe-Shoshone rights to reservation resources. The joint council also was able to force full production of oil wells on tribal land, to obtain the tribes' income (largely from leases and royalties) in per capita payments, to augment reservation acreage, and to forestall termination proceedings in the 1950s. The era culminated in another successful legal suit, this time filed by the Arapahoes and Cheyennes against the United States for the occupation of the tribes' lands in Colorado.

During Commissioner John Collier's term of office (1933–45), somewhat more lenient policies toward Indian tribal governments were instituted. As Robert Friday put it, "We might say that we have a slack rope, that we can go a little further. Things seem to be moving and giving the Indians more rights and voice in their own matters."[28] Nonetheless, the gains made by the Wind River tribes were hard-won. The Arapahoe Business Council's achievements in the face of BIA opposition validated the councilmen's reputations for mastery of the social skills necessary to deal effectively with whites. And the council's success at wresting control of tribal resources from the BIA not only improved living conditions at Wind River, but also placed at the council's disposal funds that helped its members to mobilize and retain support.

Maverick Springs

The first problem faced by the council was the renewal of leases in the Maverick Springs oil field, an explosive issue on the reservation. The tribes were incensed because earlier lessees had capped the wells and produced no oil. Thus the tribes had only the income from the lease and no royalties from production. Henry Lee Tyler, in a well-received speech, reviewed the issue at a General Council meeting in 1937: "Our old Indians have been living in expectation. They have been expecting this money for the leases all these years and they are still waiting, and if these leases expire I wish to lease to some company willing to come in here who will produce and market this oil so that the Indians can have the money as soon as possible. . . . I believe this subject has been the most talked about of any subject on the reservation. I do not know about the Shoshones but I know among the Arapahoes this subject comes up whenever there is a little gathering." Shoshone councilman Charles (Dee) Driskell pointed out in the same meeting that the oil left to seep from the abandoned wells meant a loss of several thousand dollars a year. The council charged that the federal government had clearly failed to protect the interests of the Indians, and they sent a protest resolution to the secretary of the interior. Then on March 9 the Joint Business Council approved and forwarded a resolution demanding that the leases not be renewed, that the price set for oil on the reservation be equal to prices for oil off the reservation, and that leases be subject to cancellation if lessees failed to produce.[29]

The council sent several delegations to Washington to lodge further protests, and the Federated Civic Club of Lander sent Harold Del Monte to assist the council members. Nell Scott and Robert Friday, along with two Shoshones, Robert Harris and Gilbert Day, sought to convince officials in August 1937 that the Maverick Springs oil should be produced and marketed, but the Indian Office took no action. On August 19 Nell Scott commented to the *Wyoming State Journal*:

> We were getting nowhere. We were called in to a session of heads of departments, not even introduced to them so that we knew who they were or what they represented, and told to listen to the discussions they had relative to the Maverick oil field. From these talks we soon learned that there was little that could be done, as it appeared that everything was against us. It was finally agreed that they would hear what Mr. Del Monte had to say through the representation of the Indian Affairs Department that he represented the Indians and had facts and figures to lay before them. We found Mr. Del Monte of great assistance. . . . Mr. Del Monte never stopped, was active night and day and saw people we could not even approach, gaining interviews and conferences.

The BIA, Del Monte reported, "while lukewarm at first, became convinced that the Indians had been dealt with unfairly when they faced up with the figures that showed that vast quantities of black oil had been marketed in this trade area from fields brought in from new wells drilled since the Maverick Springs field had been bottled up twenty years ago." He predicted that the fields would be opened to production.[30]

Pressure from constituents intensified until in 1938 Nell Scott informed Superintendent Stone that the people had told the council there was to be "no compromise" on the Maverick Springs issue. Robert Friday and Gilbert Day were selected to attend a hearing on January 10, 1938, in Washington on the Maverick Springs matter. They advised Secretary of the Interior Harold Ickes that the future effectiveness of the council could very well ride on the outcome: "These present leases have done nothing but ferment trouble between our people and also between our people and . . . the government and the white race. As strong leaders have developed from our Indians, they have thrown their weight against this problem, with the result that when they failed, their own people have suspicioned them of being bought off. There are a number of 'fallen leaders' among both tribes today that will never be able to hold positions of respect and leadership again on this account. We feel that *we are faced with the same hazard ourselves,* if your decision is unfavorable."[31]

The meeting, attended by oil company representatives and their attorneys, federal officials, and Harold Del Monte, resulted only in a visit by Oscar Chapman, assistant secretary of the interior, to the reservation to meet with the tribes. The oil companies had attempted to convince Chapman and the tribal representatives that the Maverick Springs oil would not bring a good price and that the tribes would make more money from a few dollars' increase per acre in the lease. The tribal representatives were not convinced, and were further outraged by the revelation that the original lessees had sold their interest to a national corporation, a transaction amounting to almost one million dollars—none of which was received by the Indians. Nell Scott recalled, "Now, the assistant secretary of the interior, Oscar L. Chapman, fought us like a tiger. Now he came out here just before we went up to Washington, D.C., and met with the whole tribes down here in the gym and said there was no market for the oil, had sulfur and all that stuff, and he would not recommend it open. So we took a trip out to the field and he had the same attitude."[32]

In February 1939 the joint council sent Nell Scott, Robert Friday, Bruce Groesbeck, Jerome Oldman, and five Shoshones back to Washington to resume the struggle.[33] The 1939 delegation was successful, and the opening of these fields eventually was to bring the tribes a sizable increase in income from oil royalties. The delegates succeeded also in convincing their constituents that they could win battles the old council could not. And in obtaining a $40 per capita payment that year, they further reinforced the image of the new council as an effective advocate for the Indian people. But the pressure on the council to accomplish tangible economic gains did not abate.

The Land-Buying Program

In 1927 the Shoshone tribe won congressional consent to file a claim for damages against the United States, citing the violation of the Treaty of July 3, 1868. By the terms of this treaty, the Eastern Shoshones relinquished a reservation of 44,672,000 acres, located in what are now the states of Colorado, Utah, Idaho, and Wyoming, in return for the United States' pledge that the Shoshones would have exclusive occupancy of a 3,054,182-acre reservation in Wyoming.[34] But in 1878, without the formal consent of the Shoshones, the commissioner of Indian affairs allowed the Northern Arapahoes to settle permanently at the Shoshone Agency. Despite repeated Shoshone protests, the Arapahoes shared in the Shoshones' annuities, in payments from the land cessions of 1896 and 1905, and in the allotment of lands. In fact, the two tribes were treated by the government as equal beneficiaries of reservation resources.

In 1937 the Shoshones' attorney, George Tunison, won the suit and the Eastern Shoshones were awarded $4,408,444 in damages. The decision relieved the Arapahoes' anxiety about their rights on the reservation. They had long smarted under Shoshone accusations of trespass. Arapahoe spokesmen tried from time to time to justify the tribe's position at the Shoshone Agency by pointing out that the Arapahoes had shared their rations and annuities with the Shoshones after the Shoshones' right to receive provisions had run out. The settlement of the suit forced the Shoshones at last to recognize the Arapahoes' title to Wind River. In fact, at this time the reservation's name was officially changed— the Shoshone Agency was now known as the Wind River Agency.[35]

By an act of July 27, 1939, the judgment funds and $155,080.61 in accrued interest—after attorneys' fees, $4,191,132.83—were to be distributed in this fashion: $1 million to purchase land; a payment of $2,450 ($100 in cash and $1,350 [$500 to each minor] in credit to be applied to the purchase of land, housing, equipment, seed, livestock, or support for the aged and incapacitated, and $1,000 to the individual account of each Shoshone for purposes approved by the secretary of the interior); $125,000 for a loan fund; the remainder to capital reserve funds to be used with the consent of the secretary of the interior. Reservation lands were placed in trust for both tribes and Shoshone funds used for the purchase of land were to be reimbursed from joint funds of the Shoshones and Arapahoes at 4 percent interest per year to the Shoshones.[36]

Thereafter, by purchase and by restoration of ceded lands, the reservation acreage was increased. In 1939 the Arapahoes were pressured by the Indian Office to borrow $500,000 from the Shoshones at annual interest of 4 percent, in order to participate along with the Shoshones in the purchase of lands then owned by non-Indians. On April 17, 1940, the secretary of the interior signed an order of restoration that returned approximately 1.25 million acres in the ceded portion to joint tribal ownership. These developments in land acquisition eventually enhanced the status of both the Shoshone and the Arapahoe business councils, though at first the land-purchase program was unpopular among members of both tribes.

The major land purchase engineered by the BIA was that of the Padlock Ranch and other properties adjacent to and within the northeastern corner of the reservation. Both tribes contributed half of the purchase price, the Arapahoes borrowing the necessary funds from the Shoshones. The Shoshones resented being pressured into helping the Arapahoes and were angry because they had received so little cash from the settlement of their claim. The Arapahoes were not enthusiastic about taking on such a large debt, or about BIA plans to establish a ranching cooperative on the newly acquired Padlock lands. The joint council members were particularly resentful of coercive tactics used by BIA personnel to pressure them into approving the purchase of particular tracts of lands. Nell Scott described the BIA efforts as "a knife held over our heads." The purchase price for all land was determined by government appraisers. Scott related the council's frustration thus: "Now we had to go through all this trouble—we had to meet here and there about what we was paying too much for the land. It didn't do no good to say, 'We won't.' They [the BIA] took the appraiser's word."[37]

As a means of generating income for the Arapahoes, the Indian Bureau proposed to help the tribe to develop a cattle ranch. Although the Shoshones were to have joint ownership of the land occupied by the ranch, the cattle enterprise was to be owned by the Arapahoes and ranch profits were to go only to them. When Arapahoe councilmen resisted the proposal, government officials suggested that their cooperation might improve the chances for a per capita payment. When the subject of the ranch was raised in a General Council meeting, a councilman declared that acceptance of the BIA plan might result in "a benefit for the old people"; he urged, "We should take this grant and buy the cattle so we can get the per capita payment." Government officials also reminded the Arapahoes that they were now the poor relations of the Shoshones, with a bleak economic future unless they cooperated with the BIA advisers. After requesting that several elders participate in the meeting, the Business Council voted to approve the purchase of the ranchland and properties in August 1940, and in November the Arapahoe General Council gave its authorization.[38]

The ranch properties were purchased in 1940, and in the following year the Joint Business Council assigned to the Arapahoe tribe irrigated farmlands and ranch base properties and issued grazing permits, for which the Arapahoes were to pay the standard reservation fees. The commissioner advanced $290,000 in federal rehabilitation funds under a trust agreement for the purchase of livestock and equipment and to pay the first year's operating expenses. The BIA appointed a white manager, and the Arapahoe Ranch began operations in 1941 with 4,939 head of cattle. By 1947 the Arapahoe tribe had repaid the Shoshones the money it had borrowed to buy the land. Even though the ranch had originally been started only under pressure from the BIA, the Arapahoe Business Council could take credit for authorizing a venture that was clearly successful. The ranch became a source of pride to the Arapahoes, and its success bolstered the tribe's esteem both within reservation society and in the local non-Indian community. Within a few years the herd had doubled and was profitable enough to pay a regular dividend to each enrolled Arapahoe (see Table 6). On matters of common interest, white ranchers in the area have had to consult with the Arapahoes on the ranch board of trustees. The enterprise also figures importantly in ranching and farming operations on the reservation itself. The Shoshone cattlemen, who dominated the livestock business before the establishment of the Arapahoe Ranch, had to cooperate (and at times compete) with the ranch. [39]

The Arapahoe Business Council seized on the opportunity presented by the ranch enterprise to expand the scope of its authority and press for greater self-determination. Its success in wresting control of the ranch from the BIA bolstered its influence with its constituents. When the ranch began operations, the Indian Bureau viewed the enterprise as a means of improving the economic position of the Arapahoe tribe. Officials felt that the ranch should be operated with maximum efficiency so that profits would be as great as possible. The first manager appointed by the BIA apparently felt that maximum efficiency required white ranch hands. Angered at seeing the jobs on their own ranch go to whites, the Arapahoe Business Council began to pressure the BIA to relinquish control of the ranch to the tribe.

In 1941 an Arapahoe delegation to Washington persuaded officials to permit the Arapahoe council to act as trustees of the ranch, but to the councilmen's indignation, their decisions were consistently overruled by the manager and the commissioner. The central conflict continued to be the manager's refusal to hire Arapahoes, who he was convinced were unreliable. Seven more years passed before the council members, with the help of their attorney, finally succeeded in obtaining the authority to select the manager and make policy decisions. The 1951 council initiated a policy of giving preference to applicants for the manager's position who had previously worked successfully with Indians. In 1954 the Arapahoe Business Council transferred the trusteeship to a board of three Arapahoe trustees, whom they selected. By 1965, under the management of the trustees, the ranch, consisting of 343,000 acres of range and 4,500 acres of irrigated land, was making

Table 6
Per capita payments and ranch payments
received by each enrolled Arapahoe, 1947–64

Year	Per capita payments	Ranch payments	Total
1947	$ 361	$ 35.00	$ 396.00
1948	285	100.00	385.00
1949	425	148.00	573.00
1950	239	82.00	321.00
1951	314	121.00	435.00
1952	364	164.00	528.00
1953	357	0.00	357.00
1954	1,320	unrecorded	1,320.00
1955	705	unrecorded	705.00
1956	1,106	25.00	1,131.00
1957	342	40.00	382.00
1958	602	50.00	652.00
1959	540	59.96	599.96
1960	552	41.70	593.70
1961	552	64.00	616.00
1962	612	42.00	654.00
1963	540	42.00	582.00
1964	1,488	0.00	1,488.00

Source: Records of the Office of the Bureau of Indian Affairs, Fort Washakie, Wyo.

a sizable profit each year and employed predominantly Arapahoe workers.[40]

Although both the BIA and the Arapahoe tribe were eager for the ranch to make a profit, they did not agree on its ultimate purpose. Government officials had hoped that it would provide training or at least an example of good management techniques for Arapahoes interested in starting individually owned and operated farms and ranches. The Arapahoes viewed the ranch as a communal effort. It is clear from the statements of Arapahoes in General Council meetings in the early 1940s that those who supported the enterprise viewed the ranch as one more way in which the Arapahoes pooled their resources and shared with each other. One speaker in a General Council meeting in 1940 compared the ranch to earlier communally organized work groups: "You Arapahoe people are noted for your unity. Unity to work. In history I can look back anytime in the line of agriculture.

When you were interested, fifteen or twenty or thirty of you would get together with your teams, your farm machinery or equipment. . . . In three days the ground was plowed and then seeded; . . . you went from place to place as a community band working hand in hand for each other." Members of the tribe consistently opposed the government's efforts to help individuals to begin ranches; they viewed such attempts to aid individual enterprise as a threat to tribal unity. In 1948, when Shoshone ranchers urged the joint council to reduce the amount of range assigned to the Arapahoe Ranch, so that individual Indian ranchers of both tribes could expand or begin operations, an Arapahoe leader stated the consensus of the tribe that individual advancement would result in socially disruptive economic differentials within Arapahoe society. He argued, "If we have to break up the ranch, the Arapahoe [tribe] will lose. I am as much in favor as anyone of helping the Arapahoe stockmen. . . . I am bringing that up to point out that if everyone is allowed to expand to the extent that they will be economically [well] situated, only a few will survive. The rest will have to go somewhere else." And in 1951, despite BIA urgings that the ranch dividend should be paid in one large sum to be used as capital by individuals who wished to improve their farms, the Arapahoe Business Council insisted that the money be paid in small installments throughout the year, so that families could use it to meet subsistence needs.[41]

In short, the Arapahoe Business Council's management of the ranch served to implement economic policies that perpetuated the leveling of economic differentials among the tribe's members and promoted the distribution of tribal resources as widely as possible within the Arapahoe community. In Arapahoe eyes the success of the ranch helped to justify the merits of these economic policies, and bolstered the status of the councilmen as well.

Per Capita Payments

When the new council took office, members of both tribes clamored for the distribution of tribal income in the form of per capita payments. The BIA ignored their demands. As Gilbert Day, Shoshone councilman, put it, "We Indians ask for money, beg for money, send telegrams asking for money, and can't get it; even then the tribe can't get it. It is getting to be the song of the reservation, 'Can't Get It.'"[42]

Pressure from constituents was particularly intense because of the people's awareness of their low standard of living and of poor health conditions on the reservation. As one Shoshone, John Trehero, told the joint council, "We find that our people have an awful heavy load. They are down somewhere in the ditch, and they can't lift the load. I was talking to an Indian the other day, and while he was talking he was quivering, just shaking, and he says, 'My friend, I do not know what I am going to do.' Still they say we have lots of money on this reservation. Who can we go to for help? It does not seem right that we should not be as well off as we used to be because we have smarter men on the council now." The superintendent reported that in 1943, 77 percent of the Indian families had an average income of less than $1,000 per year. This figure represented an improvement over previous years but stood in sharp contrast to the apparent prosperity of neighboring non-Indians, many of whom were farming or running stock on leased reservation lands. In the winter of 1940 a BIA survey of 218 Arapahoe homes found that most Arapahoe households, ranging in size from one to ten persons, lived in either one-room log houses (sixty-nine households) or tents (sixty-two households). A few families lived in larger log or frame houses. The water supply came from irrigation ditches or the river, into which flowed untreated sewage. Health problems were immense, and it was not until 1946 that a concentrated effort was made to eradicate disease. In that year the joint council passed an ordinance requiring any person thought to be suffering from a communicable disease to undergo treatment.[43] Nell Scott, always adept at devising a joke at the expense of whites, gave this account of some of the difficulties encountered in the effort to control disease, as well as to counter local discrimination against Indians:

> The Indians, there was one time that they couldn't eat in restaurants. They couldn't go in anyplace in the town—any public place to use. So Mr. Stone and I met with the commissioners in Riverton. And Riverton seemed to me the worst town. Lander did not treat the Indians as bad as Riverton did. So we met with them and they said we had so much disease here, the white people wouldn't eat with them in the restaurants. These people that had stores. We had a letter from a Dr. Hunt that was "governor" there and it said if we didn't clean our reservation up he'd have to ask us to stay here—put a ban on us going across. So we had then a meeting. Dr. Wilson of Denver came and met with us and said for us to put in a communicable disease code, which we did. And we cleaned up the reservation. We had a blood test and we had an X ray for TB. We had all of that to go through. And believe me, it was a hard thing to go through. We was criticized by everybody, outside of the towns. So I said after we had cleaned up, "Now if the white people comes over, they'll have to have a health certificate to show *they're* all clean!"[44]

Aggravating the problem was a staggering increase in population. Although the reservation death rate from tuberculosis and pneumonia was many times higher than that of Wyoming or the United States, the rate of population growth was high. Table 7 indicates the number of births per 1,000 population, the birth rate corrected for infant mortality, and the actual rate of population increase for 1937—43. In 1936, the Arapahoe population on the reservation was 1,128; in 1937, 1,164; in 1943, 1,307; and in 1953, 1,699 (see Figure 4). (The Shoshones increased from 1,133 in 1936 to 1,286 in 1953.) The council was under great pressure to get tribal income distributed in per capita payments, so that their constituents could support their growing families.

The Bureau of Indian Affairs still had not agreed to a per capita payment by 1945. The council angrily refused to charge fees to traders on the reservation, since the fees would be deposited in the U.S. Treasury, along with the other joint tribal funds, which were inaccessible to the tribe's members without government consent.[45] They requested aid from local whites and from elected officials of the state of Wyoming. Then in March 1947, Nell Scott, Ben Friday, Scott Dewey, Paul Hanway, Ike Bell, and Elk Redman (the Arapahoe Business Council members) and Shoshone councilmen Robert Harris, Maud Clairmont, and Reuben Martel, with attorneys George Tunison and Kenneth

Table 7

Crude birth rate, birth rate corrected for infant mortality,
and rate of population increase, Wind River Reservation, 1937–43
(per 1,000 population)

| Year | U.S. birth rate | Wind River Reservation | | |
		Crude birth rate	Births minus infant deaths	Rate of population increase
1937	16.9	38.0	30.4	- 2
1938	17.5	46.8	40.8	+17
1939	17.6	42.8	34.0	+15
1940	17.6	46.4	37.4	+15
1941	18.6	45.2	38.3	+16
1942	19.5	36.8	31.5	+12
1943	—	42.4	34.6	+20

Source: Superintendent's Annual Report to Commissioner of Indian Affairs, 1944, p. 61, Bureau of Indian Affairs, Fort Washakie, Wyo.

Simmons, went to Washington. The BIA was still insisting that tribal funds be held in trust and spent only with BIA approval. The council delegates were determined to get two-thirds of their money in semi-annual payments to each enrolled member of each tribe. Congressman Frank Barrett of Wyoming testified on behalf of the tribes, which at that time had $1,040,396.75 in trust in their joint account. Barrett introduced a bill providing for division of joint funds, with the funds of each tribe to be managed separately; the retention of one-third of the joint funds in trust under BIA control; and the distribution of the remainder in per capita payments.

Nell Scott was the main spokesperson for both tribes, and she set out to convince the House Subcommittee on Indian Affairs of her tribe's dire need. She informed the committee that there was an acute shortage of food, clothing, and fuel among the Arapahoes, and that many needy persons were ineligible for relief from the state. Scott's testimony presented a dramatic picture of tribespeople crowded together in tents, "sleeping on gunny sacks" or old coats. Schoolchildren were known to "faint in the schoolroom for want of food." Ben Friday and Scott Dewey spoke briefly in support of Nell Scott's account of Arapahoe poverty. Scott also testified that the problems of her tribe were in large measure due to the ineptitude of BIA officials who were unable or unwilling to respond to the Indians' plight: "We are over-burdened with regulations. We almost have to go for a regulation there in order to breathe. The Arapahoe people felt that if they had to go under the regulations and the rules of the Indian Department, it would be far better for them to turn this money down. We are not here asking for sympathy of you gentlemen; we are asking for the money to be paid out as rightfully is due us. . . . We have no help in any way. We wonder who is starving the Indians. It is the Indian Office, or the government itself that is starving the American Indian." She reminded the congressmen of the sacrifice and contribution of the Indian men who fought for the United States during World War II: "Our boys fought for freedom, they fought for democracy, and yet when they come home they find their parents starving or half starved."

In her attack on Indian Bureau policy on the use of tribal funds, she employed a series of powerful visual images that portrayed the BIA officials as ineffectual and even a hindrance in efforts to cope with reservation problems. Her testimony was aggressive, yet tempered by wit; she put opponents on the defensive without arousing overt antagonism in members of Congress:

> Mr. Tunison talked about our population. Our Arapahoe population is 1,395, but if we do not get relief, we probably will not have that many. Of course, it

is coming spring now, and they can get out and eat prairie dogs or something similar to that. But we are asking you to support our bill. We have drafted this bill with our congressmen, and we drafted it, as I said before, with the Arapahoe people. They have had a little money from the Padlock ranch, but we have had to go for it to the Indian Service. The Arapahoe people were told last year by the Indian Service to plow the lands so they could do farming. We did; we [the council] granted them loans, and by the time the loans came in for the Indians to buy their seed, it was in August. If you gentlemen can farm in August out in Wyoming, we will have you come out there. . . . If we get our money, the Indians can buy their own seed. They can go along and do not have to wait for this red tape to be taken off their neck, and the shackles off their legs, to go and buy some seed. We feel that if we are not capable now of handling our money, I want to ask you congressmen when shall we ever be able to handle our own money and spend it to our advantage. . . . The Indian Office officials sit there with roses on their desks, they do not know what the Indian has in his house, and they will never know until they go out there. . . . If these regulations were taken from the Indians' necks so they could survive, they could go along very nicely. I do not think the Indians will spend their money as foolishly as the Indian Office has spent its money. . . . In the past they have had nothing to look forward to except pen and ink in the Indian Office. That is all we have had to look forward to in the Indian Office.

A Shoshone delegate, Maud Clairmont, embellished the attack on the BIA, particularly its policy of issuing Shoshones purchase orders rather than cash from the claim settlement: "The purchase order was a very bad thing among the Indians because they were set up at a definite amount to be spent at some definite place. When you bought your article, sometimes it was not the exact amount, so then you had to buy something else to supplement it to fill out that purchase order, something that you probably would never have bought otherwise. . . . It took all of their initiative away from them." She pointed out that many of the unwanted items were eventually sold at less than cost to local whites.[46]

Acting Commissioner William Zimmerman argued against the proposed per capita payment: "To require the payment without any regard to what the income might be, and also to what other uses might be made of it, seems to me undesirable from the standpoint of a prudent trustee." He also commented that the delegates exaggerated the severity of economic conditions on the reservation, and suggested that per capita payments would be foolishly spent. The payments were authorized by Congress in May 1947 but limited to a five-year period, after which the tribes' conduct would be evaluated to determine whether or not they should be continued.[47]

In the months before Congress was to reconsider the issue, the tribes and their allies gathered evidence to support their case. The Joint Business Council prepared a report to the secretary of the interior in 1951 which included affidavits from more than sixty local white businessmen, testifying that Indians spent their money wisely. (Of course, the per capita payments bolstered the local economy.) According to Nell Scott, a BIA representative who was sent during the time the affidavits were being taken was determined to produce a report critical of the tribes:

> We was on trial for five years. When the five years was up, then we had to go after it. We had pro and con. . . . They sent that old devil down from Billings [the BIA area office]. . . . He didn't want to have any of us go with him, see, so the superintendent said, "Well, the tribe, the council, that's who nominated these two [Scott and Clairmont] to go with you. . . ." We went out there. Lord have mercy! He didn't want us to go. Everywhere they treated him like a dog. . . . Oh, he was an old devil. He was bound that we wasn't going to go with him, in order to make it hard. . . . And he run off in the briar pit down here by Ethete. Run into the briar pit. He was trying to scare the hell out of us. And [he] put the heat on! Said, "Are you comfortable?" "Oh, yes," Maud said. We was cooking! Our feet was just aburning. So pretty soon he got pretty hot. He said, "I wonder if that heat is on?" "I don't know," I said. "Why, it is!" he said. "Why didn't you girls tell me?" I said, "We didn't feel it." We did. Oh, we was burning up. He just didn't want us to go with him, see. We always stood back. We didn't go to the door with him 'cause they were always so nasty to him. Some of them was real nasty to him, you know, [he was] seeing how we spent our money. . . . So Maud took her own car the next day![48]

Backing for the extension of per capita payments was particularly strong from Wyoming's Department of Public Welfare, which saw the payments as a means to relieve the state of the burden of relief to needy Indians. The department's report noted that in 1940 all but ten Arapahoe families were on relief or relief labor and that many were living in tents, wearing "rags" and using old coats as bedding. Between 1947 and 1951, however, the per capita payments built thirty-seven new homes at Ethete and fifty at Lower Arapahoe, and 162 families on the reservation had electricity installed. By 1951 only five families were on relief. Summer nomadism to obtain wage work was no longer necessary, and Arapahoes moved onto their allotments and lived there all the year.

During the struggle for an extension of the per capita payments, the Business Council was particularly alert to potential aid from the Wyoming congressional delegation. The council met in the fall of 1950 to plan strategy with Congressman William H. Harrison, a member of the Committee on Interior and Insular Affairs. They also enlisted the aid of the Shoshones' attorney, George Tunison, and the Arapahoes' attorney, Kenneth Simmons. When the Wyoming congressional delegation sponsored legislation to extend the per capita payments, Secretary Oscar Chapman's office told the Committee on Interior and Insular Affairs that there was no assurance that the tribes' income would continue and that, despite the good reports about the tribes' use of their money, the "unearned income" might have an adverse effect on attitudes toward social responsibility and parental obligation. He also attempted to introduce a provision in a subsequent bill (H.R. 4636) that would have required the tribes, in return for their per capita payments, to pay one-third of the cost of BIA services on the reservation, and would eventually have withdrawn federal assistance altogether (if possible, by 1954). Tunison appeared at the congressional hearing on July 23, 1951, and he and Harrison succeeded in having the payments extended. An act of August 30, 1951, provided that the semiannual payments were to be made for an additional five years and that the tribal income from sources other than oil royalties was also to be distributed in this fashion.[49]

With the help of attorneys and the Wyoming congressional delegation, the Joint Business Council continued to press for an increase in the per capita payment. In 1953, with the endorsement of the council, Congressman Harrison sponsored a bill to increase the proportion of tribal income distributed to members of the tribe to 80 percent. In hearings before the Committee on Interior and Insular Affairs on March 18 and April 1, the BIA and the Department of the Interior opposed the increase. Per capita payments, they insisted, should be made contingent on termination of federal assistance to the tribes. The average annual income per person at Wind River was $1,200, "higher than usual for reservations." The Indian Bureau representatives met with the council in the fall of 1952 but failed to secure any cooperation in the effort to lessen federal responsibility. Congressman Harrison argued that the tribes already contributed 20 percent of the agency's operating costs (primarily in expenses for law enforcement, agricultural and industrial assistance, administration of trust lands, and property maintenance) yet exercised no control over policy or personnel. And he pointed out to the other committee members that the United States was paying 4 percent interest on the funds deposited in the Treasury, an expenditure that would be reduced if more of the tribes' income were released to them. With the assistance of Frank Barrett, who had become a senator, Harrison's bill was enacted into law on July 17, 1953.[50]

Two years later, on August 9, 1955, Congress enacted legislation that provided for quarterly per capita payments, and thus the per capita payments became a more regular source of subsistence income. The Business Council then directed its efforts toward preventing the secretary of the interior from exercising liens on the per capita money of individuals without the council's consent. Relying particularly on attorneys Marvin Sonosky (employed by the Shoshone tribe) and Glenn Wilkinson (employed by the Arapahoe tribe), the council sought to prevent the withholding of per capita payments from individuals to pay irrigation charges or reimbursable loans, or the withholding of the funds of minors and persons who, in the opinion of the secretary, were in need of assistance in conducting their affairs. In hearings held in June 1956, Lewis Sigler, Secretary Douglas McKay's representative, ceased his objections to the per capita payment and did not oppose a proposed amendment (H.R. 10182) to raise the percentage of income distributed from 80 to 85 percent, but insisted on the continuation of his authority to exercise liens on individual payments. Sonosky and Wilkinson accompanied the Wyoming delegation in meetings with the Department of the Interior and argued the Business Council's aims. The tribes contended that the lien for irrigation charges was unfair because white people with delinquent charges were not penalized and because some people were being charged for water they had not requested and had not used. The tribes also held that control over the minors' money was unwarranted since the secretary's office had admitted that the tribes' adults had not spent their money foolishly. They also objected to the secretary's attempt to charge them for the cost of administering the payment, pointing out that this was a governmental function delegated to the Indian Bureau by Congress, and similar to the issuing of social security checks.[51]

The Committee on Interior and Insular Affairs engineered a compromise bill (H.R. 11928) without the wholehearted support of the council, leaving a final determination until 1959. In an act of July 25, 1956, the per capita payments were extended to May 19, 1959, the percentage of income for distribution was raised to 85 percent, and the secretary of the interior retained for two years his authority in regard to the per capita payments due to minors and persons unable to conduct their own affairs and maintained the right to apply liens for reimbursable Treasury loans and for irrigation charges, although only for water requested and used.[52]

Finally, in 1958, the act was amended so that as of January 1, 1959, payments were made monthly and no liens were applied on minors' money. In 1959 the tribes were at last assured of receiving tribal income in the form of per capita payments indefinitely, and these payments augmented their income considerably (see Table 6).[53]

In obtaining the per capita payments, council members had scored a tremendous victory over the Indian Office and in so doing had buttressed the council's prestige among its constituents. The per capita payments were referred to as *chéé'eyóóno* ("what they issue you") by most Arapahoes, and the money was regarded as subsistence due the tribe from the government. The councilmen, then, established without doubt their effectiveness as intermediaries. Moreover, a portion of the 15 percent of tribal income not distributed was budgeted by the Business Council to provide for needy constituents and to hire expert help in future battles over reservation policy. By the end of the era, many Arapahoes were relying on the per capita payments and on Business Council aid for subsistence.

"Termination"

In January 1945 Commissioner Collier was forced to resign by congressional opponents who favored a return to the policy of assimilation and pressed for a reduction of BIA costs. Congress asked his successor to prepare a list of tribes that were sufficiently well organized and self-sufficient to allow for the termination of federal services and the withdrawal of federal supervision of trust property. The commissioner was also asked to work for the eventual "termination" of all tribes. With termination, reservation lands could be sold and would be subject to local property taxes. Concrete action on the termination policy was taken in 1953, when the House passed Concurrent Resolution 108, expressing Congress's determination to free the federal government from responsibility toward Indian tribes and directing that legislation be enacted to carry out the termination policy. In the next session of Congress, several bills to end federal guardianship of specific tribes were introduced and passed. In 1969 President Richard Nixon repudiated the termination policy, but throughout the 1950s such services as health care and education were transferred from the Indian Bureau to other agencies, and the bureau pressed individual Indians to relocate to urban areas.[54]

The rise in the standard of living on the Wind River Reservation contributed to congressional efforts to end the trust relationship with the Wind River tribes. During the hearings on the per capita payment between 1947 and 1959, delegates were pressured by several congressmen to indicate their willingness to end their relationship with the

Bureau of Indian Affairs and to remove reservation land from collective tribal ownership in return for congressional approval of the per capita payment. But the delegates refused to agree to consider terminating the trust relationship.

On September 29, 1954, a special subcommittee on Indian affairs of the House Committee on Interior and Insular Affairs issued a report that listed the Wind River tribes among those qualified to handle their own affairs without federal assistance. Warned of the danger by the Association on American Indian Affairs, the Joint Business Council sent Nell Scott and Robert Harris to try to convince Congress that the Wind River tribes should not be terminated. Nell Scott recalled: "Bob and I cried on everybody's shoulder. We had [Congressman] Keith Thomson behind us then to help us. And this [Congressman E. Y.] Berry, I think, of North [South] Dakota, was really insulting, like we were wooden Indians sitting there. . . . We finally got that settled. Now all that we had to do was to cry on the shoulders of the [congressmen]. Tell them, 'Well, we haven't got no education. We got a lot of old people that isn't educated. Why don't you let it go for awhile.' So they did."[55] This crisis past—at least for the time being—the Arapahoe council attempted to obtain redress for the broken treaties about which the old people had complained for generations.

The 1961 Claim

On November 1, 1955, the Arapahoes filed a petition with the Indian Claims Commission, which had been established in 1946 to hear tribal grievances and award damages to tribes whose rights were found to have been violated. The Northern Arapahoes and Cheyennes and the Southern Arapahos and Cheyennes asked summary judgment respecting the proper construction and effect of the September 17, 1851, Treaty of Fort Laramie. The tribes argued that they had never been fully compensated for the lands lost to whites in Colorado, southeastern Wyoming, western Kansas, and Nebraska (see Map 1). The commission ruled that the Treaty of 1851 had given to the United States only the right of passage over the lands in question and that the United States accepted, acknowledged, ratified, and confirmed the petitioners' aboriginal title and right of occupancy, possession, and use to this territory. Then in 1961 the commission ruled that after the tribes ceded these lands—the Southern tribes in 1861, 1865, and 1867, the Northern tribes in 1868— they were not paid full value. All parties to the case stipulated that the value of the lands should be determined as of October 14, 1865. The commission set the fair market value at $23.5 million and found that the Northern Arapahoes had not received the full payment to which they were entitled under the 1868 treaty. On the basis of relative population, the Northern Arapahoe tribe received 24.07 percent of the land value, less the payments received under the provisions of the 1868 treaty. The shares of the other three petitioners were similarly calculated. In 1964, each enrolled Northern Arapahoe received his or her share of the judgment money, twelve monthly payments of $124 each.[56]

"We're Not Kids, I Said":
Relations between the Business Councilmen and Non-Arapahoes

The improvement of the tribe's economic position aided the councilmen's efforts to broaden the scope of their authority within the reservation community and at the same time to validate that authority. Relations with whites began to change, as well. More combative tactics replaced the conciliatory stance previously taken by the Arapahoe business councils. And as the Arapahoe councilmen became as assertive as the Shoshones in dealing with whites, the dynamics of the Joint Business Council began to change.

Tribal leaders were able to make use of the tribe's newfound income to hire attorneys to offset the actions of the Bureau of Indian Affairs. The council also persuaded Wyoming state officials to intercede for them in Congress when the BIA opposed the tribe's goals. In these new times, the Business Council no longer found itself at the mercy of the Indian Office. The Arapahoe councilmen were able to take a firm stance in their dealings with whites, not only because their access to tribal income made them less dependent on the BIA, but also because such individuals as Nell Scott were not tolerant of condescending, patronizing federal agents. Nell Scott remembered one meeting between the council and members of Collier's staff when the division of joint tribal resources was discussed: "And old [W. F.] Woehlke said, 'Now that-there's an apple and you cut it in two. Shoshones take this one, you take that.' I said, 'Now you know we're not kids,' I said. 'When I first went to school we used to count on little beads. But,' I said, 'we don't have to now, Mr. Woehlke.' Oh, he hated me. That makes me mad when they make [it appear that] we're stupid Indians."[57] That kind of overt expression of resentment and self-assertiveness did not occur in the days of the old council.

Relations between Arapahoes and local whites were ambivalent at best. Despite the townspeople's assistance during the struggle to obtain per capita payments, Indians were discriminated against and there was considerable prejudice, particularly against Arapahoes. One prominent Landerite went so far as to suggest that an infusion of "white blood" was necessary if Indians were to progress beyond "savagery": "The admixture of white blood will increase the ambition of these people to equal the standards of the whites." Most local whites who married Indians chose Shoshone mates; the Arapahoes were viewed as more "savage." The tribes' growing spirit of independence and desire to exercise control over their own resources was reflected in the Joint Business Council's decision to implement fish and game regulations. Despite the antagonism of local townspeople, the council voted in 1937 to require whites to buy permits to fish on the reservation. Superintendent Stone commented, "You were the first council with the nerve to do it." The fishing regulations were only the first of several measures taken by the council to assert the tribes' jurisdiction over reservation resources.[58]

Both the Arapahoe and the Shoshone business councils sought to present to their constituents an image of assertive, "educated" leadership. At Superintendent Stone's urging, they were instructed in Robert's rules of order in 1937. Thereafter, meetings were conducted according to parliamentary rules. Almost all of the Arapahoe councilmen—in fact, almost all of the Arapahoes—were bilingual. Gradually English came to be used exclusively during Business Council meetings, although outside the council meetings Arapahoes often conversed in the native language.[59]

The Arapahoe councilmen worked to find ways of cooperating with the Shoshone Business Council, despite cultural and political differences, and at the same time to end the old pattern of allowing Shoshone councilmen to take responsibility for militant confrontations between the joint council and federal agents. The Shoshone and Arapahoe councilmen had to work together on joint goals, despite the fact that the orientations of the two tribes were dissimilar in many ways. The members of the Shoshone Business Council were much younger than the Arapahoe councilmen: in 1937, the ages of the six Shoshones were 25, 28, 29, 34, 45, and 64; the ages of the Arapahoes were 46, 49, 56, 57, 57, and 66. Ten years later the Shoshone councilmen ranged in age from 28 to 44 and the Arapahoes from 40 to 58. In contrast to the Arapahoes, Shoshone councilmen by and large favored policies geared toward helping nuclear families set up farms and businesses. As Robert Harris put it, "The Shoshone has never sanctioned any [communal] enterprise. . . . They are individualists, and instead of building up large capital assets for the tribe, our position of councilmen should be to build up a more substantial capital asset for each member of the tribe."[60] In interactions with whites, the councilmen often exploited their differences so as to have a favorable influence on both whites with an assimilationist philosophy and those who were sympathetic to retention of Indian culture. In the congressional hearings the Shoshones stressed the help that per capita payments would provide to progressive individuals who wanted to expand their business enterprises and become financially independent; the Arapahoes stressed the desperate need for the payments to relieve the extreme poverty of the traditional Indian. With Nell Scott's election to the council, the Arapahoes had a spokesperson who was able and willing to assume an overtly assertive, combative posture toward whites. She shared the chairmanship of the Joint Business Council with the Shoshone councilman Robert Harris for most of the 1940s and 1950s. The growing self-confidence of the Arapahoe business councilmen during those years became manifest in the development of reservation programs and policies that were increasingly independent of those of the Shoshone councilmen.

CULTURAL CONTINUITY AND THE "NEW" POLITICS

After 1937 new political opportunities and increased income from the per capita payments produced extensive changes in Arapahoe society. The changes were potentially disruptive in at least three respects. First, both the desire of younger people to increase their involvement in reservation politics and the government's pressure toward detribalization and assimilation (particularly in the 1950s) threatened to undermine the ceremonial and age hierarchies and to promote disunity. Second, the Business Council's new powers to use the tribe's money to fund community programs were worrisome because they threatened the nondirective and noninitiatory orientation of traditional Arapahoe politics. Third, the start of regular per capita payments made the criteria for enrollment in the tribe of increasing importance, and the enrollment issue sparked considerable dissension. As in the past, the elders assumed responsibility for maintaining cultural continuity and social order.

"All Striving for One Thing": Preserving Tribal Unity

Despite the changing times, the ceremonial elders were convinced that the ceremonial and age hierarchies must persist if the Arapahoes were to prosper as a people. At the same time, the elders took a flexible position toward nonnative rituals and toward innovation in the native ceremonial order.

The ceremonial elders did not oppose participation in Christian and peyote rituals. A commitment to Christianity or peyote did not necessarily conflict with traditional ritual obligations. In fact, the Arapahoes suspected that their prayers were more effective when they used two or three mediums than when they used only one. Molly Stenberg noted in the 1940s that although the Catholic priests opposed non-Christian forms of worship, the Arapahoes commonly went their own way: "The priest told me I couldn't come to communion if I attended peyote meetings. But I go anyway. I have a right to worship where I please." She also observed that neither peyote nor Christianity had supplemented the "tribal faith"; rather, they were additional forms of worship, and nothing took precedence over the Sacred Flat Pipe.[61]

To perpetuate the Arapahoe religion the ceremonial elders opened new avenues to Arapahoes who wished to acquire ritual authority, primarily by relaxing some of the rules that governed the transfer of some ritual offices. When Collie Judson's second wife died in 1935, he went through a period of mourning so severe that people doubted his ability to care for the Sacred Pipe. One elderly Arapahoe explained it this way: "When his wife died, he felt so bad that he lost his wife that he wouldn't stay home. Maybe he'd come home for a little while and he'd go back out, stay out in the hills. And then this Oscar White went down there and brought the pipe up [to his place]. So naturally when he got back to his mind again, when he got over his sorrow and was trying to come back after it, he came back up to take it back down there, but this old man told him that he didn't have no woman no more, so he was going to keep it." White died in 1937, soon after taking the pipe, and his daughter Jane Wallowing Bull—not considered to be of the *béesóowú'unenno'*—assumed the role of keeper, with her husband, Fred, and her stepbrother, Luke Smith, performing the rituals. One of White's relatives told Inez Hilger in 1940 that the woman took custody of the pipe because the "Pipe follows the blood like the sap in a tree, for wherever the blood goes that is where the Pipe goes." Hilger apparently misunderstood this to mean that the earlier keepers were "blood relatives" of the White family. Jane died in 1959 and Fred in 1961; the ceremonial elders then selected Adam Shakespeare, a great-grandson of Weasel Bear, as keeper of the Sacred Pipe.[62]

Beaver Dodge died in 1939, still in possession of the Sacred Wheel. His Sun Dance grandson, Ralph Piper, took custody of it. He returned it to the ceremonial elders a few years later (sometime after 1950), and the elders allowed Ben Goggles (who was a high-ranking ritual authority in the Sun Dance but not of the *béesóowú'unenno'*) to serve as keeper of the Sacred Wheel.

During this era the role of Sun Dance chief formally became one of the most important positions in the ceremonial hierarchy. Bart Sitting Eagle served in this capacity. Having pledged (vowed to sponsor) and completed the Sun Dance seven times, he was acknowledged by other ceremonial elders as qualified to direct the ritual with the assistance of two other priests. Upon his death in 1956, Ben Goggles, who had also qualified by pledging the Sun Dance seven times, became Sun Dance chief.

In effect, these changes permitted ceremonial authority to be diffused among more individuals than would have otherwise qualified for the highest positions in the ceremonial hierarchy and possibly stimulated participation and involvement in native rituals. The ceremonial elders also were careful to try to keep among their ranks a roughly equal number of elders from the Lower and Upper Arapahoe areas. The two highest positions, held by Coal from Lower Arapahoe and Shot Gun from Upper Arapahoe, passed to Frank Addison and Morris White Plume.[63] With the deaths of these two men, ritual authorities selected four replacements from the two residential areas: West Shakespeare, Anthony Iron, Sidney Willow, and Ben Goggles. Thus the number of people who held the highest ritual positions was doubled. The men chosen were referred to as the "four old men," a title symbolically associated with the four supernatural beings that figure in Arapahoe mythology and thus very effective in reinforcing the priests' authority.

The elders' influence was also bolstered by their role as orators at tribal ceremonies and by the Arapahoes' perception that they spoke the native language "better" than the younger people. Although most elders were bilingual by this time, they refrained from speaking English in certain contexts (for example, at tribal gatherings, at religious ceremonies, and even sometimes at Business Council meetings).[64] Younger Arapahoes showed their deference by translating English speech into Arapahoe for the elders. Ceremonial elders were considered to be not only particularly proficient in the Arapahoe language, but, because of their wisdom and training, less likely to make errors of speech that could be disastrous in a sacred context. Mature adults (in their late forties and fifties) were considered to be particularly proficient in English, and therefore less likely to be deceived in dealings with whites. These views had important political implications. In crisis situations, elders broke into the native language, which worked to intimidate opposition, discredit disruptive individuals, and reduce anxiety and fear.

During the Collier era, the government put considerable pressure on the Arapahoes to modernize their political relations; in particular, Superintendent Stone vigorously tried to persuade the tribe to institute political districting, so that councilmen would be more "representative" of and responsible to a group of constituents. The elders viewed this plan as inevitably disruptive because it would encourage favoritism; that is, councilmen would help only a few Arapahoes rather than all. To them it was apparent that Arapahoe cultural continuity and social order depended on their ability to prevent the districting plan. Stone urged the Ethete, Mill Creek, and Lower Arapahoe residents to vote by district for three slates of candidates, each of which would represent one district. Each district would send its two representatives to sit on the six-member Business Council and would not be allowed to vote for candidates from the other districts. In 1937 the Arapahoes rejected Stone's plan. Andrew Brown (Lone Bear's son) spoke for the tribe: "And the opinion of the people is that they do not want to segregate the tribe into different districts for the simple reason that the council acts for both tribes in whatever action they take. It would be different if each district has a problem of its own. Regardless of where the candidates are from, they are all striving for one thing—the tribal welfare, rather than one district." Despite Stone's admonition that under the old plan no district could be certain of electing anyone, the Arapahoes would not yield. Stone's fears were unrealized. In the election of 1937, in which almost all men and many women voted, two candidates from each of the three districts were elected at large, and in all subsequent elections the districts were usually equally represented. Tribal unity was a primary goal, and the elders worked hard to prevent conflicts and to check the growing power of the councilmen in order to prevent abuse of the Business Council position.[65]

Compartmentalization of Authority

During Collier's term the BIA encouraged the Joint Business Council to assume many responsibilities for reservation economic development, health, education, and welfare which were once those of the bureau. In its enthusiasm, the joint council of 1937–38 tried to extend the sphere of Business Council authority to include supervision of all tribal celebrations and sodality activity. In an effort to legitimize the proposed innovations, the council drafted a constitution and by-laws that outlined the council's role in supervising ceremonial activity. They were never implemented, and contrary to the Arapahoe Business Council's hope, authority became clearly compartmentalized, with committees of Arapahoes exercising authority in all spheres of community life that did not pertain to Arapahoe–federal relations. In supervising the committee activity, the elders reinforced the traditional age hierarchy.

In the early twentieth century, social dances and community service activities were organized by individuals or sodalities. By the late 1930s, most of these activities were under the supervision of the Dance Committee (also referred to as *heches-néécheeno'*, "little chiefs"). The Dance Committee was made up of male elders, mature men, and a few younger men. The elders supervised the younger men, who were viewed as apprentices. The Dance Committee brought together people from Ethete, Mill Creek, and Lower Arapahoe; when celebrations were held by people in only one of these communities, the Dance Committee members who resided in that community took responsibility. Family and neighborhood groups also spent time and energy in raising funds for tribal feasts and celebrations, and donated money to the "old and orphans," as a writer for the reservation newspaper put it. *The Wyoming Indian* frequently reported these activities. For example:

One day last week at Cornelius Vanderbilt's log house on Mill Creek: The entertainment got under way about 9:00 P.M. and lasted for seven hours. On the program was a hand guessing game until about 12 o'clock. During this particular game Ora Manderson was the star player, and John Shakespeare was the guess against Ora; both teams started from scratch with ten tallies a side and each side composed of four people. So this game was bound to be interesting with two such outstanding players pitted against each other plus some very lively music. On the first guess Ora and another teammate scored two tallies; the second guess, Ora scored alone, and the third pass finds Ora still playing, thereby giving his partners a chance to play again. Ora was on his prayer bones and swaying his body to the rhythm of the music and it was very evident that he had the attention of all the players as well as all the lookers-on. The rest of the game ran pretty much like the first part only as the game progressed it created a spirit of real fun; one of the women on Ora's side got up and fanned his face as it could be readily seen that he was getting pretty warm! The guesser, John Shakespeare, began to look very sheepish and thinking that he needed a rest, suggested to his teammates that one of them pinch-hit for him but they could not see it that way and he had to remain as guesser. Believe it or not, the twenty tallies soon melted to zero and the game was over, making Ora the star of the game, upon which he proudly acclaimed his power to the four winds. After the game we moved on to the Rabbit [dance], Wolf [dance], and Competitive dancing. In the contest Ora was again to be reckoned with but there was a strong rival in the person of Bruce Groesbeck, who stole some of the honors from Ora. Andrew Brown assumed the role of the jokester and handled his role without giving an inch. During all this merry-making

refreshments were served at ten cents for sandwiches, ten cents for cake or
pie, and ten cents for coffee; all proceeds derived from this sale was turned
over to the Christmas fund and it amounted to twelve dollars, so you see it was
a successful party in every manner.

Because these occasions sometimes ended in quarrels, tribal leaders
sought ways of controlling them. The elders sought to end "private
doings," and instead encouraged social activities held at the community
dance halls under the supervision of the Dance Committee.[66]

The people in the three residential areas chose the men on the
Dance Committee; leaders of these committees were sometimes selected
in a drum ceremony. Until the 1950s, the names of committee members were submitted to the Arapahoe Business Council as a matter of
courtesy. There were three subcommittees: the Sun Dance Committee,
the Fourth of July Committee, and the Christmas Committee. Some
committee members worked for all three; others concentrated their
efforts on one kind of ceremony. The Sun Dance ritual itself was conducted by the ceremonial elders, but the Sun Dance Committee prepared the campground and performed other kinds of secular functions
associated with the ceremony. The Fourth of July celebration included
a rodeo and races, and the committee members also cooperated with
white organizers of Fourth of July parades in the neighboring towns by
sending Indian dancers and singers to the town events. The Christmas
Committee members of each residential community sponsored dances
and feasts and distributed gifts for the "old, young, and disabled,"
as *The Wyoming Indian* put it, during Christmas week in their residential areas. It was also the duty of the members of the Dance Committee to hunt for game to provide meat for tribal feasts. The state
game warden issued special permits to the committee members.[67]

Committee leaders as well as Business Council members were expected to be "good men"—to be generous, selfless, and modest, and to
behave in ways supportive of tribal consensus. A speech by forty-nine-
year-old Dave Headley, selected by the Lower Arapahoes for the 1938
Christmas Committee, illustrates the unassertive manner in which
leaders were expected to present themselves: "I have been chosen to
make a talk today and before I commence I will not hesitate to admit
of not being worthy before making a talk to such a large crowd nor I
am not too familiar in wording as an adviser. . . . First of all I have no
idea why I was elected for I always considered myself a poor speaker,
in fact I don't class myself as an outstanding figure among my people.
However, I say that I am appreciative to the Christmas Committee for
the honor to make this speech and saying prayers for all the people. We

select people as leaders and we should respect them because in doing any misconduct we [leaders] deny ourselves in our own respect toward our people." Committees were expected to provide liberally for the people during the all-tribal celebrations, just as councilmen were expected to help constituents in need. Robert Friday noted that individuals were allowed to serve on the committees only as long as their behavior was acceptable to the Arapahoes: "Those men are recognized by the tribe and if at any time, any of the committee does not do right, is crooked or money sticks on his hand, we take him off and put someone else on."[68]

From the late 1930s through the 1940s, three separate spheres of Arapahoe leadership developed: sacred offices, committee positions, and Business Council offices. Participation in committee work could help an individual build a reputation as a "good man" and eventually gain support for election to the Business Council, but most of the men prominent in committee work never served on the council. Committee positions by custom went to many of the same individuals year after year. From 1935 to 1940 Andrew Brown and Lynn Norse (Upper Arapahoes) and Luke Sun Roads (from Lower Arapahoe) headed their district dance committees. Joe Arthur and Frank Tyler, two young members of the committees in 1939—in a sense, apprentices to the older men—were to be prominent in the committee sphere for over thirty years.[69] Continuing to serve in the 1960s and 1970s, they became elders who directed the activities of the Dance Committee. Similarly, those who achieved positions of ritual authority had apprenticed themselves to ritual leaders and did not hold council positions.

The Arapahoe Business Council's effort to control the committees was a clear attempt to expand its authority. The constitution and by-laws prepared by the Joint Business Council in 1938 provided that the dates of any tribal religious ceremony were to be set by the business council of that tribe and that "the council shall have the power to appoint all social and dancing committees." Moreover, "each council shall have power to remove any member or members of such committees whose conduct is not reflecting credit to their respective tribe." Robert Friday tried to convince the tribe that authority over all aspects of tribal government should be centralized: "There is one or two things I would like to state to the tribe. One of the things is that if the council don't appoint the committee, it might be someone that might not try to conform. He might set a time for the Sun Dance when the people are the busiest. There is another way that we would like to protect the people. Suppose a white man came from away off and tried to take a certain percentage of the Indians to come to another town and make a bad name for the tribe." His speech skillfully employed several images that were likely to sway public opinion. Much of the controversy over the Sun Dance in previous years had centered on the superintendents' claims that the ritual interfered with work; now Friday suggested that without council supervision a naive committeeman might revive white opposition to the Sun Dance. Council supervision would prevent groups of Indian performers from being exploited, on the one hand, and would inhibit performers from behaving in ways detrimental to Indian–white relations, on the other. The BIA refused to approve this section of the document, arguing that it was a violation of "Constitutional rights," that is, the provision for separation of church and state. The proposed constitution for the tribes also stipulated that "all associations and organizations of a tribal nature are subject to the review by and the recommendations of the Business Council." The bureau did not object to this section, but the 1938 constitution failed to win final approval from the tribes' general councils, and in any case, the Arapahoes ignored the councilmen's suggested innovations in regard to committees. The Sun Dance and the activities of the social committees evolved as spheres of authority separate from Business Council concerns. The ritual and committee leadership also served as a check on the scope of Business Council authority.[70]

Beginning in 1951, the Arapahoe and Shoshone tribes instituted elections to choose the members of each tribe's dance or entertainment committee. The Arapahoes elected six Entertainment Committee members every two years at the same time that they elected councilmen. The men were elected at large, usually three from the upper and three from the lower communities. The Entertainment Committee developed into an organization of elders. Responsibility for the various tribal celebrations was assumed by sodalities or clubs that were supervised by the Entertainment Committee. From the tribal income the Arapahoe Business Council budgeted funds to the Entertainment Committee and several clubs. This arrangement also helped to curtail private doings to raise money for feasts and dances. While the Entertainment Committee supervised secular preparations for the Sun Dance, other celebrations were organized by the clubs.[71]

The involvement of Arapahoes in club activity was extensive. Some individuals became active in many such groups. The Christmas clubs of both Ethete and Lower Arapahoe sponsored the Christmas week celebrations. The Ethete Memorial Club gained new importance through its increasing involvement in funeral ritual. Because of its members' participation in ceremonies to honor servicemen, they became known as *niiwohóóyeneséíno',* or "flag women." New clubs were organized, as well. Peyotists started a charity committee (*niithêyeebiihiiho'*, "they help people") to aid the needy.[72] Veterans who returned to the reservation after World War II were particularly eager to become leaders in the community even though they were still "youths." Two American Legion posts were formed by several of these men. The Legion members were called *beniinênno'*, or "soldier men"; the posts were named for Arapahoe youths killed in the war: Trosper Redman Post at Ethete and Arthur Antelope Brown Post at Lower Arapahoe. Female relatives formed an auxiliary (*beniinêseino'*, or "soldier women") for each Legion post, and the women cooked and helped to prepare for Legion-sponsored events. In the late 1950s, youths excited by the Pan Plains intertribal celebrations on other reservations also organized a powwow committee in each residential area, which replaced the old Fourth of July committees. The postwar involvement of young people and the increased income that was available to the tribe and its members spurred sodality activity. The elders encouraged the formation of sodalities, which worked for the benefit of the tribe. Naming the groups was one way of honoring the clubs for their service to the community. One of the first members of the Altar of the Rosary Society, a women's club formed at Lower Arapahoe, explained that the "old, real old men" named her club *nôôkôôxúúséino'* ("morning star women" or "cross women") because they served St. Stephen's and had purchased a wooden cross for the church.[73]

"We Might Split Our Relationships": Controversy over Enrollment

The Arapahoes wanted to limit enrollment in order to maximize the size of their per capita payments. The problem of establishing requirements for enrollment was taken up in 1946 by the General Council, which at that time approved or rejected all requests for enrollment. In a meeting on November 21 it was decided that parents who wished to enroll a child should be required to file an application accompanied by a birth certificate. The following year the General Council began to consider a set of proposed criteria for enrollment. "Foreign Indians" (who in former times were accepted as members of the tribe if they conformed to tribal values) now were resented if they sought enrollment, and their applications were rejected. And, following the example of the Shoshones, the General Council now considered requiring a minimal amount of Indian ancestry or "blood." This question and the decision on what the other qualifications for enrollment should be were referred by the General Council to the elders of the tribe. Apparently no formal decision was made, although a consensus was developing. Then, in 1952, a committee composed of members of the "younger generation" (two of whom were councilmen) was appointed by the General Council, and the committee proposed four criteria for enrollment. First, an application accompanied by a birth certificate had to be submitted to the General Council within two years of an applicant's birth. Second, the applicant had to demonstrate at least one-fourth degree (25 percent) Arapahoe "blood." Third, one of the applicant's parents had to be an enrolled Northern Arapahoe. And fourth, the applicant had to be the child of a lawful marriage. These recommendations generated dissension, particularly the last; some Arapahoes proposed that in addition the enrolled parent ought to be the father. Because of the lack of unanimity on these issues, the matter was referred to another committee of twelve men and women, who tried to mobilize consensus.[74]

Finally, after discussion throughout the Arapahoe community, the General Council met on April 22, 1954, and by a vote of 151 to 41 set enrollment criteria. The requirements that an applicant must have "one-fourth degree" Arapahoe blood and an enrolled Northern Arapahoe parent were adopted. A compromise on the legitimacy issue was reached in order to accommodate persons who married by "Indian custom" rather than legal ceremony: a child could be enrolled if his parents married before they applied for his enrollment or if he were adopted by his mother's husband (provided he was Indian). But the pressure to limit enrollment in order to prevent reductions in the per capita payments grew. A consensus was building that the children of women married to non-Arapahoes should be excluded. Proponents of this change presented it in public meetings as "for the benefit of the older people," and in fact, the elders did support this position. Before the per capita payments began, few Arapahoes had married outside the tribe; by 1957, approximately seventy-five women and sixty-five men had non-Arapahoe spouses and their children were enrolled. Arapahoes generally felt that many outsiders who married Arapahoes were motivated by a desire to share in the payments. On August 10, 1956, the General Council modified the enrollment criteria. Now an applicant had to have an enrolled Northern Arapahoe father, and the parents of a child born out of wedlock had to marry within two years of the birth. Applications for enrollment were to be processed by the Arapahoe Business Council.[75]

Five years later, several Arapahoes with young relatives who did not qualify for enrollment protested to the General Council. The issue was troubling to Arapahoes. One speaker in the council advised the people, "I think we're getting just a little out of hand here—getting a little bit radical. It's time we settled down. Let's talk sense because this enrollment is something that is a very touchy question. It's going to be a rough day. We might split our relationships today. That's the reason I'd like to have you people settle down and talk sense and settle some of these things in a nice way." He was urging the dissident group to conform to the wishes of most Arapahoes. One man, who had nonenrolled grandchildren, persisted in moving that children of unmarried women and of women married to non-Arapahoes be permitted to enroll. Another individual requested, without success, that the vote be by secret ballot (so that those who disagreed with the elders would not have to do so publicly). At this point a respected elder stood and exclaimed that the matter had already been decided. The motion was defeated, 186 to 72. An Arapahoe councilman then asked the crowd to agree never to discuss the enrollment issue again—in short, to accept without bitterness the General Council's decision. Only six persons refused to vote in favor of the motion.[76] Only one councilman opposed the elders' wishes; he was not reelected subsequently to the Business Council. Throughout the crisis the elders kept conflict under control and publicly supported the General Council's final decision in 1962. While not all Arapahoes were pleased with the enrollment restrictions, they could not complain without appearing to oppose the elders.

At the same time that the availability of per capita payments in the 1940s and 1950s brought about a reexamination of cultural identity, the new income also brought into question the nature of the councilman role. Part of the tribal income that was not distributed in per capita payments was used by councilmen for social programs. These funds gave the councilmen considerably more economic leverage in the community than they had previously had. By the 1960s the Arapahoes saw their success in gaining control over tribal income as both a boon and a potential problem. They encouraged the council's management of tribal money, yet tried to ensure that the councilmen remained "good men," as well as forceful advocates in relations with whites.

PART II

POLITICS TODAY, 1965–78

5

"What They Issue You": Political Economy at Wind River

Despite the monthly issue of per capita payments and the greater degree of independence possible for the Arapahoes since the Collier era, economic life is precarious and self-government is still limited. In 1934, one of the Arapahoes who spoke during the meetings about the IRA portrayed the tribe as being circled by a predatory wolf. He expressed in metaphor fears that make Arapahoes rely on tribal leaders for protection from external, hostile forces. These anxieties and fears still persist. In the words of one leader, unless the legal and economic status of the reservation community is preserved, "there's nothing else but the alleys and trash cans of Lander"—nothing but social discrimination and poverty. Arapahoe political culture and the organizational forms of tribal government are conditioned by the fact that both individually and as a group the Arapahoes must rely on oil and gas royalties and bonuses, that on many levels Indian self-determination is threatened by whites, and that Arapahoe-Shoshone relations are strained. Now as in earlier eras, the Arapahoe Business Council is depended on as protector and provider.[1]

The Arapahoe Business Council still manages tribal funds and represents and defends Arapahoe interests in relation to federal, state, and local governments, as well as white interest groups in general. Operating without a constitution and by-laws, the Business Council is authorized by the tribe to represent the Northern Arapahoes vis-à-vis the federal government and to make decisions in areas that by custom include economic development; the leasing, purchase, and sale of land; conservation of natural resources; and some aspects of health, education, and welfare. Major expenditures of tribal funds and matters of particular significance or controversy are attended to by members of the tribe over the age of eighteen in a general council, which is usually convened by the Business Council. Matters affecting both tribes are dealt with by a joint business council, comprised of the members of the Arapahoe and Shoshone business councils.[2]

Since 1937, members of the Arapahoe Business Council have been elected by popular vote every two years. The Shoshone tribe conducts its election separately but at the same time. All enrolled members of the tribe eighteen years old and older are entitled to vote. Before 1972 candidates were nominated in community meetings at each of the Arapahoe residence clusters (Ethete and Lower Arapahoe). In accordance with a decision made by the General Council on August 23, 1972, potential candidates have had to register to participate in a primary; the twelve winners compete in the council election in November. At this time, Arapahoes vote for six candidates at large. The voting is by handwritten ballot and is usually supervised by respected elderly women. When the six newly elected councilmen take office in January, they choose a chairman from their group to preside over meetings. Councilmen receive no salary, but are paid $30 per diem each time they meet. The joint Shoshone and Arapahoe council employs a bookkeeper and clerical workers to staff the Tribal Office.

THE WIND RIVER RESERVATION TODAY

Wind River Reservation, fifty-five miles from north to south and seventy miles from east to west, lies east of the continental divide at the foothills of the Rockies in west-central Wyoming, and encompasses high mountainous terrain in the west, vast areas of range, and some irrigated farmland in the east. The distant mountains form a purple, snow-capped ring around Wind River country. There is a pervasive stillness and, despite the clusters of extended family settlements, a sense of great space. Indian settlement is largely in river valleys to the south (see Map 6).

In April 1976 there were 3,093 enrolled Northern Arapahoes, approximately three-fourths of whom resided on the southeastern portion of the reservation in two communities, Ethete and Lower Arapahoe, and along the road that connects them.[3] Almost every Arapahoe household included some members who were not enrolled in the tribe, mostly children whose mothers married outside the tribe and children born out of wedlock—543 individuals altogether.[4] Most of the 700 or so Arapahoes who were living off the reservation at that time were married to and living with non-Arapahoes or had temporarily left Wind River for job training or employment.[5]

To the southwest is the residential area of the Eastern Shoshones, who in April 1976 had 2,202 enrolled members. Approximately 1,454 of these people and 271 nonenrolled individuals were living in a widely dispersed pattern in the vicinity of the BIA headquarters, Tribal Office, and Public Health Clinic at Fort Washakie, and throughout the Burris, Morton, and Crowheart areas. Several hundred of the enrolled Shoshones resided off the reservation, as well.

Along the road from the Ethete community eastward, frame houses, one after the other, sit surrounded by an assortment of items put aside until needed—unused furniture, discarded automobile parts, camping stoves, and tipi poles. Clotheslines heavy with freshly laundered clothing thrash against an interminable wind. Horses wander, aimlessly grazing alongside the houses, and dogs of all sizes run about. Groups of young cousins ride horses or run back and forth between the houses.

On the north side of the Ethete road is a small Catholic church, painted in symbolic geometric designs by Arapahoe artists. Here the priest comes from St. Stephen's to say mass. Where the road turns south, a community center called Blue Sky Hall stands opposite the Arapahoe-decorated St. Michael's Mission, a post office, and an Indian-owned gas station, laundry, and cafe (periodically closed). Farther to the south is an elementary school for Ethete children, and to the east is the Sun Dance Grounds, where the lodge frame of the last ceremony stands, far apart from the houses. Twenty miles farther along the road is Great Plains Hall, the community center for the Lower Arapahoes, and a small public health clinic. Two miles to the south is a post office and small grocery store, opposite an elementary school for Lower Arapahoe children. Here the highway connecting Riverton and Lander is visible, the speed of the cars and trucks noticeably greater than the more leisurely pace on the Ethete–Arapahoe road. Three miles from Riverton at some distance from the highway, nestled among shade trees, is St. Stephen's Mission, now the site of an elementary school staffed with St. Stephen's personnel but since 1976 operated as a community-controlled contract school by Arapahoe parents.

During the last decade an extensive federally sponsored home-building program has resulted in far-reaching improvements in living conditions. In 1965 most people were living in small log or frame houses or in trailers, and a few still used canvas tents as extensions to their houses. Not all homes had electricity, plumbing, or gas heat. Today most families have larger, remodeled frame houses or prefabricated split-level or ranch-style homes, or live in one of the new housing projects. Jokingly termed Easter-Egg Village by the Arapahoes, the

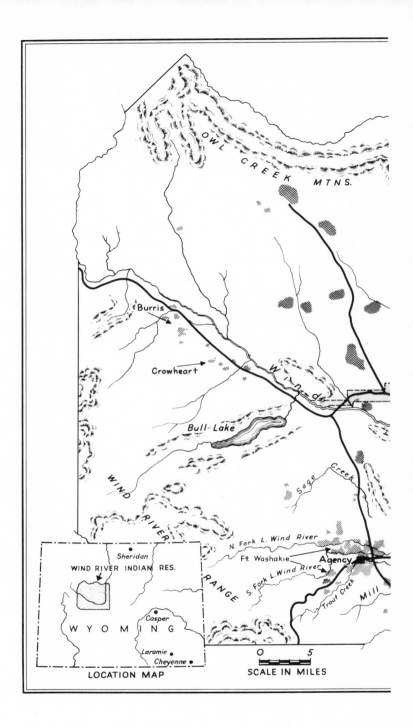

OWL CREEK MTNS.

Burris

Crowheart

W i n d *r.*

Bull Lake

WIND

RIVER

RANGE

Sage Creek

N. Fork L. Wind River

Ft. Washakie

S. Fork L.Wind River

Agency

Trout Creek

Mill

LOCATION MAP

Sheridan

WIND RIVER INDIAN RES.

WYOMING

Casper

Laramie

Cheyenne

0   5

SCALE IN MILES

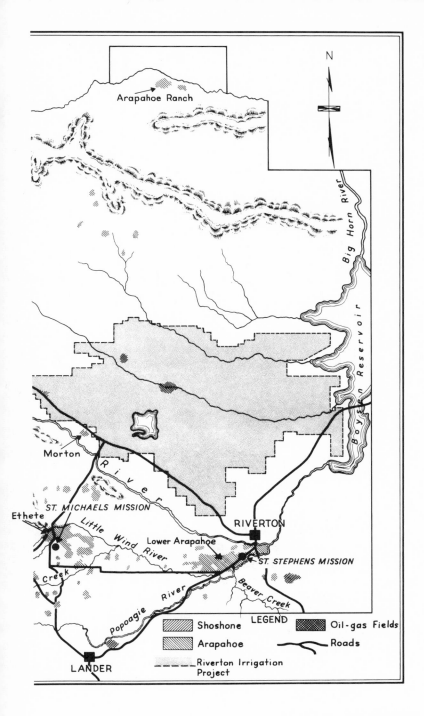

N

Arapahoe Ranch

Big Horn River

Boysen Reservoir

Morton

River

St. Michaels Mission

Ethete

Little

Wind River

Lower Arapahoe

RIVERTON

ST. STEPHENS MISSION

Creek

Popoagie River

Beaver Creek

LEGEND

LANDER

▨	Shoshone	▨	Oil-gas Fields
▨	Arapahoe	∿	Roads
	Riverton Irrigation Project		

Map 6. Wind River Reservation, 1965–78. Source: Office of the Bureau of Indian Affairs, Fort Washakie, Wyo.

Ethete project stands opposite St. Michael's and has twenty-one pre-fabricated units brightly painted in blue, pink, green, or yellow. At Arapahoe there is a similar project, of comparable scale although painted in more subdued colors, and several units for elderly Arapa-hoes, termed in jest Geritol Heights. A new natural-gas line to Ethete and an expanded system of power lines are other recent developments. Television sets are common, telephones less so.

Despite these improvements, the economic situation of the tribes-people is still precarious. The 1970 per capita income on the reserva-tion averaged $1,281, $2,640 below the national average and $2,275 below the per capita income for the state of Wyoming;[6] Shoshone in-come was higher, so that Arapahoe income averaged even less. Arapa-hoe families have good reason to depend on councilmen for aid in emergencies. The income to the tribe from mineral royalties allows for considerable flexibility in economic planning, but these resources are limited. To alleviate the economic problems of the Arapahoes, tribal funds must be expended cautiously, new sources of revenue must be sought, and enrollment criteria must be conscientiously enforced lest the tribe's membership swell beyond the present capacity of reserva-tion resources.

The Economics of Reservation Life

Tribal income is derived primarily from deposits of oil and gas. Leases are issued to national corporations, which pay the tribes royalties and bonuses, half to the Arapahoes and half to the Shoshones. Before 1974 this income was deposited in the U.S. Treasury at 4 percent interest. Now the funds are managed by an investment coordinator, who sees that the money earns the highest rate of interest available. In 1976 the Arapahoe share of these funds was about $4.5 million, 85 percent of which was used for per capita distribution. Per capita payments are paid directly to each enrolled Arapahoe on a monthly basis. In 1976 each person received $90 every month. (The Shoshones, with a smaller population, received $136 each.) Fifteen percent of the tribal income is designated for operating expenses (the Arapahoe Business Council budget in 1976 totaled $379,150) and for augmentation of capital reserve funds. These funds are allocated by the Arapahoe Business Council (and the Shoshone share by the Shoshone Business Council).[7]

The council seeks to maximize the income from mineral resources by employing an oil consultant, who works with the law firms re-tained by the Arapahoe and Shoshone business councils to pursue the tribes' interests. The policy of the joint council is to refer applications and bids to these specialists, who have been very effective in increasing the tribes' income.[8]

The joint council is periodically under pressure to invest tribal funds in order to stimulate economic development as well as to augment income. But in the Arapahoe view, after years of victimization by local whites and mismanagement of tribal resources under BIA directives, expenditures should be made only with great caution. The rejection of an effort to use tribal funds to erect a potato-processing factory on the reservation in 1969 was typical of the fate of proposals for economic development. When the BIA representatives and local white businessmen repeatedly argued the feasibility of the project, a member of the joint council offered this evaluation: "On this potato factory, if they want Indians to put money in it there must be something wrong with it." A second Arapahoe councilman concurred: "I'm riding the same horse as you"; and a third remarked, "I'm on that horse, too."[9]

Such cynicism is reinforced by such incidents as the tribes' support of an electronics factory in Riverton. The company, Datel, needed the tribes' endorsement to secure funds from the Economic Development Agency, whose support was contingent on the consent of the "depressed area" (the reservation community). The tribes endorsed the project and the EDA made a grant of $95,000 plus a sizable loan to match the amount raised by Riverton businessmen. In return for the support of the joint council, Datel promised 150 jobs for Indians by the end of 1967 and 300 jobs eventually. But only thirty Arapahoes and Shoshones were selected for training (out of seventy-five applicants), and only half that number (most of whom were Arapahoe) successfully completed the program. Datel hired only nine of the trainees, and shortly afterward these nine were laid off. A few Indians were hired later. (In late 1969, twenty Indians were employed.) Business councilmen have harbored considerable bitterness over the alleged discrimination and the company's failure to live up to the agreement that the council felt had been made.

The per capita payments are vital to family subsistence, particularly since the rates of unemployment and underemployment are high. The Arapahoe Business Council assumes the responsibility of alleviating its constituents' anxiety about these payments. The amounts fluctuate and the number of enrolled Arapahoes is increasing. For example, the payment declined from $49 in 1965 to $40 in 1969. The recent rise in the price of oil enabled the tribes to raise more revenue from the renegotiation of mineral leases, but the future rate of production is uncertain.

As an increase in enrollment can produce a decline in the size of the per capita payment, the council carefully checks each enrollment application. In contrast to the situation among many other tribes, such as the Eastern Shoshones and the Northern Cheyennes,[10] decisions about enrollment are not "political." Despite occasional pressure, especially from families with Arapahoe children whose parents did not marry, the Arapahoe councilmen do not deviate from the criteria set in 1956. Cases in dispute always are referred to the tribe's attorney; his decision is accepted by the councilmen. (As we shall see, legal enrollment and "degree of blood" are not considered central criteria for *cultural* identity.)

The concern over keeping the enrollment down was magnified by a suit brought by an Arapahoe woman in an attempt to force the tribe to enroll her children, fathered by a non-Arapahoe.[11] In fighting the suit, councilmen were seen by their constituents as protectors not only of the tribe's solvency, but also of the Arapahoes' "sovereign government."[12] An Arapahoe wrote in response to a letter to the editor of the *Riverton Ranger*, "You say the BIA has the last word concerning all our tribal laws; you're right to a certain degree, but we still have a few laws of our own that still hold true and one of them is enrollment, and that's what you women are fighting against."[13] And one man explained the tribe's position in this way: "The suit would do away with tribal law." To the council's relief, the case was dismissed in 1971.

It is also the Arapahoe Business Council's responsibility to ensure that the tribe's income is expended in ways acceptable to its constituents, that is, in culturally prescribed ways. Allocation takes the form of institutionalized sharing. The process of redistribution serves as a leveling device. This strategy is evident in employment policies, the budgeting of tribal funds for grants and loans, and policies of land management.

High unemployment is a central concern of the council. The per capita payment does not cover living expenses, and unenrolled family members are not entitled to such benefits as tribal loans and grants, tribal scholarships, most reservation jobs, and the right to hunt on the reservation and to fish without a license. A March 1975 BIA report indicated that of an available labor force of 1,125, 375 men and 210 women were employed, and 292 men and 248 women unemployed. These figures represented a 48 percent unemployment rate, about the same rate of unemployment reported for the same month in 1968.[14]

A recent survey reported that 43 percent of the total jobs held on the reservation in 1974 were in agriculture, 31 percent in government and services (food preparation, aide work, protective service, janitorial work), and 7.7 percent in minerals and mining.[15] Most of the jobs held by Indians are tribally funded (roughly three-fourths), followed by BIA and U.S. Indian Health Service positions. A high job turnover and high incidence of absenteeism are routinely tolerated in the reservation-based jobs. Indians are rarely hired off the reservation except as seasonal agricultural workers. Fremont County is heavily industrialized, with a large percentage of jobs in iron and uranium mines and oil and gas fields; these positions are held primarily by whites. Locally, Indians are hired in the most menial jobs, largely because of discrimination, the disinclination of many Indians to work at the same job for long periods of time without absenteeism,[16] and the reluctance or inability of Indians to commute forty to sixty miles daily to jobs off the reservation.

Educational levels among the Arapahoes lag behind those of Wyoming residents; for Wind River Indians in 1970, the United States Census indicates a median of 10.3 years of schooling. Recent federal and tribal incentives, however, have spurred higher educational attainments. In 1968 twelve Shoshones and three Arapahoes had B.A. or M.A. degrees; by 1970 the comparable figures were thirty-eight Shoshones and eighteen Arapahoes.[17] Employment opportunities for most Arapahoes—even those with degrees—are still better on the reservation than off, and employment is most likely in tribal or federal positions. Yet the reservation jobs generally offer low pay and many are only part-time.

The joint business councilmen budget a sizable portion of the tribes' income for salaries. In addition, they expend great efforts to obtain federal grants and, more recently, state funds with which to hire Shoshones and Arapahoes. Since 1971 the council has pressed successfully for funds from the state office of the Department of Public Assistance and Social Service. Indians were hired to staff the food-stamp program (which replaced commodity distribution in 1974), the meals program for the elderly, Aid to Families with Dependent Children, and the program to insulate the homes of the elderly. The hiring of staff is generally done by the councilmen, all twelve of whom act as an employment committee; and the people they recommend for Indian Health Service or BIA jobs are often hired. Since 1975 the council has used federal grant money (Comprehensive Employment and Training Act funds) to give temporary employment to more than three hundred Indians.[18]

In selecting employees, the Arapahoe Business Council places priority on the financial need of the applicants and on frequency of prior employment—the needy and those who have had little employment are often hired before the less needy, and in fact before the more qualified or experienced. Reputation for participation in the sharing network is also a factor in hiring. People who can be counted on to be generous in helping others in the tribe are considered to be entitled to a job or some other form of aid; people who do not share with other Arapahoes can expect little tribal aid. The councilmen work toward maximum hiring rather than a minimum wage level. For example, in 1974, when the BIA employed fifty-one Indians and paid them $462,800 in wages, approximately the same amount ($476,440) was expended by the Business Council for salaries for five times as many people. A person is usually not penalized for leaving a job; job turnover permits a wider distribution of the funds available for employment. One of the council's main objectives is to allocate jobs impartially; that is, when hiring is done, jobs are allocated among as many families as possible. If several brothers apply for jobs in a work crew, only one is selected. And by custom councilmen abstain from the selection process if a close relative is an applicant.

Thus the council's aim is to distribute tribal income in some form or other to as many Arapahoes as possible. Both in employment policy and in the allocation of grants to clubs, ceremonial groups, and individuals, councilmen give concrete expression to the Arapahoe view that resources are to be shared throughout the tribal community and that economic differentials are destructive to the tribe in both a social and a spiritual sense.

The first of each month Arapahoe families wait in line at the post office to receive their per capita checks. The entire amount is usually spent within the week, and families (particularly those with no employed members) may then resort to pawning property or asking merchants for credit. But for the most part, Arapahoes count on a system of institutionalized sharing, and petition the councilmen for tribal aid. People with money or food are expected to share with relatives or friends upon request. Thus the meals program for the elderly functions to distribute food throughout the community almost daily,[19] and those with jobs help those without. The sharing process is institutionalized in the "donation dance": families who need money to meet an emergency (usually for travel expenses for a serviceman or a visitor from another tribe) spread a blanket in the center of the dance hall or camp circle, and other members of the tribe place contributions on it. In a discussion of contemporary Arapahoe patterns of exchange, Sara Hunter notes pervasive networks of reciprocity reinforced by a high value placed on generosity. "One informant said his grandmother always told him to share whatever he had: 'If someone comes to your door and wants to borrow flour, even if you only have a little, share with him. . . .' Another informant said her grandmother always told her: 'Don't be afraid to give. Even your most prized possession. Something will always come back to you.'"[20]

The Arapahoe council budgets funds both directly, to aid needy individuals, and indirectly, to aid other leadership groups to make distributions. Money is allocated to sodalities to help them to finance communal feasts and celebrations. This practice in turn buttresses the leadership status of the sodalities. Tribal celebrations are held at least once a month, at which time money, property, and food are given away. (Recipients who are particularly hard-pressed may inconspicuously sell or hock property received on these occasions.) Each of the clubs—often with aid from the council, occasionally with the help of local non-Indian merchants or with funds they raise themselves from contributions or from such money-making ventures as selling soda and coffee at tribal events—is responsible for sponsoring one or more celebrations on such holidays as Christmas, Veterans' Day, and Memorial Day. At a Flag Day celebration recently sponsored by one of the women's auxiliaries, the women purchased and cooked one whole cow; they made a potato salad of 100 pounds of potatoes and fourteen dozen eggs; they distributed 150 loaves of bread, several pounds of fried bread, twelve dozen sweet rolls, a large quantity of canned tomatoes, and several gallons of soup, coffee, and fruit punch. A family that attends such a function may accumulate enough groceries to last a day or two.

Individuals may apply to the council for grants for all sorts of personal needs, including groceries, unpaid bills, travel money, health care, school clothing, and funeral expenses. The grants to individuals and families are made by the Welfare Committee, composed of all six councilmen. Families, like clubs, are obligated to make generous periodic distributions to other Arapahoes. Every family sponsors a large giveaway and a feast for the tribe as part of the mortuary ritual for a deceased relative, and holds another giveaway several months after the death as a memorial. Clubs and individuals assist with expenses, but even families with more than average means may go heavily in debt to fulfill the obligation. Families also hold giveaways for relatives who return from military service or who have been honored in some way.

The funds available for the council's loan program are limited and not every loan request can be met, but the council-appointed members of the Arapahoe Credit Committee attempt to distribute the available money as widely as possible. In General Council meetings, this guide-line is periodically reinforced by members of the tribe. At a meeting on September 28, 1968, an Arapahoe expressed dissatisfaction with the committee's failure to approve a loan to every applicant: "The reason why I brought it up was that it appears to me there's a lot of us here that's being deprived on a loan because you're a drunk, you're a gambler, or you have opposed the superintendent or you have op-posed the council. It's not right. I think a man, I mean he's going to go out here to, well, supposing if I was a drunk, but I went out here to say, 'Well, I think I'm going to go out and get me a loan for cows or a house,' well, I believe they should give this guy a loan."[21] When applications for loans are being considered, the spending patterns of applicants or the likelihood of their making repayment are not weighed as heavily as need and reputation.

An additional thrust of council activity is the preservation of the tribe's land base and the allocation of land to members of the tribe so that the majority benefit, rather than the few. It is the policy of the joint council to buy land from individuals who wish to sell their allot-ments or their portion of land that they have inherited, and thus to prevent the sale of reservation lands to non-Arapahoes or non-Sho-shones. Land purchases are made with the funds at the tribes' disposal in the U.S. Treasury, and more recently with additional funds obtained through federal loan programs. When individually owned trust land is put up for sale, the council has the right to match the highest bid and to acquire the property. In fact, the vast majority of reservation land now is owned not individually but in trust by the tribes. The joint council makes assignments of this land for homesites, so that individ-uals without allotments are not homeless.

In 1976 the Wind River Reservation contained 2,268,000 acres, with 1,778,096 acres (a little over 78 percent) jointly owned in trust status by the Arapahoe and Shoshone tribes. This acreage represents an increase of 4,753 acres since 1968. In 1976 individual Arapahoes and Shoshones owned 106,982 acres in trust status. Non-Indians and a few patent-in-fee Indian owners had 381,626 acres (about 6,582 acres were owned by Indians). Non-Indians own most of the land in the Riverton reclamation area (see Map 6). And 1,296 acres were reserved by the BIA for the agency site at Fort Washakie. The aim of the coun-cil is to buy back as much of the fee-patent and non-Indian-owned land as possible. Moreover, the council gives enrolled Indians preference in leasing tribal land for grazing, farming, or business, and non-Indians who obtain leases pay a higher fee. In 1975, 1,752,582 acres were as-signed by the joint council to Indians and 18,173 acres to whites. Only a few Arapahoes have grazing leases, and the amount assigned to individuals is adequate for only very small herds. In 1967, for example, 22 Arapahoes owned 1,782 head of cattle (the median number owned was 42), while 10,356 head were owned by 89 Shoshones. A large portion of the range is assigned to the Arapahoe Ranch, where the stock is tribally owned and the profits are divided equally among all Arapahoes.[22]

In all respects, then, the Arapahoe Business Council attempts with the means at its disposal to maximize the tribe's resources, and so far as possible to allocate those resources in roughly equal shares, with priority placed on aiding the most needy. The results are a general leveling process, on the one hand, and the potential for councilmen to wield considerable economic power, on the other.

Indian–White Relations

The council member's role as an intermediary between the tribe and the white society is colored by the tribe's economic deprivation relative to neighboring whites, periodic threats to cultural and what remains of political autonomy, and challenges to tribal pride. Whites are viewed as adversaries, and the present-day anxieties about the whites' intentions and the expectation that intermediaries must be capable of effective advocacy are reinforced by the elders who describe Arapahoe leaders of the past as men who struggled to prevent, offset, or resist the harm that whites sought to do. One frequently told story about Sharp Nose provides a kind of charter for the councilmen's dealings with whites. When Sharp Nose knew he was dying, he sent for a friend and left with him his last message to the Arapahoes. This is one elderly Arapahoe's version of the story:

> "Now you carry what I tell you." He told that to Sitting Eagle, his friend. They're about the same age. "I'm going to tell you about white people. . . . I picked this place to be my reservation. So they bring us up here, but the white people going to watch us; agent, to protect us and learn us what they're doing now. But I tell you, people—tell them—the white people sometimes they get tricky," he said. "They might cheat you out of something and they might cheat you. But always watch out for that tricky stuff. I heard about white people cheating themselves and they going cheat Indians too." And that's happening now. Been happening right along. That's what he told him. And in a couple days, he died.[23]

Today councilmen "watch out" for their constituents against the "tricky" whites in an aggressive and sometimes combative manner, in sharp contrast to the cooperative and conciliatory strategy of earlier times. The income from royalties and bonuses provides the council with the means to intervene effectively on behalf of the tribe. Councilmen vigorously seek to recoup past losses, to strengthen the degree of political independence they have managed to attain, and to augment the benefits that accrue to a federally recognized tribe living on a reservation.

Reservation Status: The Implications of Legal Separatism

The federal government is charged with preventing the alienation of Indian lands held in trust, with protecting tribal resources, and with providing certain services in the area of land management, health, education, and welfare. Federal agents periodically encourage the tribe's representatives to assume more responsibility, particularly financial responsibility, in providing services. The council pressures the federal government to exercise its responsibilities more competently and to assume more of the costs of managing the reservation (while at the same time relinquishing authority to the tribe in some areas). Much of the substance of contemporary reservation politics revolves around these maneuverings.

BIA services are looked upon as "treaty obligations," not as gratuities.[24] Councilmen are expected to press the government to fulfill its obligations to the tribe. As one Arapahoe explained to me, "Indians feel they are owed."

Arapahoes often expect unequivocal aid from BIA employees. For example, tribe members occasionally solicit help from the BIA's Road Department to gravel the roads leading from their homes to the highway. The department's policy is to furnish the gravel, equipment, and technical aid, but not the labor. The Arapahoes consider the BIA's refusal to complete the graveling process as typical of the government's failure to meet its obligations to Indians.

The council tries to make sure that the BIA and other federal agencies assume as many as possible of the expenses incurred by the tribe. For example, in response to repeated Indian complaints about health care, in 1969 Public Health Service officials tried to persuade the council members to share the responsibility of planning the health program on the reservation and of explaining the policies and the program to their constituents. The council rejected the proposal. The federal government was bound "by treaty" to assume the full burden for health care, the councilmen contended, and sharing of responsibility would weaken this historic obligation. One Business Council member noted that the council's best strategy was periodically to petition Public Health for additional benefits, and a joint planning program would appreciably weaken its role as petitioner.

New programs often are perceived as long-due "treaty" benefits. In recent years, as part of a general policy to grant Indians more self-determination, the federal government has contracted with tribes for the operation of schools. In 1972 a contract high school was established at Ethete, despite opposition from the Riverton and Lander public school officials, who were wary of losing Indian students and with them the federal funds designated for their education. One elderly Arapahoe man viewed the Wyoming Indian High School as part of the payment due the tribe for land cessions: "The government made a deal with Sharp Nose and Washakie, they's going to be Indian schools built so they could learn talk English and numbers, read and write. . . . And they donate all around pasture, farming land. . . . The treaty was all Indian schools appropriated by the government. Up through first grade, to high school, to college schools. They'd be furnished, appropriated by the government. That's the treaty. . . . Now they [Riverton and Lander] kicking us about that high school. I know they couldn't very well do it. That's Indian money and the treaty says they're going to go through education for all Indians." In the minds of many Arapahoes, the people involved in the effort to acquire the school were pressuring the federal government to honor "the treaties."[25]

Many Arapahoes also viewed the per capita payments as income due them because of their status as Indians. Until recently, the per capita checks were issued by the BIA with the consent of the councilmen, who did not wish to bear the administrative expense. The Arapahoes refer to the per capita payment as *chéé'eyóóno,* "what they hand out to you" or "what they issue you." This is the same term that was used to refer to the annuity payments prescribed by treaty in former times. The BIA superintendent is referred to as *chéé'eyééhinen,* "he who gives [it] out." Councilmen are credited with achieving the distribution of per capita money by "standing up to the government." They mediate between the people and the government, and when they are successful, "issue" in various forms is the result.

The Arapahoes conceive of federal benefits and services as "payments" to which they are morally and legally entitled. In contrast, proposals for aid to be extended by private groups or individuals usually are rejected. The councilmen and their constituents resent "do-gooders."

In expressing the conviction that the Arapahoe people need leaders who are able to resist intimidation and behave aggressively toward non-Indians, one Arapahoe man put it this way: "The people *them-selves* won't rock the boat; they'll sit back and take their licks." The controls still exerted by the superintendent and his staff are viewed as irksome and heavy-handed interference. Councilmen are expected to offset BIA interference in their constituents' personal lives. In one man's words, "We need somebody to get out and go in the white world and not back down."

Under certain circumstances the superintendent of the BIA office at Wind River can withhold funds from the individual Indian money accounts, in which individuals' income from the sale and lease of trust land is deposited. Funds can be withheld for debts to the United States or the tribes, and on the recommendation of the BIA Social Service Department in the case of minors, the elderly, or the mentally handicapped. The superintendent can require an individual to submit a family budget acceptable to BIA staff members before funds from the individual account are released. Moreover, the BIA can institute unpopular conservation measures or limit the number of livestock that can be grazed on reservation lands. The BIA also selects individuals for many job-training programs and administers federal scholarships— activities that frequently raise accusations of unfair treatment.

It is in this context, then, that Arapahoe councilmen personally intercede with the BIA staff on behalf of individual Arapahoes. A "councilman," the Arapahoes say, is "one you can come to with a problem." Councilmen "speak up" for their constituents, and by the grant and loan programs they administer, as well as their watchfulness in relation to per capita payments, they compensate for the uncertainty about access to the money in individual accounts.

The councilmen are generally successful today in offsetting actions of the Fort Washakie BIA which affect the tribe as a whole. The business councils' procedure is to notify the tribes' attorneys in Washington, D.C., when there is a conflict. These legal representatives then petition BIA officials in the office of the commissioner of Indian affairs or the secretary of the interior. Almost without exception in recent years, controversial regional and local BIA decisions have been reversed. The fact that the Wind River tribes did not organize under the Indian Reorganization Act has resulted in increased flexibility. Because their actions are not limited by by-laws, the attorneys have more room to maneuver to offset policies that the Business Council opposes.[26]

The council's success in dealing with BIA representatives is also due in part to the fact that the Arapahoe councilmen almost invariably act unanimously. They decide among themselves on a course of action, and, having reached a consensus, approach the BIA staff—or, when necessary, the attorneys—from a position of unity. In matters of interest to the joint council, the Shoshone and Arapahoe business councils often present a solid front, as well—at least in matters defined as "Indian versus white."

Councilmen also work to defend tribal sovereignty in relation to state, Fremont County, and municipal interests. Although most adult Arapahoes avoid face-to-face conflict with neighboring whites, there are periodic court battles over legal jurisdiction. The trust status of reservation lands—exempt from local property taxes—is irksome to many local whites, and they eye reservation resources with interest and hope to profit from the needs of Indians as consumers. Whites view the federal protection of Indian lands as unfair, and particularly resent the fact that Indians do not "use" or "develop" the land. One Lander resident whose family settled in the area in the mid-nineteenth century expressed his frustration thus: "They [nomadic Indians] were in [this part of] Wyoming two or three weeks out of the year, at the most three months out of the year. Whereas my family at that time was here the whole year round. When they talk about indigenous and things like that, it's ridiculous."

Local and state interests frequently conflict with tribal interests. The council has been successful in holding local whites at bay by means of the legal assistance furnished by its attorneys; in former times, when the federal government was the tribe's only recourse, they were less successful. One recent conflict involved the joint council's suit to overrule the county's issue of a liquor license to a prominent white businessman who wanted to operate a bar on the reservation. The businessman's repeated disregard of council instructions about health problems angered the councilmen, and in 1974 they took the issue to court to establish their jurisdiction on the reservation. The attorneys argued successfully that the county could not grant a license to a business in the reservation community, even though it was on nontrust land. In a similar case not yet settled the Shoshone and Arapahoe tribes claim jurisdiction in a right-to-access dispute involving a business that was established on fee-patent land but which claims access from the public highway through land held in trust.[27] A current concern is the issue of water rights. The tribes are seeking to prevent the state from attaining control over the use and allocation of the water from the rivers that rise in the mountains in the western sector of the reservation.

"Don't Tell Them White People about It": The Implications of Social Separatism

The conflict over jurisdiction reinforces and is conditioned by the strained relations and misunderstandings between Indians and whites in general. There are white families living on the reservation and in two adjacent towns, but there is little contact on a personal level: few friendships are formed and no joint activities take place. Each group clings to stereotypes and assails the moral worth of the other. Blatant economic exploitation, social discrimination, and prejudice against Indians is countered by Arapahoe leaders—both councilmen and elders—on a number of levels.

Arapahoes have about 434 non-Indian neighbors on their section of the reservation. Some operate small farms and live among the Arapahoes, and some are members of the staffs of the two elementary schools and live in the school compounds. Few whites have married Arapahoes and moved onto the reservation. An additional 360 or so whites reside on the Shoshone section of the reservation. A handful of Indian Public Health Service and white BIA employees reside in the government compound at Fort Washakie. There is virtually no social interaction on a personal level between the adult Arapahoe and white residents of Wind River. Both Indians and whites pick up mail at the post offices and attend the mission churches, but they usually do not visit each other's homes or attend weddings or funerals together. From time to time friendships are formed with transient whites—in recent years a few Public Health physicians and their families, and occasionally a teacher. These ties are looked at askance by the other whites. Many of the white children attend the elementary schools at Ethete and Arapahoe, and in recent years there has been occasional conflict between white and Indian children.

Riverton, with a population of about 10,000, is actually within the reservation boundary, but the 100 or so Arapahoes who live there consider themselves "off the reservation." Most of these families intend only temporary residence in Riverton, and frequently move back to Ethete or Arapahoe. Lander has a population of about 8,000, including about 40 Arapahoes. A few Arapahoe and Shoshone young people commute to attend high school and reservation residents do their shopping in these towns, but Indians do not attend the churches there or join their social clubs. Indian patients are admitted to hospitals in the two towns, with Public Health assuming the cost, although Indians and Public Health officials have complained of discrimination. Indians and whites rarely visit with each other on the street or in the stores. Despite physical proximity, the two groups keep to themselves.

Local whites assail the moral worth of Indians in innumerable ways, thereby justifying their differential treatment of Indians and whites.[28] Indians are categorized as financially irresponsible. Local whites call the per capita payments a "dole," implying that it is unearned and therefore immoral. Although townspeople are repeatedly informed that the payments come from proceeds of the tribes' own resources, comparable to the stock dividends received by many non-Indians, they continue to cite the Indians' acceptance of the payments as evidence of their lack of moral fiber. Indian values and attitudes in regard to work differ from those of whites. Employment is valued, but reporting for work does not take precedence over family or ceremonial commitments. When sharing is a moral imperative, saving is not possible, and therefore when families come to town with money they have little incentive to refrain from spending it. To whites, these aspects of Indian behavior are clear evidence that Indians are lazy and improvident. Some local businessmen do not hesitate to overcharge an Indian when they know he has just received his per capita payment or a tribal grant or loan. And some merchants encourage Indians to buy on lay-away or pawn property, knowing that the debt may not be paid and thus the initial payment or property may be forfeited. While such practices may be regarded as immoral in transactions with whites, Indians are fair game.

As the yards around Indian homes usually lack landscaping and are used as storage areas, the homes themselves are described by whites as "dirty." In the view of whites, Indian families are "disorganized" and parents do not "discipline" their children. Actually, child care is shared by many relatives, with young cousins ("brothers" and "sisters," as they are called and thought of by Arapahoes) frequently rotating their residence from one household to another. Adults usually employ indirect methods of correction and often delegate older children to look after younger ones.

Drinking behavior is another area of conflict. Indians sometimes drink to excess in town and are unable for one reason or another to return the twenty or so miles to the reservation. They are labeled "drunks." Whites who drink to excess usually are quietly escorted by the police to their homes in town.

Compounding these difficulties are the disputes over jurisdiction. The special status of Indian lands and the relationship between the tribe and the federal government are sources of resentment to the whites.

Many whites view the Indian status as "anti-American," and feel that Indians should be treated the same as other citizens. Note this comment by one local white: "This idea of saying that because we happen to have a whole band of them who are associated in tribal ancestry, they're different, I just don't buy that. I don't agree with it. . . . There is no more Indian heritage that I can think of to doing anything that they refer to as Indian heritage than there is to cowboy heritage for me to do such things. I don't plan to live in a sheep camp but a large number of my forebears did all their lives." Discriminatory treatment of Indians by whites is justified by whites' categorization of Indians as "different"; yet whites also resent Indians for their special status vis-à-vis the rest of the population.

The Arapahoes are aware of the negative white stereotypes and the resentments. They, in turn, harbor a series of stereotypes about whites. Whites are viewed as "materialistic." They are seen as lacking strong feelings for kin. Whites' emphasis on nuclear-family relationships and on sharing with the immediate family and with lineal sets of relations more often than with collateral kin is viewed as "stinginess." Self-sufficiency and economic independence is seen not in positive terms, but as another indication that a white person "only thinks of himself." Whites are regarded as "pushy" and "mouthy." A person who is out-going and affable even with strangers is well thought of among whites, but Arapahoes, who view modesty and reticence as central to social harmony, view such a person with suspicion. Thus the moral worth of whites is challenged, and although Indians are not in a position to discriminate in off-reservation contacts, breaches of social norms in relation to whites are more often excused than similar transgressions against other Arapahoes.

Arapahoes also view their own way of life as morally superior to that of whites because of the special tie between the Arapahoes and the Great Mystery. The relationship between the supernatural and whites is more distant. Elders particularly reinforce these sentiments. Note, for example, this account by an elder, who stresses that although whites are disrespectful of Indian religion, they are confounded and worried by it just the same:

> That museum over there, there's a lot of stuff in there. I don't know where they got it. But there's some stuff they shouldn't bother. There's a beaver hide and some medicine in there, and this white fellow took it out and had it on display. My grandson told him, "You better put that back in there. It don't belong on that table here." So he put it back in there and they wrapped it up again. . . . In the evening when they turn the lights off in that museum, I think about eight o'clock or nine o'clock, they turn the lights off. Later on, there's

light in there again, in the whole building. They said, "They often wonder what causes that." And I told them, I says, "Those people that had those things [the "medicine"] are the ones that turned the lights on again," I told them. "But you don't have to tell them white people about it; they'll find out themselves," I told them.[29]

Elders, in their interpretation of Arapahoe–white relations, perpetuate the values of the Arapahoe way of life and reinforce Arapahoe cultural identity through their stories. One old man told this story to young Arapahoes:

You hear the old people say *nootinei, nootinei.* He married his own daughter. He told his family, "You roll me up and hang me up in a tree." He says, "There's a man coming. His name is *koo'ookunnootinei,* One-Eyed Sioux. And you want to give him our daughter so they'll get married and then he can make a living for you." So, he played like he was dead. So they wrapped him up and hanged him on a tree. Then later on he unraveled himself, kept following this camp. They moved one place then another place. Later on, he'd come to the camp and he was trying to talk Sioux, but he couldn't talk very good. But this old lady, his wife, said, "Oh my, when this Sioux is going to come, why he told me to marry my daughter off to him so he could make a living for us." So he married this girl that was his own daughter. And then one morning I guess he slept late. But, he put mud on his eye, so he just had one eye. And this girl said, "Mama, he looks like my dad." "No, your dad died long ago. That ain't him." "No, I think it's him." So they went over and looked at him. And it was him! So his wife took a club and started clubbing him. That's where that story comes from. Maybe that's the reason why these white men, you know, marry Indian women. How they put mud in their eye, you know. That's what they say, you know. They tease people that way— *"koo'ookunnootinei."* That's One-Eyed Sioux.[30]

The implication of the story is, first, that whites, like the trickster figure who marries his own daughter in this old Pan Plains story, are exploitive (that is, they marry Indian women in order to profit from economic benefits these women receive from the tribe). And second, whites, like the trickster, are both powerful and foolish: they violate the moral laws of well-ordered society, and thus, while they may succeed in their deceptions for a time, ultimately their transgressions are exposed.

The councilmen's efforts to bolster pride in Arapahoe cultural identity are evident in several ways. They try to insulate the tribe's members as much as possible from economic exploitation and social embarrassments. A liberal policy regarding grants and loans helps to minimize the need for Arapahoes to seek financial aid from local whites (although such help is sometimes sought). When an Arapahoe mother offers a child for adoption or when a home situation so far deteriorates that Arapahoe leaders acknowledge that the children should be removed, councilmen make sure that whites do not obtain the children. They are placed with Indian families. In the few cases of Indian-white marriage, the council may place limitations on the white parents' access to their children's per capita payments. In cases of divorce, the children's payments may be placed in a trust account until the children reach adulthood. The council enthusiastically supports and grants funds to clubs that sponsor tribal celebrations; reservation-oriented recreation is considered preferable to exposure to stressful town situations (although Indian families do enjoy trips to town to shop and to patronize drive-in fast-food establishments). Councilmen try to prevent "insults" to Indian people, as such incidents reflect adversely on their abilities as protectors.

When councilmen personally represent the tribe in interaction with local whites, they are expected to conduct themselves with skill and dignity. The two local newspapers, the *Riverton Ranger* and the *Wyoming State Journal* (published in Lander), carry the names of the day's arrests in each town. Indian families read these papers regularly and show keen interest in the columns that give the names of people arrested and the charges brought against them. A councilman's arrest for public intoxication or any other legal offense in one of the towns is a most serious breach of trust. Such a thing rarely happens. If councilmen drink socially, they are careful not to do so off the reservation. In fact, councilmen rarely appear at official town functions. Avoidance lessens the chance of a social slight. Councilmen are also charged with controlling the behavior of whites on the reservation. They harass employees who annoy Indians and they work to prevent the hiring of whites who do not interact graciously with Indians.

In short, local whites' discriminatory behavior and prejudice toward Indians figure in the Indians' expectations in regard to the role of councilman. Today councilmen are more aggressive and less tolerant of slights than they were in past eras.

Shoshone Neighbors

Despite 100 years of proximity, the Shoshones and the Arapahoes are still socially and culturally distinct. The members of the two tribes have not learned each other's language. There has been no significant diffusion and almost no intermarriage: in 1968, sixty-three Arapahoes were married to Shoshones (see Table 8).[31] While Arapahoes and

Table 8
Number of Arapahoes with Shoshone spouses,
by age group and sex, 1968

Age group	Males	Females	Total
69 and older			
58–68		1	1
48–57	3	2	5
38–47	12	5	17
28–37	11	8	19
18–27	12	9	21
Total	38	25	63

Source: Arapahoe Tribal Census Roll, Shoshone-Arapahoe Tribal Office, Fort Washakie, Wyo.

Shoshones sometimes attend peyote meetings together, strong ties between families are apparently not formed. Forced by circumstances to share limited reservation resources, they have periodic conflicts and harbor resentment and suspicion toward each other.

Shoshone households—nuclear or extended families—are scattered along the tributaries of the Wind and Little Wind. Shoshone homes are much farther apart than those of the Arapahoes. The dispersed settlement pattern accompanies a loose, flexible social organization. In contrast to the Arapahoes, the Shoshones have no cross-cutting institutions (such as sodalities) that mediate kinship divisions, nor do they hold frequent tribal gatherings or tribal giveaways.[32] Reciprocity is found more often within the family. The Shoshone Sun Dance ritual is much more individualistic than the Arapahoe ceremony.[33] And political factionalism corresponds in large part to the residential areas of Trout Creek, South Fork (of the Little Wind), North Fork (of the Little Wind), Sage Creek, Morton, Crowheart, and Burris. Often political activity centers on disadvantaging a rival faction. Thus Shoshone sociopolitical organization stands in sharp contrast to the Arapahoe pattern of consensus and consolidation.

Many Shoshones today, as in past generations, marry whites. The tribal census indicates that over three-fourths of the Shoshones have some white ancestry. And many enrolled Shoshones have less than

"one-fourth degree" of Shoshone "blood." Shoshones classify themselves as either "full blood" or "mixed blood"; these are largely social,
not biological, categories. The groups have different lifestyles, political
strategies, and economic orientations.[34]

In contrast, Arapahoes intermarry very little (in 1968 about seventy
Arapahoes were married to whites—few of whom were local residents—
and most of these Arapahoes were living off the reservation); about
48 percent are enrolled as full-blood (see Table 9); and while several
hundred Arapahoes have some white ancestry, few are classified as
mixed-bloods. The Arapahoes, unlike the Shoshones, have not tried to
adapt to economic, social, and political discrimination by extensively
participating in white institutions or by intermarriage with local whites.
And individual or family ranching is much more common among Shoshone families—who are not morally obliged to participate in intratribal sharing—than among Arapahoes, for whom wage work is more
practical in view of the leveling mechanisms operating in the tribe's
economics.

Given the nature of the relationships between these two tribes, each
perceives the other as a potential threat to its own political and economic well-being. Shoshones still on occasion refer to Arapahoes as
"trespassers," and periodically talk of trying to put them off the
reservation. Continued resentment toward Arapahoes is abetted by the
Shoshones' awareness of the growing numerical strength of the enrolled
Arapahoes. At the time of settlement, the Shoshones outnumbered the
Arapahoes, but today there are three Arapahoes for every two Shoshones, even though Shoshone criteria for enrollment are less strin-
gent.[35] Shoshone women can enroll their children in the tribe even if
the father is not Shoshone. Moreover, approval of applicants is sometimes based on political considerations, rather than conformity to the
established criteria. The Shoshones also view the increase in political
and economic strength of the Arapahoes as a challenge to their continued well-being.

Similarly, the Arapahoes' anxiety about their own economic predicament is intensified by the Shoshone presence. Despite their smaller
population, the Shoshones share equally in all reservation resources,
including BIA and tribal jobs. Thus the Shoshone per capita payment is
$135, considerably higher than the $90 paid to Arapahoes. The Arapahoes sometimes are denied work when the Arapahoe job quota (by a
"gentlemen's agreement" among joint council members) is filled, even
though there may not be enough Shoshone applicants to fill the available jobs. Range assignments are an additional source of conflict.

Table 9

Arapahoe population enrolled at Wind River Reservation,
December 1968, by degree of Arapahoe blood and age group

Degree of Arapahoe blood	Age group								
	0–9	10–14	15–20	21–34	35–44	45–54	55–64	65 and older	All ages
8/8	293	149	164	309	163	94	58	65	1,295
7/8	224	104	113	111	30	12	2	0	596
6/8	99	59	54	55	18	20	10	12	327
5/8	46	25	25	30	11	4	0	0	141
4/8	16	27	44	22	11	15	6	9	150
3/8	24	18	29	11	6	4	1	0	93
2/8	5	20	13	18	15	7	0	1	79
1/8	0	0	33	8	0	0	0	0	41
All Arapahoes	707	402	475	564	254	156	77	87	2,722

Source: Arapahoe Tribal Census Roll, Shoshone-Arapahoe Tribal Office, Fort Washakie, Wyo.

Shoshones who wish to expand their cattle operations are thwarted by the large acreage assigned to the Arapahoe Ranch.

In joint council proceedings, Arapahoe councilmen generally vote as a block. The Shoshones are aware of this tendency and often are anxious about the potential damage to their interests. If the Shoshone vote splits along factional lines, as it often does, the Arapahoe councilmen can dominate the proceedings. Moreover, since the time of Nell Scott's service on the council, the Arapahoes have increasingly tended to assume an assertive stance in relation to whites, no longer allowing Shoshone "mixed-bloods" the principal spokesman role. These considerations increase the insecurity that the Shoshones feel in regard to sharing Wind River with the Arapahoes. Yet the Arapahoes frequently forbear to take advantage of Shoshone factionalism; they sometimes compromise in order to maintain long-range cooperative relations, so that in conflicts with whites the two tribes' resentment of each other does not work against their joint interests. In this spirit, by custom the chairmen of the councils alternate the job of presiding over joint council meetings.[36]

POLITICAL STRATEGIES

In manipulating the symbols surrounding the "protector" and the "provider" aspects of council leadership, councilmen minimize dissent and generate support for policies and programs. As advocates for the tribe vis-à-vis the federal government, they seek to demonstrate their vigilance in furthering tribal interests. For example, in 1969 the Arapahoe Business Council refused to allow the BIA Law and Order Department to use the tribe's motor vehicles. If BIA personnel were to drive the cars owned by the tribe, constituents would have felt that the council was sharing responsibilities that at that time belonged to the federal government. Moreover, individual councilmen sometimes make a point of ridiculing or berating the agency superintendent in public places where their Arapahoe constituents can watch. A few minutes later, the two may be amicably talking about agency business in an office out of public view.[37]

In 1968, problems between local whites and Indians caught the attention of the governor of Wyoming, and he established the Governor's Advisory Council, a committee of reservation people, to act as liaison between the tribes and his office. From names submitted by the superintendent at the request of the council, three Arapahoes and three Shoshones were chosen by the joint council to serve on the committee. Several BIA employees urged that the people selected should be, in one official's words, "educated people who could talk, rather than accepted Indians in the community. . . . Indians can't express themselves." The superintendent suggested two councilmen and one former councilman as the Arapahoe members of the committee. Actually, the Arapahoes were extremely reluctant to serve, and two of the three resigned shortly after their appointment because of "conflict of interest." One of the replacements was considered to be loyal to Arapahoe interests and concerns; the other was a "mixed-blood" who had little contact with or understanding of the tribal community.

For the most part, the committee worked to attain state welfare benefits for Indians without jeopardizing the trust status of Indian lands. By 1969 the Arapahoe Business Council was wary of the group. The councilmen objected to the Advisory Council's efforts to deal independently with state officials and to seek benefits for Arapahoes. They also feared that involvement with the state might weaken the tribe's claims on federal aid. Success on the part of the advisers would undercut the position of the councilmen as intermediaries. Councilmen began to remark to their constituents that there were no "full-bloods" on the committee, that the members were not "doing any good," and that "they might want to take on too much." In other words, they could not be trusted and they would abuse their authority. At a meeting on April 16, 1969, one Advisory Council member pessimistically said, "I question what the council would give us the authority to talk about. . . . Too many times the Business Council can slant things and get a scapegoat." Soon after that, Arapahoe participation on the committee declined.

During a Shoshone General Council meeting in 1968, a Shoshone game warden made several derogatory remarks about Arapahoes, and word of the episode soon circulated through the Arapahoe community. At that time there were two other game wardens, both Arapahoes. Subsequently, in a joint business meeting, the Arapahoe council retaliated by proposing that the man's job be abolished—officially for disobedience to a council order, actually for insulting the Arapahoes. Five Arapahoes (one other was acting as chairman) and two Shoshones, who were members of a faction hostile to the game warden and his relatives, voted to abolish his job. The action put a tremendous strain on intertribal relations. For a time it was rumored that one of the two Arapahoe wardens would be fired in order to even things out. Eventually the council hired a Shoshone as the man's replacement and appointed him supervisor over the two Arapahoes. In this way the Arapahoe councilmen avenged the slight to their constituents' satisfaction, yet repaired their relations with the Shoshones.

Arapahoe councilmen frequently suggest that individuals who oppose their policies and decisions endanger the security of the tribe by inviting interference not only from whites but also from Shoshones. To gain support against their critics, the councilmen call them "radicals" and either suggest that they are dangerous deviants or tell anecdotes that hold the critics up to ridicule.

Councilmen can also circumvent criticism by attributing to Shoshone or non-Indian influence any decision that displeases individual Arapahoes. They are quite adept not only at manipulating federal officials into accepting responsibility but also at using these officials to better relations with their constituents. For example, when the Arapahoe Credit Committee was organized to act on applications for moderate and large loans, the council asked the BIA superintendent to sit on the committee with veto power. When a would-be borrower is considered to be a bad risk, the superintendent's veto can be blamed for the denial of the loan, while the Arapahoe committee members—and the councilmen who appointed them—avoid criticism. The superintendent wields his veto power very sparingly and takes into account the wishes of the committee in selecting those applications to be denied.

Constituents may apply some of the same tactics to influence the behavior of the councilmen. In 1970 several Arapahoe men, leaders in a peer group of men in their late thirties who were eager to gain political influence, began to generate support for a contract high school and pressured the federal government to finance it. The councilmen initially opposed the efforts of these ambitious "youths." But as the elders began to favor the plan and local whites and Shoshones opposed it, the councilmen changed their position. As soon as the proposal generated opposition from parties hostile to the tribe, the council felt obliged to assume a protective stance. The supporters of the school manipulated the opposition, even organizing a "camp-in" at the state capitol and releasing statements to the local press that provoked negative reaction from whites. The councilmen's reputations soon were linked with the success of the proposal to establish the school, and they supported the venture.

Councilmen also attempt to demonstrate their efficacy as providers by personally delivering council services so that they as individuals are associated in their constituents' minds with specific benefits. Old people who are granted a sum of money by the council may be presented with the authorization in person by one of the councilmen. Councilmen also may drive individuals to the agency and help them to deal with their difficulties with the superintendent.

Because the council carefully guards its prerogative to provide for its constituents' welfare, the councilmen were wary of the community health representatives or CHRs—three members of each tribe who, beginning in 1969, served as liaison between the Indian community and their employer, the Indian Health Service. When the CHRs solicited toys from local merchants to be used as prizes in a children's toothbrushing contest, the Arapahoe councilmen told them to stick to their job. The councilmen consider the distribution of goods—toys or anything else—to be their task; they may delegate it but they do not look kindly on those who assume it unasked. Similarly, when a club established by Arapahoe men in their thirties began to distribute firewood to elders, the council again took effective action to prevent infringement on a service customarily provided by the council.

Constituents are constantly alert for any failure on the part of the council to fulfill its responsibilities. In the spring of 1969 some people criticized the council's agreement to provide a trailer to be staffed by a Public Health physician and used as a first-aid station at tribal gatherings. Critics remarked, "We shouldn't have to furnish the trailer. That's Public Health's job. The council shouldn't have agreed to that." In order to avoid criticism while publicly displaying their accomplishments as providers, Arapahoe councilmen have to walk a very fine line indeed.

Finally, councilmen seek to manipulate the Arapahoes' negative attitudes toward the Shoshones in ways that buttress their pride in their cultural identity as Arapahoes. Since they are in frequent contact with Shoshones at Fort Washakie, they may entertain their constituents with tales of Shoshone ineptitude at the agency or Tribal Office and with reports of comments from outsiders about the richness of Arapahoe tradition in comparison with the Shoshone cultural tradition.

In sum, Arapahoe adaptation to a precarious socioeconomic situation results in a relationship between council and constituency that in some respects is a patron–client relationship. Councilmen are obliged to intercede for and provide for a constituency that in return is obligated to support the council's actions. As one councilman commented, "A tribal employee has no business not backing up the council." Recipients of any form of aid are similarly expected to be loyal. During the last generation, the Business Council has had unquestioned authority in secular matters. Opposition is checked and factional divisions are circumvented both by the councilmen's economic levers and by their skill in keeping the Shoshone and white communities sufficiently at bay so as to minimize the anxiety of their constituents.

At the root of the council's legitimacy is the fact that the tribe's elders sanction its authority in the secular realm. Of equal importance are the cultural constraints on abuse of the council's powers. To be recognized and supported as a councilman (or a leader in one of the sodalities), an individual must manage to acquire a reputation that reassures other Arapahoes of his social and moral fitness for the position. An individual who aspires to leadership must "make a name for himself."

6

"To Make a Name": The Cultural Context of Contemporary Leadership

Business councilmen and many sodality leaders are selected by ballot in public elections, but this process can hardly be said to parallel the electoral campaigns in the national society. Rather, from the Arapahoe viewpoint, balloting tends to formalize group consensus. Those who are regarded by their fellows as "good men"—those who have a "good name" or reputation—are chosen as councilmen. People who lack a good name are hard-pressed to generate support, no matter how well educated and highly motivated they may be. The importance the Arapahoes place on reputation is revealed in this exchange between two Arapahoes who discussed with me an impending council election:

"Things are pretty much cut and dried the way people will vote before the election."

"The old people decide before the election anyway."

The actions of individual Arapahoes are constantly being evaluated by others. In fact, the interpretations are as important as the acts themselves in determining reputation or "name." Behavior is interpreted in the context of a value system, a set of moral imperatives rooted in a conceptual framework in terms of which Arapahoes understand the world around them. Yet the framework provides room for maneuvering on the part of individuals who seek to attain leadership positions or to mobilize support for community goals. Hence, individuals can manipulate the ways others understand and evaluate their capabilities.

In efforts to construct and reconstruct reputation, relations between the old and the young are fundamental. Elders, and especially ceremonial elders or ritual authorities, are particularly involved in monitoring reputations and effecting behavioral transformations. Soon after birth, children are given a name (an "Indian name," in addition

256

to the legal name that appears on the tribal roll)[1] by an elderly relative, who selects a name that portends a "good life" (see Plate 13). The name may be that of an Arapahoe (one of the child's ancestors, usually) who had a long, successful, and respected life, or it may represent a "good thought" of the elderly person who names the infant. Occasionally an adult is given a new name by an elder in an attempt to help the person through a particularly difficult undertaking. Ceremonial elders, in addition to elderly relatives, continue to influence an individual's actions throughout his lifetime by offering counsel and, in the case of the ritual authorities, religious training. Relatives may take it upon themselves to request such guidance for a kinsman who is troubled in some way. From birth the Arapahoe is carefully observed by other Arapahoes and his behavior is constantly discussed both in his presence and in his absence. When a man is nominated for an office or when he is urged to register for the Arapahoe Business Council primary, he has already been acknowledged to have the right qualities for the office. One candidate for a recent council election put it this way: "The people know more about me than I do myself."

THE CONCEPTUAL ORDER

To ordinary Arapahoes, the universe operates in ways that can be affected by humans who have the requisite knowledge. A pervasive power or life force—*béétee* or Great Mystery Above (or Old Man, *hiicheebee nih'óóOoo*)—invests the universe.[2] *Béétee* on earth is first and foremost manifest in and resident in the Sacred Pipe (also referred to by priests as "the Old Man"). The pipe symbolizes the order of the universe and the Arapahoe tribe's covenant with the Great Mystery Above. The bowl of the pipe is circular, conceptually parallel to the universe itself, which is comprised of a center, from which radiate the "four corners" (cardinal directions; also the path of the sun), an above, and a below (earth).

In prayer the pipe is offered first to the four directions, then to the above and below, and then returned to the center (and the pipe is in ritual symbolically equated with the center and with the Great Mystery or Creator). The four directions may also be addressed as the "four old men," who represent all deceased ceremonial elders (or in earlier times apparently all deceased keepers of the Sacred Pipe). Prayers are for a "good" life journey, one in which the "four hills or ridges of life" are completed. Thus the life cycle is equated symbolically with the order of the universe, the progress of seasons and of the sun, the completion of self wherein one returns to one's beginning.[3] Even the problems brought by contact with the dominant white society can be alleviated by proper relations with the supernatural. For example, while Sun Dance vows are most commonly vows for the recovery of a sick relative, it is not unheard of for an individual to participate so that a relative will be released from prison.

In return for proper "respect" and supplication, the cosmic, natural, and social processes operate harmoniously and the individual's life journey is facilitated. For example, one is respectful toward animal life—the permission and goodwill of a sacrificial dog is sought before the animal is killed for a ceremony. One is respectful toward ritual objects—Arapahoes are careful never to cross the path of the Sacred Pipe. And controlled, harmonious relations between Arapahoes, especially during ritual acts, facilitate the supplication process. Violence toward another Arapahoe damages one's spiritual state. One elderly Arapahoe explained to me the consequences of an act of murder for one individual: "He killed a man. He went to Oklahoma and only comes back here for two days. He only comes out at night. And bad things have been happening to him since. His house burned down. Two children died and two are in prison."

The Sacred Pipe (the main object in the tribal medicine bundle) is symbolic of the life of the people. It contains and reminds the people of the Great Mystery, of the supernatural power accessible to the cooperating tribal group through correct and properly performed ritual acts executed by priest-intermediaries. The powers of the tribal bundle supersede any powers attained by individuals; in fact, Sacred Pipe rituals counteract power from any other source. Thus, while Arapahoes deny that any medicine man or *bééteet* today would or could commit destructive or "bad" acts against the social order or against the welfare of any individual, they still take care to check the potential use of *béétee* in this way by participating in pipe ritual.[4]

Access to *béétee* is the prerogative of priests (*bhe'iihoho'*, "old men"), men who occupy ritual offices for life. These ceremonial elders are intermediaries between the people and the Great Mystery Above. Individual prayer can be effective, but priestly mediation facilitates the supplication process. Today priests include the keeper of the Sacred Pipe, the keeper of the Sacred Wheel, Sun Dance medicine men, and keeper of the tribal drum.

Priesthood (and any position of ritual authority) is still attained through gradual acquisition of ritual knowledge by progression from one degree of knowledge to another, higher degree. Each degree necessitates a kind of ordeal, a difficult sacrifice or offering made as the result of a vow to the Great Mystery Above or to the Sacred Pipe. Progression through the degrees requires an apprenticeship of sorts to those who have already attained the higher degrees of supernatural knowledge sought, and who can teach the prescribed songs or ritual forms to the novice. Progression through degrees takes time and preparation, and is associated with increasing age. Successful performance of priestly duties requires great control and composure, not only during ritual acts, but in one's personal life as well. Mistakes, anger, or "bad thoughts" are likely to result in ineffective supplication, inclement weather conditions or a natural catastrophe, or disaster for the entire tribe or for the priest's family. Elders, who are best able to control their emotions, are best suited for priestly office.

The hierarchical principle, expressed in the institution of the priesthood, pervades Arapahoe ceremonial life and limits individualistic ritual expression. Yet it is tempered by the reciprocal relations between priest and novice. The senior authority, who is termed "elder" (or "grandfather") regardless of actual age (in fact, the highest authorities are elderly), is obligated to "respect" his junior, the novice. If the novice makes the proper supplication, to refuse or to fail to act in harmony with the interests of the novice would be disruptive of the priest's own relationship with the supernatural. Moreover, gifts received by ritual authorities properly are redistributed to others, never hoarded. Concomitantly, any individual who behaves in a careless or disrespectful way toward the supernatural or toward ritual authorities, or who acts in ways destructive of social harmony, may bring on himself supernatural retribution.[5]

BEING ARAPAHOE: CULTURAL VALUES AND POLITICS

Arapahoes put considerable pressure on each other to conform to cultural ideals regarding social relationships. Such ideals are an inherent part of the socialization process. Among the most important of these value orientations are the imperative of suppression of overt hostility and conflict; the stress on a persuasive rather than a directive style in interaction; the importance of deference to elders and conformity to role expectations associated with age categories; the need for acceptance of role expectations associated with sexual identity; and the necessity of meeting obligations of reciprocity and of behaving generously toward others. These values figure importantly in political relations, and they influence behavioral norms generally.

"Getting Along with the People"

Among the stories told by elders today is this one about an incident involving the nineteenth-century chief Black Coal: "He got jealous over a woman down the line somewhere . . . jealous of another man, an Arapahoe. He thought he was fooling around his wife. So he took a gun and shot that Arapahoe, shot him in the leg. But the man got all right; he didn't break a bone, flesh wound. So that spoiled him [Black Coal] for being chief, later, spoiled him. . . . He want to split the tribe. . . . He got jealous and pretty near killed his own tribe. So that, you know, kind of fired him from being a leader. Spoiled himself, see. He just spoiled himself."[6]

Black Coal continued to be recognized as "head chief" in dealings with the government, but the Arapahoes attribute the equal importance of Sharp Nose and other subchiefs influential in internal political affairs to the violent behavior of Black Coal, which led to his loss of status. The story reinforces the elders' admonitions against overt displays of hostility. And harsh words are considered to be as potentially damaging as violent acts.

While there is ample potential for dispute and disagreement, and tensions erupt into family quarrels from time to time, elders and respected persons in general are always ready to intercede, to urge individuals to "let it go." Persons who ignore insult and injury are generally praised. In sodality and Business Council meetings there is strong pressure for all to agree. One Entertainment Committee member expressed it this way: "We have meetings and the commitee votes on whatever they want to do. If all agree, well, OK. . . . If we can't agree, we have to table it and take it up another time or go to the Business Council and they decide. There's never been a case [of a split vote] that I can remember." Another Arapahoe explained why individuals should suppress criticism or opposition this way: "White people can debate for or against, take either side and think nothing of it; if you win, that's all right, and if you lose, that's all right. An Indian can't. He thinks he has hurt someone's feelings. And he won't talk again if he is offended. That's our nature." When votes are taken, the result is a unanimous decision, because the decision was reached before the voting, in informal discussion, where the recommendations of the senior members are generally followed.

It sometimes happens that a decision reached in the General Council becomes unpopular. To say so publicly would imply criticism of the person or persons responsible for proposing or supporting the policy or act in question. So a common procedure is for several Arapahoes respectfully to ask that person to move to rescind his original motion or to agree that others may do so. It would be unseemly for him to refuse.

Unsuccessful candidacy for the Arapahoe Business Council or occasional conflict among sodality members often is attributed to inability to "get along with the people," or failure to cooperate with others. One man's repeated failure to win election to the council was explained as follows: "He has a chip on his shoulder. . . . It seems like he thinks, 'I'm ready to try anybody.' He has a long face. People seem to want to veer away from it because of that." The man in question is considered to be a troublemaker because he goes against the grain of group sentiment. All Arapahoe leaders attempt to display sociability and an even temper, and are reluctant to advocate anything their constituents oppose.

It is particularly important for a person seeking a council position not to appear to be more comfortable with people from his own residential area than with those from the other Arapahoe community, and not to express negative feelings toward the other community. The repeated failure of a man from Lower Arapahoe to win election was generally attributed to his disregard of tribal sentiment on this issue. One Arapahoe explained, "He won't get on [the council]. He tries it, but doesn't get anywhere. He knocks these people up here [Ethete], that's why."

In recent years a man who had served as councilman for a term and whose name had been frequently mentioned as a good choice for future councils attempted to do serious injury to another man with whom he had quarreled. As the Arapahoes said, he "ruined himself." He was never again elected to the council. Aggression by "mature adults," even verbal aggression, is acceptable only in encounters with non-Arapahoes.[7] Leaders who appear to intimidate whites are acting according to Arapahoe ideals of proper conduct, but serious intratribal conflict is deplored.

"Helping out" with one's time and material goods is viewed as evidence of one's ability to "get along with others." Participation in community activities suggests to the Arapahoes that one "knows how to deal with people." Cooperative, harmonious interaction facilitates ritual acts and strengthens tribal unity, both of which are important for the perpetuation of the life and wellbeing of the people. One can offer a man no higher praise than to say of him, "He gets along with the people."

"Keeping a Low Profile"

Arapahoe children are taught and adults reminded not to be obtrusive in their dealings with others: they must avoid direct eye contact and loud, disruptive speech. Arapahoes avoid asking too many or too pointed questions. To give an order is an extremely offensive act; one must try to persuade others to do what one wants them to do, never to tell them to do it.

Persons seeking positions of leadership try particularly to avoid appearing too self-confident or knowledgeable. It is a serious charge indeed to say that one "tries to run the whole show." An individual who tries to be boss is resented and spoken of derisively. "I'm an Indian; I know as much as he does" is the way one Arapahoe put it. In the Legion posts it is the custom to rotate the position of commander so that the organization, while military-oriented, has an egalitarian focus. Councilmen are especially eager to acquire a reputation for modesty. They do not attempt to persuade others to vote for them. As one man explained, "The candidates never go around and speak for themselves. . . . People here know everyone from *A* to *Z*." And in exercising Business Council duties, councilmen take care not to appear to wield excessive power. One elder explained that the council delegates some governmental tasks to the Entertainment Committee in order to diffuse authority: "The council *and* the Entertainment Committee are the leaders. No one person wanted to take the whole leadership." Moreover, councilmen do not serve as officers in sodalities while they are on the council.

The scope of authority associated with leadership groupings—ritual offices, sodalities, and the elected offices (the Arapahoe Business Council and Entertainment Committee)—is limited and narrowly defined. As one Arapahoe man put it to me, "There is no one outstanding person on the reservation. If there is a certain function, the person in charge is sort of a boss—the president or chairman." When asked how one goes about making a request or accomplishing something, another man explained, "Arapahoes have no influential people. It depends on what you want to do."

In the allocation of authority, Arapahoes distinguish between groups that have responsibility in sacred matters and those that have responsibility in secular matters: "They are separate." In fact, individuals tend to concentrate their efforts in one or the other of the two spheres. While councilmen have generally participated fully in such rituals as the Sun Dance, and several have served from time to time as grandfathers, they do not enter the priesthood. Only two priests in the

1965–78 era had served on the council, both when they were much younger, before they had ritual authority; one served only one term.

Men in ritual offices are as wary as those in secular offices about the misuse of authority. Recently a rash of deaths within a short span of time was attributed to a breach in form on the part of several officials who presided over a particular ritual. All of the deceased were relatives of the ceremonial officials. The officials were accused of taking too much responsibility on themselves by performing the ritual without the consent and participation of all of the "four old men." Even speaking ill of another Arapahoe's performance in an office can bring disaster. The death of a ceremonial elder's son was attributed to the father's private criticism of another priest. Modesty and goodwill are as important in a priest as in a councilman.

Each priestly office has a set of prerogatives and duties associated with it. The keeper of the Sacred Pipe cares for the pipe and directs many aspects of rituals that involve the pipe. All ceremonies with the pipe require the permission and participation of the keeper, even though some aspects of pipe ritual may be known to other priests. Phases of the Sun Dance are the charge of specific priests—the medicine men (the "four old men"), who handle the dancers' pipes; the Sun Dance chief, who directs most other phases of the ritual; the keeper of the wheel, who is currently the Sun Dance chief and who cares for the Sacred Wheel, which is used in the Sun Dance. The keeper of the tribal drum directs aspects of ritual involving the drum. The drum is not to be used in a tribal ceremony without the permission of the keeper. Several old women serve as ceremonial elders, performing those aspects of tribal ceremonies for which women are needed. All ritual authorities have the right to perform only those rituals for which they have qualified.

In the secular realm, the elected members of the Business Council and the Entertainment Committee are viewed respectively as the most important and second most important leadership groups outside the ceremonial sphere. Both groups serve as intermediaries between members of the tribe and non-Arapahoes.

The power of the Business Council is checked by the General Council, which can override Business Council decisions (although it very seldom does so) and is called upon to decide major issues, including investment of tribal funds.

The Entertainment Committee coordinates and supervises the community celebrations that are under the direction of the clubs and sees that the money allocated to the clubs by the council is not misspent and that the community halls at Ethete and Arapahoe and the

Sun Dance Grounds at Ethete are maintained satisfactorily. They may request support from white businessmen and they purchase supplies from town merchants. Non-Indian groups from neighboring towns arrange with the committee to provide Indian entertainers for local parades or other special programs. The six committee members are elected every two years in the same manner as the members of the Business Council; they elect their own president, vice-president, and secretary-treasurer. Members are paid per diem, but meet less frequently than the council—usually before a tribal celebration.

The clubs are responsible for arranging the tribal celebrations (social dances and feasts) throughout the year, for distributing resources over which they have control, and for helping persons in need generally. Each club assumes responsibility for one celebration or type of celebration, so that authority in this sphere of activity is circumscribed as it is in other spheres. The influence of the clubs peaks at certain seasons: the powwow committees are most important during the summer, the American Legion posts in the fall, the Christmas clubs in winter, and the memorial clubs in the spring, although the memorial clubs are active throughout the year. The Ethete club is comprised of upwards of forty women, and their activities center around funeral ritual, providing help for those in need (particularly servicemen), and cooking for tribal celebrations. Membership is controlled by several of the elderly members, who exercise what amounts to veto power over potential members. The group sponsors a tribal celebration on Memorial Day, and often prepares the food for tribal events sponsored by other clubs. The Memorial Club at Arapahoe has a membership of about forty men. They are responsible for upkeep of the graveyards, particularly that of St. Stephen's Mission. They also sponsor a celebration on Memorial Day (the members of a women's sodality cook the food that is distributed at the event).

The members of the Ethete Powwow Committee—some thirty men—enlist the aid of their wives in sponsoring a powwow a few days after the Sun Dance in July. Indians from Montana, South Dakota, Oklahoma, Idaho, and elsewhere camp on the powwow grounds for three to four days and participate in intertribal dancing and games. The Powwow Committee (with the help of the Entertainment Committee) is responsible for issuing rations to the visitors, organizing the games and giveaways, raising prize money and selecting judges and announcers for the events, setting up the dance arbor and camp facilities, and arranging for camp security. In August a similar powwow is held at Lower Arapahoe, sponsored by the Arapahoe Powwow Committee, a group of comparable composition and size.

In the fall each of the American Legion posts, with the assistance of their women's auxiliaries, sponsors a tribal celebration, usually on Veterans' Day. The Legion posts—each with about thirty members— are responsible for conducting military ritual during funerals of servicemen and veterans and for ceremonies accompanying the display of the American flag at all tribal celebrations. Each year they conduct military ceremonies at the graves of the old army scouts, and they occasionally sponsor competitive athletic events. Formal membership in the Legion is confined to veterans who served during World War I, World War II, the Korean War, or the Vietnam conflict, but other servicemen may volunteer to help the posts with their activities. Female relatives of members may join the women's auxiliaries. Each has approximately twenty members. In addition to assisting the Legionnaires (by cooking for tribal celebrations, among other things), they offer assistance to persons in need.

The Christmas clubs at Ethete and Arapahoe have about twenty male members each, and female relatives assist when they are needed. These groups sponsor the winter dances, which begin shortly before Christmas and continue till New Year's Eve. At this time the Christmas clubs give away clothing, money, and dress goods to "old people, invalids, orphans, and unenrolled children," and provide a feast for the tribe.

The clubs in each of the two communities are organized so that authority is widely diffused and quarrels over allocation of responsibilities during tribal celebrations are less likely to break out between the people at Ethete and Arapahoe. While the residents of one community may attend the celebrations held in the other (particularly if they have in-laws there), responsibility for organizing the celebrations is clearly that of the residents of the community in which the event is held. But the Arapahoes stress that the residents of Ethete and Arapahoe must cooperate and "get along" with each other. Elders particularly take it upon themselves to generate support for councilmen from each community because these six councilmen must do business for all Arapahoes, regardless of residence.

Arapahoes feel that it is best to vote for candidates from both Ethete and Arapahoe, and all councilmen or candidates for a council position seek and draw support from both communities. So do the members of the Entertainment Committee. As Table 10 shows, in virtually every election held in this era (as in previous ones), an equal number of councilmen are chosen from each settlement. And, as we shall see, this principle operates also with regard to ritual offices.

Table 10
Members of Arapahoe Business Council, 1965–78,
by place of residence

Term	Arapahoe	Ethete
1965–66	Jess Miller Scott Dewey Ernest Hanway Steven Duran	Eugene Ridgley Arnold Headley
1967–68	Jess Miller Ernest Hanway Herman J. Moss	Nell Scott Arnold Headley Ben Friday
1969–70	Jess Miller Ernest Hanway Herman J. Moss	Arnold Headley Eugene Ridgley Felix Groesbeck
1971–72	Jess Miller Ernest Hanway John Warren	Eugene Ridgley Felix Groesbeck Hubert Friday
1973–74	Jess Miller Ernest Hanway John Warren	Arnold Headley Felix Groesbeck Hubert Friday
1975–76	Jess Miller* Ernest Hanway Ernest Sun Rhodes	Arnold Headley Hubert Friday Felix Groesbeck* Burnett Ridgley† John Lee Whiteman†
1977–78	Jess Miller Ernest Hanway Herman J. Moss Joseph Oldman	Felix Groesbeck Arnold Headley* Burnett Ridgley†

*Resigned.

†Replacement.

Source: Records of the Office of the Bureau of Indian Affairs, Fort Washakie, Wyo.

"First to the Elders"

The organization of Arapahoe society in four broad age groups still affects all social interaction. One Arapahoe explained "Indian politics" this way: "When I want something to get done, I talk first to the elders, then the younger generation, and then maybe the young people." Associated with each age group is a specific kind of leadership potential. (Children have no political role.)

People who have lived over sixty years usually are considered to have the greatest amount of wisdom. They must be wise to have lived so long; and having lived so long, they may have acquired knowledge of spiritual matters. Their judgments, when given, are most respected. Their opinion is still required on most tribal matters of any importance. They are called upon to recall and interpret past events—to monitor tradition. The Arapahoes also expect elders to exert a tempering influence on the "younger generation," although elders generally do not try to control behavior directly.

The ceremonial elders—the "old people," who have ultimate authority in all tribal religious rituals—are considered to have completed the requisite "degrees" to communicate most directly and effectively with the supernatural. One priest, in recalling his selection by the old people to replace one of the "four old men" who had died, remarked:

> Four is picked out by Arapahoe tribe. Four old men. . . . Those that earn it with their religion, and their pledges. . . . You don't know if anybody he's looking at you on the reservation and sometimes they pick out that kind of old people. They pick them out, they're the one. He's the one, and this old man's supposed to pray for them. Get up every morning before sunup and pray. I do that. They picked me. I was surprised. They picked me to be one of them old people, old men, at ceremonial doings. At Sun Dance, I have to be there. What I say, when I talk to people, if I want someone to know, I got to tell them the truth. I got to say what's good. That's what I'm supposed to do. That's a rule. You can't say nothing but good.[8]

This elder makes clear the importance of the four old men: each must think good thoughts and speak good words so that relations between the Arapahoes and the Great Mystery Above will be proper and harmonious.

The Arapahoes are wary of persons other than ceremonial elders (or their apprentices) who seek through fasting and prayer to have visions. The vision experience is closed particularly to "young people." During 1974–75 a few young Arapahoe men formed a chapter of the American Indian Movement (AIM) at Wind River and some went into the hills to fast. The elders expressed grave apprehensions that they would err or misuse supernatural power, and thereby bring disaster on the tribe. Elderly ritual authorities, and Sun Dance grandfathers of any age, have special responsibilities to preserve social order. It is their responsibility to counsel younger people and "grandsons" against socially disruptive or violent acts. Ceremonial elders, guardians of tradition, are also considered to be legitimately endowed with the right to change tradition. Today, as in the past, old men may innovate in the ceremonial realm, and because of the supernatural sanction given to their acts (as long as disaster does not follow), these changes are not considered to be in conflict with the "Arapahoe way" of doing things. At the close of a recent Sun Dance, for example, a storm was moving toward camp, and the participants knew they would have to hurry to get the Sacred Pipe safely under cover before the storm broke. By custom the pipe is carried on the back of a female relative of the keeper, but the most influential of the medicine men authorized the use of a pickup truck so that the rain would not fall on the pipe.

At the funeral of an old woman whose husband was important in tribal ceremonials, an Arapahoe leader acting as announcer said, "The old people are what holds this reservation together. We must listen to them and respect them." He was reaffirming before a tribal gathering the belief that wisdom, supernatural beneficence, social harmony, and perpetuation of Arapahoe tradition—all are linked with advanced age. Thus elders play a key part in monitoring the reputations of their juniors, and the "younger generation" and "youths" defer to them and are constantly attuned to their interpretations and reactions.

The "younger generation"—persons in their mid-forties to late fifties—are thought to be not so capable of a life of "good thoughts" but more skilled in dealing with whites (and in speaking English). Success in dealing with the white world is indicated by completion of military service, educational attainment, or achievement in some other sphere of activity involving interaction with the institutions of the wider society. Education is of value only when it is applied on behalf of the tribe, and when it does not interfere with "common sense." Common sense is indicated by one's deference to the elders and by demonstrated loyalty to the Arapahoe community. As the wife of one councilman remarked proudly, "He came home from college to be an Indian." Thus individuals are "educated" if they are successful in dealings with whites and use this success to help other Arapahoes; education is not necessarily related to progress in school, nor does lack of formal education keep one from acquiring a reputation as an "educated" person. People of the "younger generation" are considered to be mature enough to become apprentices to the ceremonial elders.

"Young people" under forty are not considered to be fully mature. They occasionally apprentice themselves to sodalities and help with club projects, but they are still presumed to be too unstable to take on responsibilities of any significance. As one elder explained when talk turned to a man in his early thirties who was known to want a leadership position, "He is kind of liquid, unsettled, and this affects his frame of mind." The position of young Arapahoes today (as in the past) is often frustrating. As one individual commented, "You find all over this reservation if a young guy tries to say something they snicker and say he is too young. It makes a guy want to quit." Young people, however, may motivate older Arapahoes to accept innovations.

Together with childhood, these age categories are viewed as the "four hills" or stages of life. "All the Arapahoes go through the four stages of life. And that's what they pray for. . . . To grow up to pass through the four stages of life, or four hills of life." Arapahoes with "common sense" accept the limitations and responsibilities of each stage. They respect their elders and proceed with caution, engaging only in activities appropriate to their chronological and personal development.

Individuals interested in positions of leadership are advised to "watch on" and thus to earn the respect of others by accumulating experience. A Business Council position is acquired through years of service in the clubs, which are viewed as stages on the avenue leading to a council position. One elderly Arapahoe made this observation: "If you start out from the bottom, like on the Powwow Committee, and really work, you have a chance." And another Arapahoe remarked, "If you want to be a leader, throw your hat in the ring. You can join a club and get your name used." Persons who become impatient fail to earn the respect of others. Individuals who run for the council and lose are frequently characterized as "too fast": they behaved inappropriately for their age or "experience."

Elders aid an individual at birth, at death, and whenever they are exposed to dangerous or threatening experiences. At a tribal gathering an older man, a veteran of World War II, gave his Indian name to a youth who was leaving for military duty in Vietnam. The naming ceremony was performed to help ensure the young man's safe return. As the name was associated with the veteran's successful battle experiences, so it would aid the youth in similar circumstances.

Younger club members defer to older members and newer councilmen defer to those with more years of service. A newly elected councilman is a kind of apprentice to his colleagues. There have been occasions when two classificatory siblings have served at the same time on the Business Council, and the younger of the two felt an obligation to defer to his senior and to refrain from participating extensively in his presence. In 1969–70, when I attended all council meetings, the youngest and most recently elected council member had the least responsibility and status. He was almost always the one who ran errands for the other members. He sat closest to the door and frequently left meetings to check on something for the other councilmen or to summon someone into the council room. By the late 1970s he was one of the senior councilmen; he had worked his way up. I observed the same pattern in Entertainment Committee meetings that I attended. The clubs often have one or two elderly advisers, who may hold the group's funds. Members explain this arrangement by saying that they need an older person to watch over them.

The ceremonial officers, the Entertainment Committee, the Business Council, and each of the sodalities are associated with age categories and are thought of as comprised predominantly of either elders or the younger generation. The elderly ritual authorities have apprentices and "helpers" of the younger generation. The apprentices follow the instructions of the elders; they have no authority of their own.

The Entertainment Committee, which mediates between sacred and secular activities, is an organization of elders (with one or possibly two younger members who serve as apprentices). The Arapahoes feel that the men who oversee the tribal celebrations should have considerable knowledge of music and dance, and that they should be of especially calm disposition to interact smoothly with all of the various sodalities. This group also acts as liaison between the council and the ceremonial elders during the Sun Dance preparations.

The Arapahoe Business Council is made up of members of the younger generation who are thought to have accumulated experience and shown marked level-headedness. Most of them are veterans, and have the reputation of being sociable and even-tempered in their relations with other Arapahoes. Council members exhibit deference to elders and may consult them on important tribal business, particularly on proposed innovations, even though this kind of business is supposedly for the Business Council alone to decide.

The Ethete Memorial Club is composed primarily of elderly women and is categorized as a club of elders. The sodality has a central role in mortuary ritual, and elders—with their prayers and other supportive behavior—are viewed as necessary participants in this rite of passage, as well as on other such occasions. Thus Arapahoes often comment that it is "respected" more than the other clubs, or that it "does the most for the people."

The members of the other clubs range in age from the late thirties to late fifties, and these organizations are labeled "younger generation" clubs. In fact, although membership in the American Legion is open to veterans who served in Vietnam, by and large these youths feel that it is inappropriate for them to participate. In practice participation in Legion activities is confined to veterans of Korea and World War II.

Being "Fair-minded"

Sexual identity is clearly associated with behavioral prerogatives and expectations that have political significance. Women are thought to be properly oriented toward family, while men properly strive to extend social ties beyond the kin group.

It is the women that effectively exert pressure on councilmen for various forms of aid for family members. They are in all respects advocates for their relatives, while men tend to avoid appearing to press for benefits for their own relatives. When quarrels between people of different family groups escalate to the point where the parties appear in Tribal Court,[9] women come forward to defend their kin. Men urge the parties to "let it go," or at least they avoid appearing in court. The parties in conflict often appear with one or more elderly female relatives, whose presence is likely to affect the outcome of the case. The judge's decision may be influenced as much by the social standing of the old women as by the particulars of the case. In General Council, it is most often women who make complaints; men promote unity. Women's reputations are important to family interests as well as those of men, despite the fact that women customarily do not seek elective office. On the other hand, aggression toward whites is a matter for male attention; abrasive public confrontations with whites would be viewed as immodest for women. (Nell Scott—who did not live like a "real Arapahoe"—was not subject to this constraint.)

Potentially disruptive feelings and dissension usually are channeled through the actions of women, although public conflict is infrequent. Early in the morning, women and girls (female "youths") travel from one kinsman's or friend's household to another to visit, to obtain water from houses with water pipes, or to drop small children off for the day. More visits are paid at the end of the day. During these visits, the news of the community and the events of the day are related and commented on. People who have behaved in socially disapproved ways are inevitably confronted by their elderly female relatives, who sometimes tease or gently chide and at other times greet the transgressor with stern silence or admonitions. Thus women are important instruments of social control; they help to induce conformity through gossip and occasional public ridicule. Men are expected to avoid such behavior, although teasing is permitted. Councilmen are not supposed to express feelings of rivalry; through gossip, however, their female relatives can damage the reputations of other councilmen. Institutionalized boasting is permitted in the giveaway and at honor dances, which women manage and in which they are most prominent. Before these ceremonies women prompt the announcer on the accomplishments or reputation of the person in whose honor the giveaway is held. Women also dance with the flag of a serviceman in order to acknowledge his sacrifice and contribution.

Women play a central role in the Sun Dance, which is an occasion when social harmony is stressed. By exchanging food with households not related to them by kinship during all-tribal religious rituals, women symbolically reinforce tribal unity and promote social solidarity.

The values associated with male and female roles are reflected in the formation of sodalities. Clubs are sex-specific. Only men's clubs— the Legion posts, the Christmas clubs, the Powwow committees, and the Arapahoe Memorial Club—draw their membership from all family groups and thereby cross-cut kin divisions (although wives may help with some of the work). Arapahoes explain that women's sodalities restrict their membership to "people who are related," although women from all households supposedly are eligible. The women's sodalities are the Ethete Memorial Club, the Legion auxiliaries, and the Altar of the Rosary (which assists the work of the Arapahoe Memorial Club and which is affiliated with St. Stephen's Mission at Arapahoe). Women's sodalities occasionally sponsor all-tribal events but the men's groups ask the women's groups to prepare the food for all of the tribal celebrations. At Ethete the Memorial Club and the Women's Auxiliary are asked alternately to cook. When a women's club does sponsor a dance, it usually does so in conjunction with a male club. Women's clubs feel the obligation to provide assistance to anyone in serious need, regardless of kinship. A death in the family or the destruction of a home by fire qualifies a family as seriously in need. And the Ethete Memorial Club and women's auxiliaries honor all servicemen.

Arapahoe business councilmen are expected to be "fair-minded," to disregard kinship when allocating resources. In praising the record of one councilman, an elder remarked, "If he wasn't fair-minded his kids would all have jobs." Arapahoes are reluctant to place close relatives on the council; during the 1970s only two individuals closely related (classificatory siblings) served at the same time. Few of the councilmen assumed a position once held by a father or brother.[10] Relationship to a former councilman does not seem to have much bearing on a man's ability to generate support; his own reputation is paramount.

Only one woman has been elected to the Arapahoe Business Council since Nell Scott, and no woman has ever served on the Entertainment Committee, although women are not legally barred from these offices. One elderly man gave this justification for the exclusion of women from important political positions: "It is always men who do the planning. If women want to help, they can, but not in the planning. They always disagree—but not like whites, not about the planning. But about personal things. We keep the women out because they break things up." He is suggesting that whereas Business Council and Entertainment Committee members are expected to be "fair-minded," to allocate financial resources equitably and to reconcile divergent points of view, women are expected to be advocates for their own extended families. The role of elected officials in dealings with whites is also viewed as an inappropriate one for women.

No important religious ritual is possible without female participation, both in the ceremony itself and in the preparations for it. In fact, Arapahoe religious ritual expresses the complementary nature of male and female life forces. But women who as ceremonial elders are qualified to participate in sacred ceremonies—to sing, for example—are not permitted to direct and perform important rituals with the symbols of tribal unity, the pipe, wheel, and drum (see Plate 14).

"Helping Out"

Arapahoes place great stress on the obligation to be generous. In the Arapahoe view, sharing is an expression of tribal loyalty—one's well-being depends on the well-being of all. As one elder explained it, "A person tries to survive, to get food for his family. It's the same with the tribe. It has to survive. The individual is just one unit of the tribe." Requests from relatives or friends are very rarely refused, and ideally aid is given to others whenever possible. Those who earn a good living are expected to give conspicuous and liberal financial aid to others. Arapahoes often express this imperative thus: "Whenever anybody tries to get ahead, everybody tries to pull him down."

The recent increase in income, due to the per capita payments, has not been used primarily to improve family economic status, but has been channeled into the tribal network of reciprocity. Elderly people frequently comment that the food and gifts that were distributed at the Sun Dance before the days of per capita payments were much less plentiful than they are today. Families spend several hundred dollars on the food and gifts that are exchanged among participants in the Sun Dance. A novice can expect to receive considerable aid from friends and from almost all lineal and collateral relatives. In commenting on this fact, one old man noted: "If he wants to join in any kind of ceremonial doings like this Sun Dance, he's got to furnish his own material that he's going to use—some dress goods, anything that he needs, he's supposed to furnish himself. Nowadays, it's different now. They help each other, you know. People help him. Like these Sun Dance people. They put up carry-in dinner for those that's going to put up the Sun Dance. . . . All those that want to donate anything, why, they can donate. . . . It's way different now."

Similarly, funerals have evolved from private ceremonies attended by relatives and close friends,[11] at which time the property of the deceased was given away or destroyed, to large-scale tribal ceremonies. Everyone is expected to attend if possible, and children are excused from school. The family, with the help of others in the community, purchases and gives away hundreds of dollars' worth of material goods and provides a large meal for the whole tribe.

People who at any time appear laggard in participating in the networks of reciprocity are labeled "stingy" or "out for themselves." The strength of their commitment to the tribe is questioned. One man who for a time was the butt of considerable criticism was described this way: "He lives like a white man. His children said they didn't need the per capita. Their father's salary is enough for them to spend on what they want. People said they should get off the reservation if they are that good off." The man lived no more "like a white man" than many others, but members of his family had become too boastful about their economic situation, and community pressure was exerted to censure this immodesty and to encourage a generous donation to the next tribal celebration.

Similarly, people who are enrolled but not full participants in reciprocal exchange may be called "breeds" or "just like a breed" (that is, *kho'nih'óóOoo,* "half white man"). People remark, "The breeds, they don't know you when you're in distress." When the child of one such family wanted to compete in the regional Frontier Days Rodeo, the Entertainment Committee refused to sponsor him. "It would be like that money just went right out of the tribe. We wouldn't get anything back."

Arapahoes who wish to earn respect must demonstrate generosity above the norm. And people in positions of leadership are expected to aid any Arapahoe or "foreign Indian" on request. As one elder put it, "If you want to be an important man, you give away. . . . This is to keep your name known to the people, to let them know what you are going to do for the tribe. You give away if you want to be recognized. . . . Not to say thanks for electing me, but for your judgment, your recognition of me." Failure to reassure other Arapahoes of one's generosity is, for business councilmen, a sure way to damage one's reputation. One councilman who failed to win reelection was criticized before the election for repeatedly refusing to give aid when he was asked for it. One woman who was refused use of the man's telephone remarked, "He only thinks of himself."

Similarly, the sodalities' most important role is to extend aid to all members of the tribe: "The present-day societies, they're supposed to be there to help out." Elders, who with the wisdom of advanced years are thought to be the most generous, use their influence to promote intratribal sharing. An Entertainment Committee member noted that his group (an organization of elders) had the responsibility of supervising the expenditure of sodality funds: "We try to watch their money so they use it where it is supposed to be used. . . . In the first place, it's not their money, it's tribal money." The position of club treasurer often goes to an elder, specially invited to "help out." Explaining the selection of an elder as treasurer in a younger-generation women's sodality, one member remarked, "She was elected because she is the only one they all trust with the money."

One of the striking features of Arapahoe political life, compared to that on many other Plains reservations, is the absence of public accusations of graft on the part of the council leadership. During the 1965–78 era, no council member failed to be reelected or resigned because of misuse of tribal funds; departures from the council are usually due to personal problems or to difficulty in bearing up under the pressure of council duties. One councilman, sent to an eastern city to attend a conference, failed to attend the meeting and instead used his expense money for personal entertainment. The other councilmen and the elders took him so severely to task that he soon repaid the sum to the tribe's account. By repaying the money the man atoned for his "mistake."

These moral imperatives—getting along with people, keeping a low profile, respecting the elders, being fair-minded, and helping others by sharing—influence behavioral choices. The degree to which an individual conforms to these ideals, or convinces others that he conforms to them, affects his reputation in the community and thus his perceived readiness for leadership. Political opposition is expressed in accusations of unsociability or dissension, immodesty or an overbearing manner, inattentiveness to the teachings of elders, favoritism, or stinginess.

Political success depends on the degree to which people are reassured of an individual's commitment to tribal life and values. During one recent election, one candidate generated considerable negative comment. The following remarks were typical: "He doesn't want to be Arapahoe. He talks like he could go to Washington and he will be a businessman someday. He won't stay Arapahoe. Probably will go to Denver. He probably won't even take his per capita payments or anything that's Arapahoe." In fact, the man was no more skilled in the English language, no more successful occupationally, and no less dependent on the per capita payment than many men who were far more respected. But he was at that time unskilled in reassuring others, through appropriate behavior, that he could be relied on to conform to Arapahoe ideals of political behavior. The observation that "he won't stay Arapahoe" is telling in another respect. It is quite possible that cultural identity can change and that an individual can alter Arapahoe perceptions and evaluations of his character.

In political life, and in social relations in general, Arapahoes attempt to manipulate shared public symbols in appropriate social contexts to reaffirm cultural values. Reputations are enhanced and diminished, traditions reshaped, and change interpreted in the course of the display of those symbols.

SYMBOLIC STRATEGIES

All-tribal celebrations are particularly appropriate occasions for individuals to influence the way other Arapahoes evaluate their leadership potential. In the fall, winter, and spring, these events are held in one of the community halls. Chairs are placed in a circle, leaving the center of the room clear for the drum and the participants in the ceremony.

When a person enters the hall, his choice of a place to sit is important to the construction of a reputation. Younger-generation men demonstrate their leadership potential by escorting their families to seats near their relatives and then going to stand with a group of peers who have reputations for helping out, getting along, and so on. In this way an individual publicly signals that his ties extend beyond his family. Friendship has especially important political implications; recruitment into sodalities is often on this basis. It is in his age peer group that a man makes a reputation for getting along with others. Men who sit only with their relatives during tribal celebrations are viewed as too "shy" or even too "backward" for a leadership position.

While relations with kin figure in one's reputation, there is room for maneuver. "Relations" include all persons bilaterally related.[12] But there is leeway in how one associates with one's relations and variation in "closeness." At all-tribal celebrations, a young married couple that aspires to high status will position themselves with respected elders for a while before the husband leaves to join his peers. If both spouses have grown up in the same community, they usually sit with the elders of highest status.[13] A person who has married into the residential community sits with the elder relations of his or her spouse. Every Arapahoe has many relations, but exercises the option to emphasize or de-emphasize particular relationships, depending on personal goals. One elder commented that he had a "half-breed" niece, and jokingly remarked, "But I drive faster when I go by her house."

Giveaways are a common feature of all-tribal celebrations. By large distributions to nonrelatives, families display their support of the relative in whose honor the giveaway is held and affirm ties of mutual obligation and affinity with other Arapahoes. Members of the sponsoring family stand with their goods in the center of the camp or hall, and an announcer (often an elder) gives a formal speech recounting the family's reason for the ceremony and indicating their gratitude to those in attendance for their support. The family distributes gifts first to elders, thus exhibiting deference to and respect for old people (see Plate 15). Just before the distribution, honor songs are often sung, while the family members and all who wish to affiliate themselves with the family slowly and with great dignity dance in a circle around the drum. Individuals seeking to gain political or social recognition and stature are very visible participants.

Business councilmen, in addition to their distribution of tribal resources (in as public a fashion as possible), seek to validate their status by individual displays of generosity at powwows and other tribal celebrations. They frequently donate money to the drum group or the sodalities. At tribal celebrations songs may be dedicated to the councilmen ("chiefs' songs"). After such an honor, the individuals singled out are expected to donate money "to the drum" (to the singers at the tribal drum). Club leaders, who often operate concession stands at tribal events and visibly take in considerable amounts of money, often make large donations to the gathering, and the gift is announced to the crowd.

Conspicuously absent from giveaways and all-tribal celebrations (with the possible exception of the Sun Dance) are persons termed by the Arapahoes "one-day Indians." These people (almost always "mixed-bloods") are not regular participants in institutionalized sharing and in community rituals. They are viewed as estranged, and, being unpredictable and uncommitted, are suspect. The term "one-day Indian" refers to the fact that the per capita payment is distributed on the first day of the month; people who collect their checks and then ignore their obligations to the tribe are exploiting their enrollment status. "They come down and pick up their pay and make fun of Indians," said one elder.

The term "half-breed" is also applied to deviant individuals. Many Arapahoes have some white ancestry, but as long as their loyalty is not suspect, they are identified as "really Arapahoes," even as "full-bloods." Few adult individuals (fewer than fifty, by my count) are permanently categorized as "mixed-bloods" or "half-breeds"; but the label can be applied from time to time to embarrass dissenters and induce conformity, or to discredit a political opponent.

Some people are also occasionally referred to as "foreign Indians." A large number of Arapahoes have ancestors who were members of other tribes yet are considered "full-blood" Arapahoes as far as cultural identity is concerned. To antagonize other Arapahoes, however, is to leave oneself open to the accusation of being "really a foreign Indian." Alluding to "foreign" ancestry is a political tactic used to discredit opponents. Such a label suggests that a person's loyalty to Arapahoe values and institutions is in question. In fact, the word used for a non-Arapahoe Indian is *hoowóóOenennin,* "stranger."

During all-tribal celebrations people take note of who is present and who is not. Public behavior is evaluated, and when elections are held or ritual leaders selected, this understanding figures in judgments of the candidates' suitability for office. In the weeks before a recent election, rumors were circulating that if a certain candidate were elected, he would "open up the enrollment" and "sell the reservation." These fears were in reality groundless: only the General Council can sanction a change in enrollment criteria, and almost all reservation lands are in trust. But the charges that the man would endanger tribal economic security were symbolic of his failure to behave in ways that would have reassured people that he could be trusted in a council position. Skilled in business enterprise but only a rare participant in community activities, he was unable to construct a political persona that reflected predictability. People were not sure what the man would do with power if he had it.

Other men, more skillful in interpersonal relations, have overcome such potential handicaps as predominant white ancestry or a white wife. One such man returned to the reservation after distinguished military service in World War II and began a small ranching operation. His conspicuous donations to tribal ceremonies and his financial aid to several people brought him to the attention of the elders, and he was nominated for the Business Council. Once on the council, he acknowledged the old people with frequent visits and with personal presentations of benefits voted them by the council. He diligently attended all-tribal ceremonies, including all funerals, and appeared at peyote meetings periodically, although he was not a peyotist. Several of his close relatives were referred to as "half-breeds" by other Arapahoes, and he carefully avoided associating with them, even excluding them from family celebrations. At an important religious ceremony he arranged for an elder to announce publicly that he and his immediate family had renounced their "white blood" and that they wanted to be considered Indian only. By his adeptness at orchestrating events, such as the elder's announcement and the presentation of benefits to the elders, he won recognition as a person who "really respects the old people," and his public displays of generosity brought him a reputation for always "helping out."

The public addresses at tribal gatherings are opportunities for individuals publicly to display their respect for and deference to the elders. After a giveaway at a recent celebration, a member of the family sponsoring the event spoke to the crowd. He had been in the process of "making a name" for himself for several weeks, and he used this occasion to display his oratorical ability, his readiness to "speak up." In English he told a story about his grandmother, who had counseled him during the long winters of his youth. He acknowledged the old woman's wisdom and ceremonial knowledge, and related an incident he said had guided him in all of his attempts to work for the tribe. As he had sat beside his grandmother he had worried about what it would be like to go into the white man's schools. One day his grandmother called to him, "Quick! There's *nih' óóOoo*! Step on him!" A little brown spider was crawling across the floor, and he stepped on it. His grandmother was pleased. After the speech, many people in the crowd commented on the merits of the story. The word for spider in the Arapahoe language is *nih'óóOoo*, but *nih'óóOoo* is also the word for white man.[14] The speaker had chosen his story carefully. He symbolically linked educational qualifications and ability to deal with the white world, resistance to the demoralizing experiences in Indian–white contacts, and commitment to Arapahoe culture and society. And throughout the story he affirmed his respect for elders by his emphasis on his grandmother's great influence in his life.

Less successful in mobilizing support was a group of young Arapahoes who organized a reservation chapter of the Jaycees in 1964. Probably the key factor in the group's failure to survive was the threat that they appeared to pose to the position of the elders. Club membership included about twenty men between the ages of twenty-six and thirty-five whose educational and occupational attainments surpassed those of most Arapahoes of their age. Although they had decided to organize their chapter after visiting the non-Indian Lander chapter of the Junior Chamber of Commerce, their activities were oriented toward reservation needs and did not merely parallel Jaycee activities in Lander and Riverton. They assisted Indian families in need, acquired firefighting equipment for the community, and delivered firewood to the elderly. They also proposed political innovation: they suggested that a primary election be held and that the council chairman's position be salaried and full-time. The group also negotiated with firms in an attempt to bring retail stores to the reservation. The educational needs of Indians were an additional concern of the Jaycees, and they successfully ran two young Indian men for seats on local school boards.

But by 1969 the Jaycees' membership was dwindling. In the face of strong opposition from Arapahoe Business Council members and lack of support in the community at large, participation in Jaycee activities declined. The Business Council withheld permission for the Jaycees to use a community hall for meetings and to operate a concession stand at tribal celebrations, courtesies routinely extended to other clubs. It rejected the group's proposal that the Jaycees raise funds for a rodeo grandstand. One councilman charged, "If the Jaycees spend this much, they will want to take over the whole rodeo." Recalled one former Jaycee, "They said we had wild ideas."

The Jaycees' efforts to initiate change and to take on responsibilities not delegated by the elders or supported by community sentiment signified to the Arapahoes that the young men were a disruptive influence. When members of the group ran for election to the council, they were labeled "Jaycee candidates" and "radicals." Councilmen viewed their proposals for economic and political innovation as infringements on the council's prerogatives that implied criticism of a "senior" leadership group. The elders resented the failure of these "inexperienced young people" to seek out and defer to their judgments on Jaycee programs. By labeling them "radicals," the Jaycees' opponents effectively mobilized community sentiment against them: the term suggested both disruptive change and links with the violent social protest in the wider society during the 1960s.

Yet a few years later, in 1972, many of the former Jaycees organized as the Wind River Indian Education Association (WRIEA) and successfully enlisted the tribe's support for an Indian-controlled high school to be located at Ethete. Their accomplishments resulted also in fundamental political reorganization. The WRIEA is the first sodality of "young people" to gain the support of the elders, and its members have used the organization as a base from which to generate support for election to the council. The WRIEA has been successful primarily because the changes introduced were advocated in a manner that conformed to Arapahoe notions of how the political process should work. Its members were careful this time to approach the elders first and to ask for their consent before they went ahead with their plans. Then they talked over their ideas with members of the other sodalities and with the Business Council. Having obtained some support, they were not viewed as threatening to the political order, as the Jaycees had been. These young men were thought to be particularly qualified on the education issue because, unlike most of the older Arapahoes, several had completed high school or vocational programs, and most were regularly employed.

These young men led a demonstration at the state capitol to protest state opposition to the school. The demonstration was in sharp contrast to the conciliatory stance the tribe has long taken toward the surrounding white community, yet the Arapahoe community supported the Education Association in its confrontations with the state. Opposition to the school came from local school districts, which received considerable federal funding from the enrollment of Indian students. The young WRIEA organizers were aware of the tribe's need for continued protection and aid from the federal government, but they were also sensitive to the deep resentment felt by the tribespeople as a result of the treatment they received locally. Their attack on the state government's position gave expression to their people's anger without arousing apprehension about "radical" tactics in dealings with the United States government. In fact, the WRIEA, without the aid of the Business Council, secured federal funding for the school despite local protests.

In this way the young men found a niche in the Arapahoe political order. In linking their efforts with the education of Indian children, they appealed to the elders' recognition of the need to provide realistic opportunities for young people in contemporary society. Government policy in the reservation schools had been to eradicate Indian culture, and students were punished for speaking the native language or exhibiting other forms of Indian culture. Community control of the high school represented cultural persistence to the Arapahoes. The members of the Education Association say that the goal of the Wyoming Indian High School is to teach basic skills—such as reading and mathematics—and career-oriented subjects, but in such a way as to kindle pride in Indian heritage and to involve the entire community in the educational process so that the school is not viewed as an alien, threatening institution. Today many elders join in making policy and implementing programs.

There has been one other attempt on the part of young Arapahoes to form a new sodality—a local AIM group. These efforts to generate tribal support came to a peak at a General Council meeting. The events on this occasion illuminate some of the ways in which particular kinds of actions provoke cultural judgments and articulate political goals. Although the day was hot and dusty, most of the adult Arapahoes attended the meeting. People were unusually quiet; low whispers replaced the usual chatting and joking. The question to be decided was whether or not to concur with the Shoshone tribe in closing the reservation to non-Indian recreation. Such a move, already decided upon by the Shoshone General Council, would effectively prohibit whites in the area from fishing, hiking, or riding on reservation lands.

Influential old men sat in a row against the wall, chairs tipped slightly back, hats forward, almost covering their eyes. The ceremonial leader of the Arapahoes—the keeper of the Sacred Pipe—was there, as well as the Sun Dance chief, the medicine men, and most of the elderly men of the tribe. The old women in their dark shawls, their hair braided, sat with their grandchildren tumbling around them or dozing at their feet. Cigarettes in their mouths, the grandmothers inhaled deeply, lips tightly pursed, and avoided glancing around the room. Pacing back and forth behind a long table at the front of the meeting hall were several men in their early fifties, dressed in Western shirts and jeans and broad-rimmed hats—the younger generation. But the attention of the crowd was focused, though inconspicuously, on a small group of young men seated in the center of the room. In sunglasses and tall "reservation hats," the bands decorated by feathers or AIM buttons, with long hair braided or hanging loosely, some wearing ribbon shirts, they openly gazed about the room.

One of the middle-aged men at the long table, the chairman of the Arapahoe Business Council, called the meeting to order and sat down. The crowd looked at the young men and waited. One member of the American Indian Movement stood up. He was a young man, not quite thirty. In English he began to speak in favor of closing the reservation to non-Indian recreation. He said that the Arapahoes had been subjected to abuse by the people in Riverton in retaliation for the action of the Shoshones, and that he was tired of not fighting back. "We are just like a pack of sheep," he said. "We should stand up and fight and close the reservation." One by one the young men rose and supported the speaker's position. The remarks signified rejection of current Arapahoe leadership; the youths intimated that tribal interests were not aggressively pursued against non-Indians, and they demanded an end to all forms of accommodation with the neighboring white towns.

The elders sat in silence while the speakers harangued the crowd in English. Before the third man had finished, one old man stood, in an apparent signal to the chairman of the meeting. The chairman interrupted and cut the speaker short—an act recognized by everyone as a very demeaning affront to the speaker. The old man, a ceremonial elder, walked slowly to the front of the room. Although bilingual, he spoke in the native language. He spoke eloquently in the formal oratorical style, one not heard in everyday conversation. He spoke of people who had forgotten Arapahoe ways, who did not speak the Arapahoe language, who did not respect the tribe's elders. He said, "Why was I not consulted by my younger relative before he announced to the people that he stood for closing the reservation? And you," pointing to the second speaker, "can you speak your language? Why don't you answer me?" He paused. The young man could not understand the formal oration and of course could not answer. The old women began to laugh.

A man about the age of the council members moved to reject the closing of the reservation and suggested instead a meeting between representatives of the towns and the two tribes to discuss the situation. The motion was carried. Someone moved that the meeting be closed; someone seconded.

The AIM leaders left hurriedly. In fact, many left the reservation community and stayed away or out of public sight for several weeks. Later both tribes agreed to raise the price of licenses sold to non-Indians, but to permit the recreational activities to continue.

The actions of the women were particularly significant. Their laughter was politically devastating. Old grandmothers normally are a young man's strongest support. Their ridicule dramatically expressed to the whole tribe the elders' rejection of AIM's tactics, which were an affront to the elders.

In their rebellion against the hierarchical authority structure dominated by elders and implemented by the younger generation, the young

AIM leaders demonstrated an assertive confidence and combative oratorical style. Their behavior worried and alienated the Arapahoe community. Like the Jaycees, the American Indian Movement failed to
achieve sodality status.

POLITICS AND RELIGION

The ceremonial elders employ an array of ritual symbols in reinforcing
values associated with political office and they use these symbolic
forms to check abuses of the authority vested in political or ritual
office and to resolve social conflict. When accidents or deaths directly
affect councilmen or other leaders, the elders may interpret such events
as supernatural sanction. In short, they make judgments as to whether
or not misfortunes are connected with failure to conform to the ideals
of leadership. Their controlling influence is buttressed by a compelling
set of symbols that surround ritual office. The highest ritual authorities, the "four old men" (however many they may be), mediate between humans and the supernatural in the rituals of the Sun Dance,
just as they have always done. The "old men" at the tribal drum are
referred to as the "Eagles"; they also facilitate good relations with the
Great Mystery Above, as did their predecessors.

Elders today have effected an association of other symbolic forms
with the prerogatives of priestly office. For example, the native language is used to symbolize sacred authority. All elders are bilingual and
most people of the "younger generation" speak fluent Arapahoe as
well as English. Choice of language is determined by social context.
The language of secular politics is English, and councilmen speak it
fluently. But the language of religious ritual is Arapahoe; in fact, it is
in part archaic. Elders are considered to have more control over the
native language and to use it more correctly. Thus they are more effective in ritual acts of prayer. Younger people, whether or not they speak
Arapahoe, must rely on elders to communicate and interpret in ritual
contexts. In times of crisis, as in the meeting to discuss the use of the
reservation's recreation facilities by whites, elders augment their influence over others by speaking in the native language, although they are
perfectly capable of articulate communication in English.

Today the authority of the elders appears to be at least as great as
it was in former eras, perhaps greater. The elders have gradually introduced innovations that have resulted in increased centralization of the
authority of the ceremonial elders. Within this generation the drum
groups of Mill Creek and Ethete were consolidated and that of Lower

Arapahoe was relegated to secondary status. The Upper Arapahoe drum became known as "Drum Number One," and the head of the drum group became known as the keeper of the tribal drum. The Eagles—the old men who attend the tribal drum—became an elders' leadership group. In this way the authority of the drum group was bolstered. Although the sodalities are in charge of organizing social dances, they depend on the keeper of the drum to start all-tribal celebrations (all of which involve the drum and the elderly male and female singers), including the Sun Dance.

In times of stress, ritual authorities use their influence to prevent serious schism. After a series of tragedies during 1976, several Arapahoes began to agitate for the transfer of the Sacred Pipe to another custodian. At a community meeting the custodian's supporters spoke of his outstanding qualifications and service, and his critics offered counterarguments. When the discussion became heated, the ceremonial elders counseled that since the season was a time for earnest preparations for an impending Sun Dance, no cross words should be spoken. The matter was tabled, and by the following year the crisis had passed.

The elders discourage younger people from seeking any relationship with the supernatural that is not mediated by priests. Such an effort is viewed as potentially threatening to the social order because individuals could use medicine power against other individuals—unlike priests, who are bound to think only "good thoughts." The ceremonial elders advise that "no one today can use a curse" (although there are ceremonies to counter curses). And on rare occasions when individuals are thought to have tried by supernatural means to gain influence over others, the elders watch carefully for signs of supernaturally induced misfortune and publicly comment on any they perceive.[15]

As we have seen, the ritual elders selected to fill the highest positions in the Sun Dance Lodge are customarily chosen equally from the two residential areas in order to prevent schism. When two old men predominated, West Shakespeare was chosen from Ethete and Anthony Iron from Arapahoe. In the 1970s, the elders, possibly seeking to reinforce the symbolic association of the mythological "four old men" with the Sun Dance authorities, began to choose four elders—two from Ethete and two from Arapahoe—to direct phases of the ritual. After West's death in 1976, Ben Friday from Ethete was placed in his position (see Plate 16), and Ralph Antelope from Arapahoe and Hiram Armajo from Ethete were also chosen.

The elders are also aware of another possible source of tension: the "young people." As in past eras, there is pressure for change from young Arapahoes. The elders have continued to be flexible, accommodating their juniors to some degree, but incorporating innovations within the hierarchical structure. In the 1970s, when "youths" pressed for more involvement in the electoral process, the tribe replaced the customary nomination procedures (nominations from the floor in General Council) with a primary election. This change would allow youths to seek support from voters without the elders' approval. The old people disapproved, primarily because persons who wanted to run had to announce publicly their intention and register. To do so would be immodest. Although the primary is now part of the electoral process, it has not led to the election of any "young people." The elders are still so firmly in control of public opinion that the occasional "youth" who is not eliminated in the primary is not able to generate enough support for election. But the elders have attended to the needs of these "young people" by permitting adjustments in the ritual sphere.

A young man who has participated in the Sun Dance once is today allowed to be a "grandfather" to a novice; before the 1970s, several Sun Dance vows were required. These young grandfathers are supervised by older grandfathers. Recently the most influential of the priests influenced the selection of a replacement for one of the "old men" so that a man only in his fifties was chosen. The priest pointed out that the selection of a younger man would ensure a long period of apprenticeship and would increase the involvement of younger men in ritual matters.

The remarkable continuity of leadership is in part due to the creative role the elders play in Arapahoe society. As we saw earlier (Table 10), the forty-two two-year council positions at Wind River during 1965–78 were filled by thirteen individuals.[16] These councilmen served consecutive terms, in good standing with their constituents; only occasionally did a man resign (because of illness or personal difficulties).

Elders work constantly to prevent the formation of factions. Participation in any and all religious ritual is regarded as proper. In fact, both of the senior priests today are regular participants in native religion, peyote ritual, and Christian services. Neither religious affiliation nor political view nor ancestry forms a basis for factional alignment.

The ethos of tribal unity and harmony is central to Arapahoe social relations in both political and religious spheres. Promotion of unity is the particular responsibility of the elders. Nowhere is this more apparent than in the present-day Paint Ceremony. The ceremony is initiated by the drum group—the Eagles and several elderly female singers. The people stand in a circle around the drum while the paint is applied by the old people to their cheekbones and forehead. Red-earth paint has always been applied to relatives of deceased persons after a period of mourning. People in mourning stay apart, avoiding others and shunning tribal ceremonies. The red paint, which symbolizes life and the tribe, reintegrates the bereaved into society—that is, public life. The mourning period used to last about a year. Today, with the sanction of the elders, the Paint Ceremony is held soon after a funeral, so that the family can rejoin and participate fully in the tribal activities—and *all* members of the tribe tend to receive the paint. This innovation integrates all Arapahoes with the mourners, whether they are related or not, and works to draw individuals into the sodality and ritual activity.

7

"Beware of the Stranger and His Strange Ways": The Evolution of Political Symbols, 1851–1978

Arapahoe political life and the role of ritual leaders in political relations have undergone extensive change since the mid-nineteenth century. Leaders have developed one innovative strategy after another; tribal elders have reshaped political culture many times over in successive eras of social crisis. One of the stories told on the reservation today is of the passing of Sharp Nose. As the chief lay dying, he said, "My friend, I am dying of my battle wounds. Watch out for our children, and yourselves. Stay together, and as the Arapahoes have always, beware of the stranger and his strange ways."[1] That this story is so integral to the Arapahoes' view of their own history is, on the surface, ironic. For historically Arapahoes have in fact accommodated themselves to "strange ways" and have embraced an assortment of "strangers" as allies in one capacity or another. But leaders have ascribed traditional meanings to political or ritual innovations so as to sanction the unfamiliar, and they have manipulated cultural understandings about long-standing institutions so that the old may appear novel. The Arapahoes have stayed together—spiritually, culturally, socially— not by rejecting innovations, but by interpreting them in adaptive ways and by giving powerful symbolic expression to these interpretations.

CONCILIATION

Arapahoe leaders who served as intermediaries sought to influence federal policy and policy implementation, and the approaches they took varied with the conditions they encountered. In their efforts to cope with both pressures from whites and the expectations of their constituents, intermediaries manipulated or redefined the traditional symbols of office, and in the process revitalized their authority.

Throughout most of the period since the Arapahoes first came in contact with whites, they have sought to avoid conflict. The chief they chose to act as their spokesman in the 1851 treaty council and to receive and distribute annuity goods was a man universally acknowledged to be a "friendly chief." He was used to receiving presents from whites in return for accommodating emigrants and government representatives, and he was expected to redistribute these gifts among the tribe. Their accommodating posture was precipitated by the circumstances in which they found themselves: the Arapahoes needed peaceful relations with the whites and direct access to the goods they produced. At the same time, the words spoken at the council are not to be interpreted as expressions of renunciation of or disinterest in traditional cultural and social forms and patterns. The remarks were designed to reassure the whites and to bring the Arapahoes additional benefits. Thus the friendly chief, literally cloaked in the vestments of the intermediary—wearing a major general's uniform and carrying a document that attested to the president's favor—reassured whites that he would be loyal and at the same time reassured his constituents that he could deliver American goods and provisions. The uniform of a high-ranking officer signified to whites that Little Owl could speak for and control all Arapahoes; to Arapahoes, the impressive uniform was a valuable gift that portended more gifts to come.

By the 1870s the tribe's predicament was more serious. Relations with whites had deteriorated, yet warfare would be disastrous. Arapahoe leaders took advantage of the opportunity to serve as army scouts, and in so doing convinced United States officials that they were "friendlies," not "hostiles." The Indian wars and the preeminence of army officers in Indian relations at that time—men who found areas of mutual interest and who came to appreciate the scouts as allies in war— created a new set of circumstances on which the Arapahoes were able to play. Scouting offered a man opportunities for the war exploits he needed to build a reputation for success and for *béétee*; yet in forming personal friendships with army officers, in making "brothers" of them, the chiefs tapped resources they could use to buttress their positions as intermediaries. The scout's uniform worn with the accessory traditional emblems of success in battle—personal medicine, feathers, paint— was a mark of both a man's influence with white officials and his prowess in overcoming his enemies. In the councils with army officers Sharp Nose affirmed, "We are your friends. You must be our friends. . . .

We want to be like white men. We want plenty of ammunition to fight with and good fast horses to ride on. We want to scout in our own way." Arapahoe scout chiefs stressed their determination to remain on good terms with whites; yet clearly the military alliance that they promoted strengthened the tribe's ability to preserve some measure of political autonomy and retain many fundamental elements of Arapahoe political culture. The scouts' wages and benefits enabled them to carry out their duties as chiefs—to provide for the members of their tribe. Benefits were channeled from federal officials to scouts, who publicly distributed goods to others during a tribal gathering.

Settlement on the reservation gradually weakened the influence of the chiefs: as Indians became less of a threat militarily, their needs and the commitments made to them became less important to government agents. In the early days on the reservation, Arapahoe leaders tried to manipulate the government's fears of an Indian outbreak by comparing themselves favorably with the Sioux, who were still causing trouble for the government. Although they made a show of being antagonistic to the Sioux, in reality the Arapahoes continued to entertain large parties of Teton Sioux visitors and to borrow or purchase ritual forms from them. In speeches to government officials the council chiefs stressed the Arapahoes' desire to learn farming, to send their children to school, and to become Christians—in short, to be "good Indians." Black Coal's address to the governor in 1878 was typical: "Once I was wild. Then at last I found the white man's trail. It is better than the red man's." Thus they conveyed a message of conciliation and the desire to cooperate. In reality, the farms that to whites signified "civilization" were communal efforts that buttressed the traditional redistributive exchange. The public distribution ceremonies reinforced the value of sharing rather than that of individual enterprise. Similarly, "educated" youths were put in service to the chiefs and acted as scribes or interpreters, subordinate to their elders. And Christianity never supplanted the native religion; rather, the chiefs used the resources of the churches to validate their positions and church rituals were added to an array of ritual obligations, always subordinate to the tribe's covenant with the Sacred Pipe. Black Coal, aware of how agents interpreted signs of "civilization," pointedly attended both mass and the Episcopal services, and he arranged for agents to observe him in the fields or bringing his harvest to the agency. The Arapahoes' willingness to accept the allotment and cession of land was a gratifying indication to federal officials that the tribe wished to travel the white man's road. To the Arapahoes, these agreements signified that their home at Shoshone Agency was secure and that provisions were guaranteed for a while longer.

As the influence of the council chiefs waned, a new kind of leader arose, the business councilman. There was no need now for a reputation based on battle exploits or on one's ability to present oneself to whites as a valuable ally in their struggle against "wild" Indians. The symbol of Business Council leadership came to be not the scout's uniform, but the "chief's little book," in which leases were recorded. The leasing of reservation land by a business council was part of the process by which Indians accommodated themselves to the end of annuities and rations and tried to convince the agent that they were "progressive" and business-minded. The councilman's lease book signified the ability to deal with whites, to conduct business, and thereby to secure economic aid for members of the tribe. To constituents, leases represented payment for the whites' infringement on natural resources that legally belonged to the tribe (grass, water, coal, and wood), and the councilmen watched over these money-making activities, facilitating the distribution of assets in the form of cattle purchases, seed, and so on. In fact, lease money was viewed in the same way as the rations and annuities of former times: the councilman's role was to augment this income and see to its equitable distribution. During the 1920s, Arapahoe leaders began to encourage white visitors to attend tribal ceremonies, and they publicly adopted and bestowed Indian names on a few particularly prominent or powerful whites. Such acts minimized the estrangement these whites felt toward Indians, and, as the Arapahoes had intended, persuaded them to intercede for the tribe in their struggles with the federal government. The adoption ceremony symbolized to both whites and Arapahoes the beginning of reciprocal expectations and obligations. To whites, attendance at ceremonies, and particularly adoption, was a romantic adventure; to Arapahoes, the invitations were political strategies that evolved in response to the intensification of government attempts to repress cultural traditions.

In the tribe's effort to appear "progressive" so as to reduce repressive measures on the part of federal agents, several sodalities of "youths" or "younger generation" Arapahoes came into being during the early twentieth century. Each such group bore two names—an Arapahoe name and an English name that reassured whites of the tribe's progressive bent: Christmas Club, Memorial Club, Fourth of July Committee, and later, after World War II, the American Legion. These groups' activities, however, served to perpetuate the traditional leadership roles and to abet the redistribution process, as the Arapahoe names given the groups seem to reflect.

During the post-Collier era, the Business Council was able to take a more aggressive, less conciliatory position vis-à-vis the Bureau of Indian Affairs. In their struggle with the BIA, councilmen stressed that the tribe was competent to manage its economic affairs. Capitalizing on ties with the tribe's attorneys and with congressional delegations, the council concentrated during the 1940s and 1950s on attaining per capita payments. In the Arapahoes' view, the per capita payments represented the government's recognition of its obligation to the tribe; these payments (known to Arapahoes as "that which is issued") also reinforced the position of councilmen as protectors of tribal solvency and as providers for all Arapahoes. At congressional hearings the councilmen tied the payments to the economic self-sufficiency of individuals and to the entry of Arapahoes into the American mainstream. Nell Scott argued, "Our boys fought for freedom. They fought for democracy, and yet when they come home they find their parents starving." The Arapahoes needed "this red tape to be taken off their neck, and the shackles off their legs, to go and buy some seed." With the consent of Congress the councilmen stripped the BIA of control over the per capita payments and at the same time buttressed the authority of the Business Council. In the 1970s, the council, following the initiative of an Arapahoe sodality, pressed the government to contract the operation of a high school to the tribe. To government officials the school symbolized the tribe's desire for independence from federal supervision and for greater participation in the wider society. In the view of many Arapahoes, the school brought more economic benefits and the fulfillment of old treaty agreements.

Thus throughout the successive eras of Arapahoe–white contact the intermediary leaders have relied on an assortment of symbols that have assisted them both to interact effectively with whites and to convince their constituents of their ability to protect the tribe's interests. The friendly chief, with his documents of good conduct, medals, and suits of clothing, displayed his ability to acquire provisions and generously distribute them. The distributions were ritual occasions, with a prescribed order of presentation and accolades by the elders. The occasions were symbolic of the relationship between leaders and constituents. Similarly, the scout, with his prerogatives of rank and the open patronage of his officer brother-friends, assured other Arapahoes of his ability to provide and protect. The reservation council chief, who had the ear of the agent, was able to distribute publicly the resources he acquired by virtue of the government's acknowledgment of his council chieftainship and to relieve the tribe's anxiety about the threat of removal from the reservation. The lease book of the government-instigated business council was a record of incoming funds and expenditures on cattle, seed, clothing, and the like; it also signified the councilmen's ability to provide. The sodalities—"they who hang up presents," "those who fix up graves," and so on—were oriented toward generous distribution as well. Today the council's long-standing role in the distribution and protection of the per capita payments and the acquisition of federal money and resources is central to the status of councilman. Thus the intermediary role, when most successful, has always been associated with symbolic activities or forms that signify to Arapahoes that these leaders are effective advocates who can be counted on to make generous and fair distribution, and at the same time signify to whites that they will be cooperative.

LEGITIMIZATION

The legitimization process has, at least indirectly, been the responsibility of the elders, particularly the ritual authorities, who helped to revitalize and validate the criteria of legitimacy for intermediary offices in new social contexts. In fulfilling the duties of their offices, the ceremonial elders recharged ritual symbols with new meaning and introduced them into contemporary politics. In making traditional religion relevant and responsive to new conditions, they strengthened the authority of priests and the influence of senior males over their juniors.

The Arapahoes experienced intensive contact and hostile encounters with whites relatively late, compared with the Teton Sioux and the tribes in the upper Missouri and Saskatchewan areas. The white Americans, with their awe-inspiring weaponry, may have influenced the Arapahoes toward conciliation. Whatever the reason, Arapahoe priests appear to have encouraged a strategy that mitigated in some respects the federal assault on Arapahoe cultural traditions. The situation was far more repressive on other reservations where the tribes were overtly uncooperative with federal agents. In the reservation era, when federal agents were bent on eradicating or reducing the influence of native ritual authorities, ceremonial elders publicly endorsed the government's proposal that the Arapahoes take up farming. They agreed to eliminate some religious practices that whites found objectionable, such as the torture phase of the Sun Dance, and they supported the efforts of the missionaries; they even requested baptism. Thus whites often were placated, and Arapahoes were not threatened with loss of the native priests' support when they attempted to adapt to new times.

By monitoring the selection and actions of intermediaries, ceremonial elders helped to generate public support and thereby strengthened the intermediaries' influence with government officials. The ritual symbols used by priests in validating secular authority worked also to curb its abuse. When Little Owl was selected as head chief in 1851, an elder linked support for him with the tribe's continued good relationship with the supernatural. For Little Owl, aid from the Great Mystery Above was also necessary to his success as chief; failure indicated supernatural disfavor. After reservation settlement only chiefs of whom the ceremonial elders approved could use the scepter that symbolized the wisdom and authority of the aged. Such a scepter helped the leader to mobilize support. When a "business council" was introduced during the twentieth century, government officials were hopeful that a small group of councilmen—induced to make decisions independently of the elders—could be manipulated to support policies opposed by most of the tribe. But while the councilmen were presented to the agents as "elected" officials, the ceremonial elders actually selected them "by the drum," and in so doing sanctioned the new councilman role. As a sacred symbol, the drum both induced sentiment to support the councilmen and influenced the councilmen themselves to respect the teachings of the ceremonial elders. In the past as in the present a leader in secular affairs had to legitimize his authority by a public display of generosity. Such a display could be validated only by elders. Elders always presided over the giveaway, announcing and singing songs of praise and receiving the first gifts. Their participation was essential to the satisfactory performance of the ceremony and to the public acknowledgment of the status of those who were "giving away." Despite generations of oppression, the giveaway and its association with any form of public distribution (government annuities, mission benefits, Business Council programs) persisted, under the elders' direction.

The ceremonial elders have curbed the influence of dissenters by symbolically associating them with danger not only to tribal security, but also to the natural order of things. Warriors who declined to be "good Indians" were called "foolish" or "crazy"—that is, they were accused of behavior counter to orderly social relations. Individuals who occasionally were slow to cooperate with "progressive" strategies were "kickers," futilely resisting the inevitable. The elders, fearful of losing their influence over young, "educated" Indians fluent in English and adept in dealings with whites, dismissed the rebellious as "schoolboys," immature and untrustworthy. Today nonconformists are termed "radicals," and associated with disruption and disorder.

The ceremonial elders also helped to keep order by a flexible approach to ritual innovation. When the water-sprinkling old men died without legitimate successors in the late nineteenth century, other elderly ritual authorities assumed their duties. When the social functions of age grades atrophied, the priests transformed the ceremonial lodges into purely religious sodalities for age peers and relaxed some of the criteria for membership. In the twentieth century, the priests allowed the ritual duties of the Big Lodge People to be assumed by others, thus diffusing ceremonial offices more widely throughout the society. They validated the leadership status of social sodalities by bestowing names on the groups. The ceremonial elders not only accepted revitalization movements, but took on supervisory roles in them. Thus, while young people could find new outlets for religious expression and social ambition, the participants were under the watchful eyes of the native priests. Similarly, in recent times the ceremonial elders have permitted more extensive participation by "young people" in the Sun Dance, even in lesser positions of ritual authority, as grandfathers. Three and four times as many men participated in the Sun Dance in the 1960s and 1970s as in the 1940s and 1950s. Elderly Arapahoes recall that at the turn of the century only a handful of young men participated because of the necessity of "respecting" the ceremony. By their flexibility in permitting and even legitimizing change, the priests contained or resolved successive crises when young Arapahoes impatiently pressed for change and for a more satisfying role in Arapahoe society.

The ceremonial elders have consistently reaffirmed their right and ability to mediate between their people and the supernatural. Over the years their authority has actually increased. In the nineteenth century, a man's pipe was an implement of his personal bond with the supernatural and was used to cement political ties with non-Arapahoes; thus chiefs often insisted on smoking with white officials or gave pipes as gifts. But in the reservation era, pipes and their ritual use came to be reserved for religious ceremonies supervised by the priests. Whereas in the past the sacred and secular spheres of leadership were closely intertwined and related to a chief's success, they were now compartmentalized. Intermediaries began increasingly to rely on the prayers and prophesies of ceremonial elders in relations with the supernatural. The symbolic association of priests with the "four old men" has been emphasized in recent years, when "young people" threatened rebellion, by the actual selection of four men as tribal medicine men. Similarly, the three drum groups have given way to a tribal drum, Drum Number One. In short, the priests have employed these old, traditional symbols of the tribe's relationship to supernatural forces—the pipe, the drum, the "four old men"—in new ways so as to reinforce priestly authority, particularly in times of crisis.

The Arapahoes were able both to appease federal officials and to perpetuate the overriding authority of the ceremonial elders. In external relations, leaders successively created several new ways to symbolize a conciliatory stance toward federal officials. In appearing to change, to "progress," leaders attempted to mitigate federal dominance and repression. In the guise of innovation, the symbolic forms and activities associated with positions of leadership served not only to placate or influence whites but also to perpetuate features of traditional political culture. The ceremonial elders, in coping with the dramatic changes imposed on the Arapahoes by contact and reservation conditions— changes that threatened their authority over their juniors—creatively defined contemporary conditions as continuity and used symbols associated with past tribal life to serve new functions. The old symbols reinforced the role of the priests as legitimate innovators; the new symbols of conciliation or progress concealed from whites the perpetuation of old political values.

"FIRST THE ELDERS, THEN THE YOUNGER GENERATION, THEN THE YOUNG PEOPLE": AGE GRADING AND CULTURE CHANGE

Throughout the reservation period, membership in the Arapahoe Business Council has shown remarkable continuity. The council's stability was not disrupted by the change from selection by the drum to election by ballot or by Collier's program and the new controls and funds acquired by the council. The position of councilman has been a respected one, with many councilmen serving until death or retirement; in fact, since the inception of the council in 1908, all of its terms of office have been filled by fifty-one individuals. And the Arapahoe community lacks the devisive factions—old against young, sect against sect, conservative against progressive, mixed blood against full blood— that are found on many other Plains reservations. The Arapahoes' success—the willingness of elders to support innovations and of the younger generation dutifully to accept the elders' guidance—is in large part attributable to an age-grading tradition.

The association of leadership roles with age categories persisted even after the age-grade system collapsed. Arapahoes continued to rely on respected elders, as well as priests, to aid them in living successful lives. The aging process has always been correlated with a gradual increase in potential for wise counsel and for authority in the sacred realm. Although a changing social environment precipitated revisions in Arapahoe ideas about the particular social roles that were appropriate to the various age categories, relations between "elder" and "younger generation" Arapahoes remained complementary. "Youths" were excluded from important positions of secular leadership but given new ritual roles. In earlier times certain political responsibilities were delegated to particular men's lodges; important secular duties were assigned to "younger generation" age sets and the highest ritual authority was reserved for the elder set or the priests. Youths achieved prestige by devoting themselves to warfare and raiding.[2] Today Business Council leadership is the prerogative of men of the younger generation, and only elders have authority in the sacred realm. Although ceremonial authority is hierarchical, the elders are expected to indulge their juniors to a considerable extent. In effect, age groups act both to buttress and to constrain each other's authority.[3]

Henry Elkin's 1936 study of Arapahoe society, with its emphasis on the acculturation process, obscures this fundamentally important aspect of Arapahoe culture and society. Elkin argues that the "equilibrium" of men's lives was shattered by reservation life, and thus that "middle-aged men are far more personally disorganized" than elders, "and have achieved a passive and listless adjustment." According to Elkin, "the young men under thirty fare the worst. A good part of their lives has been spent in school, and now that they have left, there is nothing to turn to. The older people treat them like children. They get drunk frequently and are apt to be involved in auto crashes and fights."[4] Yet those "passive" and "listless" Arapahoes are today's respected elders, and the unruly youths are today's councilmen and sodality leaders. In the Arapahoe scheme of things, men's roles are directly associated with age, or stage in life. Eventually youth becomes younger generation, and people of the younger generation become elders. Over the last 160 years the association of leadership roles and prerogatives with age has been regarded as part of the natural order.

The way Arapahoes view age-group relations has facilitated the centralization of both secular and sacred authority, offset strains toward social schism, and contributed to political stability. Elders' views are most important in singling out "good men"; thus their support of the selection of a few council chiefs and then of six councilmen who spoke for all Arapahoes helped those intermediaries to maintain the confidence of the tribe. Armed with their right to mediate between Arapahoes and the supernatural, elders intervened in times of social conflict, holding in check any troubles between bands (as in the Waterman–Fast Wolf case and the dispute between the Upper and Lower Arapahoes) so that quarrels did not escalate into factional alignments.[5] The influence of the elders contributed to the widespread conformity to the set of values that defined Arapahoe cultural identity and to the general acceptance of the enrollment criteria set in 1956.

Thus "mixed-bloods" were never significantly influential or numerous on the reservation. Elders also, by reinforcing values of generosity, contributed to the leveling process that has mitigated differentials in wealth in Arapahoe society. For its part, the younger generation took on intermediary roles; as a result, more educated leaders were dealing with whites, and the elders and priests were insulated from criticism if the council's actions became unpopular. With roots in the age-set/age-grade tradition, cross-cutting institutions in the form of twentieth-century clubs, as well as the Sun Dance grandfather–grandson relationship, contributed to consensus formation and tribal unity.

The kind of relationship that prevailed between the younger generation and the elders, between intermediary and ritual authorities, was important in the Arapahoes' adaptation to the changes brought by white society. Federal agents were not able to create long-lasting breaches between old and young, or to enlist the aid of young men in eroding the influence of the old and undermining traditional leadership. The elders, the younger generation, and the youths relied on each other for certain skills and ministrations. Thus Arapahoe society is without the "progressive" and "conservative" (or "traditional") interest groups that clash in other reservation communities. Each age group's particular input in reservation society is seen as sanctioned by "tradition," as well as important and necessary to the tribe's well-being.

Walter Sangree's work on the political reorganization of the Tiriki of Kenya describes a similar case in which an age-group system proved adaptive in colonization and rapid sociocultural change. According to Sangree, Tiriki elders lost less ground to youth than other elders elsewhere in Africa, in large part because the political roles of the age groups are complementary rather than competitive.[6] Traditionally, Tiriki age groups supplied the principal political and ritual bases for corporate action, and administrative roles were functionally specific. In Kenya the British policy of indirect rule delegated a considerable measure of authority to native leaders, and institutions of leadership were buttressed rather than eroded. The British supported the administrative and executive authority of young men and the judiciary authority of elders. The elders' roles were secularized, no longer based on supernatural sanction, during the colonial era. In the United States, in contrast, there was severe repression, and the status of leaders and the political cultures that defined the criteria of legitimacy for leadership roles were harshly attacked. Arapahoe intermediaries had no autonomy, and much of the political power in the reservation community was in the hands of the agent. Real autonomy persisted only in the supernatural realm. The intermediaries relied on the ceremonial elders, not the United States government, for legitimization of what secular authority they did have.

Generalizations made by anthropologists about Plains politics so far have been based on studies of groups that lacked age-grade systems—the Teton Sioux and the Cheyennes in particular. We have seen that Northern Arapahoe political history contrasts sharply with that of these and many other Plains peoples. An understanding of Arapahoe political history is an important beginning in the effort to make sense of the full range of political variation in the Plains area; however, further study is needed. I have argued that the form the Arapahoes' politics took stems largely from their age-grading tradition and its particulars. The complementary nature of age-group relations is found among the Arapahoes and Gros Ventres but to a lesser extent among the other age-graded peoples, the Blackfeet, Mandans, and Hidatsas. Research has shown that among the Gros Ventres, centralized intermediary leadership was well institutionalized and deep divisions between old and young or "conservatives" and "progressives" were absent.[7] Further studies are needed of political reorganization among the age-graded tribes and of the ways these societies differed politically from those that lacked a tradition of age grades. Surprisingly, no published work on Plains peoples has yet recognized that adaptation to contact with whites may have varied according to the presence or absence of an age-grade tradition.

In the reorganization of their political life the Arapahoes have shown great creativity in developing innovative strategies and accommodating these innovations to cultural orientations so that they retained a sense of continuity with their past. In a repressive colonial experience, this continuity was articulated largely through symbolic processes, through what Abner Cohen terms "symbolic strategies."[8] Arapahoe political change cannot be fully understood without awareness of what actions and events *meant* to the Arapahoes and to those who had political relations with them. Change has been monitored and interpreted by the elders, who, in helping the people "stay together" and in making the strange familiar, transform traditions in ways acceptable to the Arapahoe people.

APPENDIX

Arapahoe Orthography

Arapahoe phonemes are as follows:

Vowels:

ee	Lower mid-front, unrounded; approximately as in *there*.
e	Lower mid-front, unrounded; approximately as in *bet*.
oo	Low back, slightly rounded; approximately as in *law*.
o	Low central or back, slightly rounded; approximately as in *bought* or *cup*.
ii	High front, unrounded; approximately as in *seed*.
i	High front, unrounded; approximately as in *sit*.
uu	High central or back, unrounded; similar sound in Southwest English *food* or Japanese *u*, as in *Fuji*.
u	High central or back, unrounded; similar sound in Southwest English *foot*.

Consonants:

b	Bilabial stop, voiced initially, intervocalically, and following another consonant; in the final position it is voiceless (i.e., phonetically a *p* in this position); as in *bat*, finally as in *top*.
t	Voiceless dental stop, aspirated finally, and with prolonged closure in intervocalic position after a short vowel associated with a high-pitched prosodeme; as in *stop* or *pot*.
k	Voiceless velar stop articulated according to the following vowel between the prevelar and mediovelar points; finally and as the first member of a cluster it has an aspirated allophone; as in *skill* or *book*.

'	Glottal stop; in the final position it has an aspirated allophone.
ch	Voiceless alveopalatal affricate; as in *choke*.
O	Voiceless interdental spirant; as *th* in English *thin* or *z* in European Spanish.
s	Voiceless alveolar groove spirant; as in *sap*.
x	Voiceless velar spirant; as in German *Buch*.
h	Glottal spirant; as in *hat*.
n	Nasal dental continuant, voiced nonfinally; as in *nap*.
w	Bilabial semivowel, voiceless in final position and voiced elsewhere; as in *watch*.
y	Mediopalatal semivowel, voiceless in final position and voiced elsewhere; as in *you*.

Accent indicates raised pitch, but the phonemic analysis of tones is not complete.

A technical description of Arapahoe phonology is Zdenek Salzmann (1956). The analysis here—which follows Ives Goddard's interpretation of Arapahoe phonology (personal communication)—differs slightly.

Notes

The following abbreviations are used in the notes:

CF   Central Files, 1907–39, Shoshone Agency, Records of the Bureau of Indian Affairs, Record Group 75, National Archives.

DC   George Dorsey Correspondence, Field Museum of Natural History, Chicago.

DI   Inspection Division, Reports, 1881–1924, Records of the Office of the Secretary of the Interior, Record Group 48, National Archives.

FRC   Wind River Files, Records of the Bureau of Indian Affairs, Record Group 75, Federal Archives and Records Center, Denver.

HRPD   Historical Research and Publications Division, Wyoming State Archives and Historical Department, Cheyenne.

LG   Legislative History Files, Committee on Interior and Insular Affairs, Records of the U.S. House of Representatives, Record Group 233, National Archives.

LR   Letters Received by the Office of Indian Affairs, 1881–1907, Records of the Bureau of Indian Affairs, Record Group 75, National Archives.

LR-DI   Letters Received by the Secretary of the Interior—Indian Division, Records of the Office of the Secretary of the Interior, Record Group 48, National Archives.

LR-DS   Letters Received by the Office of Indian Affairs, 1824–81, Dakota Superintendency, Records of the Bureau of Indian Affairs, Record Group 75, National Archives.

LR-RC   Letters Received by the Office of Indian Affairs, 1824–81, Red Cloud Agency, Records of the Bureau of Indian Affairs, Record Group 75, National Archives.

LR-SL   Letters Received by the Office of Indian Affairs, 1824–81, St. Louis Superintendency, Records of the Bureau of Indian Affairs, Record Group 75, National Archives.

LR-UP   Letters Received by the Office of Indian Affairs, 1824-81, Upper Platte Agency, Records of the Bureau of Indian Affairs, Record Group 75, National Archives.

LR-WS   Letters Received by the Office of Indian Affairs, 1824-81, Wyoming Superintendency, Records of the Bureau of Indian Affairs, Record Group 75, National Archives.

LS   Letters Sent by the Office of Indian Affairs, 1824-81, Records of the Bureau of Indian Affairs, Record Group 75, National Archives.

LS-FF   Letters Sent, Post Records of Fort Fetterman, Records of the U.S. Army Continental Commands, 1821-1920, Record Group 393, National Archives.

LS-FL   Letters Sent, Post Records of Fort Laramie, Records of the U.S. Army Continental Commands, 1821-1920, Record Group 393, National Archives.

LS-FW   Letters Sent, Post Records of Fort Washakie, Records of the U.S. Army Continental Commands, 1821-1920, Record Group 393, National Archives.

NAA   National Anthropological Archives, Smithsonian Institution, Washington, D.C.

OAG   Records of the Office of the Adjutant General, Record Group 94, National Archives.

PJ-FF   Daily Journal of Events, Post Records of Fort Fetterman, Records of the U.S. Army Continental Commands, 1821-1920, Record Group 393, National Archives.

RCIA   *Reports of the Commissioner of Indian Affairs.* Washington, D.C.: Government Printing Office, 1846-1906.

RT   Ratified Treaty File, Records of the Bureau of Indian Affairs, Record Group 75, National Archives.

SC   Special Cases, 1821-1907, Shoshone Agency, Records of the Bureau of Indian Affairs, Record Group 75, National Archives.

WHRC   Western History Research Center, University of Wyoming, Laramie.

INTRODUCTION

1. The files for several Montana tribes (Cheyennes, Fort Peck Assiniboines, Blackfeet, Fort Belknap Assiniboines, and Gros Ventres) contain some such correspondence. Very large files of letters of protest exist for other tribes, including the Crows in Montana and the Teton Sioux on Rosebud and Pine Ridge reservations in South Dakota.

2. See Henry Elkin, "The Northern Arapaho of Wyoming."

3. Merwyn S. Garbarino, *Native American Heritage,* p. 452. In *Indian Americans,* Murray L. Wax concludes that Plains tribal governments "have a difficult time existing and maintaining sufficient communal support to transact business" (p. 74). See also Joseph G. Jorgensen, *The Sun Dance Religion.*

4. Women were not organized into age grades but upon maturity could join the women's sacred society, which may have had political as well as religious

functions. Unfortunately, anthropologists and other observers of nineteenth-century Arapahoes did not inquire into the role of women in Arapahoe political life.

5. The complementary nature of relations among Arapahoe age grades contrasts with the situation reported for most African age-graded societies. Some scholars argue that in the African societies, the distribution of privileges among men of different grades is overwhelmingly unequal, so that an inordinate amount of power is vested in older men, and older men control all significant social activities. In this kind of situation the young resent the old (see Paul Spencer, "Opposing Streams and the Gerontocratic Ladder: Two Models of Age Organization in East Africa"). At transition points, a preceding age set resents the initiation of a junior set. Elder men see the progression of younger men as a challenge or threat. Passage to the final age grade often brings a loss in status. In contrast to the situation among the Arapahoes, the decision to allow a set to pass from one grade to another is made not by the initiates themselves but by the elders—a situation that results in conflict and social discord (see Anne Foner and David Kertzer, "Transitions over the Life Course: Lessons from Age-Set Societies").

6. Elizabeth Colson, *Tradition and Contract,* pp. 84-86.

7. Clifford Geertz, *The Interpretation of Cultures,* pp. 12, 91-95. The interpretation of past culture from contemporary historical documents is complicated by the difficulty of drawing conclusions from fragmentary data and of verifying data in documents, particularly the statements of Arapahoes that were recorded by whites. I have tried to come to terms with these problems by an exhaustive search for documentary accounts hitherto unused; by placing available data within the context of general and comparative anthropological perspectives on the Plains; by paying particular attention to contemporarily recorded statements of the Arapahoes themselves; and by not relying on documents in which transcribed statements reportedly made by Arapahoes were translated into English by an interpreter whose veracity or skill is in doubt.

8. Feliks Gross, "Language and Value Changes among the Arapaho," pp. 12-13, 15. Gross's conclusions also are disputed by Zdenek Salzmann, "Contrastive Field Experience with Language and Values of the Arapaho."

9. Ralph Linton, *Acculturation in Seven American Indian Tribes,* p. 256.

10. F. G. Bailey applies the term "parapolitical situations" to those cases in which political structures "are partly regulated by, and partly independent of, larger encapsulating political structures" ("Parapolitical Systems," p. 281).

11. In this work "political" activities are broadly defined as those that are involved in the formulation and implementation of public goals (see Marc J. Swartz, *Local-Level Politics,* pp. 1-6). For a more thoroughgoing discussion of Euro-American concepts of authority, see Walter B. Miller, "Two Concepts of Authority," pp. 275-76, and for a discussion of Euro-American concepts of political process, see William O. Farber, "Representative Government: Application to the Sioux," pp. 124-25. Robert H. Lowie examines the role of religion in native North American political organization ("Some Aspects of Political Organization among the American Aborigines").

12. Edwin James, *James's Account of S. H. Long's Expedition of 1819–20,* vol. 16, pp. 201, 208-10, and vol. 17, pp. 161, 166.

13. John R. Bell, *The Journal of Captain John R. Bell,* p. 197.

14. James, *James's Account,* vol. 17, p. 166.

15. Ibid., p. 161. Although neither James nor Bell mention age-graded men's societies, George Bird Grinnell's report of an Arapahoe with a "Flat War Club" who helped to lead an expedition of Arapahoes and Cheyennes against the Kiowas in 1837 possibly refers to a member of the Arapahoe age grade known as the Tomahawk Lodge (*The Fighting Cheyennes,* p. 70). George Bent (Grinnell's informant) sketched the man's club for George Hyde; the drawing is that of the wand carried by the "honored dancer" (the "sword man") of the Tomahawk Lodge (Bent to Hyde, August 7, 1914, Box 2, folder 33, Bent Papers, William Robertson Coe Collection, Yale University Library).

16. In the view of Arapahoes, the life cycle is one manifestation of the oneness of all life. The "four directions" of the universe and the perceived course of the sun from daybreak to dark and season to season parallel the "four hills" of life and the course of the individual from birth to death. As the sun is "reborn" each day and the earth renews itself, so human life is constantly renewed. In fact, M. Inez Hilger reported that the Arapahoes believed that a person who died when very old returned to earth to live again in a newborn child (*Arapaho Child Life and Its Cultural Background,* p. 6).

17. Regina Flannery also makes this point for the Gros Ventres, who separated from the Arapahoes proper before the nineteenth century (*The Gros Ventres of Montana: Part I, Social Life,* p. 39). Among the Arapahoes, an age set is a group of peers who as youths are formally inducted into the first age grade (or ceremonial "lodge") and together move through a series of age-grade categories (*beeyóóowu'*, or "all the sacred lodges"). The group members refer to each other as "friends" or "comrades" and share certain constraints, privileges, and obligations associated with their particular grade, and they owe each other assistance all their lives. For a more extensive discussion of age-set and age-grade systems, see Frank Henderson Stewart's cross-cultural study, *Fundamentals of Age-Group Systems.* See also David I. Kertzer, "Theoretical Developments in the Study of Age-Group Systems."

18. Fred Eggan, ed., *Social Anthropology of North American Tribes,* pp. 53-54; Hilger, *Arapaho Child Life,* pp. 75-76.

19. In Plains studies, intergenerational relations are usually ignored or, if mentioned, discussed without detail. I also find that, without having done research on the communities described in other studies, it is difficult to evaluate what is said about relations between generations. These reservations aside, it is not uncommon to find in the literature references to "young" and "old" factions and to a diminished role for elders in reservation political life. For example, in *The Indian Elder, a Forgotten American,* a survey of the problems of elderly Indians today, the National Indian Conference on Aging concludes that elders have less respect and less input in the political life of their communities than they did in earlier times (pp. 11, 15). Graham D. Taylor characterizes much of the conflict that occurred over the introduction of elective tribal governments and political and economic reforms

urged by Commissioner of Indian Affairs John Collier in 1934 as divisions between young Indians and their elders, who were more "full-blood" (*The New Deal and American Indian Tribalism*, p. 50). Stephen E. Feraca identified a young, educated faction in opposition to the older traditionalists among the Pine Ridge Teton Sioux ("The History and Development of Oglala Sioux Tribal Government," pp. 31-32). Political factions identified as old and young Northern Cheyennes are mentioned by Ann Sawyier Straus ("Being Human in the Cheyenne Way," p. 246) and are also discussed by Katherine Weist ("The Northern Cheyennes: Diversity in a Loosely Structured Society," p. 142). Donald J. Berthrong observes that among the Southern Cheyennes in Oklahoma, young educated Cheyennes competed with elderly leaders for the political support of tribal members (*The Cheyenne and Arapaho Ordeal*, p. 324). Malcolm McFee concluded that among the Blackfeet positions of political power are held by young educated men; elders, while they are respected as authorities on tradition, are peripheral to the political process (*Modern Blackfeet: Montanans on a Reservation*, pp. 112-14).

20. The most important object in the tribal medicine bundle is the Sacred Flat Pipe. The pipe and other sacred objects are wrapped in many cloths to form a bundle. The tribal medicine bags contained several small sacred objects (see Alfred L. Kroeber, *The Arapaho*, p. 207). I take exception to Kroeber's characterization of the water-pouring old men as an age grade (the eighth grade). Membership was not open to all men of advanced years, only to those who had been specially trained for the priests' offices, and only seven men could serve as tribal priests (see Stewart, *Fundamentals*, pp. 130-32).

21. Among the Northern and Southern Cheyennes, native religion reportedly was challenged and its relevance eventually undermined by converts to the peyote religion, who began to dominate tribal politics; among the Northern Cheyennes, Christian (Protestant) converts formed a third interest group (Berthrong, *Cheyenne and Arapaho Ordeal*, p. 324; Weist, "Northern Cheyennes," pp. 54-55, 119). According to McFee, Blackfeet leaders in native ritual play no role in politics today; council leadership positions are held by Christians (*Modern Blackfeet*, pp. 112-14). In the view of Feraca and Powers, at Pine Ridge sacred and secular authority exist apart from one another, as the Sioux believe that supernatural power is not adequate to accomplish political goals (Feraca, "History and Development," p. 20; William K. Powers, *Oglala Religion*, p. 205). Among the Mandan, however, Edward M. Bruner observed that the hereditary heads of clans, who own medicine bundles, remain an important leadership group apart from the elected tribal council ("Mandan," p. 265); he does not say whether the two leadership groups are hostile or mutually supportive.

22. In 1851 one of the three chiefs who were officially recognized was from the southern bands of the tribe; the others were from the northern bands. Subsequently, the federal government began to deal with the northern and southern divisions separately and each had its own intermediaries. The southern bands eventually settled permanently in Oklahoma and the northern bands in Wyoming. These two divisions also have adopted different spellings of the tribal name: Southern Arapaho and Northern Arapahoe. Both spellings appear in the literature in reference to both of the divisions.

23. For a general discussion of white notions of "good Indians," see Robert E. Berkhofer, *The White Man's Indian.*

24. Wax, *Indian Americans,* p. 75. The resistance to centralized tribal government seems most intense among the Teton Sioux groups, for which tribal identity was less developed than among the Cheyennes, Blackfeet, and Arapahoes. At Pine Ridge, political identity is based on band rather than tribal membership (Raymond J. DeMallie, Jr., "Pine Ridge Economy: Cultural and Historical Perspectives," pp. 274, 294-95; Powers, *Oglala Religion,* p. 119; Feraca, "History and Development," pp. 26, 37, 76-77). Taylor points out that when decision making by consensus was replaced by majority vote, dissidents were resentful and debates bitter (*New Deal,* pp. 49-50). And Ernest L. Schusky notes that in fulfilling their duties, tribal councilmen on Lower Brule Reservation (and at Pine Ridge, according to Feraca) alienated themselves from the electorate because the councilman role—modeled after Euro-American standards—was incompatible with the role of the "good man" (*Politics and Planning in a Dakota Community,* pp. 61-62). See also Farber, "Representative Government," pp. 132, 138. Bruner observed that among the Mandan-Hidatsas at Fort Berthold, hereditary clan leaders function independently of councilmen, and the effectiveness of the tribal organization is thereby weakened ("Mandan," p. 265).

Reservation factionalism is often characterized as a "mixed-blood"/"full-blood" division, with the "mixed-bloods" more willing or able to fill elective tribal offices. (These categories refer to *social* identity, not to biological characteristics.) The conflict between "blood" groups, however, is not always accompanied by a conflict between the political ideals and expectations of traditionalists and those of proponents of the elective tribal governments introduced by federal officials. Although "mixed-blood" and "full-blood" factions exist among the Cheyennes and Blackfeet, elective tribal council government is not opposed by "full-bloods," or traditionalists. The traditional values associated with chiefly behavior are subscribed to by elected councilmen among the Northern Cheyennes (Weist, "Northern Cheyennes," pp. 60, 140; Taylor, *New Deal,* p. 60). Like the Cheyennes, the Gros Ventres at Fort Belknap (before the Indian Reorganization Act, or IRA) accepted elective tribal council government without conflict; here there was no "mixed-blood"/"full-blood" political conflict until a few years after the acceptance of the IRA (Loretta Fowler, "'Look at My Hair, It Is Gray': Age Grading, Ritual Authority and Political Change among the Northern Arapahoe and Gros Ventre"). For the Blackfeet, the Western form of elective government has replaced traditional decision making by unanimity or consensus (McFee, *Modern Blackfeet,* p. 113). As discussed in later chapters of this book, the Northern Arapahoes do not have political factions composed of "mixed-bloods" and "full-bloods."

25. See Taylor, *New Deal,* p. xiii. Robert Burnette and John Koster also suggest that tribes that rejected political reorganization under the provisions of the IRA escaped difficulties rather than sacrificed benefits (*The Road to Wounded Knee,* p. 187). Taylor argues that basically the same benefits accrued to non-IRA tribes as to those that accepted reorganization.

26. Jean Baptiste Trudeau, "Journal of Jean Baptiste Trudeau among the Arikara Indians," pp. 46-47. Before Trudeau and other traders from the Missouri

penetrated Arapahoe country, Arapahoes had been in occasional contact with Spanish traders to the south, but I know of no written accounts of Arapahoe relations with the Spanish-speaking traders (the Arapahoe term for Mexican was not *nih'ôôOoo*, but rather *chô'chooniinên*, or "breadman"); James, *James's Account*, vol. 16, pp. 208-09; vol. 17, p. 157; Jacob Fowler, *The Journal of Jacob Fowler*, pp. 54, 55, 59, 62, 70.

27. Trudeau, "Journal," p. 31. Antoine Soulard in 1795 located the Blue Bead Nation just to the south of the "Little Missouri River" (that is, the Cheyenne River, according to Perrin du Lac) near wandering bands of Arikaras and Cheyennes (for the three versions of the Soulard map, see John Logan Allen, *Passage through the Garden*, pp. 150-51; Abraham P. Nasatir, *Before Lewis and Clark*, vol. 1, p. 46; Carl I. Wheat, *Mapping the Transmississippi West*, vol. 1, map 235a; see also W. Raymond Wood, "Notes on the Historical Cartography of the Upper Knife-Heart Region," pp. 11-15). At about this time, Edward Umfreville reports the Gros Ventre division of the Arapahoes on the south branch of the Saskatchewan in Canada, where they had been for at least a generation (see Flannery, *Gros Ventres*, pp. 3-4).

28. In 1821, when a "chief" greeted Jacob Fowler by saying, "Me Arapahoe," "Arapahoe" had already become the term by which whites recognized a people who called themselves *hinono'eino'*, or "the people." According to James Mooney's interviews in 1890, there were at one time five divisions—Nakasinena (Sage People), Nawunena (Southern People), Hitunena (Begging People), Basawunena (Big Lodge People), and Hanahawunena (meaning unknown) (*The Ghost-Dance Religion and the Sioux Outbreak of 1890*, pp. 954-56). It is difficult to identify any but the Hitunena (Gros Ventres) in the early accounts of the traders. Tokaminabiches (*tUhkaNIhnâ:wish*) was the Arikara word for Arapahoes; it meant "colored stone village" (Douglas Parks, personal communication). Edwin James noted that the Hidatsas referred to the Arapahoes as e-ta-leh, or "Bison-Path Indians" (*James's Account*, vol. 16, p. 215); according to Douglas Parks, the correct transcription is probably *ita'ari:* or *ita:ri:*, which means "his path." The term for the Gros Ventre division (in Long, A-re-tear-o-pan-ga) is *ati:htia ruxpâ:ka*, "big lodge people." In 1810 John Bradbury—whose associates were from Crow country—referred to the "Arapahoes or Big Bead Indians" who lived near the Rocky Mountains (*Travels in the Interior of America in the Years 1809, 1810 and 1811*, 5:139) and in 1812 Manuel Lisa—who had a fort on the Bighorn branch of the Yellowstone, also in Crow country—mentioned trade with the "Arapaos" (Herbert E. Bolton, "New Light on Manual Lisa and the Spanish Fur Trade," p. 65). The Crows referred to the Arapahoes as *Alappahô*, or "many tattoos" (G. H. Matthews, personal communication). Hugh Lenox Scott concluded that the name Arapahoe was adopted by whites from the Crows ("The Early History and the Names of the Arapahoe," pp. 556-57). (In 1801, Peter Fidler noted that the Blackfeet and Crow sign for a group of eighty lodges living between the Musselshell and Yellowstone was Tattooed Indians; see D. W. Moodie and Barry Kaye, "The Ac Ko Mok Ki Map," p. 15). Since the early nineteenth century, the members of the tribe have designated themselves as Arapahoes in their dealings with whites.

Charles Le Raye located the Kananawesh (whom he also refers to as Gens-di-vach or Buffalo People) on the headwaters of the Cheyenne in 1801 ("Journal of Charles Le Raye," p. 159); Pierre-Antoine Tabeau noted in 1804 that the Caninan-biches and the Squi-hitanes, who he says spoke the same language, roamed with other wandering tribes between the Yellowstone and Platte rivers (*Tabeau's Narrative of Loisel's Expedition to the Upper Missouri,* pp. 154-55); Meriwether Lewis and William Clark state that in 1804 the 190 lodges of Canenavich or Blue Beads and Staetan, numbering 2,900 people, were found on the Yellowstone, Cheyenne, and particularly the headwaters of the Loup branch of the Platte (*Original Journals of Lewis and Clark Expedition, 1804-1806,* vol. 1, p. 190, and vol. 6, p. 101; Alexander Henry noted in 1806 that the Cheyennes told him that 500 lodges of Caveninavish or Buffalo Indians ranged the sources of the Platte and another "large river to the south," presumably the Arkansas ("The Manuscript Journals of Alexander Henry and of David Thompson, 1799-1814," vol. 1, p. 384).

29. Trudeau, "Journal," pp. 31-32. Trudeau noted that in 1795 the Arapa-hoes were near the Cheyennes, Kiowas, and western Pawnees (Pitapahato), all of whom lived on the branches of the Cheyenne River. According to George Bent, who interviewed elderly Cheyennes at the turn of the century, when the Chey-ennes first came to the Missouri they found the Arapahoes already visiting in the Arikara and Mandan villages (Bent to George Hyde, August 3, 1914, in Box 2, folder 33, Bent Papers).

30. The Arapahoes were known to bring horses, robes, and some furs to trad-ers as far north as the Hudson Bay posts in Canada and south to the Spanish traders from New Mexico. On trade relations, see M. Perrin du Lac, *Voyage dans les deux Louisianes,* p. 206; Fidler in Moodie and Kaye, "Ac Ko Mok Ki Map," p. 15; Tabeau, *Narrative,* p. 158; Henry, "Manuscript Journals," p. 384; James, *James's Account,* vol. 15, pp. 282, 285, and vol. 17, p. 156; Jacob Fowler, *Journal,* p. 65. See also Virginia Cole Trenholm, *The Arapahoes, Our People;* Donald J. Berthrong, *The Southern Cheyennes;* and Joseph Jablow, *The Cheyenne in Plains Indian Trade Relations, 1795-1840.*

On the Arapahoe-Cheyenne alliance, see Le Raye, "Journal," p. 159; Lewis and Clark, *Original Journals,* vol. 6, p. 100; Henry, "Manuscript Journals," p. 384.

31. In December 1812 Robert Stuart, traveling through southwestern Wyo-ming, encountered "Arapohays" from the Platte; he was informed by Joseph Miller that they numbered probably 2,700 in all (*The Discovery of the Oregon Trail: Robert Stuart's Narratives,* pp. 86, 192). A map made in 1811, which is associated with Stuart's expedition, places the "Arropolous" on the headwaters of the Platte, just southwest of the Absarokas (Crows); the Oue-ta-pa-ha-to (Pawnees) on the Padouca branch of the Platte; and southeast, on the Platte, the "Ka-ne-na-vich" (Stuart, *Discovery,* p. cxix). Also at this time, H. M. Brackenridge located 5,000 "Kan-ne-na-wish" on the headwaters of the Yellowstone, presumably to the south of the Crows (*Views of Louisiana,* p. 147). In 1810 Bradbury reported the Chey-ennes in the Black Hills, on the headwaters of the Cheyenne River (*Travels,* vol. 5, p. 139). In 1829 the secretary of war reported that the main body of Chey-ennes was north of the Arapahoes and still north of the Platte (*Report of the*

Secretary of War, Senate Executive Document 72, 20th Cong., 2d sess. [1829], p. 104).

32. José Francisco Ruiz, *Report on the Indian Tribes of Texas in 1828,* pp. 16–17.

33. Berthrong, *Southern Cheyennes,* p. 18.

34. George Bird Grinnell, "Bent's Old Fort and Its Builders," pp. 15, 42. See also the map in Henry Dodge, "Report on the Expedition of Dragoons, under Col. Henry Dodge, to the Rocky Mountains in 1835," *American State Papers, Military Affairs,* vol. 6 (1836).

35. Bell, *Journal,* pp. 198, 203.

36. *Report of the Secretary of War* (1829), p. 104.

37. Dodge, "Report," p. 141.

38. Ibid. The names of the "principal chiefs" were Buffalo Bull That Carries a Gun (ena-cha-ke-kuc), Old Raven (oe-che-ne), Strong Bow (e-thaw-ete), Black Dog (waw-lau-nah), Mad Bear (waw-hin-e-hun), and Buffalo Belly (naw-tuh-tha). Old Raven and Buffalo Bull were noted Southern Arapaho leaders. The Arapaho population given by Dodge was a little over half the population estimated in 1829. It is possible that the group Dodge encountered on the Arkansas River comprised only the southern-division Arapahos, or that the figures reflect the loss of population from a smallpox epidemic about 1830.

1. "THEY HELD UP THEIR HANDS": WAR CHIEFS AND FRIENDLY CHIEFS, 1851–77

1. John C. Frémont, *A Report of the Exploring Expedition to the Rocky Mountains in the Year 1842 and to Oregon and North California in the Years 1843–44,* p. 145; J. W. Abert, *Report of Lieut. J. W. Abert of His Examination of New Mexico in the Years 1846–1847,* p. 118; George Ruxton, *Ruxton of the Rockies,* p. 249.

2. Rufus B. Sage, *His Letters and Papers, 1836–1847,* vol. 4, pp. 190, 220, 222–23; Theodore Talbot, *The Journals of Theodore Talbot, 1843 and 1849–52,* pp. 22, 32 (see also Frémont, *Report,* p. 77); Sage, *His Letters and Papers,* vol. 5, pp. 54–55; *RCIA,* 1848, p. 8 (see also Thomas Fitzpatrick to Thomas Harvey, June 27, 1848, and October 19, 1847, in LR-UP, microfilm M 234, roll 889; Frémont, *Report,* pp. 282–83).

3. Frémont, *Report,* p. 128; S. W. Kearny, *Report of a Summer Campaign to the Rocky Mountains in 1845,* p. 212; *RCIA,* 1846, pp. 80–81; Lewis H. Garrard, *Wah-to-yah and the Taos Trail,* p. 119; D. D. Mitchell to Commissioner of Indian Affairs, October 13, 1849, in LR-SL, microfilm M 234, roll 755.

4. Francis Parkman, *The Oregon Trail,* p. 304; Abert, *Report,* pp. 99, 111; Fitzpatrick to Harvey, December 18, 1847, in LR-UP, microfilm M 234, roll 889; Garrard, *Wah-to-yah,* p. 120.

5. Sage, *His Letters and Papers,* vol. 5, p. 67; Parkman, *Oregon Trail,* p. 321; Fitzpatrick to Harvey, June 27, 1848, in LR-UP, microfilm M 234, roll 889;

Augustus M. Heslep, "The Santa Fe Trail: Letters and Journals of Augustus M. Heslep," pp. 371-72; Charles Edward Pancoast, *A Quaker Forty-niner,* pp. 192-93.

6. Philip St. George Cooke, *Scenes and Adventures in the Army,* p. 401; Kearny, *Report of a Summer Campaign,* pp. 211-12; Parkman, *Oregon Trail,* p. 238; John T. Hughes, *Doniphan's Expedition: Containing an Account of the Conquest of New Mexico,* p. 60.

7. Garrard, *Wah-to-yah,* p. 88. See also Ruxton, *Ruxton of the Rockies,* p. 231.

8. Francis Parkman, *The Journals of Francis Parkman,* vol. 2, p. 469; Fitzpatrick to Harvey, May 22, 1849, in LR-UP, microfilm M 234, roll 889; Heslep, "Santa Fe Trail," p. 373; Pancoast, *Quaker Forty-niner,* p. 191.

9. Fitzpatrick to Commissioner of Indian Affairs, February 13, 1848; D. D. Mitchell to Commissioner of Indian Affairs, May 29, 1849; Fitzpatrick to Harvey, May 22, 1849, all in LR-UP, microfilm M 234, roll 889; Garrard, *Wah-to-yah,* pp. 88, 314; Abert, *Report,* p. 113.

10. A. L. Kroeber, *Ethnology of the Gros Ventre,* p. 232; Fitzpatrick to Harvey, June 27, 1848, in LR-UP, microfilm M 234, roll 889. See also Frémont, *Report,* pp. 285-88; Talbot, *Journals,* pp. 20, 23; Sage, *His Letters and Papers,* vol. 5, p. 66.

11. Alfred L. Kroeber, *The Arapaho,* pp. 151-227; Talbot, *Journals,* p. 25 (see also Parkman, *Oregon Trail,* p. 322); "Arapaho Material Culture," in folder 1, A1, box 2, George Dorsey-Cleaver Warden Collection, Field Museum of Natural History, Chicago.

12. Sage, *His Letters and Papers,* vol. 5, p. 256; Talbot, *Journals,* p. 21; Garrard, *Wah-to-yah,* p. 314; Parkman, *Oregon Trail,* pp. 113-56. See also Frémont, *Report,* pp. 29-30.

13. Fitzpatrick to Harvey, June 27, 1848, in LR-UP, microfilm M 234, roll 889; Talbot, *Journals,* p. 26.

14. Articles of Treaty, Documents Relating to the Negotiation of the Treaty of September 17, 1851, in RT; Report of D. D. Mitchell, November 11, 1851, in ibid.; *RCIA,* 1850, pp. 20-21, and 1851, p. 71. Father De Smet said that 10,000 Indians were present (Hiram Martin Chittenden and Alfred Talbot Richardson, *Life, Letters, and Travels of Father Pierre Jean De Smet,* vol. 2, p. 681). Mitchell estimated that 8,000 to 12,000 Indians were present (*RCIA,* 1851, p. 63).

15. Documents Relating to the Negotiation of the Treaty of September 17, 1851, RT (the Shoshones attended the council but were not requested to sign the treaty); *Missouri Republican,* November 30, 1851. In August 1853, Fitzpatrick met with "a large portion" of the Cheyennes and Arapahoes' on the South Platte and obtained their consent to the amended version (*RCIA,* 1853, pp. 359, 366).

16. *Missouri Republican,* November 9, 1851. The map is in the National Archives, Record Group 75, no. 251.

17. *Missouri Republican,* October 26, November 2, and November 9, 1851; Articles of Treaty, in Documents Relating to the Negotiation of the Treaty of September 17, 1851, RT; *RCIA,* 1853, p. 366. The Arapahoe interpreter was John Poisal, married to a Southern Arapaho. Cut Nose was not present at Fort Laramie

on August 31, 1853, when Little Owl and Big Man made their marks on the amended treaty.

18. *Missouri Republican,* November 2 and November 23, 1851.

19. Percival G. Lowe, *Five Years a Dragoon,* pp. 87-88 (see also Chittenden and Richardson, *Life, Letters, and Travels,* vol. 2, p. 683); Report of D. D. Mitchell and Articles of Treaty, in Documents Relating to the Negotiation of the Treaty of September 17, 1851, RT; *Missouri Republican,* November 2, 1851.

20. *Missouri Republican,* October 22, 1851; Chittenden and Richardson, *Life, Letters, and Travels,* vol. 2, pp. 687-91; Le Roy R. Hafen and W. J. Ghent, *Broken Hand: The Life Story of Thomas Fitzpatrick, Chief of the Mountain Men,* pp. 248-50.

21. *RCIA,* 1853, p. 368, and the following letters in LR-UP, microfilm M 234, roll 890: Thomas Twiss to A. B. Greenwood, August 16, 1859; John Poisal to Commissioner of Indian Affairs, April 12, 1860.

22. John Whitfield to Secretary of Interior, March 6, 1855, in LR-UP, microfilm M 234, roll 889. On the dishonesty of the agents, see the affidavits in Alfred Cumming to Charles Mix, March 31, 1856, in ibid., roll 889; John Royal to J. Thompson, November 12, 1860, and William Dole to C. B. Smith, March 24, 1862, in ibid., roll 890; and the following letters in ibid., roll 891: Robert Campbell to Dole, September 25 and October 23, 1863; Vital Jarrot to Dole, July 15, 1865; George Williams to Commissioner of Indian Affairs, May 7, 1866. On the withholding of annuities and the ban on trade, see Twiss to Cumming, November 14, 1855, in ibid., roll 889; the following letters in ibid., roll 891: H. B. Branch to Dole, June 12, 1863; John Loree to Dole, June 30, 1864; Jarrot to Dole, July 15, 1865; and *RCIA,* 1855, pp. 82-83; *RCIA,* 1864, p. 220; *RCIA,* 1865, pp. 181, 183.

23. *RCIA,* 1855, p. 82. Robert Munkres, who examined diaries kept by travelers during this era, finds no evidence that Arapahoes attacked whites before the 1860s ("The Plains Indian Threat on the Oregon Trail before 1860"); *RCIA,* 1859, p. 130. On the Indian-white hostilities of the 1860s, see Loree to Dole, February 5, 1863, in LR-UP, microfilm M 234, roll 891; *RCIA,* 1863, pp. 134-35, 144-45; *RCIA,* 1864, pp. 216-17, 233.

24. *RCIA,* 1864, p. 225 (see also James C. Murphy, "The Place of the Northern Arapahoes in the Relations between the United States and the Indians of the Plains, 1851-1879," and Lewis B. Hull, "Soldiering on the High Plains: The Diary of Lewis Byram Hull, 1864-66," pp. 36, 47); Albert D. Richardson, *Beyond the Mississippi,* p. 173; letter of April 18, 1865, in Agnes Wright Spring, *Caspar Collins,* p. 172; Albert M. Holman and Constant R. Marks, *Pioneering in the Northwest,* pp. 31-38; James A. Sawyers, "Official Report of James A. Sawyers," pp. 261-62.

25. Ferdinand Hayden, "Arapohos," p. 323.

26. A. F. C. Greene, interview with Sherman Sage, in "The Arapahoe Indians," pp. 32-40, HRPD. On intertribal hostilities, see Whitfield to Cumming, July 11, 1854, in LR-UP, microfilm M 234, roll 889; *RCIA,* 1858, p. 95; *RCIA,* 1863, p. 134; *RCIA,* 1864, p. 252; John Pulsipher, *Diary of John Pulsipher,* p. 198.

27. Twiss to Greenwood, September 26, 1859, and Loree to Dole, October 15, 1862, in LR-UP, microfilm M 234, roll 890. Medicine Man also was known to whites as Roman Nose, but he probably was not the Roman Nose mentioned by Talbot in 1843.

28. See William Hoffman to A. Pleasonton, August 8, 1856, in LS-FL. From 1859 through the early 1870s the important intermediary chiefs were Medicine Man and Black Bear, and lesser intermediaries (probably leaders of men's age sets) were Little Wolf, Sorrel Horse, Littleshield, Black Coal, and Knock Knee—all accused by whites of attacks on emigrants or settlers (see H. E. Palmer, "History of Powder River Indian Expedition of 1865," pp. 214–20; Collins to Commissioner of Indian Affairs, May 12, 1865, in Spring, *Caspar Collins,* p. 167 (here the principal chiefs are named as Medicine Man, Black Bear, Littleshield, and White Bull); Margaret Irvin Carrington, *Ab-sa-ra-ka,* p. 132; George Bent to George Hyde, December 5, 1904, in Box 1, folder 2, Bent Papers, William Robertson Coe Collection, Yale University Library; H. G. Nickerson, "Early History of Fremont County," p. 3. On the effect of the Sand Creek massacre on Indian–white relations, see *RCIA,* 1864, pp. 24, 51. Little Raven, Southern Arapaho chief, said there were eight lodges of Arapahos at Sand Creek and thirty men, twenty women, and sixteen children killed (Dawson Scrapbooks, bk. 1, Colorado State Historical Society, Denver); for the version of Goes in Lodge, a Northern Arapahoe who claimed to have been at Sand Creek, see "Farlow Memoirs," in L. L. Newton Collection, WHRC.

29. William Marshall Anderson, *The Rocky Mountain Journals of William Marshall Anderson,* pp. 222–23; Talbot, *Journals,* pp. 20–21; Diaries of John Gregory Bourke, vol. 20, frames 1952 and 1965, U.S. Military Academy Library, West Point.

30. Anderson, *Rocky Mountain Journals,* p. 222; Talbot, *Journals,* p. 21; Sage, *His Letters and Papers,* vol. 5, pp. 300–303; interview, translated by John Goggles, Michelson MS, no. 1910 (hereafter cited as Michelson MS), NAA.

31. Sage, *His Letters and Papers,* vol. 5, p. 299; Diaries of John Gregory Bourke, vol. 20, frames 1966–67. The name that Bourke indicates Friday finally took was *téenokúhú'*; this is translated Sits Brooding by Nickerson Shakespeare (author's field tapes, August 21, 1975).

32. Michelson MS; Cooke, *Scenes and Adventures,* p. 401; Pulsipher, *Diary,* pp. 198–99; W. R. Raynolds, *Report on the Exploration of the Yellowstone River,* p. 64; Hayden, "Arapohos," p. 322.

33. *RCIA,* 1863, p. 136; Frank A. Root and William Elsey Connelley, *The Overland Stage to California,* p. 347; *RCIA,* 1864, pp. 219, 223, 236; *RCIA,* 1865, pp. 432–34; Jarrot to Dole, July 15, 1865, in LR-UP, microfilm M 234, roll 891; *RCIA,* 1868, p. 181.

34. Richard Irving Dodge, *Our Wild Indians,* pp. 285–86, 293–96.

35. The Arapahoes' attack on Fort Kearny was led by Black Coal and Eagle Head (George Bent to George Hyde, December 5, 1904, in Box 1, folder 2, Bent Papers). See also Grace Raymond Hebard and E. A. Brininstool, *The Bozeman Trail,* vol. 1, p. 339.

36. Hayden, "Arapohos," p. 321; Greene, interview with Sherman Sage, in "Arapahoe Indians"; Sage interview in Inez Hilger Field Notes, August 5, 1940, NAA.

37. *RCIA,* 1862, pp. 230-31; *RCIA,* 1863, pp. 122, 131-32. See also Donald J. Berthrong, *The Southern Cheyennes.* The southeastern section of the 1869 reservation shown in Map 2 was assigned to other tribes in 1872.

38. Henry Maynadier to D. N. Cooley, May 8, 1866, in LR-UP, microfilm M 234, roll 891; P. E. Connor, "General Connor's Report of the Tongue River Battle," pp. 46-47 (other observers estimated the dead at sixty-three, but this figure appears greatly exaggerated); the following letters in LR-UP, microfilm M 234, roll 892: Alfred Sully to N. D. Taylor, April 28, 1867; John B. Sanborn to Taylor, June 16, 1867; and N. C. Kinney to Acting Adjutant General, February 9, 1867; Greene, interview with Sherman Sage, in "Arapahoe Indians."

39. Greene, interview with Sherman Sage, in "Arapahoe Indians," p. 34.

40. George Bird Grinnell, *The Fighting Cheyennes,* p. 271; John Hallam, "Kinan, the Great Arapahoe Medicine Man," Newberry Library, Chicago; Hayden, "Arapohos," p. 325 (compare the native terms recorded by Hayden with those recorded by Kroeber: Biitahanwu or Spear Society, Hahankanwu or Crazy Society, Hecawanwu or Dog Society, Banuxtanwu or Buffalo Society).

41. Indian Treaty Commission, Special Files, Report, vol. 1, September 13 and November 12-13, 1867, Indian Division, Records of the Office of the Secretary of the Interior, Record Group 48, National Archives; Lewis L. Simonin, *The Rocky Mountain West in 1867,* pp. 118-19.

42. Jay Cooke and Co. to Taylor, July 11, 1868; Sanborn to Mix, June 4, 1868; and Ashton White to O. H. Browning, April 14, 1868, all in LR-UP, microfilm M 234, roll 893. Apparently only two of the eight commissioners, John Sanborn and William Harney, actually met with the Arapahoes; see James C. Olson, *Red Cloud and the Sioux Problem,* p. 75.

43. Charles J. Kappler, ed., *Indian Affairs: Laws and Treaties,* vol. 2, pp. 1012-15. See also Olson, *Red Cloud.*

44. Murphy, "Place of the Northern Arapahoes," p. 225; John Campbell to Commissioner of Indian Affairs, November 20, 1869, in Governor J. A. Campbell Letter Books, HRPD; William McE. Dye to George Ruggles, September 30, 1868, and Caleb H. Carlton to Ruggles, November 22, 1868, both in LS-FF.

45. Carlton to Ruggles, November 22, and November 25, 1868, January 6 and February 10, 1869; Carlton to Dye, November 22, 1868, all in LS-FF.

46. PJ-FF, April 9, April 13, October 1-2 (here the Indian delegates are given as Medicine Man, Sorrel Horse, Black Bear, Friday, and "one other"), and October 30, 1869; January 9, 1870 (the visits of Arapahoe leaders Medicine Man, Black Bear, Friday, Sorrel Horse, and Black Coal are mentioned throughout the post journal, November 1868-December 1869); *Cheyenne Leader,* November 8, 1869; Campbell to Commissioner of Indian Affairs, November 20, 1869, in Campbell Letter Books; *RCIA,* 1870, pp. 175-76; John Campbell, "Diary—1869-75," pp. 66-67.

47. Nickerson, "Early History of Fremont County," pp. 3, 6-11; Alexander

Chambers to Ruggles, May 6 and June 8, 1870, enclosed in E. D. Townsend to Secretary of the Interior, May 21, 1870, in LR-UP, microfilm M 234, roll 895; Campbell to E. S. Parker, April 30, 1870; Secretary of War to Secretary of the Interior, May 5, 1870; and Campbell to Parker, May 7 and May 26, 1870, all in ibid., roll 896; *RCIA,* 1870, p. 176. See also Robert B. David, *Finn Burnett, Frontiersman,* pp. 245, 248, 251; statement of Sherman Coolidge, in Indian Files, Episcopal Diocese, Laramie; PJ-FF, May 2 and June 5, 1870.

48. *RCIA,* 1870, pp. 176, 201; Chambers to Ruggles, June 8, 1870, in LR-UP, microfilm M 234, roll 895; Campbell to Parker, May 26, 1870, in ibid., roll 896; PJ-FF, June 5, June 7, December 15, and December 29, 1870, and February 14, February 18, February 23, March 25, April 25, 1871; Peter Koch, "The Journal of Peter Koch—1869 and 1870," pp. 150-51, 156-57; John Hunton, *John Hunton's Diary,* vol. 1, p. 30; Chambers to Commissioner of Indian Affairs, December 19, 1870, in LS-FF; John E. Smith to Ruggles, March 22, 1871, in LS-FL.

49. *RCIA,* 1871, pp. 26, 697; *RCIA,* 1872, pp. 75-76, 267; *RCIA,* 1873, pp. 153, 244; *Report of the Special Commission to Investigate the Affairs of the Red Cloud Indian Agency,* pp. 375-77, 435, 438, 449; PJ-FF, January 14, February 11, February 27, February 28, and May 21, 1874; Indian Scouts, Fort Fetterman, Box 2345, Regular Army Muster Rolls, OAG (all but Little Dog deserted in late July 1874, after Bates Battle). A few families moved south after a delegation of five Arapahoes and ten Cheyennes went to Washington and on November 18, 1873, signed an agreement to move to the Indian Territory. The Arapahoe signers were Powder Face, Yellow Bear, Little Wolf, Medicine Pipe, and Fool Dog ("Cheyenne and Arapahoe Indian Reservation," Letter from the Secretary of the Interior, House Executive Document 12, 43d Cong., 1st sess. [1873]).

50. "Medical History of Camp Brown," Fort Washakie File, WHRC (the sketch on which Figure 1 is based is also in this file).

51. Tacetta B. Walker, *Stories of Early Days in Wyoming,* pp. 11, 15; interview with Nickerson Shakespeare, August 21, 1975, author's field tapes; "Mrs. Broken Horn," File B-B78, L. L. Newton Collection.

52. *Report of the Special Commission,* pp. 216-18, 261, 377, 449, 454; PJ-FF, July 27 and August 21, 1874.

53. Diaries of John Gregory Bourke, vol. 20, frames 1969-70; Ada A. Vogdes, "The Journal of Ada A. Vogdes, 1868-71," p. 14; Dodge, *Our Wild Indians,* pp. 132, 134; William Philo Clark, *The Indian Sign Language,* pp. 41, 183-84, and see also p. 355 on the Southern Arapahos.

54. On the generosity expected of intermediary chiefs, see Clark, *Indian Sign Language,* pp. 185-86, and Vogdes, "Journal," p. 14; *Report of the Special Commission,* pp. xxxvii, xxxix, lx; *RCIA,* 1868, p. 253; Dye to Ruggles, February 3, 1869, in LS-FL.

55. Sorrel Horse and Littleshield led sixty-seven lodges into Fort Fetterman (Dye to Adjutant General, June 11, 1868, in LS-FF), and at Fort Laramie, Medicine Man, Sharp Nose, Friday, and Little Wound each came in to receive daily rations for forty lodges, Big Eagle for eighteen lodges, and Plenty Bear for ten

lodges (Smith to Ruggles, March 22, 1871, in LS-FL); Carlton to Ruggles, February 10, 1869, in LS-FF; Campbell Letter Books, November 20, 1869.

56. Diaries of John Gregory Bourke, vol. 5, frame 611; Carlton to Ruggles, November 22, 1868, in LS-FF; *Report of the Special Commission,* pp. 376-77; *RCIA,* 1874, p. 97.

57. *Report of the Special Commission,* p. 377; Diaries of John Gregory Bourke, vol. 3, frame 11; William A. Graham, *The Custer Myth,* pp. 109-12 (see also Greene, interview with Sherman Sage, in "Arapahoe Indians"); interview with Salt Friday, August 12, 1940, in Inez Hilger Field Notes.

58. *New York Times,* October 1, 1875, and July 15 and September 22-23, 1876; *Message from the President of the United States, communicating the Report and Journal of Proceedings of the Commission Appointed to Obtain Certain Concessions from the Sioux Indians,* Senate Executive Document 9, 44th Cong., 2d sess. (1876), pp. 21-23, 34-35. See also Olson, *Red Cloud.*

59. *RCIA,* 1873, p. 155.

60. John G. Bourke, *On the Border with Crook,* p. 390; Indian Scouts, Camp Robinson, boxes 2262 and 2363, Regular Army Muster Rolls. Some scouts were men from other tribes married to Arapahoes; for example, Spoonhunter was a Sioux married to Sage's sister.

61. Diaries of John Gregory Bourke, vol. 3, frame 11; vol. 14, frames 1363 and 1400; vol. 15, frame 1507; vol. 16, frame 1589; vol. 17, frame 1640; vol. 20, frames 1979-83; Bourke, *On the Border,* p. 406; interview with Winnie Sharp Nose, August 27, 1936, and interview with Salt Friday, August 12, 1940, both in Inez Hilger Field Notes. In 1868 the agent mentioned that two small bands of Arapahoes headed by Sharp Nose and Big Heart were hunting with Two Strikes's band of Sioux (M. T. Patrick to H. B. Denman, December 25, 1867, in LR-UP, microfilm M 234, roll 893). But since in 1872 Sharp Nose was reported to have died along with Medicine Man, the Sharp Nose of 1876 was probably a relative (perhaps a successor) of the earlier Sharp Nose.

62. *New York Herald,* December 11, 1876, and *Cheyenne Leader,* December 20, 1876; Diaries of John Gregory Bourke, vol. 14, frames 1415-27; vol. 17, frames 1658 and 1696; vol. 24, frames 29 and 68; Bourke, *On the Border,* pp. 391-95, 405, 421; Papers of Richard J. Dodge, Powder River Winter Campaign, Diary, bk. 1, November 29, 1876, in Graff Collection, Newberry Library, Chicago; Greene, interview of Sherman Sage, in "Arapahoe Indians."

63. Diaries of John Gregory Bourke, vol. 14, frames 1370-73, 1404; vol. 15, frame 1508; vol. 20, frame 1938; Bourke, *On the Border,* pp. 405-06.

64. Diaries of John Gregory Bourke, vol. 15, frame 1507; vol. 16, frame 1589; vol. 19, frames 1858 and 1904-5; vol. 20, frames 1938 and 1941; personnel file of Goes in Lodge, Records of the Bureau of Indian Affairs, Fort Washakie; R. S. Mackenzie to Secretary of the Interior, March 17, 1877, and P. H. Sheridan to Secretary of the Interior, March 27, 1877 (Sheridan acknowledges the peace between Arapahoes and Shoshones but opposes Mackenzie's effort to settle the Arapahoes in Wyoming), enclosed in George McCrary to Secretary of the Interior, April 3, 1877, in LR-RC, microfilm M 234, roll 721.

65. Council with the President, September 26–27, 1877, File S1061 1/2, in LR-DS.

66. Ibid.; *New York Times,* October 2–3 and October 6, 1877.

67. George Crook to E. A. Hayt, October 19, 1877, and James Irwin to Hayt, October 26, 1877, both in LR-DS, microfilm M 234, roll 259; Irwin to Hayt, October 27, 1877, in LR-RC, microfilm M 234, roll 721.

2. "OTHERS TELL ME WHAT I AM TO SAY": CHIEFTAINSHIP IN THE RESERVATION CONTEXT, 1878–1907

1. H. R. Lemly to Adjutant General, November 27, 1877, and William T. Sherman to Philip Sheridan, October 27, 1877, both in LR-WS, microfilm M 234, roll 955; James Patten to Commissioner of Indian Affairs, January 14, 1878, in ibid., roll 956.

2. Patten to Commissioner of Indian Affairs, February 21, March 18, and March 20, 1878, in LR-WS, microfilm M 234, roll 956; "Medical History of Camp Brown," vol. 2, May 15, 1878, in Fort Washakie File, WHRC.

3. Baptismal Record of St. Stephen's Mission, bk. 1, 1886–98, office files, St. Stephens, Wyo.

4. Interview with Anne Wolf, August 5, 1942, in Inez Hilger Field Notes, NAA; interview with Orlo Amos (1894–1976), May 28, 1975, author's field tapes.

5. Interviews with Nickerson (West) Shakespeare (1903–76), August 21, 1975, and Ralph Grasshopper (1910–), April 6, 1977, author's field tapes.

6. John W. Hoyt to Commissioner of Indian Affairs, July 17, 1878, in LR-WS, microfilm M 234, roll 956 (see also John McNeil to Commissioner of Indian Affairs, February 16, 1881, in File 3728, and Sanderson Martin to Commissioner of Indian Affairs, May 20, 1885, in File 11848, both in LR). The agents' reports indicate that the tribespeople resisted efforts to induce them to abandon native rituals, disband extended-family camps, and cease sharing provisions.

7. *Cheyenne Daily Leader,* May 17, 1889. Army officers also had trepidations when Sioux visited the Arapahoes (see Mary Jackson English, "Prairie Sketches or Fugitive Recollections of an Army Girl of 1889," HRPD); Patten to Commissioner of Indian Affairs, January 14, 1878, and August 2, 1879, in LR-WS, microfilm M 234, rolls 956 and 957; "Black Coal," in John Roberts Collection, WHRC. Black Coal assisted in Waterman's surrender to federal authorities, although they had not demanded his arrest. Commissioner E. A. Hayt wrote Patten that there was no law applicable to the case and suggested that the murderer be put in military custody; but the military commander at Camp Brown refused to accept the responsibility, and Waterman was released. See LS, September 4, 1879, microfilm M 21, roll 150.

8. English, "Prairie Sketches," pp. 60–66; Charles Hatton to Commissioner of Indian Affairs, September 5, 1881, in File 16258, LR; P. H. Ray to Commissioner of Indian Affairs, June 30, 1894, in File 26220, LR. Visiting bands numbering

upwards of 200, led by Red Cloud, Red Shirt, American Horse, High Wolf, Show Bull, and Blue Horse, came to trade and visit.

9. Lemly to Adjutant General, November 27, 1877, in LR-WS, microfilm M 234, roll 955; Patten to Commissioner of Indian Affairs, May 8, May 12, May 13, June 5, and July 12, 1878, in ibid., roll 956. Eventually the discontented in the Cheyenne camp were permitted to join the main body of Cheyennes; see Post Returns, September 1878, Fort Washakie, Returns from U.S. Military Posts, 1800–1916, in OAG, microfilm M 617, roll 1363.

10. Cyrus White Horse to Commissioner of Indian Affairs, August 12, 1884, in File 16088, LR. Cyrus, son of Chief White Horse, had learned to read and write at Carlisle Indian School in 1881. The "violence" attributed to the Shoshones is probably more properly attributed to a group of "mixed-bloods" who lived among the Shoshones. Several agents characterized the "mixed-bloods" as "lawless."

11. Ellis Ballou to Commissioner of Indian Affairs, November 25, 1880, in LR-WS, microfilm M 234, roll 958. Ballou noted that Black Coal had been urged by one of his relatives in Oklahoma to send children to Carlisle as the Southern Arapahos had done.

12. Patten to Commissioner of Indian Affairs, February 28, 1881, in File 8780, LR; Student Information Cards, Carlisle Indian Industrial School Records, Records of the Bureau of Indian Affairs, National Archives. Two Shoshone boys also accompanied the Arapahoe children, although the Shoshone leaders withheld support for the venture.

13. Hoyt to Commissioner of Indian Affairs, August 14, 1878, in LR-WS, microfilm M 234, roll 956; Hatton to Commissioner of Indian Affairs, January 26, 1882, in File 2255, LR; council proceedings, February 10 and February 14, 1882, in File 650-651, LR-DI; Martin to Commissioner of Indian Affairs, May 20, 1885, in File 11848, LR.

14. Patten to Commissioner of Indian Affairs, February 21 and March 2, 1878, in LR-WS, microfilm M 234, roll 956; "Edward J. Farlow Manuscript," p. 43, HRPD.

15. Patten to Commissioner of Indian Affairs, August 2, 1879, in LR-WS, microfilm M 234, roll 957 (see also Edward T. Gibson to George Kellogg, March 8, 1880, in ibid., roll 958); Hatton to Commissioner of Indian Affairs, December 30, 1881, in File 340-1882, LR. When the Arapahoe delegation went east in 1882, Iron went in place of Friday, and White Horse also accompanied Black Coal and Sharp Nose. The elderly Little Wolf was the fifth member of the group (see Arapahoe file, nos. 184, 186, 189, 191b, and 193, Photograph Collection, NAA).

16. A. F. C. Greene, "Irrigation Development on Wind River Indian Reservation," July 15, 1941, pp. 2-3, Works Progress Administration Interviews, no. 1453, HRPD; minutes of council meeting, August 10, 1927, p. 2, in Tribal Councils 064, 1927-29, Box 196, Archives, FRC. The ditches were destroyed several years later when the government began to build a network of irrigation canals on the reservation.

17. The information on band names and locations is from elderly Arapahoes living today.

18. On Littleshield, see "Farlow Manuscript," p. 42, HRPD. Eagle Head was the son and namesake of the man who went east with the delegation of 1851; Little Owl was not the chief chosen in 1851.

19. James Mooney, *The Ghost-Dance Religion and the Sioux Outbreak of 1890,* p. 956. Both White Horse and Wallowing Bull were leaders among the Greasy Faces. According to the Indian Census Roll of 1890, Wallowing Bull had a younger brother named Spotted Horse, but he was an adolescent (Indian Census Rolls, 1885–1940, Records of the Bureau of Indian Affairs, microfilm M 595, roll 498). The name Spotted Horse may have been used in succession by several prominent people in the band.

20. Alfred L. Kroeber, Arapaho Notebooks, bk. 26, p. 4, manuscript no. 2560-A, NAA. The council chief's headdress and scepter described in Kroeber's notebook are in the collections of the American Museum of Natural History, New York (see Figure 2).

21. Patten to Commissioner of Indian Affairs, August 20, 1878, in LR-WS, microfilm M 234, roll 956; H. R. Lemly, "Among the Arrapahoes," p. 494; interview with Orlo Amos.

22. English, "Prairie Sketches," pp. 42–44. Sharp Nose, who spoke English, translated for Black Coal.

23. Charles Dickson to Commissioner of Indian Affairs, February 15, 1886, in File 5764, LR; James Irwin to Commissioner of Indian Affairs, November 21, 1883, in File 21841, LR; Martin to Commissioner of Indian Affairs, July 17, 1885, in File 17169, LR; E. C. Watkins to Commissioner of Indian Affairs, November 9, 1878, in LR-WS, microfilm M 234, roll 956.

24. E. Ballou to C. M. Carter, January 9, 1881, in File 1277, LR; M. A. Thomas to Secretary of Interior, October 6, 1886, in File 28154, DI; Dickson to Commissioner of Indian Affairs, February 15, 1886, in File 5764, LR; Patten to Commissioner of Indian Affairs, February 12, 1878, in LR-WS, microfilm M 234, roll 956; Watkins to Commissioner of Indian Affairs, November 9, 1878, in ibid.; Irwin to Commissioner of Indian Affairs, April 17, 1883, in File 7704, LR; Thomas D. Marcum to Secretary of Interior, January 16, 1888, in File 4236, DI.

25. Martin to Commissioner of Indian Affairs, May 20, 1885, in File 11848, LR; Patten to Commissioner of Indian Affairs, January 14, 1878, in LR-WS, microfilm M 234, roll 956; Marcum to Secretary of Interior, January 16, 1888, in File 4236, DI.

26. Dickson to Commissioner of Indian Affairs, February 15, 1886, in File 5764, LR; Thomas Jones to Commissioner of Indian Affairs, September 15, 1887, in SC 147, file no. 21523 (and see all correspondence in SC 143, file no. 1887-16912); *RCIA,* 1886, pp. 258–59, and 1894, pp. 336–38; Robert Gardner reported to the Secretary of the Interior that in 1884 there were twenty-six Arapahoe "farms" or gardens, each from one to five acres, where wheat, oats, potatoes, and other vegetables were grown (December 11, 1884, in File 24577, DI). By 1896 the Arapahoes were farming about 700 acres (James McLaughlin to Secretary of Interior, April 25, 1896, in File 17034, DI). As shown on Map 3, Plenty Bear's garden was especially large; his white son-in-law, Paul Hanway, probably assisted him.

27. "Diary," August ca. 1886, office files, St. Stephen's Mission, St. Stephens, Wyo.; Mary Graham, John Roberts interview: "President Arthur's Visit to the Reservation," Works Progress Administration Interviews, no. 1017.

28. Hatton to Commissioner of Indian Affairs, December 31, 1880, in File 679, LR; Roster of Agency Employees, 1879-88, in Records of the Bureau of Indian Affairs; William Quinton to Assistant Adjutant General, August 31, 1889, in LS-FW; Indian Scouts, 1883-1900, Fort Washakie, Regular Army Muster Rolls, OAG; John Hunton, *John Hunton's Diary,* vol. 6, p. 99 ("Mrs. Brand" is listed on the 1885 Arapahoe Indian Census Roll); Patten to Commissioner of Indian Affairs, July 24, 1878, and July 11, 1879, in LR-WS, microfilm M 234, rolls 956 and 957; C. F. King to Commissioner of Indian Affairs, January 21, 1886, in File 3068, LR; Roster of Indian Police, 1878-82, in Records of the Bureau of Indian Affairs; receipt from Black Coal, September 20, 1886, in Jones to Commissioner of Indian Affairs, May 19, 1887, in SC 143, file 16912.

29. On the Catholics, see "Diary," August 30, 188?, office files, St. Stephen's Mission; Jones to Commissioner of Indian Affairs, April 16, May 16, and May 19, 1887, and J. Atkins to Secretary of Interior, June 11, 1887, all in SC 143, file 16912; Paul Ponziglione to J. A. Stephan, February 26, 1887, and Stephan to Philip Turnell, May 23, 1892, in St. Stephen's files, Bureau of Catholic Indian Missions Records, Marquette University, Milwaukee; *History of the Sisters of Charity of Leavenworth, Kansas,* pp. 415, 421; Patrick A. McGovern, ed., *History of the Diocese of Cheyenne,* pp. 199-202. On the Episcopalians, see Talbot Diaries, Box 2, July 10, 1889, in Francis Donaldson Collections, WHRC; Robert Talbot to Dora Talbot, August 1, 1893, in Correspondence of Ethelbert Talbot, Box 1, Francis Donaldson Collections.

30. See *United States Statutes at Large*: vol. 24, pp. 388-91, 463; vol. 26, pp. 794-96; vol. 28, pp. 304-5.

31. *RCIA,* 1890, pp. viii, clxvi; *RCIA,* 1901, p. 6; *RCIA,* 1902, p. 4.

32. Mooney, *Ghost-Dance Religion,* p. 977; Quinton to Assistant Adjutant General, August 28 and August 31, 1889, in LS-FW; Quinton to Secretary of War, July 28, 1889, in Letters Received, OAG, microfilm M 689, roll 701; E. Kellogg to Assistant Adjutant General, December 2, 1890, in LS-FW; *Report on Indians Taxed and Indians Not Taxed in the United States at the Eleventh Census,* p. 627; Peter Moran to Commissioner of Indian Affairs, December 22, 1890, in File 39768, LR.

33. Thomas Downs to Commissioner of Indian Affairs, April 16, 1903, in File 25948, LR; W. C. Forbush to Assistant Adjutant General, December 7, 1897, in LS-FW; M. Brown to Adjutant General, November 16, 1901, and January 14, 1902, in LS-FW; *Report on Indians Taxed,* p. 633; Greene, "Irrigation Development"; *Indian Guide,* March and September 1896 and January, September, October, and December 1897, HRPD (Littleshield was the son of Chief Littleshield, who signed the treaty of 1868); McLaughlin to Secretary of Interior, April 25, 1896, in File 17034, DI. At this time the Shoshones were extensively involved in raising horses for sale (see Albert H. Kneale, *Indian Agent,* p. 117).

34. Moran to Commissioner of Indian Affairs, December 22, 1890, in File

39768, LR; Secretary of Interior to Commissioner of Indian Affairs, January 30, 1894, in SC 191, File 4449; P. H. Ray to Commissioner of Indian Affairs, April 2 and October 10, 1894, in Files 13514 and 40368, LR; Ray to Commissioner of Indian Affairs, February 19, 1894, in SC 191, File 8108; A. J. Duncan to Commissioner of Indian Affairs, December 29, 1897, in File 2257, LR.

35. Dickson to Commissioner of Indian Affairs, February 15, 1886, in File 5764, LR; John Fosher to Commissioner of Indian Affairs, July 31, 1893, in File 30442, LR. These figures are best regarded as estimates, as the agent could not validate all reports of births and deaths.

36. Proceedings of council of May 8, 1888, in Thomas Jones to Commissioner of Indian Affairs, May 10, 1888, in SC 147, File 13078; *Cheyenne Daily Leader,* May 17, 1889; Alfred Smith to J. M. Jones, April 1, 1886, in LS-FW; John Clark to Commissioner of Indian Affairs, March 29, 1895, in File 14439, LR; Richard Wilson to Commissioner of Indian Affairs, September 1, 1896, in File 34076, LR.

37. Council proceedings, January 29, 1899, in SC 191, File 6450; Broken Horn et al. to Commissioner of Indian Affairs, May 19, 1905, in File 40146, LR.

38. Quinton to Assistant Adjutant General, September 5, 1889, in Letters Received, OAG, microfilm M 689, roll 701; Chief Washakie et al. to Commissioner of Indian Affairs, January 31, 1891, in File 5896, LR; James McLaughlin to Secretary of Interior, April 25, 1904, in File 4713, LR-DI.

39. Report of the Shoshone Commission, October 2, 1891, p. 67, and October 20, 1891, in Irregularly Shaped Papers, Records of the Bureau of Indian Affairs; on Woodruff, see *Fremont Clipper,* December 29, 1893.

40. F. P. Sterling to Commissioner of Indian Affairs, February 22, 1893, and proceedings of councils, January 26, February 6-7, February 9, and February 13, 1893, in SC 147, File 10860; *Negotiations with the Shoshone and Arapahoe Indians,* pp. 3-17.

41. Commissioner of Indian Affairs to Secretary of Interior, May 5, and McLaughlin to Commissioner of Indian Affairs, April 23, 1896, in File 16453, LR; Wilson to Commissioner of Indian Affairs, October 23 and July 10, 1897, in Files 45471 and 29026, LR; H. G. Nickerson to Commissioner of Indian Affairs, August 31, 1898, in File 36300, LR; *Indian Guide,* January 1897.

42. Minutes of council meeting, April 19, 1904, in File 4713, LR-DI; H. E. Wadsworth to Commissioner of Indian Affairs, January 22, 1907, in Indian File, WHRC.

43. Minutes of council meeting, April 19, 1904, in File 4713, LR-DI. The amended version of the agreement provided that the Boysen lease on the ceded portion was exempt from these provisions; Boysen could sell the land for $10 an acre, and after eight years to the highest bidder.

44. Lone Bear to Commissioner of Indian Affairs, March 6, 1905, in File 20462, LR; Lone Bear et al. to Commissioner of Indian Affairs, December 17, 1906, in File 112990, LR; Wadsworth to Commissioner of Indian Affairs, January 28, 1907, in File 11551, LR (see also Wadsworth to Commissioner of Indian

Affairs, January 22, 1907, Indian File, WHRC); McLaughlin to Secretary of Interior, June 12, 1907, DI.

45. Wilson to Commissioner of Indian Affairs, October 23, 1897, in File 45471, LR.

46. *RCIA,* 1894, pp. 336–38.

47. Nickerson to Commissioner of Indian Affairs, June 30, 1898, and July 17, 1899, in Files 32661 and 34972, LR; on Sage, see Kroeber, Arapaho Notebooks, bk. 21, p. 3.

48. Wadsworth to Commissioner of Indian Affairs, July 27, 1903, in File 49270, LR.

49. *United States Statutes at Large,* vol. 26, p. 795; vol. 28, pp. 304–5.

50. Record of joint council, January 29, 1899, in SC 191, file 6450. See also record of joint council, December 9, 1893, and Nickerson to Commissioner of Indian Affairs, December 20, 1898, in SC 191, files 3909 and 58121. *RCIA,* 1886, mentions a six-member business council (p. 260), but I find no record of any action taken by such a council, nor are any members named. On September 19, 1889, Agent John Fosher identified six Arapahoe councilmen—Black Coal, Sharp Nose, Little Wolf, White Horse, Eagle Head, and Bill Friday—and four Shoshone councilmen (Authority no. 21248, Records of the Bureau of Indian Affairs). In March 1890 he named Black Coal, Sharp Nose, Little Wolf, Yellow Owl, Tallow, and six Shoshones (Authority no. 25340). In 1891 he named eighteen men as Shoshone councilmen (Authority no. 29457). In an 1892 council meeting Chiefs Black Coal and Sharp Nose were distinguished from "leading men" and from ten "councilmen"; yet none of those ten men spoke in the council meetings held that year (minutes of council meeting, August 19, 1892, in Fosher to Commissioner of Indian Affairs, August 23, 1892, in File 31302, LR). It seems apparent that until the leasing council of 1893 was established, the members of a "business council" and their functions varied.

The Shoshone council members were: 1893-97, Washakie, Muyahooyal, Bahugooshia, Tonevook, Hebah, Wahwannibiddie; 1898-1902, Washakie (until 1901), Bishop, Noyahozo, Timmoco, Tassitsie, Moonhabbie, Tosiah, Hebeecheechee, George Terry (after 1901); 1903-7, Dick Washakie, Hebeecheechee, George Terry, Myron Hunt, John Timbana, Seth Perann.

51. *RCIA,* 1894, p. 336; minutes of August 19, 1892, in Fosher to Commissioner of Indian Affairs, August 23, 1892, in File 31302, LR; statement by Yellow Calf's grandson from Yellow Calf's dictation, March 10, 1935, in Personnel File of Yellow Calf, Bureau of Indian Affairs, Fort Washakie; see also the correspondence in files for 1892-1907, in SC 191.

52. Report of the Shoshone Commission, September 29, 1891, pp. 56–57, in Irregularly Shaped Papers, Records of the Bureau of Indian Affairs. See also interview with Anne Wolf, August 5, 1942, in Inez Hilger Field Notes, NAA.

53. Report of the Shoshone Commission, September 4, 1891, p. 37; see also minutes of council meeting, August 19, 1892, in Fosher to Commissioner of Indian Affairs, August 23, 1892, in File 31302, LR.

54. A. Burt to Assistant Adjutant General, June 25, 1889, and July 16, 1890,

and E. Kellogg to Assistant Adjutant General, December 11, 1890, in LS-FW. See also Ignatius Panken to Secretary of Interior, December 10, 1890, in File 39955, LR.

55. Report of the Shoshone Commission, 1891, September 21, 1891, pp. 44-45, and September 30, 1891, pp. 61-62; "Comments by Col. Richard H. Wilson Relative to the Indian Treaty of April 1896," pp. 67-68 and 75, Works Progress Administration Interviews, no. 302; minutes of council meeting, April 19, 1904, in File 4713, LR-DI; Wadsworth to Commissioner of Indian Affairs, January 8, 1904, in File 1548, LR; minutes of council meeting, May 14, 1907, p. 40, in File 1908-83566, CF 54.

56. Wannibiddie et al. to Commissioner of Indian Affairs, July 19, 1900, in File 36291, LR; Wadsworth to Commissioner of Indian Affairs, August 4, 1903, in File 51056, LR.

57. Henry Lee Tyler in minutes of council meeting, January 2, 1930, p. 2, in File 1930-6905, CF 54; Nickerson to Commissioner of Indian Affairs, July 17, 1899, in File 34972, LR.

58. Nickerson's tactics were also upsetting to the Shoshones. On July 22, 1901, George Terry, chairman of the Shoshone business council, asked the Indian Rights Association to investigate "crooked" occurrences at the agency (Series 1A, reel 15, in Indian Rights Association Papers, Historical Society of Pennsylvania).

59. Mrs. Charles Coolidge to Grace Hebard, December 29, 1930, in Sherman Coolidge File, WHRC. Arapahoes living today comment that Coolidge often rebuked Arapahoes for allowing him to be captured; perhaps resentment explains in part his seeming hostility to the tribe. Coolidge's wife, Grace, wrote a novel, *Tepee Neighbors,* based on her experiences on the reservation.

60. Lone Bear to Commissioner of Indian Affairs, June 5, 1899, in File 27012, LR.

61. Nickerson to Commissioner of Indian Affairs, July 10, 1900, and May 29, 1901, in Files 34290 and 29270, LR; S. Coolidge to Commissioner of Indian Affairs, May 29, 1901, in File 29270, LR.

62. William Ketcham to Commissioner of Indian Affairs, February 11, February 13, and February 21, 1902, in Files 10096, 9970, and 11448, LR; Ketcham to F. P. Sansone, February 11, 1902, and George Garfield to Ketcham, January 12, 1902, St. Stephen's files, Bureau of Catholic Indian Missions Records. The Shoshones selected were George Terry, Charles Lahoe, and Shoyo. None were council members (Shoshone Delegation to Commissioner of Indian Affairs, March 1, 1902, in File 12804, LR).

63. N. Thomas to Mrs. John Markoe, July 12, 1911, in Episcopal Church Collection, Box 13, WHRC; Wadsworth to Commissioner of Indian Affairs, February 2, 1910, in File 1909-98148, CF 54; Superintendents' Annual Narrative Report, 1911, Records of Bureau of Indian Affairs.

64. Mooney, *Ghost-Dance Religion,* p. 775.

65. *Report on Indians Taxed,* p. 628. The account obtained by Kroeber appeared in George A. Dorsey and Alfred L. Kroeber, *Traditions of the Arapaho,* pp. 4-6. The most detailed version was obtained by Dorsey from Southern

Arapahos (George A. Dorsey, *The Arapaho Sun Dance: The Ceremony of the Offerings Lodge,* 191-212).

66. "Arapaho Material Culture," folder 1, pp. 150, 156, A1, Box 2, Dorsey-Warden Collection, Field Museum of Natural History, Chicago. The term "water-pouring old men" refers to the fact that the elderly priests prayed in sweat lodges, where they poured water over hot stones to produce steam.

67. "Notes Not Incorporated," folder 4, p. 92, A1, Box 2, Dorsey-Warden Collection. Cleaver Warden was born about 1867 and attended Carlisle from 1880 to 1887. He worked for A. L. Kroeber, then was hired by the Field Museum to work for George Dorsey. He apparently used Kroeber's publications as a guide, verifying and elaborating on Kroeber's information.

68. Alfred L. Kroeber, *The Arapaho,* pp. 418, 436, 450-51 (Kroeber gives examples of orations in which elders address the tribe in terms of the four age categories; see p. 314); Robert H. Lowie, *Indians of the Plains,* p. 158 (see also Edward S. Curtis, *The North American Indian,* vol. 6, p. 142). *Bééteet* might also acquire what the Arapahoes called "bad medicine"—power to curse or harm others.

69. Kroeber, *Arapaho,* pp. 167-68; *Indian Guide,* May 1897 (see also Kroeber, *Arapaho,* p. 316; *Indian Guide,* November 1896; record of council meeting, August 19, 1892, in File 31302, LR).

70. Kroeber, *Arapaho,* pp. 30, 209-10 (see also Curtis, *North American Indian,* vol. 6, p. 142); "Notes Not Incorporated," folder 4, pp. 1-2, A1, Box 2, Dorsey-Warden Collection.

71. "Arapaho Material Culture," folder 1, pp. 150-54 and 156, A1, Box 2, Dorsey-Warden Collection.

72. *Report on Indians Taxed,* p. 633; Kroeber, *Arapaho,* pp. 279, 303 (see also Nickerson to Commissioner of Indian Affairs, November 11, 1901, in File 73506, LR; English, "Prairie Sketches," passim); Robert C. Morris, "Wyoming Indians," p. 105; Nickerson to Commissioner of Indian Affairs, May 17, 1901, in File 27111, LR; Kneale, *Indian Agent,* pp. 155-56; Faustinus Antelope to George Dorsey, January 25, 1908, in DC.

73. Cleaver Warden to George Dorsey, December 5, 1903, DC; "Lodges," folder 6, pp. 1-6, A1, Box 2, Dorsey-Warden Collection. Warden noted that if a lodge were held in fulfillment of a vow, incumbent members of that society were called "Imitation" (for example, Imitation Spear Men) until they participated in the next lodge of the series. See also Robert H. Lowie, *Plains Indian Age Societies,* pp. 932, 973; interview with William Shakespeare (1900-1975), September 1, 1969, author's field tapes. The women's Buffalo Lodge was pledged at the turn of the century but the vow was not fulfilled.

74. Kroeber, *Arapaho,* pp. 166, 168; Lowie, *Plains Indian Age Societies,* pp. 950-51, 973; "Lodges," folder 6, p. 5, A1, Box 2, Dorsey-Warden Collection.

75. Patten to Commissioner of Indian Affairs, August 2, 1879, in LR-WS, microfilm M 234, roll 957. Inez Hilger recorded the details of a murder case in which the victim's family pressured the murderer to commit suicide (interview with Agnes Yellow Plume, August 5, 1942, in Inez Hilger Field Notes).

76. "Notes Incorporated," folder 5, A1, Box 2 (and see "Arapaho Material

Culture," folder 1, p. 155, A1, Box 2), Dorsey-Warden Collection. Warden recorded Weasel Bear's story from Black Horse, who had heard it from Weasel Bear.

77. Edward Curtis reports that Weasel Bear died in 1908 (*North American Indian*, vol. 6, p. 141), but Warden wrote Dorsey on February 25, 1905 (DC) that Weasel Bear was already dead, and the agent noted his death on the Indian census roll of 1904. See also J. Roberts to H. L. Scott, February 14, 1907, Box 46, Indian Correspondence, Hugh L. Scott Papers, Library of Congress, Washington, D.C.

78. Mooney, *Ghost-Dance Religion*, p. 986; John Roberts to Tacetta Walker, September 19, 1934, in Works Progress Administration Interviews, no. 1774; Kroeber, *Arapaho*, pp. 207, 209; "Sweat Lodge," folder 3, A1, Box 2, Dorsey-Warden Collection.

79. Antelope to Dorsey, August 8, 1910, in DC. According to Warden, Kroeber purchased medicine from the daughter of a man who had received it on pledging the Old Men's Lodge ("Sweat Lodge," folder 3, A1, Box 2, Dorsey-Warden Collection); "Dog Soldiers," folder 2, p. 52, A1, Box 2, Dorsey-Warden Collection.

80. Mooney, *Ghost-Dance Religion*, p. 961.

81. *Laramie Republican-Boomerang*, March 10, 1931 (this account names some of the Arapahoe participants in the 1904 Tomahawk Lodge); Warden to Dorsey, January 10, 1901, November 23, 1904, and December 4, 1905, and Antelope to Dorsey, October 3, 1904, and November 3, 1906, all in DC; "Dog Soldiers," folder 2, A1, Box 2, Dorsey-Warden Collection (apparently some of the novices were Southern Arapahos); interview with Ralph Antelope (1899–1980), April 6, 1977, author's field tapes.

82. Lowie, *Plains Indian Age Societies*, p. 971.

83. Interview, August 15, 1978, author's field tapes.

84. Mooney, *Ghost-Dance Religion*, pp. 791, 807–8, 817. According to Arapahoes living today, the Ghost Dance was called *ko'éinohowóot* or big round dance; Mooney says it was called *thigúnawat* or spirit dance.

85. Ibid., pp. 895–97; Fosher to Commissioner of Indian Affairs, April 3, 1891, in File 13408, LR-DI; C. F. Ashley to Commissioner of Indian Affairs, August 12, 1891, in File 30157, LR.

86. "Social Organization," folder 7, pp. 109–11, A1, Box 2, Dorsey-Warden Collection; Kroeber, *Arapaho*, pp. 368, 320.

87. Fosher to Commissioner of Indian Affairs, December 3, 1890, in SC 188, File 38007; Mooney, *Ghost-Dance Religion*, pp. 808–9. After the death of Reed in 1894, young alumni of the government boarding school interpreted for the Arapahoes.

88. Molly Peacock Stenberg, "The Peyote Culture among Wyoming Indians," pp. 142–43. See also Kroeber, *Arapaho*, pp. 320–21. Kroeber says that the peyote ceremony was learned from the Kiowas, while Goggles says that the Southern Arapahos learned it from the Caddos.

89. Stenberg, "Peyote Culture," p. 143.

90. Dorsey and Kroeber, *Traditions*, p. 6; *History of the Sisters of Charity*, pp. 417–18.

3. "GETTING ALONG WELL":
THE OLD COUNCIL, 1908–36

1. Oliver W. Toll, *Arapaho Names and Trails: A Report of a 1914 Pack Trip,* p. 3.

2. For a more extensive discussion of the history of federal Indian policy, see S. Lyman Tyler, *A History of Indian Policy.*

3. The Arapahoes did continue to inquire after redress in the matter of the "Black Hills Treaty," that is, the Agreement of 1876. In an intertribal meeting of December 15–17, 1920, the Northern Cheyenne delegates proposed that they and the Northern Arapahoes file a claim for the loss of the Black Hills apart from the Sioux claim (Black Hills Council, pt. 3, File 1917-70018, Pine Ridge, Central Files 54, National Archives). At a meeting held August 6, 1921, Arapahoe delegate Robert Friday withdrew the Northern Arapahoes from the Sioux effort to file a claim (minutes of Sioux General Council meeting, Pine Ridge, Central Decimal File .064, Records of the Bureau of Indian Affairs, Federal Archives and Records Center, Kansas City).

4. T. A. Larson, *History of Wyoming,* pp. 351–53.

5. F. H. Abbott to H. E. Wadsworth, November 23, 1911; Abbott to Secretary of Interior, February 24 and July 23, 1912, and March 18, 1913; Joseph Norris to Secretary of Interior, May 16, 1912, all in File 1911-101494, pts. 1–3, CF 341.

6. Superintendents' Annual Narrative Reports, 1920, Records of the Bureau of Indian Affairs, National Archives; Report of John W. Bale, July 24, 1920, in File 1920-64190, CF 57. In 1917 the superintendent reported that 39 patents in fee had been granted Wind River Indians; by 1919, 192 had been granted. Most Indians sold these lands (Superintendents' Annual Narrative Reports, 1917, 1920). The 1906 Burke Act (a modification of the General Allotment Act) enabled the Bureau to release Indian allottees from federal supervision and protection before the twenty-five-year trust period had expired by a declaration of competence (see *United States Statutes at Large,* vol. 34, pp. 182–83). Lands in patent-in-fee status could be sold and were liable to taxation.

7. Report of J. H. Norris, August 17, 1911, DI; see Larson, *History of Wyoming,* p. 406; Superintendents' Annual Narrative Reports, 1920, in Records of the Bureau of Indian Affairs. Congress delegated authority to the secretary of the interior to use and expend for the benefit of the Indians money obtained from the sale or lease of property in trusteeship. With the secretary's approval, the superintendent acted as "custodian" for individual or tribal funds (see *United States Statutes at Large,* vol. 36, pp. 856–60).

8. Lone Bear et al. to Commissioner of Indian Affairs, November 4, 1910, and Report of Peter Wadsworth, February 11, 1911, both in File 1911-18594, CF 154.

9. The 1876 agreement is referred to by the Arapahoes as the Black Hills Treaty.

10. Remarks of Arapahoe delegation to F. E. Leupp, March 9, 1908, in File

1908-18001, CF 56. The water-rights laws of Wyoming provided that title to water for irrigation was contingent on actual use of water for that purpose within a certain time after application was made to the state engineer (*RCIA*, 1906, p. 403). Government reports submitted after the cession indicated that in drawing Indians away from farming to work on construction of ditches, the government assumed the responsibility for securing water rights for the Indians (*RCIA*, 1904, p. 124; *RCIA*, 1905, pp. 155, 381; *RCIA*, 1906, p. 403). In 1909 the government authorized the leasing of tribal and allotted irrigable lands in order to comply with the water-rights laws: 3,900 acres out of 40,559 acres under ditch were leased in 1909 (*RCIA*, 1908, p. 56; 1909, pp. 48–49). See also Larson, *History of Wyoming*, pp. 253–54.

11. Commissioner of Indian Affairs to Arapahoe Delegation, April 2, 1908, in File 1908-18001, CF 56. "Laceration" referred to the piercing of the flesh; "indecencies" referred to ceremonial intercourse.

12. Minutes of meeting with delegates, January 23, 1913, in Council Meetings 064, 1912, Box 196, Archives, FRC; minutes of Business Council meeting, May 28, 1912, p. 8, in File 1912-71322, CF 54.

13. On per capita payments, see correspondence in File 1930-3801, CF 211.

14. Minutes of Business Council meeting, January 30, 1911, p. 5, in File 1911-18594, CF 154.

15. Minutes of Business Council meeting, May 28, 1912, p. 2, in File 1912-71322, CF 54.

16. Norris to Commissioner of Indian Affairs, January 22, 1914, in File 1913-110378, CF 54, and February 17, 1916, in File 1914-8663, CF 54.

17. See *United States Statutes at Large*, vol. 36, p. 847; minutes of Business Council meeting, March 7, 1913, pp. 1–2, in File 1913-37085, CF 54; Larson, *History of Wyoming*, pp. 396–99; Report of E. B. Linnen, February 7, 1916, DI.

18. E. A. Hutchinson to Commissioner of Indian Affairs, April 19, 1919, in File 1919-10070, CF 806.

19. Hugh L. Scott, Board of Indian Commissioners, Report on the Shoshone Indian Reservation, September 4, 1920, NAA. Water charges were applied as liens against the land of Indian owners who could not pay.

20. Superintendents' Annual Narrative Reports, 1920, 1921, in Records of Bureau of Indian Affairs. The years 1914–18 were prosperous for ranchers and farmers in Wyoming, but a drought in 1919 and serious deflation in the 1920s brought hard times (Larson, *History of Wyoming*, pp. 396–407, 411–12).

21. Henry Lee Tyler to John Kendrick, April 1, 1922, and Commissioner of Indian Affairs to Kendrick, April 15, 1922, in File 1922-17574, CF 56.

22. Scott Dewey to R. P. Haas, February 15, 1923, in File 1923-20708, CF 54.

23. Minutes of Business Council meeting, March 25, 1927, p. 5, in File 1927-18222, CF 53.

24. Haas to Commissioner of Indian Affairs, February 4, 1928, enclosed in Arapahoe General Council to Commissioner of Indian Affairs, February 6, 1928, in File 1928-6348, CF 56.

25. Minutes of council meeting, August 10, 1927, p. 7, in Tribal Councils 064, 1927–29, Box 196, Archives, FRC.

26. C. J. Rhoads to Mrs. Joseph L. Smith, March 11, 1931, in File 1930-3801, CF 211; Rhoads to Shoshone and Arapahoe delegates, February 27, 1928, in File 1928-10431, CF 56.

27. Minutes of Business Council meeting, February 20, 1913, pp. 13–14, in File 1908-83578, pt. 2, CF 315.

28. Conference with delegates, February 7, 1913, pp. 13–14, in File 1913-17651, CF 56.

29. Minutes of Business Council meeting, December 15, 1914, p. 19, in File 1914-137535, CF 54.

30. Minutes of Business Council meeting, March 8, 1915, p. 10, in File 1915-31817, CF 54.

31. William Ketcham to William McMillan, March 21, 1908; Ketcham to P. F. Sialm, January 23, 1913; William Hughes to Ketcham, August 5, 1913; J. Norris to Charles Lusk, November 9, 1914, all in Bureau of Catholic Indian Missions Records, Marquette University, Milwaukee.

32. Winfred H. Ziegler, *Wyoming Indians*, pp. 11, 38; Tacetta Walker, "The Establishing of Ethete," WHRC; Mattie P. Abbott to N. S. Thomas, December 27, 1912, in Episcopal Church Collection, WHRC.

33. Hutchinson to Commissioner of Indian Affairs, April 19, 1919, in File 1919-10070, CF 806; Frances L. Hadsall to Thomas, December 10 and December 26, 1912, in Episcopal Church Collection; and McMillan to Ketcham, March 29, 1908; J. B. Sifton to Ketcham, March 15, 1910; Sialm to Ketcham, January 27, 1913, all in Bureau of Catholic Indian Missions Records.

34. Larson, *History of Wyoming*, pp. 423-24; "Farlow's Memoirs," WHRC; on white attitudes, see *Lander Eagle*, July 4, 1913; Report of Carl Stevens, January 8-17, 1923, in File 1923-16521, CF 150; Demitri Shimkin, unpublished manuscript, Urbana, Ill.

35. Minutes of Business Council meeting, February 29, 1916, p. 7, in File 1916-25506, CF 54; and see Sheila Hart to Corina Smith, August 15, 1930, in File 1930-3801, CF 211; Commissioner of Indian Affairs to Kendrick, August 2, 1919, and Commissioner of Indian Affairs to Tim McCoy, July 26, 1919, in File 1919-64823, CF 63.

36. *Wyoming State Journal*, March 27, 1908, and April 18, 1928; record of council meeting, January 23, 1913, p. 16, in Council Meetings 064, 1912, Box 196, Archives, FRC.

37. Minutes of Business Council meeting, May 29, 1912, p. 10, in File 1912-71322, CF 54.

38. Report of C. M. Knight, November 10, 1917, in File 1918-108753, CF 101; C. F. Hauke to Secretary of Interior, October 26, 1911, and Wadsworth to Commissioner of Indian Affairs, May 8, 1911, in File 1911-2328, CF 323; Report of Joseph Norris, August 17, 1911, DI; Norris to Lusk, November 9, 1914, Bureau of Catholic Indian Missions Records.

39. *Wyoming State Journal*, November 4, 1926, and December 24, 1930.

40. Minutes of Business Council meeting, June 9, 1914, p. 6, in File 1914-69552, CF 54.

41. Minutes of Business Council meeting, August 28, 1913, p. 23; January 19, 1914, pp. 4, 7; and June 9, 1914, p. 11, in Files 1913-110378, 1914-8663, and 1914-69552, CF 54.

42. *Wyoming Churchman,* November 1923, HRPD; interview with Ethel Goggles Potter (1907-), April 5, 1977, author's field tapes.

43. Minutes of Business Council meetings: March 8, 1915, pp. 4, 9, 16, in File 1915-31817, CF 54; February 23, 1911, p. 9, and March 3, 1911, pp. 33-34, both in File 1911-2328, CF 323.

44. Minutes of Business Council meeting, April 8, 1932, p. 29, in File 1932-24695, CF 54.

45. Superintendents' Annual Statistical Reports, 1933, Records of the Bureau of Indian Affairs. Out-migration was greatest during the years of economic depression, but in all years for which statistics are available, more Shoshones than Arapahoes left the reservation.

46. Minutes of Business Council meeting, March 13, 1911, p. 45, in File 1911-2328, CF 323.

47. Indian Census Roll, Shoshone Agency, 1914 and 1931, Records of Bureau of Indian Affairs; Superintendents' Statistical Reports, 1921 and 1936, ibid.

48. Shimkin, unpublished manuscript, pp. 20, 21, 27. Also see Thomas H. Johnson, "The Enos Family and Wind River Shoshone Society: A Historical Analysis."

49. Minutes of Business Council meeting, January 9, 1913, p. 2, in File 1912-118534, CF 56.

50. Report of Joseph Norris, August 17, 1911, p. 15, DI; W. W. McConihe to Commissioner of Indian Affairs, August 20, 1912, and Wadsworth to Commissioner of Indian Affairs, March 26, 1912, in File 1909-94148, CF 54; minutes of Business Council, January 9, 1913, in File 1912-118534, CF 56.

51. Minutes of Business Council, April 22, 1935, pp. 8, 13, 17, in Files 1933-24811, CF 56.

52. The terms of office shown in Table 3 represent points in time when the membership changed for reasons other than death or retirement; in the early years, the Arapahoe Business Council did not have a prescribed term of office. The members of the Shoshone Business Council were, in 1908-12, John Lajeunesse, Joe Lajeunesse, John Timbana, White St. Clair (replaced by George Washakie), Herman Tigee, and Saul Tillman (replaced by Queba Rogers); in 1913-16, John Lajeunesse, Joe Lajeunesse, Queba Rogers, Rabbit Tail, Tisso Guina, and George Washakie; in 1917-20, Dick Washakie, Tisso Guina, John Timbana (replaced by Quintan Quay), Moses Tassitsie, Heebeecheechee, and Myron Hunt; in 1921-25, Dick Washakie, Tisso Guina, Quintan Quay, Moses Tassitsie, Heebeecheechee, and Myron Hunt (replaced by Louis Tassitsie); in 1926-30, Charles Washakie, Cyrus Shongutsie, Ben Perry, Percy Wetchie, John St. Clair, and Charles Snyder; in 1931-34, Charles Driskell, William Aragon, Lanjo McAdams, Gilbert Jesse Day, Ben Perry, and Sam Nipwater; and in 1935-36, Charles Driskell, Wallace St. Clair, William Aragon, Irene Meade, Gilbert Jesse Day, and Charles Washakie.

53. Minutes of Business Council meeting, March 13, 1911, p. 50, in File 1911-2328, CF 323.

54. Minutes of Business Council meeting, March 25, 1927, p. 3, in File 1927-18222, CF 53.

55. Remarks of Shoshone delegation, March 10, 1908, in File 1908-18001, CF 56.

56. Report of Will Tipton, May 20, 1911, DI.

57. Minutes of Business Council meeting, April 8, 1932, p. 54, in File 1932-24695, CF 54.

58. Interview with Scott Dewey (1895–), March 27, 1977, author's field tapes.

59. A1, Box 2, Dorsey-Warden Collection, Field Museum of Natural History.

60. Alfred L. Kroeber, *The Arapaho,* pp. 350–51. The fingers of the hand are potentially dangerous; Arapahoes avoid pointing with the finger and instead point with the lips.

61. Interview with Orlo Amos (1894–1976), January 20, 1973, author's field tapes.

62. See *Wyoming State Journal,* March 30, 1932.

63. Carlisle Indian Industrial School Records, student file 140, Records of the Bureau of Indian Affairs.

64. Interview with Scott Dewey.

65. Minutes of Business Council meeting, December 14, 1914, pp. 8–9, in File 1914-137535, CF 54 (also see Sam Wolfrang's statement during the same meeting); Commissioner of Indian Affairs to Arapahoe delegation, April 21, 1908, in File 1908-18001, CF 56; Hutchinson to Commissioner of Indian Affairs, May 23, 1921, and Meritt to Hutchinson, March 15, 1921, in File 1921-21418, CF 63.

66. Interview with Sherman Sage, August 5, 1940, in Inez Hilger Field Notes, NAA.

67. Minutes of Business Council, August 28, 1913, p. 23, in File 1913-110378, CF 54. The Annual Narrative Reports of the Superintendents indicate that the Sun Dance was held during Wadsworth's term. During Norris's term there were conflicting reports: the *Wyoming State Journal* of May 18, 1923, reported that the Sun Dance was not held between 1913 and 1922 (see also Commissioner of Indian Affairs to Norris, June 28, 1913, in File 1913-76665, CF 63; Haas to Commissioner of Indian Affairs, August 18, 1922, and Charles Burke to Haas, August 28, 1922, in File 1922-68021, CF 63), yet Superintendent Norris's report of 1916 indicated the Sun Dance was held, and missionaries from St. Michael's also reported witnessing the ceremony in 1916 (*Wyoming Churchman,* August 1916, HRPD). Superintendent Hutchinson opposed the Sun Dance and prohibited it (see Superintendents' Annual Narrative Reports of 1918, 1920).

68. John G. Carter, "The Northern Arapaho Flat Pipe and the Ceremony of Covering the Pipe," pp. 77–78, 89–91. The reader should be warned that Carter's article contains several errors of fact.

69. Minutes of Business Council meeting, June 9, 1914, p. 6, in File 1914-69552, CF 54.

70. On settlement patterns, see Hutchinson to Commissioner of Indian Affairs,

April 19, 1919, in File 1919-10070, CF 806, and December 4, 1920, in File 1920-92946, CF 150. Band names were obtained from Arapahoes living today. On St. Michael's Mission, see Superintendents' Annual Narrative Report, 1918, Records of the Bureau of Indian Affairs; Hutchinson to Commissioner of Indian Affairs, April 19, 1919, in File 1919-10070, CF 806; Report of James H. McGregor, November 5, 1921, in File 1921-95653, CF 150; Report of Hugh L. Scott, October 1, 1924, in File 1924-87836, CF 150; A. J. Keel to Ketcham, November 26, 1917, Bureau of Catholic Indian Missions Records.

71. Tribal Council 064, 1930, in Box 196, Archives, and Tribal Elections 065, in File 347446, Records Center, both in FRC. In 1930 Alonzo Moss received the seventh highest vote total, 56, with 40 votes from Lower Arapahoe. The other candidates received a significantly lower number of votes.

72. Interview, April 2, 1977, author's field tapes. When Judson went to Europe with the cast of *The Covered Wagon,* the pipe was cared for by his brother-in-law, Three Bulls (Avon Trumbull), who had been married to Weasel Bear's daughter Sage Woman.

73. Alice Beath, "Indians in Wyoming," Box 15, Francis Donaldson Collection, WHRC; *Wyoming Churchman,* January 1917, HRPD. The elders were opposed to the abuse of peyote, however: some youths mixed peyote with alcohol and used it outside of ritual and healing contexts.

74. William Wildschut, "Arapaho Medicine-Mirror," pp. 252-53, 257.

75. Interview with William Shakespeare (1900–1973), August 20, 1972, author's field tapes.

76. "History of St. Stephen's," 1912–22, office files, St. Stephen's Mission, St. Stephens, Wyo.

77. Carlisle Indian Industrial School Records, Student File 141, Records of the Bureau of Indian Affairs; interview with William Shakespeare.

78. See *Wyoming State Journal,* May 4, 1927, and June 6, 1928.

79. See Alfred Mokler, "Indians," p. 11, no. S296, Works Progress Administration Interviews, HRPD; interview with Ralph Grasshopper (1907–), April 6, 1977.

80. Interview, August 15, 1977, and interview with Orlo Amos, January 22, 1973, author's field tapes. According to his relatives, Yellow Calf's vision was precipitated by the trauma of the deaths of two of his children; by Mrs. Baird S. Cooper's account, the children died in 1912 and 1913 (*Wind River Reservation*).

81. Minutes of Business Council meeting, February 20, 1936, p. 6, in File 1935-37345, pt. 1, CF 54.

82. Interview with Orlo Amos, January 20, 1973. Similarly, Seth Mule was Cheyenne-Sioux (Probate Hearings, 1013761-1911, Wind River files, Bureau of Indian Affairs, Billings, Mont.).

83. Minutes of Business Council meeting, March 25, 1927, p. 4, in File 1927-18222, CF 53.

84. Minutes of Business Council meeting, March 8, 1915, p. 10, in File 1915-31817, CF 54.

85. Pension file of John Jesus Lewis, File 1923-44049, CF 725; Indian Census

Rolls, Shoshone Agency, Records of the Bureau of Indian Affairs, microfilm M 595, rolls 498–503.

86. Wadsworth to Commissioner of Indian Affairs, February 2, 1910, in File 1909-98148, CF 54; Superintendents' Annual Narrative Reports, 1910 and 1911, p. 16, Records of the Bureau of Indian Affairs.

87. Haas to Commissioner of Indian Affairs, November 18, 1922; July 21, 1926; January 14, 1927; May 19, 1927; January 7, 1929; and February 18, 1930; and Hauke to Haas, October 27, 1927, all in File 1926-1634, CF 100; Superintendents' Annual Statistical Report, 1933, and Superintendents' Annual Narrative Report, 1933, Records of the Bureau of Indian Affairs.

88. F. C. Campbell to Commissioner of Indian Affairs, January 14, 1926; Haas to Commissioner of Indian Affairs, February 4, 1926; E. B. Meritt to Haas, May 18, 1925, all in File 1925-34973, CF 54. The constitution and by-laws of 1925 are also in this file.

89. Tribal Council 064, 1930, in Box 196, Archives, FRC; Carlisle Indian Industrial School Records, student files 2515 and 1151, Records of the Bureau of Indian Affairs. A total of 124 ballots were cast by the Arapahoes.

90. The constitution and by-laws of 1931 are in the minutes of council meeting, January 5, 1931, Tribal Councils 064, 1931, Box 196, Archives, FRC; J. Henry Scattergood to Robert D. Carey, January 24, 1931, in File 1930-65191, CF 54.

91. Martin Overgaard to Commissioner of Indian Affairs, November 28, 1934, and William Zimmerman to Overgaard, January 16, 1935, both in File 1930-65191, CF 54. The constitution and by-laws of November 27, 1934, are also in this file. See also John Collier to William Aragon, January 23, 1935, in File 1936-9741-A, CF 66.

92. Minutes of council meeting, January 2, 1930, p. 5, in File 1930-6905, CF 54.

93. Commissioner of Indian Affairs to George Caldwell, May 5, 1933, and Barrett Tyler to Rhoads, October 27, 1932, in File 1932-51216, CF 806; Superintendents' Annual Narrative Report, 1930, Records of the Bureau of Indian Affairs.

94. *Laramie Republican-Boomerang,* March 10, 1931; *Wyoming State Journal,* March 11, March 18, and March 25, 1931; interview with William Shakespeare. The photograph collection in the NAA includes photographs of the novices, including Aaron Willow, Richard Friday, Clifford Hopper, Nickerson West Shakespeare, Harry Shakespeare, Elk Redman, Andrew Brown, and Boniface Brown.

95. Interview with Sherman Sage, August 7, 1940, in Inez Hilger Field Notes. The *bééteet* obtained a worm or insect into which medicine had been placed, threw the medicine at the one he intended to harm, and in this way brought about disfigurement and death.

96. *United States Statutes at Large,* vol. 48, pp. 984–88.

97. See Graham D. Taylor, *The New Deal and American Indian Tribalism,* pp. 38, 51.

98. Minutes of meeting, February 23, 1934, pp. 4, 7, 8, in File 1934-4894, pt. 2-A, sec. 1, Entry 1011, Records Concerning the Wheeler-Howard Act, 1933–37, Records of the Bureau of Indian Affairs.

99. Ibid., pp. 11-14; Report of Tribal Council, in Haas to Commissioner of Indian Affairs, February 28, 1934, ibid.

100. Minutes of Plains Congress, March 5, 1934, in File 1934-4894, pt. 2-AA, sec. 1, ibid.; *Wyoming State Journal,* March 1, 1934.

101. Minutes of March 16, 1934, pp. 2, 8, 12, in File 1934-4894, pt. 3-C, and Resolution of Shoshone and Arapahoe Tribes, in Haas to Commissioner of Indian Affairs, April 16, 1934, in ibid., pt. 3-B, both in Entry 1011, Records Concerning the Wheeler-Howard Act, 1933-37.

102. Forrest Stone to Collier, April 23, 1935, in File 1935-1935, CF 56; Collier to Tribal Councils, May 9, 1935, in File 1936-9741, CF 66.

103. W. R. Centerwall to Commissioner of Indian Affairs, June 20, 1935, in File 1936-9741, CF 66.

104. *Wyoming State Journal,* June 20, 1935.

105. Minutes of Business Council meeting, August 21, 1935, p. 22, in File 1935-56532, CF 54.

4. "THE OLD INDIANS AND THE SCHOOLBOYS": THE NEW COUNCIL, 1937–65

1. Minutes of Joint Business Council meeting, January 8, 1937, p. 8, in File 1935-37345, pt. 1, CF 54.

2. Ibid., December 1, 1936, pp. 2, 9; January 8, 1937, pp. 3, 9, both in File 1935-37345, pt. 1; February 24, 1937, p. 14, in File 1930-65191, CF 54.

3. Stone subsequently agreed that the Arapahoe Business Council could decide the number of districts and the candidates per district, but the tribe firmly rejected the districting concept.

4. Minutes of Joint Business Council meeting, December 1, 1936, p. 5, in File 1935-37345, pt. 1, CF 54.

5. Ibid., pp. 4-5. Henry Lee Tyler died July 21, 1937.

6. Ibid., February 24, 1937, pp. 7-8, in File 1930-65191, CF 54.

7. Ibid., June 30, 1936, p. 2; June 18, 1937, p. 10, both in File 1935-37345, pt. 1, CF 54. In actuality, the wishes of the old council or the former chiefs were not considered by the commissioners at these cessions.

8. Ibid., December 1, 1936, p. 5, in File 1935-37345, pt. 1, CF 54.

9. File 1937-20084, CF 55; returns of 1937 election, in Tribal Elections 065, 1936, Records Center, FRC; *Wyoming State Journal,* April 1, 1937. In contrast to the retention of the four Arapahoe councilmen, only two Shoshone councilmen were reelected.

10. Henry Elkin, "Northern Arapaho of Wyoming," p. 252.

11. See minutes of Joint Business Council meeting, June 23, 1937, pp. 7, 11, in File 1935-37345, pt. 1, CF 54. In fact, the 1935 Business Council had appointed her to an Education-Employment Committee to deal with problems of unemployment (minutes of Joint Business Council, February 13, 1935, p. 5, in File 1935-12529, CF 54).

12. Interviews with Nell Scott (1888–1978), April 25, 1975, and June 28, 1972, author's field tapes. On May 6, 1969, she remembered that the two other elders who asked her to serve on the council were George Wallowing Bull and Anderson White.

13. John Wertz to Commissioner of Indian Affairs, October 29, 1898, and A. C. Tonner to Wertz, December 6, 1898, in File 1908-20096, CF 53. Sherman Coolidge, reportedly found on the same occasion, stated that he and Julia were children of the same father, an Arapahoe named Big Heart, but that they had different mothers (see File 1936-1847, CF 350). John Felter owned a dairy farm in Evanston during the late nineteenth century (Minnie Groscurth Hammond, "Some Memories of a Native Wyomingite from 1868 to 1937," April 20, 1937, Works Progress Administration Interviews, no. 773, HRPD).

14. Interview with Nell Scott, April 25, 1975.

15. See File 1908-20096, CF 53.

16. Interview with Nell Scott, April 25, 1975.

17. Ibid., March 25, 1977.

18. M. Inez Hilger, *Arapaho Child Life and Its Cultural Background,* p. 63.

19. Minutes of Arapahoe General Council meeting, July 30, 1939, p. 3, in File 1935-37345, pt. 3, CF 54; Forrest Stone to Commissioner of Indian Affairs, December 2, 1936, in File 1936-9741, CF 66.

20. Minutes of Joint Business Council meeting, April 7, 1938, pp. 16, 19-21, and September 27, 1938, pp. 21-22, both in File 1935-37345, pt. 2, CF 54; Fred Daiker to Stone, March 13, 1940, in memorandum of February 20, 1940, File 1936-9741A, CF 68; interview with Nell Scott, April 27, 1975. Stone objected particularly to Section IIIB, which stated that enrollments were subject to review and action by the business council of the tribe concerned. Stone believed that the general councils should decide enrollments (see Constitution, in minutes of Joint Business Council meeting, May 11, 1938, pp. 5-6, in File 1935-37345, pt. 2, CF 54).

21. Minutes of Joint Business Council meetings, December 1, 1936, p. 10, in File 1935-37345, pt. 1, CF 54.

22. Ibid., February 24, 1937, p. 14, in File 1930-65191, CF 54.

23. Ibid., June 18, 1937, p. 9, and April 19, 1939, p. 11, in File 1935-37345, pts. 1, 3, CF 54.

24. Minutes of Joint Business Council meeting, May 31, 1939, p. 13; September 17, 1940, pp. 1-5; and November 1, 1940, pp. 3-9, all in File 1935-37345, pts. 3 and 5, CF 54; Stone to Collier, June 12, 1935, in File 1936-9741, CF 66; interview with Nell Scott, November 5, 1974. Although there was no official constitution and by-laws, a draft document prepared in 1938 allowed the council to replace one of its members.

25. Minutes of Arapahoe General Council meeting, July 30, 1939, pp. 1-4, and minutes of Joint Business Council meeting, August 8, 1939, both in File 1935-37345, pt. 3, CF 54. Scott's application for enrollment with the Shoshones was public knowledge but she did not discuss the matter with the elders.

26. Interviews with Nell Scott, March 25, 1977, and April 25, 1975. Profanity

was rare among Arapahoes; Scott's use of it is an indication of her assertiveness in Indian-white relations.

27. Minutes of Joint Business Council meeting, August 8, 1939, p. 4, and minutes of Arapahoe Business Council meeting, June 23, 1937, p. 3, both in File 1935-37345, pts. 1 and 3, CF 54.

28. Minutes of Joint Business Council meeting, August 12, 1936, p. 4, in File 1935-37345, pt. 1, CF 54.

29. Minutes of General Council meeting, February 24, 1937, pp. 7, 9 and Joint Business Council to Commissioner of Indian Affairs, March 9, 1937, both in File 1930-65191, CF 54. The oil and gas leases in the Maverick Springs oil field, located in the ceded portion of the reservation, were issued between January 21, 1918, and December 15, 1920.

30. Minutes of Joint Business Council meeting, July 20, pp. 8-11, and September 23, 1937, p. 11, in File 1935-37345, pt. 1, CF 54; *Wyoming State Journal,* August 12, August 19, and September 30, 1937.

31. Stone to Commissioner of Indian Affairs, September 28, 1938, in Councils 064, Acts of 1927-37, in File 347446, Records Center, FRC; minutes of Business Council meeting, December 30, 1937, pp. 12-13, and Robert Friday and Gilbert Day to Oscar Chapman, January 17, 1938, in minutes of February 14, 1938, in File 1935-37345, pt. 2, CF 54 (italics mine).

32. Minutes of Joint Business Council meeting, February 14, 1938, in File 1935-37345, pt. 2, CF 54; interview with Nell Scott, April 25, 1975.

33. Tribal Delegations 066, in File 347446, Records Center, FRC.

34. The Shoshones agreed in 1874 to cede an additional 700,642 acres.

35. U.S. Court of Claims Reports, vol. 82, p. 23, and vol. 85, p. 331; William Zimmerman to delegates, Tribal Delegations 066, in File 347446, Records Center, FRC. After the suit was settled there was some talk of dividing the reservation into Shoshone and Arapahoe sides, but this plan was abandoned.

36. U.S. Senate, Committee on Indian Affairs, *A Bill to Provide for the Distribution of the Judgment Fund of the Shoshone Tribe of the Wind River Reservation in Wyoming and for Other Purposes: Hearings* (76th Cong., 1st sess., 1939); *United States Statutes at Large,* vol. 53, pp. 1128-30. The act of July 27, 1939, also directed the secretary of the interior to restore to tribal ownership all undisposed-of ceded lands except those within any reclamation project.

37. Minutes of Arapahoe General Council meeting, September 6, 1940, in File 1935-37345, pt. 5, CF 54; interview with Nell Scott, April 27, 1975. The Padlock ranch was in Hot Springs County, north of the reservation boundary. See also report of conferences with Shoshone and Arapahoe delegates, May 2-9, 1941, in Box 15, Archives, FRC. Several other cooperatives were also established at this time: a cannery, a general store, and a craft business.

38. Minutes of Arapahoe Business Council meetings, August 7 and 13; minutes of Arapahoe General Council, November 23 and 25, 1940, pp. 6, 8, all in File 1935-37345, pt. 5, CF 54.

39. For a history of the Arapahoe Ranch, see Loretta Fowler, "The Arapahoe Ranch."

40. Report of conferences with Shoshone and Arapahoe delegates, May 2–9, 1941, in Box 15, Archives, FRC; minutes of Arapahoe General Council meeting, September 23, 1948, and January 11, 1949; and minutes of Arapahoe Ranch Board of Trustees meeting, November 28, 1951, all in Records of the Bureau of Indian Affairs, Fort Washakie. See also Fowler, "Arapahoe Ranch."

41. Minutes of Arapahoe General Council meeting, November 25, 1940, p. 16, in File 1935-37345, pt. 5, CF 54; minutes of Joint Business Council meeting, April 8, 1948, and minutes of Arapahoe Ranch Board of Trustees, March 21, 1951, p. 2, both in Records of Bureau of Indian Affairs, Fort Washakie.

42. Minutes of Joint Business Council meeting, June 18, 1937, p. 11, in File 1935-37345, pt. 1, CF 54. Occasional small per capita payments were made at the discretion of the commissioner ($30 in 1937, $15 in 1938), but none was made in 1940. These payments represented only a fraction of the funds in the tribe's account (see File 1930-65191, CF 54).

43. Minutes of Joint Business Council meeting, March 9, 1937, p. 5, in File 1935-37345, pt. 1, CF 54; Superintendent's Annual Report to the Commissioner of Indian Affairs, 1944, pp. 17, 79, and resolution of joint tribal council meeting, January 18, 1946, Nell Scott Papers, both in Records of Bureau of Indian Affairs, Fort Washakie. The survey of living conditions also reported that Shoshone housing was of a higher standard, though still inadequate.

44. Interview with Nell Scott, April 27, 1975.

45. Homer A. Mathiesen to Commissioner of Indian Affairs, February 8, 1945, in File 1936-9741A, CF 68.

46. U.S. House of Representatives, Subcommittee on Indian Affairs, Committee on Public Lands, *Trust Funds, Shoshone and Arapaho Indian Tribes: Hearings* (80th Cong., 1st sess., March 15, 1947), H.R. 1098 (hereafter cited as *Trust Funds Hearings*), pp. 2, 14–19.

47. *Trust Funds Hearings*, p. 29; *United States Statutes at Large*, vol. 61, p. 102.

48. Interview with Nell Scott, April 27, 1975.

49. William E. Warne to J. Hardin Peterson, June 30, 1950, pursuant to H.R. 7522, 81st Cong., 2nd sess., LG; W. C. Smart to Oscar Chapman, June 18, 1951; E. H. Schumenan to John Murdock, July 13, 1951; and transcript of hearings before the Subcommittee on Indian Affairs, July 23, 1951, pursuant to H.R. 4636, 82nd Cong., 1st sess., all in LG; *United States Statutes at Large*, vol. 65, pp. 208–9 (see also *Congressional Record*, vol. 97, pt. 7, p. 8645).

50. Transcript of hearings before the Subcommittee on Indian Affairs, March 18 and April 1, 1953, pursuant to H.R. 444, 83d Cong., 1st sess., LG; *United States Statutes at Large*, vol. 67, p. 179.

51. *United States Statutes at Large*, vol. 69, p. 557; transcript of hearings before Subcommittee of Indian Affairs, June 21, 1956, pursuant to H.R. 10182, 84th Cong., 2d sess., LG.

52. *United States Statutes at Large*, vol. 70, pp. 642–43.

53. Ibid., vol. 72, pp. 541–42. Total Arapahoe money distributed was $515,723 in 1947, $420,656 in 1948, $650,828 in 1949, $385,474 in 1950, $526,590 in

1951, $637,841 in 1952, $651,385 in 1953, $2,518,590 in 1954 (including retro-active payments), $1,395,387 in 1955, $2,261,350 in 1956, $1,447,572 in 1957, $1,425,283 in 1958, $1,346,054.48 in 1959, $1,361,213.50 in 1960, $1,446,022 in 1961, $1,573,394 in 1962, $1,453,122 in 1963, and $3,569,338 in 1964 (in-cluding a share of the award from the Indian Claims Commission). The Shoshones' per capita payments were higher than the Arapahoes' because the Shoshone popula-tion was smaller.

54. On the termination policy, see Robert F. Berkhofer, *The White Man's Indian,* pp. 187, 189, and Harold E. Fey and D'Arcy McNickle, *Indians and Other Americans,* pp. 164-65.

55. Interview with Nell Scott, March 25, 1977.

56. *United States Statutes at Large,* vol. 60, p. 1049; see Commission find-ings, in Indian Claims Commission, *Arapaho-Cheyenne Indians,* pp. 227-342.

57. Interview with Nell Scott, April 25, 1975.

58. A. F. C. Greene, "Fremont County," October 4, 1941, Works Progress Administration Interviews; minutes of Shoshone Business Council meeting, June 22, 1937, p. 5, in File 1935-37345, pt. 1, CF 54; Stone to Commissioner of Indian Affairs, May 31, 1938, in File 1936-11649, CF 54. These fishing regulations were approved by the Bureau of Indian Affairs on April 7, 1938.

59. Stone to Commissioner of Indian Affairs, April 22, 1937, in File 1935-37345, pt. 1, CF 54.

60. *Trust Funds Hearings,* p. 23. The members of the Shoshone Business Council were, in 1937-38, Robert Harris, Lynn St. Clair, Gilbert Day, Charles Washakie, Ben Perry, and Frank Enos; in 1939-40, John Boyd, Lanjo McAdams, Pete Aragon, Gilbert Day, Charles Washakie, and Cyrus Shongutsie; in 1941-42, Maud Clairmont, Marshall Washakie, Charles Washakie, Hunting Hill, Gilbert Day, and Charles Driskell, who was replaced by Lynn St. Clair; in 1943-44, Maud Clairmont, Gilbert Day, Robert Harris, Marshall Washakie, George Harris, and Herman St. Clair; in 1945-46, Robert Harris, Gilbert Day, Herman St. Clair, Mar-shall Washakie, Lynn St. Clair, and George Harris; in 1947-48, Robert Harris, Gilbert Day, Reuben Martel, Tony Lajeunesse, Maud Clairmont, and Hunting Hill; in 1949-50, Robert Harris, Maud Clairmont, Reuben Martel, Ben Henan, Hunting Hill, and Amos Bonatsie; in 1951-52, Robert Harris, Reuben Martel, Herman St. Clair, George Harris, Maud Clairmont, and Gilbert Day; in 1953-54, Gilbert Day, Robert Harris, Enos Enos, Maud Clairmont, George Harris, and Sam Nipwater; in 1955-56, Robert Harris, Maud Clairmont, Reuben Martel, Hunting Hill, Herman St. Clair, and Gilbert Day; in 1957-58, Delmer Wesaw, Robert Harris, George Harris, Bert Harris, Maud Clairmont, and Gilbert Day; in 1959-60, Maud Clairmont, Del-mer Wesaw, Frank Enos, Robert Harris, Gilbert Day, and Suzette Wagon; in 1961-62, Robert Harris, Suzette Wagon, Frank Enos, Alfred McAdams, Starr Weed, and Gilbert Day; in 1963-64, Robert Harris, Herman St. Clair, Alfred McAdams, Frank Enos, Starr Weed, and Hunting Hill.

61. Molly Peacock Stenberg, "The Peyote Culture among Wyoming Indians," p. 132.

62. Interview, April 2, 1977, author's field tapes; Hilger, *Arapaho Child Life,*

p. 159. John G. Carter, "The Northern Arapaho Flat Pipe and the Ceremony of Covering the Pipe," p. 74, is in error in naming Luke Smith as the keeper of the Sacred Pipe.

63. Howard Lee Wilson, in "Notes on the Arapaho Sun Dance," Indian files, Episcopal Diocese, Laramie, names White Plume, who directed the Sun Dance in 1950; the names of the other leaders were obtained from Arapahoes living today.

64. Feliks Gross, "Language and Value Changes among the Arapaho," pp. 11-13.

65. Minutes of Joint Business Council meeting, February 24, 1937, pp. 12-32, in File 1930-65191, CF 54. Nell Scott was not closely associated with a particular residential area; she resided at Fort Washakie, where she bought land next to the home of her sister, who was married to a Ute.

66. *The Wyoming Indian,* November 30, 1936, pp. 5, 8, in File 1936-9741, CF 66; minutes of Business Council meeting, September 17, 1940, p. 2, in File 1935-37345, pt. 5, CF 54.

67. Minutes of Joint Business Council meeting, March 14, pp. 6, 8, and May 9, 1940, pp. 10-11, in File 1935-37345, pt. 4, CF 54; Fiestas, Festivals, Feasts 072, Box 15, Archives, FRC.

68. *Wyoming Indian,* 1938; minutes of Joint Business Council meeting, October 26, 1937, pp. 10-11, both in File 1935-37345, pt. 1, CF 54.

69. The following people served on the Dance Committee between 1935 and 1941 (the lists for some years are incomplete): in 1935, Andrew Brown, Lynn Norse, Carey Shot Gun, Pete White Plume, Orlo Amos, Iron Piper, Hayes Goggles, Henry Snake, Joe C. Bearing, and Harry Behan; in 1936, Andrew Brown, Carey Shot Gun, Pete White Plume, Luke Sun Roads, Bliss Black, and Wilson Crook; in 1937, Andrew Brown (Mill Creek), Black Bitner (Ethete), and John Yellow Plume (Arapahoe); in 1938, John Yellow Plume, Dave Headley, Leonard Warren, Alonzo Moss, and Tom C. Hair; in 1939, Andrew Brown, Lynn Norse, Scott Ridgley, Ed Aragon, Joe Arthur, West Shakespeare, Silvester Button, Leonard Warren, Frank Tyler, Bill Friday, Ora Manderson, Basil Harris, Mike Goggles, and Clark Trumbull; in 1940, Andrew Brown, Scott Ridgley, Lynn Norse, Aaron Willow, Luke Sun Roads, Bliss Black, William Thunder, Sam Friday, Bruce Groesbeck, and William Shakespeare; and in 1941, Scott Ridgley, Joe Arthur, Ed Aragon, Carlos Harris, Otto Revere, Sidney Willow, Mike Antelope, Joe Shakespeare, Tom C. Hair, Dave Headley, Leonard Warren, Dan Oldman, and Andrew Headley (see minutes of Joint Business Council meeting, May 9, 1940, in File 1935-37345, pt. 4, CF 54; *Wyoming Indian,* 1938, Nell Scott Papers; Fiestas, Festivals, and Feasts 072, Box 15, Archives, FRC).

70. Constitution and by-laws in minutes of Joint Business Council meeting, May 11, 1938; minutes of Joint Business Council meeting, October 26, 1937, p. 11, and April 19, 1939, pp. 9-13, all in File 1935-37345, pts. 1-3, CF 54.

71. *Wyoming State Journal,* October 19, 1950.

72. Stenberg, "Peyote Culture," p. 130.

73. Interview with Ethel Goggles Potter (1908-), April 5, 1977.

74. Minutes of General Council meeting, November 21, 1946, September

17, 1947, and March 7, 1952, in Records of the Bureau of Indian Affairs, Fort Washakie.

75. Minutes of General Council meeting, April 22, 1954, and August 10, 1956; Arapahoe Census Roll, all in Records of the Bureau of Indian Affairs, Fort Washakie.

76. Minutes of General Council meeting, January 19, 1962, pp. 25, 31, in Records of the Bureau of Indian Affairs, Fort Washakie.

5. "WHAT THEY ISSUE YOU": POLITICAL ECONOMY AT WIND RIVER

1. Unless otherwise indicated, quotations and facts cited in this chapter and Chapter 6 are from my field notes taken during 1967-78.

2. Before 1972 the required age for political participation, including the right to vote, was 21.

3. A few Arapahoes living in the Kinnear area, a few miles east of Morton, are considered to be residents of Ethete.

4. These figures, as well as those on the Shoshones and the subsequent estimates on white population, are computed by the Bureau of Indian Affairs and the Tribal Office.

5. See Loretta Fowler, "Arapahoe Migrants," pp. 5-8.

6. Data from an unpublished report of Hurlbut, Kershich, and McCullough, Consulting Engineers (*Inventory of Water Resources: Wind River Indian Reservation, Wyoming*), cited in Veronica Evaneshko, *Exploring Recruitment and Retention of Indian Nursing Students,* p. 5.

7. Additional income from sources other than joint tribal resources may be credited to one tribe only, as in the case of the 1964 claim award to the Arapahoe tribe. The Business Council budgets must be approved by a delegated representative of the secretary of the interior; his approval is normally routine.

8. Royalties ranging from 12.5 to 30.0 percent have been obtained in these negotiations.

9. Minutes of Joint Business Council meeting, April 30, 1969, Records of the Bureau of Indian Affairs, Fort Washakie, Wyo. The Arapahoe tribe recently invested money in an industrial park; the tribe has had great difficulty attracting industry to the site.

10. See Ann Sawyier Straus, "Being Human in the Cheyenne Way"; Katherine Weist, "The Northern Cheyennes"; Thomas H. Johnson, "The Enos Family and Wind River Shoshone Society."

11. Sarah Jean Chamberlain Slattery v. Arapahoe Tribal Council and Secretary of the Interior, Walter J. Hickel, *Federal Reporter,* 2d ser., vol. 453, p. 278. In this case, the federal court refused jurisdiction.

12. *Riverton Ranger,* letter to editor, October 14, 1969.

13. Ibid., October 16, 1969.

14. Labor Force Reports, 1968 and 1975, Bureau of Indian Affairs, Fort

Washakie. These statistics count only women who are not classified as "house-wives" as part of the available work force. The superintendent's Report to the Commissioner for 1964 stated that 25 percent were permanently employed during that year.

15. Evaneshko, *Exploring Recruitment*, p. 5.

16. See Loretta Fowler, "The Arapahoe Ranch," and also Evaneshko's survey of Indian attitudes toward work in *Exploring Recruitment*, pp. 35-36.

17. Bureau of the Census, *Census of Population, 1970*, vol. 2, "Subject Report, American Indian," p. 143; Evaneshko, *Exploring Recruitment*, p. 21.

18. Sara Hunter, "Northern Arapahoe Grandparents," pp. 47, 55.

19. Ibid., p. 50.

20. Ibid., p. 25.

21. Minutes of Arapahoe General Council meeting, September 28, 1968, Office of the Bureau of Indian Affairs, Fort Washakie.

22. Office of Land Operations, Bureau of Indian Affairs, Fort Washakie. The Riverton reclamation project is administered by the U.S. Bureau of Reclamation. In 1953 the lands in the reclamation project that were not being used were restored to the tribes; in 1958 the mineral rights to the reclamation area were restored.

23. Interview with Orlo Amos, May 28, 1975, author's field tapes.

24. Also see Hunter, "Northern Arapahoe Grandparents," pp. 44-45.

25. See Loretta Fowler, "Arapahoe Political Activists"; interview with Orlo Amos, August 13, 1975, author's field tapes.

26. Interview with the tribe's attorney, Glenn Wilkinson.

27. U.S. v. Mazurie et al., Supreme Court, *United States Reports*, vol. 419, p. 544; Dry Creek Lodge, Inc., v. United States, *Federal Reporter*, 2d ser., vol. 515, p. 926, and Dry Creek Lodge, Inc., v. Arapahoe and Shoshone Tribes, ibid., vol. 623, p. 682.

28. Niels Winther Braroe, *Indian and White*. Braroe has discussed in detail white definitions of Cree Indians as "profane" persons whose "dignity may be assaulted with impunity" (p. 35). His study focuses on Cree and white attempts to construct morally defensible self-images in a socially stratified community. Braroe concludes that such an adaptive strategy enables the Cree to cope with their subordinate status and that whites, "in large part through ignorance, are able to maintain an image of Indians as profane persons" which "justifies a special treatment of band members that violates the usual norms governing interpersonal behavior" (p. 183).

29. Interview with Nickerson Shakespeare, August 21, 1975, author's field tapes.

30. Ibid.; see also George A. Dorsey and Alfred L. Kroeber, *Traditions of the Arapaho*, pp. 82-86.

31. Since 1968 there have been marriages between Arapahoes and Shoshones, but the exact number I do not know.

32. There is an American Legion post whose members are Shoshones and whites who live on the reservation. There is one powwow to which other tribes are invited. On this occasion the Arapahoe drum groups are invited to perform.

33. The Shoshone dancers are permitted much more autonomy than the Arapahoes; for example, Shoshone dancers paint themselves according to a personal vision rather than according to the direction of ritual leaders, and their dance styles vary. When the religious symbolism of the dance is explained to the Shoshone dancers by the Sun Dance chief, other shamans may offer different interpretations. See Joseph G. Jorgensen, *The Sun Dance Religion.*

34. See Thomas H. Johnson, "The Enos Family and Wind River Shoshone Society."

35. Ibid.

36. This description of Shoshone culture and social organization is based on observations and interviews made during my fieldwork between 1967 and 1978; most of my contacts with Shoshones were limited to councilmen. I made no intensive study of Shoshone life.

37. These observations pertain to the years before 1977; in 1977 a Cheyenne replaced the white superintendent at the Wind River Agency.

6. "TO MAKE A NAME":
THE CULTURAL CONTEXT OF CONTEMPORARY LEADERSHIP

1. The Indian name is not used in address, nor is it employed to reinforce moral worth in the face of white prejudice, as Niels Winther Braroe explicates for the Cree in *Indian and White.*

2. There seems to be some confusion here between the culture hero *nih'óóOoo* and the notion of a supreme being or creator. But the term *hiicheebee nih'óóOoo* was recorded by John G. Bourke before contact with missionaries (Diaries, U.S. Military Academy).

3. The same symbolic associations are inherent in the Sweat Lodge ritual, in the Sun Dance, and in Sacred Pipe ceremonies. See also Ann Sawyier Straus, "Being Human in the Cheyenne Way."

4. An Arapahoe without ritual authority recently acquired from Sioux in South Dakota knowledge of the Yuwipi ceremony and has held several curing ceremonies, attended by Arapahoes and Indians from other reservations. The man's medicine power is viewed as potentially destructive.

5. This sketch of beliefs that are shared by most Arapahoes of the "younger generation" and older reflects the layman's view, rather than that of the priests. The reader can consult Straus, "Being Human in the Cheyenne Way," for a more detailed and systematic discussion of Cheyenne beliefs, although Cheyenne and Arapahoe belief systems are by no means identical.

6. Interview with Orlo Amos, January 22, 1973, author's field tapes.

7. Violence during a state of intoxication usually is an exception—the person is regarded as "not himself." Intoxication, however, is more prevalent and more tolerated among "youths" than among "mature adults."

8. Interview, April 6, 1977, author's field tapes.

9. The tribal court handles all offenses on the reservation that do not come

under the jurisdiction of the federal court. The judges, one from each tribe, are appointed by the superintendent on the recommendation of the Business Council.

10. Felix Groesbeck is the son of Bruce Groesbeck; Ernest Hanway is the son of Paul Hanway; Herman J. Moss is the son of Alonzo Moss.

11. For a description of a funeral in the 1920s, see "William Penn Is Dead: An Indian Funeral," in Indian Files, Episcopal Diocese, Laramie.

12. See Fred Eggan, *Social Anthropology of North American Tribes,* pp. 35-95.

13. It may be to a man's advantage to sit conspicuously with his wife, particularly if he has previously damaged his reputation by behaving in an irresponsible or wanton manner.

14. "Spider" and "white man" are the historically secondary meanings of *nih'ooOoo*; the Proto-Arapaho-Atsina form *ni'hooOyo* or *ni'hoOyo* and Proto-Algonkian *wi'sahkecyahkwa* had the meaning "the name of the culture hero" (Ives Goddard, "An Outline of the Historical Phonology of Arapaho and Atsina," pp. 107-8).

15. See note 4, above. This man recently suffered a debilitating illness that many old people interpreted as due to misuse of medicine power.

16. Five of the six Arapahoe councilmen elected for the 1972 term were still serving on the council in 1976. At Crow Agency, in contrast, only one of fourteen continued to serve in the 1972-76 period; at Blackfeet Agency, two of seven; at Fort Belknap Reservation (Assiniboines and Gros Ventres), two of twelve; at the Cheyenne reservation, four of eleven; and at Rocky Boy (the Cree reservation), three of nine.

7. "BEWARE OF THE STRANGER AND HIS STRANGE WAYS": THE EVOLUTION OF POLITICAL SYMBOLS, 1851-1978

1. This account is from Bill Shakespeare's version of the story, but it does not differ substantially from others. See the version in Chapter 5, for example.

2. Paul Spencer suggests that when young men in age-graded societies have active and prestigious roles as warriors, their resentment of the authority of older men is minimized (*The Samburu*).

3. Among Plains peoples generally, elders are greatly respected and middle-aged men are given more responsibility than youths (see, for example, Ernest L. Schusky, *The Forgotten Sioux,* pp. 214-17, and Ann Sawyier Straus, "Being Human in the Cheyenne Way"); but among the Arapahoes (and many other groups with an age-grading tradition), age-group relations are more formalized and the authority of the elders is more firmly linked to the well-being of the entire tribe. Ann Gayton's study of the less egalitarian Yokuts in California (*Yokuts-Mono Chiefs and Shamans*) indicates the potential for abuse of authority when secular and ritual leaders are more directly allied; the Yokut system worked to intensify wealth and power differentials. Among the Arapahoes, however, sacred and secular leaders held each other's authority in check.

4. Henry Elkin, "The Northern Arapahoe of Wyoming," pp. 245–46.

5. Robert H. Lowie has pointed to the importance of religion as an implement of political centralization in North America ("Some Aspects of Political Organization among the American Aborigines").

6. Walter H. Sangree, *Age, Prayer and Politics in Tiriki, Kenya,* pp. 169, 236.

7. Loretta Fowler, "'Look at My Hair, It Is Gray': Age Grading, Ritual Authority, and Political Change among the Northern Arapahoe and Gros Ventre."

8. Abner Cohen, *Two-Dimensional Man.*

References

ARCHIVAL AND UNPUBLISHED SOURCES

Billings, Montana

Bureau of Indian Affairs: Probate Hearings, Wind River

Cheyenne, Wyoming

Historical Research and Publications Division, Wyoming State Archives and Historical Department
    Governor J. A. Campbell Letter Books
    Mary Jackson English, "Prairie Sketches or Fugitive Recollections of an Army
      Girl of 1889"
    Edward J. Farlow Manuscript
    A. F. C. Greene, "The Arapahoe Indians," February 15, 1941
    The Indian Guide
    Works Progress Administration interviews
    The Wyoming Churchman

Chicago, Illinois

Field Museum of Natural History
    George Dorsey Correspondence
    George Dorsey–Cleaver Warden Collection
Newberry Library
    Papers of Richard J. Dodge, Powder River Winter Campaign, diary, Graff Collection
    John Hallam, "Kinan, the Great Arapahoe Medicine Man," Ayers Collection

Denver, Colorado

Colorado State Historical Society: Dawson Scrapbooks
Federal Archives and Records Center: Records of the Bureau of Indian Affairs,
  Wind River Files

Fort Washakie, Wyoming

Bureau of Indian Affairs
    Minutes of Council Meetings
    Nell Scott Papers
    Personnel Files
    Superintendent's Annual Report to the Commissioner of Indian Affairs, 1944

Kansas City, Missouri

Federal Archives and Records Center: Records of the Bureau of Indian Affairs

Laramie, Wyoming

Episcopal Diocese: Indian Files
Western History Research Center, University of Wyoming
    Sherman Coolidge File
    Francis Donaldson Collections
    Episcopal Church Collection
    Fort Washakie File
    Indian File
    L. L. Newton Collection
        "Farlow Memoirs"
        "Mrs. Broken Horn"
    John Roberts Collection
    Tacetta Walker, "The Establishing of Ethete"

Milwaukee, Wisconsin

Marquette University: Bureau of Catholic Indian Missions Records

New Haven, Connecticut

Yale University Library: William Robertson Coe Collection; The Bent Papers

Philadelphia, Pennsylvania

Historical Society of Pennsylvania: Indian Rights Association Papers

St. Stephens, Wyoming

St. Stephen's Mission: office files

Urbana, Illinois

Demitri Shimkin, unpublished manuscript related to fieldwork on Wind River
Reservation

Washington, D.C.

Library of Congress: Hugh L. Scott Papers, Indian Correspondence, Box 46
National Archives
    Legislative History Files, Committee on Interior and Insular Affairs, Records of
        the U.S. House of Representatives, Record Group 233
    Records of the Bureau of Indian Affairs, Record Group 75
        Authorities, 1880–1907
        Carlisle Indian Industrial School Records
        Central Files, 1907–39, Pine Ridge Agency
        Central Files, 1907–39, Shoshone Agency
        Indian Census Rolls, 1885–1940, Shoshone Agency
        Letters Received by the Office of Indian Affairs, 1824–81
            Dakota Superintendency
            Red Cloud Agency
            St. Louis Superintendency
            Upper Platte Agency
            Wyoming Superintendency
        Letters Received by the Office of Indian Affairs, 1881–1907
        Letters Sent by the Office of Indian Affairs, 1824–81
        Ratified Treaty File
        Records Concerning the Wheeler-Howard Act, 1933–37
        Report of the Shoshone Commission, 1891; Irregularly Shaped Papers,
            1849–1907; Land Division
        Roster of Agency Employees, 1879–88
        Roster of Indian Police, 1878–82
        Special Cases, 1821–1907, Shoshone Agency
        Superintendents' Annual Narrative Reports from Shoshone Agency, 1907–38
        Superintendents' Annual Statistical Reports from Shoshone Agency, 1907–38
    Records of the Office of the Adjutant General, Record Group 94
        Letters Received, 1889–1904
        Regular Army Muster Rolls, Indian Scouts, 1883–1900
        Returns from U.S. Military Posts, 1800–1916
    Records of the Office of the Secretary of the Interior, Record Group 48
        Letters Received by the Secretary of the Interior, Indian Division
        Indian Division, Special Files, Indian Treaty Commission
        Inspection Division, Reports, 1881–1924

Records of the U.S. Army Continental Commands, 1821–1920, Record Group 393
  Post Records of Fort Fetterman
    Daily Journal of Events
    Letters Sent
  Post Records of Fort Laramie: Letters Sent
  Post Records of Fort Washakie: Letters Sent
Smithsonian Institution: National Anthropological Archives
  Inez Hilger Field Notes, 1936–40
  Alfred L. Kroeber, Arapaho Notebooks, 1900
  Michelson Manuscript, no. 1910
  Photograph Collection
  Hugh L. Scott, Board of Indian Commissioners, Report on the Shoshone Indian Reservation

West Point, New York

United States Military Academy Library: Diaries of John Gregory Bourke

FEDERAL DOCUMENTS

Abert, J. W. *Report of Lieut. J. W. Abert of His Examination of New Mexico in the Years 1846–1847.* Senate Executive Document 23, 30th Cong., 1st sess. (1848).
Bureau of the Census, U.S. Department of Commerce. *Census of Population, 1970,* vol. 2. "Subject Report, American Indian."
"Cheyenne and Arapahoe Indian Reservation." *Letter from the Secretary of the Interior.* House Executive Document 12, 43d Cong., 1st sess. (1873).
Congressional Record.
Dodge, Henry. *Report on the Expedition of Dragoons, under Col. Henry Dodge, to the Rocky Mountains in 1835.* American State Papers, Military Affairs, vol. 6 (February 29, 1836).
Federal Reporter, 2d ser.
Kappler, Charles J., ed. *Indian Affairs: Laws and Treaties,* vol. 2. Washington, D.C., 1904.
Kearny, S. W. *Report of a Summer Campaign to the Rocky Mountains in 1845.* House Executive Document 2, 29th Cong., 1st sess. (1846).
Message from the President of the United States Communicating the Report and Journal of Proceedings of the Commission Appointed to Obtain Certain Concessions from the Sioux Indians. Senate Executive Document 9, 44th Cong., 2d sess. (1876).
Negotiations with the Shoshone and Arapahoe Indians. House Executive Document 51, 53d Cong., 2d sess. (1893–94).
Raynolds, W. R. *Report on the Exploration of the Yellowstone River.* Senate Executive Document 77, 40th Cong., 2d sess. (1868).

Report of the Secretary of War. Senate Executive Document 72, 20th Cong., 2d sess. (February 10, 1829).

Report of the Special Commission to Investigate the Affairs of the Red Cloud Indian Agency. Washington, D.C., 1875.

Report on Indians Taxed and Indians Not Taxed in the United States at the Eleventh Census: 1890. House Misc. Document 340, 52 Cong., 1st sess.

Reports of the Commissioner of Indian Affairs, 1846–1906. Washington, D.C.: Government Printing Office.

Supreme Court, *United States Reports.*

U.S. House of Representatives, Subcommittee on Indian Affairs, Committee on Public Lands. *Trust Funds, Shoshone and Arapaho Indian Tribes: Hearings* (80th Cong., 1st sess., March 15, 1947), H.R. 1098.

U.S. Senate, Committee on Indian Affairs, *A Bill to Provide for the Distribution of the Judgment Fund of the Shoshone Tribe of the Wind River Reservation in Wyoming and for Other Purposes, July 10, 1939: Hearings* (76th Cong., 1st sess.), S. 1878.

United States Statutes at Large, vols. 24, 26, 28, 34, 36, 48, 53, 60, 61, 67, 69, 70, 72.

NEWSPAPERS

Cheyenne Daily Leader, Cheyenne, Wyoming

The Fremont Clipper, Lander, Wyoming

Lander Eagle, Lander, Wyoming

Laramie Republican-Boomerang, Laramie, Wyoming

The Missouri Republican, St. Louis, Missouri

New York Herald, New York, New York

New York Times, New York, New York

Riverton Ranger, Riverton, Wyoming

Wyoming State Journal, Lander, Wyoming

BOOKS AND ARTICLES

Allen, John Logan. *Passage through the Garden.* Urbana: University of Illinois, 1975.

Anderson, William Marshall. *The Rocky Mountain Journals of William Marshall Anderson.* Ed. Dale L. Morgan and Eleanor Towles Harris. San Marino, Calif.: Huntington Library, 1967.

Bailey, F. G. "Parapolitical Systems." In *Local-Level Politics,* ed. Marc J. Swartz, pp. 281–94. Chicago: Aldine, 1968.

Bell, John R. *The Journal of Captain John R. Bell.* Vol. 6 of *The Far West and the Rockies.* Ed. Harlin M. Fuller and Le Roy R. Hafen. Glendale, Calif.: Arthur H. Clark, 1957.

Berkhofer, Robert F. *The White Man's Indian.* New York: Vintage Books, 1979.

Berthrong, Donald J. *The Southern Cheyennes.* Norman: University of Oklahoma Press, 1963.

_____. *The Cheyenne and Arapaho Ordeal: Reservation and Agency Life in the Indian Territory, 1875-1907.* Norman: University of Oklahoma Press, 1976.

Bolton, Herbert E. "New Light on Manuel Lisa and the Spanish Fur Trade." *Southwestern Historical Quarterly* 17, no. 1 (1914):61-66.

Bourke, John G. *On the Border with Crook.* New York: Scribner, 1891.

Brackenridge, H. M. *Views of Louisiana.* Baltimore: Schaeffer & Maund, 1817.

Bradbury, John. *Travels in the Interior of America in the Years 1809, 1810 and 1811.* Vol. 5 of *Early Western Travels, 1748-1846,* ed. Reuben Gold Thwaites. Cleveland: Arthur H. Clark, 1907.

Braroe, Niels Winther, *Indian and White: Self-Image and Interaction in a Canadian Community.* Stanford, Calif.: Stanford University Press, 1975.

Bruner, Edward M. "Mandan." In *Perspectives in American Indian Culture Change,* ed. Edward H. Spicer, pp. 187-277. Chicago: University of Chicago Press, 1961.

Burnette, Robert, and Koster, John. *The Road to Wounded Knee.* New York: Bantam, 1974.

Campbell, John. "Diary, 1869-75." *Annals of Wyoming* 10, nos. 1-4 (1938): 5-11, 59-78, 120-43, 155-85.

Carrington, Margaret Irvin. *Ab-sa-ra-ka, Land of Massacre, Being the Experience of an Officer's Wife on the Plains.* Philadelphia: J. B. Lippincott, 1878.

Carter, John G. "The Northern Arapaho Flat Pipe and the Ceremony of Covering the Pipe." *Smithsonian Institution Bureau of American Ethnology Bulletin* 119 (1938):69-102.

Chittenden, Hiram Martin, and Alfred Talbot Richardson. *Life, Letters, and Travels of Father Pierre Jean De Smet.* 4 vols. New York: Francis P. Harper, 1905.

Clark, William Philo. *The Indian Sign Language.* Philadelphia: L. R. Hammersly, 1885.

Cohen, Abner. *Two-Dimensional Man: An Essay on the Anthropology of Power and Symbolism in Complex Society.* Berkeley: University of California Press, 1974.

Colson, Elizabeth. *Tradition and Contract: The Problem of Order.* Chicago: Aldine, 1974.

Connor, P. E. "General Connor's Report of the Tongue River Battle." In *Powder River Campaigns and Sawyers Expedition of 1865,* pp. 46-48. Vol. 12 of *The Far West and the Rockies,* ed. Le Roy Hafen and Ann W. Hafen. Glendale, Calif.: Arthur H. Clark, 1961.

Cooke, Philip St. George. *Scenes and Adventures in the Army.* Philadelphia: Lindsay & Blakiston, 1859.

Coolidge, Grace. *Tepee Neighbors.* Boston: Four Seas, 1917.

Cooper, Mrs. Baird S. *Wind River Reservation.* Hartford: Church Mission Publishing Co., 1914.

Curtis, Edward S. *The North American Indian,* vol. 6. Norwood, Mass.: Plimpton, 1911.

David, Robert B. *Finn Burnett, Frontiersman.* Glendale, Calif.: Arthur H. Clark, 1937.

DeMallie, Raymond J., Jr. "Pine Ridge Economy: Cultural and Historical Perspectives." In *American Indian Economic Development,* ed. Sam Stanley, pp. 237-311. The Hague: Mouton, 1978.

Dodge, Richard Irving. *Our Wild Indians: Thirty-Three Years' Personal Experience among the Red Men of the Great West.* Hartford: A. D. Worthington, 1882.

Dorsey, George A. *The Arapaho Sun Dance: The Ceremony of the Offerings Lodge.* Field Columbian Museum Publications no. 75, Anthropological Series no. 4. Chicago, 1903.

———, and Kroeber, Alfred L. *Traditions of the Arapaho.* Field Columbian Museum Publications no. 75, Anthropological Series no. 5. Chicago, 1903.

Eggan, Fred, ed. *Social Anthropology of North American Tribes.* Chicago: University of Chicago Press, 1955.

Elkin, Henry. "The Northern Arapaho of Wyoming." In *Acculturation in Seven American Indian Tribes,* ed. Ralph Linton, pp. 207-58. New York: D. Appleton-Century, 1940.

Evaneshko, Veronica. *Exploring Recruitment and Retention of Indian Nursing Students.* Laramie: Wyoming Commission for Nursing and Nursing Education, 1976.

Farber, William O. "Representative Government: Application to the Sioux." In *The Modern Sioux,* ed. Ethel Nurge, pp. 123-39. Lincoln: University of Nebraska Press, 1970.

Feraca, Stephen E. "The History and Development of Oglala Sioux Tribal Government." Unpublished report submitted to the Commissioner of Indian Affairs, 1964.

Fey, Harold E., and D'Arcy McNickle. *Indians and Other Americans.* New York: Harper & Row, 1970.

Flannery, Regina. *The Gros Ventres of Montana: Part I, Social Life.* Catholic University of America, Anthropological Series no. 15. Washington, D.C., 1953.

Foner, Anne, and David Kertzer. "Transitions over the Life Course: Lessons from Age-Set Societies." *American Journal of Sociology* 83, no. 5 (1978):1081-1104.

Fowler, Jacob. *The Journal of Jacob Fowler.* Ed. Elliott Coues. New York: Francis P. Harper, 1898.

Fowler, Loretta. "Arapahoe Migrants." Unpublished manuscript, 1971.

———. "The Arapahoe Ranch: An Experiment in Cultural Change and Economic Development." *Economic Development and Cultural Change* 21, no. 3 (1973): 446-64.

———. "Arapahoe Political Activists: 'Radical' Change within a Conservative System." Paper read at American Anthropological Association meetings, November 20, 1976, Washington, D.C.

———. "'Look at My Hair, It Is Gray': Age Grading, Ritual Authority, and

Political Change among the Northern Arapahoe and Gros Ventre." In *Plains Indian Studies: A Collection of Essays in Honor of John C. Ewers and Waldo R. Wedel,* ed. Douglas Ubelaker and Herman Viola. Washington, D.C.: Smithsonian Press, in press.

Frémont, John C. *A Report of the Exploring Expedition to the Rocky Mountains in the Year 1842 and to Oregon and North California in the Years 1843–44.* Washington, D.C.: Gales & Seaton, 1845.

Garbarino, Merwyn S. *Native American Heritage.* Boston: Little, Brown, 1976.

Garrard, Lewis H. *Wah-to-yah and the Taos Trail.* Cincinnati: H. W. Derby, 1850.

Gayton, Ann. *Yokuts-Mono Chiefs and Shamans.* University of California Publications in Archaeology and Ethnology no. 24. Berkeley, 1930.

Geertz, Clifford. *The Interpretation of Cultures.* New York: Basic Books, 1973.

Goddard, Ives. "An Outline of the Historical Phonology of Arapaho and Atsina." *International Journal of American Linguistics* 40, no. 2 (1974):102–16.

Graham, William A. *The Custer Myth.* Harrisburg, Pa.: Stackpole, 1953.

Grinnell, George Bird. "Bent's Old Fort and Its Builders." *Collections of the Kansas State Historical Society* 15 (1923):28–91.

_____. *The Fighting Cheyennes.* Norman: University of Oklahoma Press, 1956.

Gross, Feliks. "Language and Value Changes among the Arapaho." *International Journal of American Linguistics* 17 (1951):10–17.

Hafen, Le Roy R., and Ghent, W. J. *Broken Hand: The Life Story of Thomas Fitzpatrick, Chief of the Mountain Men.* Denver: Old West, 1931.

Hayden, Ferdinand. "Arapohos." In "Contributions to the Ethnography and Philology of the Indian Tribes of the Missouri Valley," *Transactions of the American Philological Society,* n.s. 12(1862):321–39.

Hebard, Grace Raymond, and Brininstool, E. A. *The Bozeman Trail,* 2 vols. Cleveland: Arthur H. Clark, 1922.

Henry, Alexander. "The Manuscript Journals of Alexander Henry and of David Thompson, 1799-1814." In *New Light on the Early History of the Greater Northwest,* ed. Elliott Coues. New York: Francis P. Harper, 1897.

Heslep, Augustus M. "The Santa Fe Trail: Letters and Journals of Augustus M. Heslep." In *Southern Trails to California in 1849,* ed. Ralph P. Bieber. Glendale, Calif.: Arthur H. Clark, 1937.

Hilger, M. Inez. *Arapaho Child Life and Its Cultural Background.* Smithsonian Institution Bureau of American Ethnology Bulletin no. 148. Washington, D.C., 1952.

History of the Sisters of Charity of Leavenworth, Kansas. Kansas City, Mo.: Hudson-Kimberly, 1898.

Holman, Albert M., and Marks, Constant R. *Pioneering in the Northwest.* Sioux City, Iowa: Deitch & Lamar, 1924.

Hughes, John T. *Doniphan's Expedition: Containing an Account of the Conquest of New Mexico.* Cincinnati: J. A. & U. P. James, 1848.

Hull, Lewis B. "Soldiering on the High Plains: The Diary of Lewis Byram Hull, 1864-66." Ed. Myra E. Hull. *Kansas Historical Quarterly* 7, no. 1 (1938): 3–53.

Hunter, Sara. "Northern Arapahoe Grandparents: Traditional Concepts and Contemporary Socio-Economics." Master's thesis, Indiana University, 1977.

Hunton, John. *John Hunton's Diary,* vols. 1-3. Ed. L. G. Flannery. Lingle, Wyo.: Guide Review, 1956.

_____. *John Hunton's Diary,* vol. 6. Ed. L. G. Flannery. Glendale, Calif.: Arthur H. Clark, 1970.

Indian Claims Commission. *Arapaho-Cheyenne Indians.* New York: Garland, 1974.

Jablow, Joseph. *The Cheyenne in Plains Indian Trade Relations, 1795-1840.* Seattle: University of Washington Press, 1950.

James Edwin. *James's Account of S. H. Long's Expedition of 1819-20.* Vols. 15-17 of *Early Western Travels,* ed. Reuben Gold Thwaites. Cleveland: Arthur H. Clark, 1905.

Johnson, Thomas H. "The Enos Family and Wind River Shoshone Society: A Historical Analysis." Ph.D. dissertation, University of Illinois, 1975.

Jorgensen, Joseph G. *The Sun Dance Religion: Power for the Powerless.* Chicago: University of Chicago Press, 1972.

Kertzer, David I. "Theoretical Developments in the Study of Age-Group Systems." *American Ethnologist* 5, no. 2 (1978):368-74.

Kneale, Albert H. *Indian Agent.* Caldwell, Idaho: Caxton, 1950.

Koch, Peter. "The Journal of Peter Koch—1869 and 1870." *Frontier* 9, no. 1 (1928):148-60.

Kroeber, Alfred L. *The Arapaho.* In *Bulletin of the American Museum of Natural History* 18 (1902-7).

_____. *Ethnology of the Gros Ventre.* Anthropological Papers of the American Museum of Natural History, no. 1 (1907), pp. 145-281.

Larson, T. A. *History of Wyoming.* Lincoln: University of Nebraska Press, 1965.

Lemly, H. R. "Among the Arrapahoes." *Harper's Monthly Magazine* 60, no. 358 (1880):494-501.

Le Raye, Charles. "Journal of Charles Le Raye." *South Dakota Historical Collections* 4 (1908):150-82.

Lewis, Meriwether, and Clark, William. *Original Journals of Lewis and Clark Expedition, 1804-1806,* vols. 1-6. Ed. Reuben G. Thwaites. New York: Dodd, Mead, 1905.

Linton, Ralph, ed. *Acculturation in Seven American Indian Tribes.* New York: D. Appleton-Century, 1940.

Lowe, Percival G. *Five Years a Dragoon.* Kansas City, Mo.: Franklin Hudson, 1906.

Lowie, Robert H. *Plains Indian Age Societies: Historical and Comparative Study.* Anthropological Papers of the American Museum of Natural History, no. 11 (1916).

_____. "Some Aspects of Political Organization among the American Aborigines." *Journal of the Royal Anthropological Institute* 78, nos. 1-2 (1948):11-24.

_____. *Indians of the Plains.* New York: McGraw-Hill, 1954.

McFee, Malcolm. *Modern Blackfeet: Montanans on a Reservation.* New York: Holt, Rinehart & Winston, 1972.

McGovern, Patrick A., ed. *History of the Diocese of Cheyenne.* Cheyenne: Wyoming Labor Journal, 1941.

Miller, Walter B. "Two Concepts of Authority." *American Anthropologist* 57 (1955):271-89.

Moodie, D. W., and Kaye, Barry. "The Ac Ko Mok Ki Map." *Beaver,* Spring 1977, pp. 4-15.

Mooney, James. *The Ghost-Dance Religion and the Sioux Outbreak of 1890.* Fourteenth Annual Report of the Bureau of American Ethnology. Washington, D.C., 1896.

Morris, Robert C. "Wyoming Indians." *Collections of the Wyoming Historical Society* 1 (1897):91-108.

Munkres, Robert. "The Plains Indian Threat on the Oregon Trail before 1860." *Annals of Wyoming* 40, no. 2 (1968):193-221.

Murphy, James C. "The Place of the Northern Arapahoes in the Relations between the United States and the Indians of the Plains, 1851-1879." *Annals of Wyoming* 41 (1969):33-61, 203-59.

Nasatir, Abraham P. *Before Lewis and Clark.* 2 vols. St. Louis: St. Louis Historical Documents Foundation, 1952.

National Indian Conference on Aging. *The Indian Elder: A Forgotten American.* Albuquerque, 1978.

Nickerson, H. G. "Early History of Fremont County." *Quarterly Bulletin of the State of Wyoming Historical Department* 2, no. 1 (1924):1-13.

Olson, James C. *Red Cloud and the Sioux Problem.* Lincoln: University of Nebraska Press, 1965.

Palmer, H. E. "History of Powder River Indian Expedition of 1865." *Nebraska State Historical Society, Transactions and Reports* 2 (1887):197-229.

Pancoast, Charles Edward. *A Quaker Forty-niner.* Ed. Anna Paschall Hannum. Philadelphia: University of Pennsylvania Press, 1930.

Parkman, Francis. *The Oregon Trail: Sketches of Prairie and Rocky Mountain Life.* Boston: Little, Brown, 1886.

_____. *The Journals of Francis Parkman.* 2 vols. Ed. Mason Wade. New York: Harper, 1947.

Perrin du Lac, M. *Voyage dans les deux Louisianes.* Paris: Capelle et Renand, 1805.

Powers, William K. *Oglala Religion.* Lincoln: University of Nebraska Press, 1977.

Pulsipher, John, *Diary of John Pulsipher.* Vol. 8 of *The Far West and the Rockies,* ed. Le Roy R. Hafen and Ann W. Hafen. Glendale, Calif.: Arthur H. Clark, 1958.

Richardson, Albert D. *Beyond the Mississippi: From the Great River to the Great Ocean.* Hartford: American, 1867.

Root, Frank A., and Connelley, William Elsey. *The Overland Stage to California.* Topeka: Published by the authors, 1901.

Ruiz, José Francisco. *Report on the Indian Tribes of Texas in 1828.* Ed. John C. Ewers. Trans. Georgette Dorn. New Haven: Yale University Library, 1972.

Ruxton, George. *Ruxton of the Rockies.* Ed. Le Roy R. Hafen. Norman: University of Oklahoma Press, 1950.

Sage, Rufus B. *His Letters and Papers, 1836–1847.* Vols. 4 and 5 of *The Far West and the Rockies,* ed. Le Roy R. Hafen and Ann W. Hafen. Glendale, Calif.: Arthur H. Clark, 1956.

Salzmann, Zdenek. "Contrastive Field Experience with Language and Values of the Arapaho." *International Journal of American Linguistics* 17 (1951):98–101.

———. "Arapaho I: Phonology." *International Journal of American Linguistics* 22, no. 1 (1956):49–56.

Sangree, Walter H. *Age, Prayer and Politics in Tiriki, Kenya.* London: Oxford University Press, 1966.

Sawyers, James A. "Official Report of James A. Sawyers." In *Powder River Campaigns and Sawyers Expedition,* ed. Le Roy R. Hafen and Ann W. Hafen. Glendale, Calif.: Arthur H. Clark, 1961.

Schusky, Ernest L. *Politics and Planning in a Dakota Indian Community.* Vermillion: Institute of Indian Studies, State University of South Dakota, 1959.

———. *The Forgotten Sioux.* Chicago: Nelson-Hall, 1975.

Scott, Hugh Lenox. "The Early History and the Names of the Arapaho." *American Anthropologist,* n.s. 9 (1907):545–60.

Simonin, Lewis L. *The Rocky Mountain West in 1867.* Trans. Wilson O. Clough. Lincoln: University of Nebraska Press, 1966.

Spencer, Paul. *The Samburu.* London: Routledge & Kegan Paul, 1965.

———. "Opposing Streams and the Gerontocratic Ladder: Two Models of Age Organization in East Africa." *Man, the Journal of the Royal Anthropological Institute* 11, no. 2 (1976):153–75.

Spring, Agnes Wright. *Caspar Collins: The Life and Exploits of an Indian Fighter of the Sixties.* New York: Columbia University, 1927.

Stenberg, Molly Peacock. "The Peyote Culture among Wyoming Indians." *University of Wyoming Publications* 12 (1946):85–156.

Stewart, Frank Henderson. *Fundamentals of Age-Group Systems.* New York: Academic Press, 1977.

Straus, Ann Sawyier. "Being Human in the Cheyenne Way." Ph.D. dissertation, University of Chicago, 1976.

Stuart, Robert. *The Discovery of the Oregon Trail: Robert Stuart's Narratives.* Ed. Philip Ashton Rollins. New York: Scribner, 1935.

Swartz, Marc J. *Local-Level Politics: Social and Cultural Perspectives.* Chicago: Aldine, 1968.

Tabeau, Pierre-Antoine. *Tabeau's Narrative of Loisel's Expedition to the Upper Missouri.* Ed. Annie Heloise Abel. Norman: University of Oklahoma Press, 1939.

Talbot, Theodore. *The Journals of Theodore Talbot, 1843 and 1849–52.* Ed. Charles H. Carey. Portland, Ore.: Metropolitan Press, 1931.

Taylor, Graham D. *The New Deal and American Indian Tribalism.* Lincoln: University of Nebraska Press, 1980.

Toll. Oliver W. *Arapaho Names and Trails: A Report of a 1914 Pack Trip.* Published by Oliver W. Toll, 1962.

Trenholm, Virginia Cole. *The Arapahoes, Our People.* Norman: University of Oklahoma Press, 1970.

Trudeau, Jean Baptiste. "Journal of Jean Baptiste Trudeau among the Arikara Indians." Trans. H. T. Beauregard. *Missouri Historical Society Collections* 4 (1912):9-48.

Tyler, S. Lyman. *A History of Indian Policy.* Washington, D.C.: U.S. Department of the Interior, 1973.

Vogdes, Ada A. "The Journal of Ada A. Vogdes, 1868-71." Ed. Donald K. Adams. *Montana* 13, no. 3 (1963):2-18.

Walker, Tacetta B. *Stories of Early Days in Wyoming.* Casper, Wyo.: Prairie Publications, 1936.

Wax, Murray L. *Indian Americans: Unity and Diversity.* Englewood Cliffs, N.J.: Prentice-Hall, 1971.

Weist, Katherine. "The Northern Cheyennes: Diversity in a Loosely Structured Society." Ph.D. dissertation, University of California, Berkeley, 1969.

Wheat, Carl I. *Mapping the Transmississippi West, 1540-1861.* 5 vols. San Francisco: Institute of Historical Cartography, 1957-63.

Wildschut, William. "Arapaho Medicine-Mirror." *Indian Notes* 4 (1927):252-57.

Wood, W. Raymond. "Notes on the Historical Cartography of the Upper Knife-Heart Region." Lincoln, Neb.: National Park Service, Midwest Region, 1978.

Ziegler, Winfred H. *Wyoming Indians.* Laramie, Wyo.: Diocesan Office [1944].

Index